Organizational Public Relations
A Political Perspective

Chapter 3.

Remember Julie said make the lit review general at beginning and then becoming more specialised as it continues through the review

Remember her funnel idea

Organizational Public Relations
A Political Perspective

Christopher Spicer
Pacific Lutheran University

 LAWRENCE ERLBAUM ASSOCIATES, PUBLISHERS
1997   Mahwah, New Jersey

Lawrence Erlbaum Associates, Inc., Publishers
10 Industrial Avenue
Mahwah, NJ 07430

Cover design by Gail Silverman

Library of Congress Cataloging-in-Publication Data

Spicer, Christopher.
    Organizational public relations : a political perspective
/ Christopher Spicer.
        p. cm.
    Includes bibliographical references and index.
    ISBN 0-8058-1837-5 (alk. paper). — ISBN 0-8058-
1838-3 (pbk. : alk. paper)
    1. Public relations. 2. Decision-making. I. Title.
HD59.D677   1996
659.2—DC20   96-23822
                                                   CIP

Books published by Lawrence Erlbaum Associates are printed
on acid-free paper, and their bindings are chosen for strength
and durability.

Printed in the United States of America
10   9   8   7   6   5   4   3   2   1

315741

This book is dedicated to my parents,
Garland H. Spicer, Jr.
and
Doris Fisher Spicer,
with whom I practiced
some of my earliest attempts
at public relations

Contents

Preface

Cheney and Vibbert (1987) noted that, "public relations has been a fact of organizational life throughout this [the 20th] century" (p. 165). This fact is key to understanding what I seek to accomplish in this book. Organizations are situated within larger environmental systems characterized in terms of economic, sociocultural, technological, and legal/political dimensions. Public relations management and communication arises from a need (or perceived need) related to the often complicated, confusing, and compelling interaction between the organization and other stakeholders in the organization's environment. The organizational public relations function is situated at the fault line where organizational and public interests intersect, sometimes in collusion, often in conflict.

As Bolman and Deal (1991) reminded us, organizations are complex, surprising, deceptive, and ambiguous. This book takes their reminder to heart. Organizational life is rife with paradoxes. It is extraordinarily exciting yet mind-numbingly boring, creative yet routine, casual yet formal, honest yet deceptive, friendly yet hostile, supportive yet demeaning, individualistic yet team-oriented, and so on through any number of descriptive adjectives we associate with life in organizations. Above all, organizational life is our way of life, it is intimately intertwined with much of what we experience on a day-to-day basis.

This book is about understanding organizations, especially the role played by organizational decision making in the development and implementation of public relations programs and activities. My goal is to increase the likelihood that the public relations practitioner will become a key player in his or her organization's dominant decision-making coalition, which is comprised of those organizational leaders with the power to establish organizational goals and influence how those goals are accomplished. A better understanding of why and how organizational decisions emerge from the black caldron of organizational "stew" will enable public relations practitioners to join the organization's dominant coalition as fully acknowledged partners.

My approach is grounded on an elaboration of organizations as political systems. Given the need for public relations practitioners to form coalitions, negotiate consensus, and advocate organizational interests, the political system metaphor is most appropriate for understanding the relationship between organizational power and organizational public relations. Research in organizational dynamics and organizational decision making from a political perspective is most advantageous in understanding the necessity for a mixed-metaphor model of organizational public relations, a model that includes a variety of approaches from which the practitioner can select given the particular demands of the situation.

Chapter 1 introduces nine assumptions on which the book is based. I use three case studies to examine the nine dimensions, indicating ways in which public relations worked or failed. In chapter 2, I examine the darker side of public relations. Public relations is all too often misused by management, leading to organizational arrogance and deteriorating relations with stakeholders and the media. This mismanagement of the public relations function is grounded in an overreliance on the technical role of public relations to the exclusion of the all-important (but often ignored) strategic, decision-making function of public relations managers.

Chapter 3 addresses the role of systems theory in the development of both organizational and public relations theory and models. To understand modern public relations, we need to understand the contributions and strengths of systems theory as well as the weaknesses inherent in such an approach. Given critiques of systems theory, especially as it applies to organizational public relations, I think we are on the verge of moving into new and exciting domains for the study and practice of public relations.

Chapter 4 begins with Studs Terkel's (1972) admonition that work creates violence—physical, emotional, and psychological. In order to better understand his admonition, I examine a contingency model of organization that leads to a discussion of individual and organizational schemata for interpreting organizational life.

Chapters 5 and 6 present a macro and micro look at organizations as political systems with a particular focus on power. In chapter 5, I elaborate on the use of the political system metaphor for understanding organizations, examining the concepts of power, interests, and coalitions. In chapter 6, I examine the nature of organizational politics on the practice of organizational public relations. This chapter includes original data about the influence of organizational politics on public relations programs and decisions from organizational public relations practitioners.

Because so much of the public relations function is externally oriented in response to actions within the larger organizational environment, chapter 7 presents an analysis of environmental uncertainty. I also discuss recent trends in stakeholder analysis, focusing on the distinctions between instrumental and resource-dependency theories of organizational environments, both of which have consequences for the public relations function vis-à-vis stakeholder management.

Chapters 8 and 9 are bookends. In chapter 8, I address the traditional approach to organizational communication from an adversarial advocacy frame. In chapter 9, I present the traditional approach to organizational communication from a collaborative frame. Each approach is crucial for public relations, each approach is appropriate given varying environmental and stakeholder demands.

In chapter 10, I discuss four concepts from organizational and management theory that have been underused in discussions of organizational public relations. These include (a) the distinctions between instrumental and symbolic outcomes of decision making, (b) the varying discourse perspectives of organizational insiders and outsiders, (c) the perception of loose coupling between organizational intent and action, and (d) the importance of understanding information and media richness in considering responses to external events and stakeholders. Each of these concepts is applied to a case study of stakeholder management in chapter 11, leading to the identification of several areas of concern for public relations managers.

Finally, in chapter 12, I address the issue of ethics as it relates to organizational public relations. I am concerned with identification of the ways in which organizational insiders perceive the moral dimensions of issues differently from those outside the organization. I argue that these differences in moral judgments lead to unintended negative consequences for the management of organization-stakeholder relationships.

Whatever occurs between an organization and its external stakeholders is, to a great extent, predetermined by actions taken within the organization, actions often grounded in the organization's political infrastructure. It is in this nether region of organizational life—the intersection of good intentions, selfishness, power, concern for others, survival, retreat, advocacy, and collaboration—that decisions about public relations are born. Understanding how to better negotiate the political system of the organization will help public relations practitioners better achieve their dual interests of serving both the organization and the public good. As one practitioner told me in an interview, "In order to get things done for the best of everyone, you've got to know what makes the whole bloomin' thing work. That's politics."

Please feel free to comment on anything I suggest. I am especially interested in examples you have experienced that might be turned into case studies. You can e-mail me at spicerch@plu.edu or write to me at School of the Arts, Ingram Hall, Pacific Lutheran University, Tacoma, WA 98447. Any and all observations are more than welcome.

ACKNOWLEDGMENTS

It is impossible to appropriately acknowledge everyone who helped me with this book. I began this project more years ago than I care to remember with a colleague, Sheila Nolan. Her advice and early enthusiasm were both infectious and invaluable and I am sorry she could not finish this with me. I am indebted to the students in my public relations and organizational communication classes who have allowed me to try out my ideas, many of which are incorporated in this book. I am equally indebted to the many professionals I have met over the years; they were always more than kind in helping me learn about organizations, public relations, and communication. The same goes for my colleagues and friends at Pacific Lutheran University and in the discipline.

The practitioner responses at the end of each chapter turned out even better than I hoped. Credit for that goes to the twelve professionals who agreed to read a chapter and craft a response.

The staff at Lawrence Erlbaum Associates has been great, beginning with my first editor, Hollis Heimbouch, who is now at Harvard Business School Press. Robin Weisberg took over as editor in the middle of this project and shepherded it to completion. I especially want to acknowledge Anne Monaghan, LEA production editor, who took a very rough manuscript and made it presentable. The friendly encouragement of her e-mails made the last bit of editing and revising easier.

My sons, Christopher and Nicholas, always asked how it was going and genuinely listened when I told them; I thank them for just being themselves. Finally, I thank Mary DeFreest for her support, insights, questions, and laughter—our time sitting on logs at the beach and working things out was well spent.

CHAPTER 1

Assumptions

It is not who you are that matters, but what people think you are.
—Attributed to Joseph P. Kennedy, advice to his children

Although not about public relations per se, Kennedy's comment is certainly indicative of the predominant cultural view of public relations prevalent in our society. Image over substance, style over content, looking good over being good. It is a cynical view, a view that is not always, or even usually, accurate. It is a view, however, that is perpetuated by what we do as well as by what we do not do.

Actions versus image? Good deeds versus glowing words? Manipulation versus caring? Perception versus reality? We so often treat these as polarized concepts, pairs of competing realities that anchor either end of a continuum. The purpose of this book is to examine how the range of perceptions on the continuum is reflected in the decision making apparatus of modern organizations. In this chapter, I present the basic assumptions that guide my understanding of organizational public relations, both what it is and what it could be. These nine assumptions form the foundation on which we build our understanding of the intersection of organizational decision making and public relations. As a means of beginning, I offer three case studies.

CASE STUDY 1.1—THE MISADVENTURES OF SELLING AN
8-TON SCULPTURE

Henry Moore's 8-ton bronze sculpture "Vertebrae," which stands at Fourth Avenue and Madison Street, has been sold to an undisclosed buyer in Japan. And the Seattle art community is outraged. (Hackett, 1986a, p. A1)

This was the lead paragraph in a story published in one of two local Seattle, Washington daily newspapers detailing the confusing, convoluted, and often contradictory efforts of two organizations to sell a sculpture many Seattlites considered their own—a piece of very public art.

Seafirst Bank, the largest bank in the state of Washington, bought a sculpture known as the "Vertebrae" in 1971 for a reported $165,000 (Hackett, 1986a). The creator of the piece, British artist Henry Moore, is acclaimed for his large (in this case 8-ton) abstract bronzes often representative of the human body. "Vertebrae" was installed in a corner of the public plaza at the Seafirst Building in full view of untold millions of people who walked by it (or children who climbed on it) over the course of its 15-year presence. "Vertebrae" became a Seattle landmark, perhaps not treasured but certainly accepted as a part of the city scene. As a newspaper editorial noted, "Although the piece was not owned by the city, it was invariably included in lists of art on public display" (Sale Threatens "Public Treasure," 1986, p. A10).

In 1983 Seafirst Bank's corporate headquarters moved into a new building a couple of blocks away. Their old building was sold to JMB Realty headquartered in Chicago. All was fine, at least in the public's view, until a story appeared in Seattle's newspapers on August 28, 1986 announcing that "Vertebrae" had been sold by JMB Realty to an undisclosed buyer for a substantial profit. More alarming was the announcement that "Vertebrae" would be packed up and crated off the following Saturday, 2 days after the story appeared.

At this point the mystery of who owned "Vertebrae," who sold "Vertebrae," and to whom it was sold gets murky. The first series of stories published in the local papers indicated that JMB Realty bought "Vertebrae" from Seafirst for $850,000. Seafirst representatives claimed to have sold the sculpture to JMB Realty with the assumption that it would remain in place (Hackett, 1986). Unexpectedly, then, JMB Realty sold it because "a client who insists on anonymity made us such a substantial offer senior management decided to take it" (Hackett, 1986a, p. A1).

The Seattle art community, as you might well imagine, was in an uproar. The director of the Seattle Art Commission's Art in Public Places Program said, "I'm shocked JMB Realty didn't bother to talk to the people in this city before selling a piece of art that is valuable to us all. They are removing a public landmark" (Hackett, 1986a, p. A5).

As more information about the sale was reported, the apparent straightforwardness of the initial report of the transaction took a very convoluted turn. From reading reports in the local newspapers, one is left with the impression that no one really knew (or would say) what was going on or who owned or sold the piece. For example:

- A JMB Realty spokesperson in Chicago was quoted as saying, "We were led to believe that if we did not purchase the piece, it would be sold to this third party, who was not from Seattle" (Noble, 1986a, p. C1).
- A spokesperson for Seafirst bank "did not know who made the initial offer." She said the bank official who handled the transaction was on vacation and could not be reached (Noble, 1986a, p. C2).
- The local JMB general manager said, "They (corporate officials) make those decisions there (in Chicago). I can only put in my input" (Noble, 1986a, p. C2).
- "Officials of the JMB Property Management Corp. yesterday made an about-face and told city officials the firm 'wasn't the buyer or the seller' of Henry Moore's sculpture 'Vertebrae' " (Noble, 1986b, p. A1).

Ultimately, it appears that JMB Realty, rather than owning "Vertebrae" outright, had the right of first refusal to any offer tendered to Seafirst, the original owner. This apparent legal arrangement came to light when the city of Seattle refused to give the company charged with moving "Vertebrae" the permits required to undertake such a massive move in a public space.

The second interpretation of the sale, a very different narrative from the first, only added to the confusion surrounding who sold or bought "Vertebrae" because suddenly there were two apparent sales. A Boston art consultant working for Seafirst confirmed that he sold "Vertebrae" to an undisclosed buyer "which in turn triggered the first right of refusal by JMB and JMB bought it" (Noble & Sevem, 1986, p. A3). Apparently, JMB matched the undisclosed offer, did own the sculpture and then resold it, perhaps to the original undisclosed buyer or to a different one.

Regardless of who really sold what to whom and when, the act itself still rankled as indicated in a September 7, 1986 editorial in the *Seattle Times*:

Art-Sale Blunder Hurts Bank Image

Someday, perhaps a textbook for public-relations people may cite the Seattle uproar over the Henry Moore sculpture "Vertebrae" as a case study in how not to enhance a corporation's image.

Fuming for days about the pending loss of the landmark sculpture from the former Seafirst building plaza, many local art lovers were led to believe that the blame for selling "Vertebrae" to an out-of-town buyer lay with the building's new owner, the Chicago-based JMB Realty Corp.

Now it turns out that—as much as anyone—Seafirst Bank bears the responsibility, a fact that contradicted earlier statements from the bank as well as JMB. (The bank issued a belated apology a week later.)

Too bad for Seafirst, since a single public-relations blunder may have undone much of the careful, patient rebuilding of the bank's image damaged in the energy-loan fiascoes of several years ago.

One irate Seattlite telephoned a suggestion that the Seafirst slogan, "Expect Excellence," should be changed to "Expect Ambivalence." (Art Sale Blunder Hurts Bank Image, 1986, p. A4)

Even though "Vertebrae" disappeared from the front pages of the newspaper, the story did not die. The artist, Henry Moore, however, did. Ironically, Henry Moore died on August 31, less than a month after the initial reports of the "Vertebrae" sale. Question: What happens to the price of an already famous artist's works when he or she dies? Answer: They skyrocket. The worth of "Vertebrae" "made a 'quantum leap' in value after Moore's death Aug. 31" to an estimated $2 million (Hackett, 1986b, p. A1). Whew!

On October 9, 1986, a month after Henry Moore's death, Seafirst Bank and JMB Realty reportedly donated an estimated $2 million to the Seattle Art Museum that, in turn, bought "Vertebrae" from an undisclosed Japanese buyer (Hackett, 1986b, p. A1). The buyer made an enormous profit, Seafirst and JMB reclaimed some of their stature, the art museum got a substantial donation, and the people of Seattle could once again pass "Vertebrae" knowing it would stay in place. All's well that ends well.

CASE STUDY 1.2—SAVING A CHILD'S LIFE SHOULDN'T BE SO DIFFICULT

Kid's Place Hospital is a nonprofit hospital devoted to the care and treatment of children under the age of 18. It is located in a quiet, largely residential upper-middle class suburb of a large metropolitan area. Kid's Place offers a wide variety of medical services, many of them nonroutine or experimental, on the cutting edge of medical technology and treatment. One of the most acclaimed services is Kid's Place emergency trauma unit. Children, especially those severely injured in accidents, such as car crashes or burns, are rushed to Kid's Place as quickly as possible from a six-state area. Given modern transportation, many of the trauma cases come to the metropolitan area by helicopter. Decisions surrounding the use of helicopters drives the plot of our story.

Helicopters, kinds of air ambulances, transport injured children to Kid's Place and land in one of three places. If the trauma is deemed not immediately life-threatening, the helicopter lands at a helipad at a downtown hospital, the patient is transferred to a waiting ambulance and driven the six miles to Kid's Place. If the trauma is somewhat more threatening, the helicopter can land in a field approximately one mile from Kid's Place emergency room. The patient is again transferred to an ambulance for the one mile ride. Finally, if the trauma is exceedingly life-threatening, if time is of the utmost essence, the helicopter will land on a small patch of grass on the campus of Kid's Place just outside the emergency room entrance. In this case, the patient is wheeled directly into the emergency room with no transfer or ambulance ride.

In 1984, Kid's Place management decided to build a permanent helipad on the grounds of Kid's Place, preferably in the grassy spot right outside the emergency room door. This sounded like a great idea to all of the senior staff at the meeting. If air ambulances could land at the emergency room door, the time delivering patients to expert care would be greatly reduced. Lives would be saved. Not just any life, but a *child's* life.

Kid's Place personnel began the internal planning process for the helipad, knowing they would have to get approval from the city. Because a helipad is little more than a concrete slab with some lines painted on it and landing lights around it, there was not a great deal of architectural design involved. Kid's Place already owned the land on which the proposed helipad was to go, so there was no need to find and purchase a suitable space. Indeed, everything seemed so simple and straightforward that the CEO of Kid's Place announced, at a small press conference in November 1984, that the hospital was building a helipad. The announcement contained all kinds of glowing generalities about how the on-site helipad would improve the care of children and so forth. You can just imagine. A leading doctor from the hospital and the head of medical services also spoke, adding the weight of medical expertise to the announcement.

In a day or two, the daily newspaper published a short story on the third page of the local news section of the paper about the proposed helipad. The story was very positive in tone; the reporter quoted copiously from the CEO and head of medical services. Kid's Place was apparently doing what it did best—caring for the needs of children. The CEO was happy with the coverage, the director of public relations was happy with the coverage, and the medical director was happy with the coverage. The plans were submitted to the city department of construction and land use for approval, approval that was expected to be routine and quick.

Some people who read the story, people who lived in the upper-middle class neighborhood where the hospital is located, were not as happy as the good folks at Kid's Place. Indeed, some of them were so upset that they got on the telephone and started calling their neighbors. Then, they convened a public meeting to give voice to their growing hostility toward the idea of helicopters hovering over their homes and their children's playgrounds at all hours of the day and night. This meeting led to other meetings of other neighborhood groups (e.g., a community club, the PTA for the local elementary school, a condominium owners' association, residents of a retirement home), who discussed the proposed flight plan for the air ambulances. These meetings, in turn, led to the formation of an umbrella group, Citizens Against Helicopters, that began a coordinated opposition to Kid's Place proposal by filing a complaint with the city's department of construction and land use.

A hastily called open community meeting to soothe ruffled feathers between Kid's Place administrators (the CEO, medical director, and public relations director) and members of the neighborhood ended in acrimonious vocal debates and increasing mistrust. The city's department of construction and land use put a hold on the necessary permits, kicking the project upstairs to the mayor's office.

As opposition mounted and time went by, Kid's Place found itself mired in a legal tangle. Among other actions, the opponents demanded that Kid's Place needed state approval, that an environmental impact study needed to be conducted, and that the Federal Aviation Administration needed to approve the flight plans. The opposition listed six major points of contention:

1. Kid's Place is insensitive to the character of the neighborhood.
2. Kid's Place is secretive in making decisions.
3. The medical need for the increased use of air ambulances has not been proven.
4. Helicopters are too expensive to operate.
5. Helicopters are too dangerous to be flying over a family-oriented neighborhood with schools and playgrounds.
6. Helicopters are too noisy.

Time passed. The seemingly straightforward decision to build a helipad was often in the news over the following year, as various city, state, and federal agencies got involved in trying to resolve the dispute. As you might guess (or know from some better-to-be-forgotten experience), when more than one governmental agency gets involved in an issue, the time needed to reach a decision is disproportionately lengthened by a multiple based on the number of letters in the agency's acronym. So, more time, in fact, a number of years passed.

During this time, the nature of the debate changed. The opposition began to focus on the fact that Kid's Place could not (or would not) provide hard data to support their claim that a permanent, on-site helipad was necessary. Kid's Place administrators could not say how many flights might land per month, what kinds of traumas would justify using air ambulances perhaps more frequently, how many children had died because of a delay in using one of the other two alternative landing sights, and so on. The argument turned from a self-serving one about increased noise in the neighborhood, to one about the use of air ambulances as an appropriate patient delivery system.

Opponents to the Kid's Place helipad seized on any and all research that indicated air ambulances might function better as a marketing tool than a medically sound lifesaving device. This argumentative tact resulted in the state health administration getting involved in the dispute by declaring that all air ambulance use in the state needed to be examined and new rules and regulations adopted. More time passed. Kid's Place continued to use an air ambulance service, landing the incoming patients at one of the three available sites, just as they had for years.

Every once in a while, city residents read in their newspaper or saw on the local television news that progress was being made or impeded. Kid's Place embarked on different projects, implementing new programs and working to rebuild the trust it once enjoyed from its neighbors. Neighborhood activists continued to dog the case, effectively denying the permit process.

Finally, in the fall of 1993, roughly 9 years after the initial announcement, Kid's Place built its helipad. Nine years to pour a concrete slab, paint some lines, and put up some lights.

CASE STUDY 1.3—WHEN YOU GOTTA GO AND THEY WON'T LET YOU

The next time you use the restroom at your local Circle K, be sure to give the toilet an extra flush in honor of Lois Rogers and the quick-thinking management of the convenience store chain. The chain, with more than 3,100 outlets in 32 states, dealt with what could have been a very smelly public relations problem in an astute and humane way. In the end, Circle K averted a great deal of negative publicity, instituted a new sensitivity training program for its nearly 23,000 employees, and enhanced its own public image.

Seattle resident Lois Rogers was shopping in her local Circle K when she felt the early warning signs that she was about to have an epileptic seizure. Rogers, who experiences mild, infrequent seizures once or twice a month, knew that she was going to need a restroom because she could lose control of her bowels during the seizure. She was prepared for the seizure, but what totally surprised her was the store clerk's response to her request to use the restroom. The clerk said no. The restroom was for employees only. Rogers asked to speak to the manager who also said no.

Rogers and the store manager got into a yelling match (with other customers looking on). Eventually, Rogers convinced the manager of her dire predicament and was allowed to use the bathroom. After her seizure was over, Rogers showed the manager a card she always carries that explains the nature of her disability. According to Rogers, the manager, who was now quite irate, threw her card across the store.

At a friend's prodding, Rogers, who felt humiliated and embarrassed by the incident, decided to complain about the treatment she experienced at the hands of Circle K personnel. She took her case to the Seattle Department of Human Rights.

Roxanne Vierra, the Seattle human rights investigator assigned to the case, gave Circle K's Phoenix, Arizona headquarters a call. Sensing an opportunity, the public relations and human resource departments convinced Circle K management to deal with the situation quickly and humanely. In a week, Circle K's attorney, Doryce Hughston and its western division human resource manager, Diane Ketterhagen, flew to Seattle to investigate the case for themselves. They met with Rogers, the store manager and clerk, and with the Seattle Human Rights Department.

According to Vierra, it seems the manager and clerk had said no because of shoplifting fears. The store is located near a school and has had a long-running battle with young sticky fingers. In addition, the manager felt that the restroom, located near the backroom storage and bookkeeping area, was vulnerable to shoplifting. A person could take stock and walk out the back door without being seen.

Hughston and Ketterhagen expressed surprise at the complaint saying that it was the first time they had ever had one like it. But the corporation did not chose to backpedal from its now public problem.

Instead, it not only formally apologized to Rogers in the form of $1,000 in damages, the maximum allowed under the law, but it also established a sensitivity training program for all of its employees.

According to Judy States, Circle K's public relations director, "We do not want to be perceived of as discriminatory. Rather, this experience with Ms. Rogers gives us the chance to establish a policy and step ahead of our competition. We now understand what we need to address in the workplace" (personal communication).

When pushed to explain why a corporation of this size would respond so quickly to an individual complaint that many other businesses would find unimportant, States revealed the public relations priorities of Circle K. During an interview, States said "Our CEO and president are very involved with communication. I meet with both of them every couple of weeks. We realize that with 3,100 stores open 24 hours a day, we are open to everything and anything. This experience was a challenge that resulted in a positive experience for us" (personal communication).

States said that Circle K had a basic American Disabilities Act (ADA) awareness training program in place. "We knew we wanted to start some kind of training on the basic tenets of the Act. It seems the Rogers' case speeded that process along."

So, what is Circle K telling its employees to do when a customer asks to use the restroom? First, they are saying that customers should have access to toilets. But, they have taken it a step further by saying that a passerby should also be given access to restroom facilities. This is a big step for Circle K, because most state health codes (including Washington State where this case occurred) require that restroom facilities be available for employees but not necessarily for customers.

Investigator Vierra believes most discriminatory acts occur because of ignorance. "It actually doesn't cost that much money to remedy these kinds of conflicts. Circle K is a marvelous example of an individual complaint resulting in a major corporate response"(personal communication).

And Shelly Cohen, legal counsel for the Seattle Human Rights Department, believes that Circle K realized that responding positively was good public relations. States did mention that Circle K was in the middle of a new public relations campaign. Rogers' case gave Circle K the opportunity to set up an innovative training program and outdistance 7-Eleven, their major competition.

Circle K's response is a gleaming example of public relations at its best. Corporate policy is established, which will have a long-term impact on how business is done, how they serve their public, and how the corporation's reputation is enhanced. All of this was done while

spending very little money and without a news release, although the
story was covered in the Phoenix and Seattle areas. It received front
page treatment in Seattle and was picked up by the wire services.

These three cases—the untimely attempt to remove an artist's sculpture, the neighborhood uproar over a hospital's plan for better service,
and one corporation's response to making restroom facilities available—are examples of organizational public relations. They are but
three examples (and relatively small ones at that) of the ways in which
organizations and publics collide. These organizational and public
interactions often seem like the random collisions of minute atomic
particles spinning around atom smashers that nuclear physicists study.
Who knows when the next one will occur or what it will bring—
random events in random motion, as illustrated in Exhibit 1.1.

Certainly in the bank's attempt to sell the Henry Moore sculpture and
the hospital's plan to build a helipad, seemingly rational organizational decisions resulted in emotional responses. As is all too often the
case, a decision grounded in the rationality of the organization, a
rationality based on a limited (e.g., tunnel vision, narrow vision,
near-sighted vision) understanding of organizational means and ends,
succeeded in creating emotional hotbeds of opposition that thwarted
the organization's ability to implement its rational decision. The seeds
for these ill-fated interactions are found in the very nature of organizations, in their structures and processes. In order to better understand
the role of public relations in shepherding interactions between the
organization and its external constituents, I propose nine assumptions
that ground much of my thinking in this book. It is to those assumptions that we now turn.

ASSUMPTIONS

As I stated at the beginning of this chapter, the ideas presented in this
book are based on certain assumptions we have about organizations
and about public relations. There are things we take for granted about
the practice of informed, competent, and ethical public relations.
These assumptions form the underpinnings on which we discuss the
interplay between organizational decision making and public relations
effectiveness.

These assumptions are grounded in my belief that the process of
public relations occurs largely in organizational settings. "Public
relations researchers and professionals, of course, have long recog-

EXHIBIT 1.1
The Public Restroom and Public Relations, Continued

Through a bit of serendipity, the fact that I was going to use the Circle K bathroom incident as a case study in a textbook found its way into a column of short business stories in one of our local newspapers. After seeing my thoughts on the Circle K incident, one of the newspaper's readers called with another "public relations bathroom example." Charlotte Steiner and her daughter Annie flew Reno Air from Las Vegas to Seattle. An incident on that flight resulted in the following letter to Reno Air:

Dear Mr. Reno Air:

September 26th—on flight 201—to Seattle, I found it imperative that I use the lavatory. The attendants were serving drinks in our cabin and the aisle was blocked. Thus, they directed me to First Class.

Would you believe the attendant in First Class, "Tom," would not let me use the facilities. "This is for First Class passengers only"????? Of course you can't believe it!!!

Question: Upon landing do they test the urine to see which comes from which class?

Sincerely,

Annie Steiner,

A Former Reno Air Passenger

Ms. Steiner did receive a return letter from Reno Air's consumer affairs department apologizing for the "inconvenience you were caused while flying with Reno Air." Perhaps all of us who work in organizations that deal with the public should check our organization's bathroom policies to avoid future embarrassment.

nized that public relations is always practiced in organizational contexts" (Trujillo & Toth, 1987, p. 199). Public relations communication arises from some organizational need (or perceived need). Public relations efforts are influenced by the culture of the organization in which (or for which) the public relations activity is produced. In order to understand why public relations activities are undertaken, why some succeed and others fail, we need to place those activities in the organizational context. We seek to better understand the public relations process by better understanding the organizational processes.

Unquestionably, a lot of communication that falls under the rubric traditionally labeled "public relations" is done on behalf of individuals rather than organizations. Politicians visit inner city homeless shelters or flag factories, celebrities gain recognition through publicity tours, individual corporate leaders are feted at special events. Certainly, in these cases, public relations activities are performed for particular individuals, in essence, to "sell" the individual and his or her idea or product to the public. They are promotional efforts, public relations used to gain maximum media exposure as Exhibit 1.2 illustrates.

Although many might wish otherwise, particularly during sound-bite election years (the 1994 congressional races were fast apace when I wrote this chapter), we accept the fact that, given our free enterprise, capitalist American society, public relations as promotion will always be with us. This aspect of public relations is *not* the focus of this book.

That a better understanding of organizational life is important for public relations practitioners is evident in a *Public Relations Journal*

EXHIBIT 1.2
Bad Press Better than No Press to Burke

The following is from an article by the *Seattle Post-Intelligencer's* television critic that speaks about the power of the publicity model:

> Delta Burke [a television actress] burns inside over her constant roasting in the media fires.

> You know the stories: compulsively fat, arrogantly bitchy, manipulated by a Svengali husband, a swell-headed fruitcake full of lies.

> It's hurtful, Burke says, but she also credits the attacks with helping her to get her own sitcom, premiering on ABC in the fall.

> "If they didn't write about me at all, I wouldn't be famous," she told a gathering of TV critics on Tuesday.

> ". . . The bad press put me where I am. I became enough of a household name, or whatever, that I'm then in a position to have a deal like this."

> . . . "I think it sucks," she said of the negative media attention. "I am not perfect (but) most of the stuff said about me is b---s---."

> . . . But no matter. Let them [reporters] lash away, she said, because it brings her what she wants: a name and fortune.

Reprinted courtesy of the *Seattle Post-Intelligencer*. John Engstrom, *Seattle Post-Intelligencer*, July 16, 1992, C1, C8.

annual salary survey (Jacobson & Tortorello, 1992). Of the 2,019 responses to the survey, 68% of the respondents report that they work for or in some type of organization—corporate, government, or nonprofit. An additional 20% work for public relations counseling firms and 3.6% are solo practitioners. My experience tells me that these public relations consultants also do a lot of work for organizations.

Another indicator of the tremendous link between organizational entities and public relations activities is found in the 1991 Silver Anvil Awards conferred by the Public Relations Society of America. All of the 40 winners were associated with an organization, however large or small. Of the 40 winning public relations programs, 30 were created and implemented with the help of public relations consultants.

Without overly belaboring the point, public relations must be understood within organizational contexts. There is a need, then, for practitioners to understand organizational dynamics, especially those that will ultimately influence their ability to effectively communicate with desired audiences. We now turn to the assumptions guiding my thinking about organizational public relations.

Assumption 1: Organizations Are Political Entities in Which Power, in Its Many Forms, Is Used to Influence Others Toward Desired Individual or Organizational Outcomes

As a caution, please do not take this assumption as a necessarily negative view of life in organizations. All too often, people talk disparagingly of organizational politics, sensing perhaps that the worst characteristics of our governmental political system is what defines organizational politics. Or, that organizational politics is associated with certain types of people in the organization, people who cannot be trusted, for example, or the movers and shakers who will do anything to get ahead. Or, that organizational politics is a dirty, demeaning, degrading aspect of organizational life that can be avoided if we just do our job to the best of our ability.

Certainly, these negative perceptions of organizational power are in some ways accurate. All of us have experienced the detrimental aspects of organizational politics and power in one form or another. We often decry the apparent necessity of politics even being a part of our organizational life. However, power and politics are very much a part of organizational life and the more we know about them the better off we will be. As Zahra (1989) suggested, "understanding the nature of organizational power and politics is essential not only because it affects one's career but also because it may impact the very survival of the company'' (p. 15).

My concern is that power and politics are an integral part of organizational decision making and that organizational decisions influence the eventual effectiveness of organizational public relations. A number of writers have suggested that there are both political and nonpolitical decisions made in organizations (Cavanagh, Moberg, & Velasquez, 1981; Mintzberg, 1985). Nonpolitical decisions are either so routine that they are carried out in the established guidelines created to guide decisions or ones that can be made without invoking an extraordinary effort to use power. Political decisions are ones in which power is necessarily incorporated into the decision-making process, usually as organizational groups or goals come into conflict as to the appropriate means to achieve an end.

Politics most often occur when the organization faces uncertainty, when there is conflict, and when decision making is not routine. As I discuss in later chapters, these are the very organizational conditions that bring about the need for public relations. It is our belief that many (if not most) public relations decisions are political ones. As such, an understanding of power and politics is essential for understanding the 'political nature' of many public relations decisions and actions.

Assumption 2: Organizational Decisions Are Made by Individuals

Well, of course they are, you say. Who else would make them? On the surface, this seems to be almost a tautological assumption in that organizations are composed of individuals who do the work (e.g., decision making) of the organization (Weiser, 1988). But, in order to understand how organizations make and take credit for decisions, and how various publics respond to an organization's decisions, we need to refocus our attention to individual decision makers.

Our understanding of the individuals involved is important on at least two levels. The first has to do with the ethical ramifications of organizational decisions. Individuals bring individual value systems to the organizations in which they work, play, or volunteer. At the same time, the organizations in which we live provide an organizational value system, often stated in vision or mission statements, but often unstated in the norms of acceptable organizational behavior. As numerous writers have suggested (Beyer & Lutze, 1993; Fritzsche, 1991; Liedtka, 1989, 1991; Werhane, 1991) the necessity of organizational decision making often puts the individual's value system in conflict with the organization's value system. The results of these clashes can be disastrous. Certainly, these potential clashes in value systems are at the heart of the Public Relations Society of America's "Code of Ethics."

Second, and equally important for public relations practitioners, is the tendency we have to reify or objectify our organizations or institutions. We talk of Seafirst Bank or Kid's Place Hospital in terms that anthropomorphize the institution under discussion. Although there is nothing inherently wrong with doing this, it does tend to obscure the fact that people work in the organization, people who are responsible for the seemingly faceless organizational facade. We lose sight of the fact that people in the organization make decisions that affect others both inside and outside the organization.

Assumption 3: Organizational Decisions Often Affect Organizational Stakeholders Who Often Have Little or No Say in the Decision-Making Process

Organizational decision making used to be so much simpler in the old days. Decisions were made based on what was best for the organization, taking into account relatively few other interests. The decision makers might consider the needs of the organization's shareholders, its primary customers or clients, whatever regulatory agencies existed, legal ramifications, or how this decision would affect employee morale (reader please note—this is obviously somewhat facetious and simplistic to make a point). Decisions were made by organizational members with little consideration of wider-ranging or long-term effects and almost entirely to the exclusion of unidentified potentially interested publics.

This is not the case anymore. Much organizational decision making now occurs in a tumultuous, uncertain, turbulent environment that demands ever-increasing attention be paid to a wide variety of organizational stakeholders (Kreiner & Bhambri, 1991; Maranville, 1989; Pauchant & Mitroff, 1992). Stakeholders "include those individuals, groups, and other organizations who have an interest in the actions of an organization and who have the ability to influence it" (Savage, Nix, Whitehead, & Blair, 1991, p. 61). Stakeholders are parties concerned about what the organization is doing and about the decisions being made by individuals in the organization. They are not only concerned, but willing and able to lay claim to a say in the decision-making process.

The administrators of Kid's Place hospital learned that there were a number of very vocal stakeholders interested in the decision to build a helipad. Seafirst Bank and JMB Realty learned that the simple matter of selling a piece of art for a profit could rouse slumbering (and ignored) stakeholder groups.

An examination of the stakeholder literature reveals that there are two competing perspectives on stakeholders as they relate to organizational decision making. The first is a continuation of traditional management theory and practice that seeks ways to identify and manage stakeholder groups, particularly those that might be opposed to a particular organizational action (Savage et. al., 1991). The second, a more radical approach to organizational theory and management practice, seeks to identify stakeholder groups so that the organizational decision-making process can be "democratized" (Deetz, 1992). The first approach attempts to manage organizational goals in light of stakeholder support or opposition; the second seeks to incorporate stakeholder goals with those of the organization. Both are profoundly important for organizational decision makers and public relations practitioners.

Assumption 4: Organizational Decisions Have Both an Instrumental and a Symbolic Function

Organizations exist in larger social, economic, legal, and technological environments that influence the ways in which the organization conducts its business or mission. Organizational members act in response to actual or anticipated or perceived changes in the organization's internal and/or external environments (Dutton & Ottensmeyer, 1987). Often, these decisions are accomplished strategically (e.g., in terms of a strategic plan); often, they are routine actions carried out time and time again; sometimes they are one-time crises that arise suddenly and without warning; occasionally they are lucky breaks the "organization" stumbles on more by chance than design. The key to understanding the instrumental function of decision making is that it produces a tangible result for the organization in terms of resources (material or human), it is the "work" of the organization.

In the Seafirst example, someone made the decision that the time was ripe to sell the Henry Moore statue. This decision was based on what we will for the moment call "rational" organization reasoning, based on profit maximization and a desire to redirect the nature of the corporation's art holdings. These reasons support the instrumental function of the decision to sell.

As the Seafirst example so aptly illustrates, however, there is more to any decision than the hard and fast tangible results of the decision itself. There was a symbolic aspect of the decision to sell "Vertebrae" that far outweighed the instrumental reward of making even a hefty profit. The symbolic function of decisions speaks to the notion that "decision makers create and communicate shared meanings for organizational members through the structures and process they design" (Dutton & Ottensmeyer, 1987, p. 358). These meanings are sometimes consistent with the instrumental function, sometimes they are far different from the intended consequences of the instrumental function.

Circle K's instrumental decision to act quickly to resolve a potentially threatening action sent the symbolic message that the organization cared about disabled or physically disadvantaged people. The symbolic meaning of the decision complemented the instrumental function. The opposite was true in the case of Seafirst's instrumental decision to sell "Vertebrae." The symbolic message inherent in the instrumental decision was interpreted in a way that did not complement the intentions of the decisions makers. The meaning assigned the decision was that the organization was acting in bad faith, trying to make a profit at the public's expense, and ignoring the organization's civic duty to the people of Seattle. Clearly, in this case the symbolic importance of the decision far outweighed the instrumental function incorporated in the decision-making process.

The distinctions between the instrumental and symbolic functions of organizational decisions go a long way in explaining why organizational decision makers are often startled by the reactions of others to their decisions. All too often, decision makers are caught up in the instrumental side of the decision-making process and pay scant attention to the often more important and potentially beneficial or harmful symbolic side. Public relations practitioners must understand both the instrumental and symbolic functions of organizational decisions, a point I elaborate later in this volume (Grunig, 1993).

Assumption 5: Organizations Tend Toward Arrogance

Deal and Kennedy (1982) pointed out that organizations have cultures that tend to insulate the organization's members from the larger environment in which the organization exists. This organizational ethnocentricism can lead to organizational arrogance in dealings with the organizational constituencies and stakeholders (Awad, 1985). As former General Motor's President, Charles Wison said in testimony before a United States Senate committee in 1952, "What is good for the country is good for General Motors, and what's good for General Motors is good for the country."

We all know and can describe arrogant people. They are overly self-centered, convinced of their own importance, act in a haughty or condescending manner, and generally treat others with a smattering of disdain. Perhaps the best recent example of a public figure described as arrogant is Leona Helmsley, convicted of income tax fraud, who dismissed her troubles with the IRS with the comment "only the little people have to pay taxes."

Organizations (or, more accurately, the people in organizations) can also be arrogant. Witness the Exxon Corporation's response to the Exxon Valdez oil spill. Exxon officials minimized the spill; downplayed its scope and significance; did not reveal that there was inadequate containment equipment stationed in the area; and issued contradictory statements as to the ongoing status of the cleanup. Finally, Exxon said it had done enough to clean up the spill and stopped work; environmental experts countered that it would take years to restore Prince William Sound (Williams and Olaniran, 1994). In an article about Exxon oil spills (in both Alaska and in a waterway between New York City and New Jersey) Yagoda (1990) wrote, "They [Exxon management] show what a combination of bad luck, *arrogance*, and ineptitude can do to a company's public image" (p. 48, italics added).

Unfortunately, even the most cursory reading of news reports about organizations—business, government, nonprofit—indicate that many organizational members hold and espouse a "feeling of omnipotence for the company. The company is all-wise and all-powerful with little thought given to those outside the company" (Maranville, 1989, p. 57). This attitude of "we know what is best," this arrogance, flies in the face of maintaining open and confirming communication with an organization's stakeholders. Organizational arrogance, I argue, is detrimental to the ultimate well-being of the organization. Organizational arrogance is also unfortunately often associated with poor public communication, both external and internal, the very heart of the public relations function.

A recent survey of Fortune 500 company managers who buy outside public relations services indicates that public relations firms themselves are not exempt from sometimes appearing arrogant to their clients (Russell, 1993). Arrogance topped the list of the ways in which public relations firms can lose a client's business. According to those who took part in this survey/discussion:

> One form of arrogance is self-promotion, i.e. when a [pr] firm basks in its accomplishments without acknowledging the client's role. . . . The second kind of arrogance is the know-it-all syndrome. That includes talking down to the client, not listening to what he or she says and presuming that you know more about the client's business, management and staff than they do. (Russell, 1993, p. 36)

A complete list of the ten ways to lose a client is included in Exhibit 1.3.

Assumption 6: Not All Organizational Decisions Are Public Relations Ones, Although All Organizational Decisions Are Communicated

Public relations is often defined as a communication function of the organization (Long & Hazleton, Jr., 1987; Baskin & Aronoff, 1992). Such a definition, although useful in describing what public relations practitioners do or attempt to do, is overly demanding of the concept of communication. Or, perhaps a better way of saying this is that such definitions are overly inclusive of what kinds of decisions count as public relations ones and what kinds of communication count as public relations communication.

Although some public relations educators and practitioners argue that public relations is inclusive of all communication in an organization, I feel a great need for distinguishing between organizational decisions and public relations decisions. There are personnel problems, management problems, accounting problems, production problems, financial problems, and so on. All are legitimate ground for organizational decision making, none are inherently public relations problems.

EXHIBIT 1.3
Ten Ways to Lose a Client

1. Arrogance
2. Dishonesty
3. Lack of results
4. Mental obsolescence
5. Technological obsolescence
6. Lack of professional standards
7. Budget hassles
8. Fail at the small stuff
9. Fail at the big stuff
10. Let relationships go stale

Reprinted by permission of *Public Relations Journal,* published by the Public Relations Society of America, New York, NY. From Anita Russell, "How firms can attract, retain, . . . or lose clients." *Public Relations Journal,* 1993, pp. 33–36. Reprinted with permission.

Can they become public relations problems? Yes. Potentially, every problem, dilemma, and decision can evolve into a situation that demands a public relations response. Long and Hazleton, Jr. (1987) suggested that "organizational problems and solutions are not inherently PR problems and solutions. Considering the potential range of problem-types, only those directly tied to symbolic resource management are within the domain of PR responsibility" (p. 10). I like this distinction and make more of it in succeeding chapters.

The decision to sell "Vertebrae" was not a public relations decision, it was a business decision involving the making of money from the timely sale of a possession. However, the communication about the sale to the community certainly indicated how an organization can mismanage its symbolic resources. The same is true of the decision to build a helipad at Kid's Place.

Assumption 7: Organizational Public Relations Is About Conflict

As Pearson (1989b) so aptly and simply suggested, "public relations practice is situated at precisely that point where competing interests collide" (p. 67). This assumption, crucial to much of what I have to say about organizational public relations, is grounded in an open systems perspective of organization. Systems theory (as discussed in greater detail in chapter 3) focuses academic and managerial energy on the relationship between an organization and its environment and on the exchange of energy and materials between the organization and its environment. The effective organization becomes one that can best manage this organizational/environmental exchange thereby meeting the organization's needs for survival. The necessity for managing this exchange brings us to the essential role of public relations in the organization's quest for success.

If organizational success is predicated on the successful integration of environmental demands and organizational needs (a simple statement to be sure), those organizational functions that link the organization with its environment are crucial to the eventual success of the organization. Public relations is one of those crucial functions. Public relations occurs in the exchange between organization and environment; public relations happens in the boundary between the organization's interests and the interests of all other potential stakeholders. This exchange is all too often characterized by ambiguity, uncertainty, mistrust, hostility, misunderstanding, ambivalence, and conflict, both real and perceived.

The connection of public relations and potential conflict is hardly new. Indeed, many argue that public relations became a field because of conflicting interests between organizations and their stakeholders (Olasky, 1987; Pearson, 1990b). I agree with Ehling (1989) who proposed that:

> The conceptual framework of public relations management, derived from an identifiable theoretical foundation, says in simple terms that conflict (and its opposite, cooperation) constitutes the unit of analysis for public relations executives. . . . In a complex, interdependent societal system, the emergence of a communication activity as a primary means for resulting disagreements or discord cannot be left to chance, for to do so is to increase the probabilities that communication will never be employed as an appropriate and legitimate alternative to other means which may turn out to be far less appropriate and often quite illegitimate. In short, this type of conflict-reducing, cooperation-inducing communication endeavor needs to be managed. (pp. 6–7, 16–17)

As demonstrated throughout this volume, the successful management (if not resolution) of organizational and environmental conflict is best understood using both a political and symbolic sense-making approach to understanding organizations.

Assumption 8: Public Relations Cannot (and Should Not) Make a Bad Organizational Decision Good

The spirit of this assumption rests in my belief that even the best public relations efforts can only do so much in the face of poorly conceived organizational decisions. All too often, public relations practitioners are asked to use their considerable talents in symbolic manipulation to cast a positive "spin" on a poor or badly handled or questionable organizational decision (Jackall, 1988).

The potential public relations consequences of any organizational decision should be continually and closely examined during the instrumental phases of the decision-making process. The potential symbolic interpretations of any organizational decision need to be anticipated (as best they can be) and incorporated into discussions concerning the best instrumental option available to the organization. Think what might have been avoided had the symbolic ramifications of the decision to sell "Vertebrae" been discussed prior to making the instrumental decision to sell (especially with representative external arts-oriented stakeholders). A case used to highlight the negative would have been one used to accentuate the positive.

My belief that public relations efforts cannot make a bad decision good should not be construed as implying that the organization must make all decisions in a manner pleasing or favorable to its various stakeholders. Organizations need to and must make tough, unpopular, and unwelcome decisions. The decision to lay off workers, the decision to close a plant, the decision to reinvest profits rather than distribute them, the decision to raise prices, the decision to eliminate a program are all decisions that organizations must make at times. They are not popular with certain stakeholders, they are not welcome, they are not good news. But, they must be made and certainly public relations practitioners should be involved in both the instrumental and symbolic aspects of the decision-making process. Public relations can and should help in the formulation and communication of these kinds of tough decisions.

These are not bad decisions in the sense that they are poorly thought out, poorly timed, poorly understood, or simply poor instrumental choices. There is a world of difference between a tough decision that has to be made for the sake of the organization and bad decisions that should not be made. Indeed, bad decisions often jeopardize the organization, both instrumentally and symbolically. Some of the examples included later in the book speak to the distinction between tough decisions and bad decisions and the appropriate role of public relations in each.

Assumption 9: The "Best" Public Relations Encourage And Enhance Consensus and Community

This assumption speaks to the heart of public relations as first and foremost a communication function that should be used to build and maintain healthy relationships. As the title of a popular introductory communication text boldly asserts: *Bridges, Not Walls* (Stewart, 1990). All too often, organizations misuse public relations communication to build walls. How often have we heard (or read) phrases like "stone-walling" or "hanging tough" or "who do they think they are" or "proprietary interests." The walls built with inappropriate communication are the result of misguided organizational decision making, arrogance, and ignorance.

Building bridges should be the mainstay of organizational public relations. Bridges are built through what Weiser (1988) called "responsible communication" that "features traits of openness, admission, information-sharing and self-assurance" (p. 740). Bridges are built using a two-way symmetrical model of public relations (Grunig & Hunt, 1984), in which the fundamental aim of communication is to "facilitate understanding among people and such other systems as

organizations, publics, or societies'' (Grunig, 1989, p. 38). Bridges are
built by keeping the dialogue going, by encouraging discussion of all
views, by helping others communicate their opinions and ideas (Pearson, 1989b). Bridges are what Kruckeberg and Starck (1988) propose
when they define public relations as ''the active attempt to restore and
maintain a sense of community'' (p. xi).

The Circle K decision makers could have easily built a wall. They
chose to build to a bridge to the disabled community. The decision
makers at both Seafirst and Kid's Place ultimately built a bridge, but
one that was less secure and stable because of the earlier walls that
were created.

SUMMARY

In this chapter I presented three case studies and nine assumptions
shown in Table 1.1. I briefly indicated why each assumption is crucial
for building a better understanding of organizational public relations.
I also briefly showed how the case studies reflected the implications of
each of our assumptions.

Undoubtedly, there are other assumptions that could be included in
such a list. There are also any number of corollaries that can be derived
from the assumptions. A corollary of Assumption 8, for example, is
that there is a time for advocacy and a time for consensus building.
This corollary is addressed extensively in chapters 8 and 9 as I grapple

TABLE 1.1
Assumptions

ASSUMPTION 1: Organizations are political entities in which power, in its many
forms, is used to influence others toward desired individual or organizational outcomes.

ASSUMPTION 2: Organizational decisions are made by individuals.

ASSUMPTION 3: Organizational decisions often affect organizational stakeholders
who often have little or no say in the decision-making process.

ASSUMPTION 4: Organizational decisions have both an instrumental and a symbolic function.

ASSUMPTION 5: Organizations tend toward arrogance.

ASSUMPTION 6: Not all organizational decisions are public relations ones,
although all organizational decisions are communicated.

ASSUMPTION 7: Organizational public relations is about conflict.

ASSUMPTION 8: Public relations cannot (and should not) make a bad
organizational decision good.

ASSUMPTION 9: The ''best'' public relations encourage and enhance consensus
and community.

with the characteristics of public relations situations. Progressing through the book, I examine the assumptions and their corollaries in more detail, expanding on the understanding of how each illustrates and illuminates a better understanding of organizational public relations.

To conclude, I quote from a delightful book by Eric Hansen (1991), *Motoring with Mohammed: Journeys to Yemen and the Red Sea.* Hansen was shipwrecked while sailing in the Red Sea from 1977–1978. Just before he was rescued by a band of would be pirates, he and his stranded shipmates buried many of their valuables, including journals Hansen kept in which he described his travels about the world. Ten years later Hansen returned to Yemen to search for his buried journals. During an airplane flight toward the conclusion of his journey, Hansen sat next to a rabbi who asked if he knew the difference between an intelligent man and a wise man. When Hansen asked the rabbi to explain the distinction, the rabbi responded, "The intelligent man is capable of overcoming problems and difficulties the wise man would have avoided in the first place" (Hansen, 1991, p. 226).

My hope is that this book prompts the reader to become a wiser public relations practitioner; perhaps not from anything I write, but from thinking more deeply about the role and function of public relations as practiced in modern organizations.

Practitioner Response to Chapter 1: Getting Into the Huddle

Bill Wortley, Senior Vice President
Washington Natural Gas Company
Seattle, Washington

THE VERTEBRAE

"The Vertebrae" is a perfect case study for young or new public relations practitioners, addressing two of the most difficult, yet most common of all PR occurences. From childhood on we learn to show respect for our elders or superiors; answering questions when asked; and most important searching for ways to satiate our deep need for approval. "The Vertebrae" demands that we fight against the very fiber of our entire family education.

At times it is very difficult to discuss issues with corporate executives or superiors. It can be even more difficult when you have to press for hard uncomfortable answers. Executives are often reluctant to discuss sensitive issues due to liability concerns or fear of relinquishing control. Loss of control or legal concern can lead to a "no comment" directive from senior management. Responding to a reporter's inquiry with "no comment" is unacceptable in any public relations response situation.

We seek approval, which translates into answering questions from reporters to meet their deadlines, regardless of the company's needs. As we mature, with experience we realize that the accuracy of our response far outweighs the pressure created by the press. In other words, a response that only meets the immediate needs of the reporter can cause even bigger public relations problems. The primary objective is to help reporters understand that with a short delay any and all questions may be answered with more substance and accuracy. Delay can also provide for the selection of the appropriate spokesperson and preparation of answers to the first series of questions. The delay tactic can also change the momentum of the issue to your benefit. Time may also enable the CEO or other executives to better understand what credible answers sound like. One of the best uses of extra time is to role play with the information sources to demonstrate what response pressure can mean for less thought out answers.

KID'S PLACE

The Kid's Place study speaks to the way decisions are often made within a closed environment. The first thing that comes to mind is the old Bell telephone approach to decision making. You may have read about the Bell Systems one time reputation of, "We don't have to care. We're Ma Bell." Decisions are often made with the best of intentions. It's not necessarily the fault of the people as much as it is the result of an "inside-out" attitude. As presented in this chapter, people "inside" begin to think that they are at the center rather than part of the whole.

Gaining support for advance research about public reaction often meets with senior-level disapproval. In this case, it seems to be much easier to apologize after the fact, than to face the possibility of long delays. I still remain amazed by how executives can read, hear, and watch daily, outrageous headlines of project delays due to lack of advance research and attention to the community concerns, yet continue to move ahead as if *they* were somehow immune. The present-day, very public process of obtaining building permits and completing environmental impact statements should be an indicator of public awareness. When activist groups are not part of the process they often react in ways to inflame specific publics who can be against any project. We all know how very difficult it is to turn public opinion once the momentum is underway.

Our best counsel is to provide, in a nonconfronting way; real projections that show actual costs and projected delays resulting from failure to addresss public impact up-front. It is necessary to encourage research for public benefits and to find groups that will most likely support a project as well as those who might be opposed. It is essential to face each of these groups with openness.

CIRCLE K AND OTHER COMMENTS

I love rapid response situations that show concern for the public and consumers. To me, this indicates the self-confidence of management and true empowerment of the frontline people. For example, the Ritz Carlton International Hotel chain gives each employee the equivalent of $1,000 to use at any time and in any way to deal with any customer concern. The window for action remains open for such a short time, and once closed, you will most often be on the defense or dealing with old news.

Larry Newman, APR, former Executive Vice President at Manning, Salvage and Lee, provided the best understanding of the incredibly important role of the public relations professional. According to Newman, the PR professional must be inside the "circle" or "huddle" where the key decisions are made. In short, until you master the "True Decision Flow," learn who the natural leaders are, and earn a seat inside the huddle, you cannot truly provide the important counsel that the assumptions outlined in this chapter clearly demonstrate.

The strategy that I use and continue to recommend when becoming a part of any corporation or organization is to quietly observe the natural flow of the decision-making process. Then carefully select a maven or sponsor to validate your need and right to timely, credible answers. The sponsor is necessary until you earn the right to walk within the decision-making circle. The right of access is an absolute imperative essential for your credibility both inside and outside the company.

CHAPTER 2
Organizational Arrogance and the Public Relations Function

In their book, *In Search of Excellence: Lessons from America's Best-Run Companies*, Peters and Waterman (1982) identified 43 excellent companies and organizations to study. Their purpose in examining these excellent companies was to better understand what organizational and human characteristics led to organizational success. To be considered "excellent," a company had to (a) be considered excellent by an informed group of observers (analysts, academicians, industry insiders), (b) be in the top half of its industry on four of six quantitative measures of profitability over a 20-year period, and (c) be regarded as having achieved a 20-year record of innovation by industry experts.

One of the companies Peters and Waterman designated as "excellent" was International Business Machines (IBM). Peters and Waterman thought so highly of IBM, especially of its commitment to customer service, that "Big Blue" was continually used as an exemplar for success. The following quotes from Peters and Waterman (1982) are typical:

> Take IBM, for example. It is hardly far behind the times, but most observers will agree that it hasn't been a technology leader for decades. Its dominance rests on its commitment to service. (p. 137)

> While people are in this position [assistant to the company's top officers], they spend their entire, typical three-year stint doing only one thing—*answering every customer complaint within twenty-four hours.* (p. 159, italics in original)

> To make sure it is in touch, IBM measures internal and external customer satisfaction on a monthly basis. (p. 161)

IBM was, in part, so successful because of its commitment to customer service. In his summary of IBM's public image, DeLamarter (1986) wrote that we see IBM as:

> Having happy customers—customers that include not only the largest and most sophisticated organizations in the world but also small firms and just common folk using personal computers. These customers trust IBM because it always puts their interests before its own. (p. xvi)

Highly touted, highly regarded, and highly profitable is IBM's service to its customer.

How then do we explain the following headlines and quotes written in the early 1990s, a mere 10 years after Peters and Waterman's (1982) highly public touting of IBM's excellence in customer service:

> "Name alone won't restore customer confidence," (subhead from an article by Fitzgerald & Hildebrand, 1992, about IBM's problems with customer service).

> IBM may not be the Rodney Dangerfield of personal computing, but the company is clearly fighting an uphill battle to regain user [customer] respect and confidence (Fitzgerald & Hildebrand, 1992, p. 1).

> Gerstner's [IBM's new chairman and chief executive] most important task is to restore customer confidence (Brousell, 1993).

Success is just as likely to produce the seeds for failure as it is for continued success (Harari, 1993a; 1993b). Certainly, IBM's well-documented collapse in the personal computer business is indication that success is often all too fleeting, even given the best of intentions and previous successes. Indeed, the hallmark of IBM's success—customer relations—became its tragic flaw, its Achilles heel. IBM's largest customers "lambasted IBM for arrogance—its unwillingness to listen and its inability to adapt to customers. . . . Instead of sweating blood to help customers, runs the most common complaint, IBM tries to bully them into doing things the Big Blue way" ("Refashioning IBM," 1990, p. 22). Big Blue, in short, acted arrogantly.

If we accept the idea of Assumption 3, that individuals are responsible for organizational actions, then we can only conclude that organizational arrogance begins with those who manage organizations (Crosby, 1992; Greenwald, 1992; Jones, 1992; Pitta, 1991; Sims, 1992; Zauderer, 1992). As Cook (1991) vividly and pointedly claimed, "most business problems today are caused by managerial arrogance" (p. 69). Managerial arrogance, Deetz (1992) suggested, is the result of the rapid and unchecked rise of corporate colonization. Deetz (1992) wrote:

the *managerialism* practiced in the modern corporation has failed. . . . With managerialism, certain interests are arbitrarily privileged, the process of reaching decisions is distorted, and meaningful conflicts are suppressed. And finally, managerialism's arbitrary authority relations demean the human character. (p. 5, italics in original)

"Arbitrarily privileged," "distorted," "suppressed," and "demean" are all words I associate with arrogance. Throughout his provoking book, Deetz (1992) takes to task the internal worldview of organizational management and its discursive practices. He amply illustrates how the managerial mindset so often works to foster arrogance, an arrogance that extends far beyond the boundaries of the organization itself.

A managerial mindset, or managerialism, is "grounded in the assumptions that (1) all work processes can and should be rationalized, (2) the means for attaining organizational objectives should be everyone's central concern, and (3) efficiency and predictability should dominate all other values" (Conrad, 1992, pp. 508–509). Deetz's (1992) argument is based on his analysis, interpretation, and extension of critical theory and postmodern ideas that are often complex and somewhat daunting to the reader. That a managerial mindset or prerogative exists, however, is one that is reinforced by more prosaic data from surveys of managers.

In a survey of 6,000 executives and managers sponsored by the American Management Association, for example, Posner and Schmidt (1984) uncovered what they term a "managerial psyche" (p. 205). Although there are minor differences between the rankings of supervisory managers, middle managers, and executive managers, Posner and Schmidt (1984) concluded that

what is more striking is the similarity in ranking of organizational goals across managers at different levels in their organizations and across hundreds of different organizations. This seems to suggest a "managerial psyche." There is a strong sense of agreement among managers about the purpose and role of organizations. (p. 205)

I will return to their finding about the overwhelming importance of organizational effectiveness in later chapters because this focus has important implications for public relations. What is important for the moment is to understand that there does indeed exist a managerial worldview in organizations, that the parochialism of this worldview often leads to organizational arrogance, and that this arrogance unfortunately is at odds with truly effective organizational public relations.

This chapter examines a number of ways in which public relations can potentially contribute to the existence and communication of organizational arrogance. It also examines how many of the negative perceptions often associated with public relations are the result of organizational arrogance and the misapplication of public relations principles and techniques. In this chapter I (a) discuss Jackall's (1988) study on bureaucratic behavior and public relations, (b) examine the unintended consequences of the over-reliance on technical public relations values and practices, and (c) assess the antagonistic relationship between public relations and the media.

AUTHOR'S DISCLAIMER

A disclaimer is in order before we proceed. Any public relations practitioner, student, or educator should become discomfited if not downright angry while reading this chapter. The cultural picture I paint of public relations is rarely a pleasing one. It is difficult to read and think that we are less than we want to be, that some of the negative perceptions might be our own fault, or that public relations often does not serve a greater good. These are truths we need to come to grips with if we are to fashion a more pragmatic and enlightened view of public relations.

My disclaimer is this: The views expressed in this chapter are not necessarily those of the author! The views are those gleaned from the larger cultural environment as well as the profession itself. Although I think it is important to understand the negative stereotypes, writing about them should in no way be taken as validation or concurrence of their continued presence in our culture. Just the opposite is true; I feel the negative perceptions and stereotypes can (indeed, must) be overcome.

PUBLIC RELATIONS AND THE BUREAUCRATIC ETHIC

I turn now to a discussion of how the organizational public relations function is perceived by one observer of modern American organizations. Robert Jackall's (1988) portrayal of public relations in his book, *Moral Mazes: The World of Corporate Managers*, amply illustrates my feeling that negative perceptions of public relations are culturally widespread. First, Jackall presents an extended definition and discussion of public relations based on his research on bureaucratic ethics and morality in large corporations. As such, he touches on both the best and worst aspects of public relations as practiced in many organizations. Second, Jackall highlights many of the moral and ethical dilemmas facing public relations practitioners, be they corporate employees or consultants, as they work to accommodate the organization's goals with the public's needs and understandings. And, third, my experiences indicate that Jackall's definition and interpretations are widely accepted by organizational participants as well as much of the public.

The multiple aspects of Jackall's definition are familiar ones given our cultural heritage and understandings. The meanings he uncovered, however disparaging (and I think flawed), are ones that are dominant in our American culture. Although he focused on American corporations (for-profit organizations), his discoveries and analyses are equally pertinent to all large organizations.

Jackall (1988) undertook his research "to understand the connections between managerial work, bureaucracy, success, and morality" (p. 7). His data consisted of 143 interviews with managers from three companies, one of which was a public relations consulting firm. In addition, Jackall made extensive use of participant and nonparticipant observations in various locations of the three companies studied (e.g., meetings, informal gatherings at meals). His attempts to understand success and morality and ethics, led him to devote more interest to public relations than he first envisioned. Indeed, his book includes an entire chapter, titled "The Magic Lantern," devoted to public relations as he observed it and his participants perceived it in large American corporations.

The chapter entitled "The Magic Lantern" is both illuminating and discouraging. As you no doubt remember from your childhood stories (or, more recently the Disney movie, *Aladdin*), the magic lantern refers to one of the tales told by Scheherazade in the *Arabian Nights*. In this tale, Aladdin discovers a magic lamp inhabited by a genie. When Aladdin accidently rubs the lantern the genie, a powerful spirit, appears from the lamp's spout. The genie, so grateful at being released from his confinement in the lamp, becomes the slave of the person possessing the lamp and is capable of granting that person's every wish. An evil magician steals the lamp and uses the genie's powers for his own selfish and destructive ends, even to stealing Aladdin's bride and castle. Eventually, Aladdin recaptures the lamp, vanquishes the evil magician, and returns the genie's powers to serving the good of Aladdin and his people.

The symbolism of the magic lantern, the genie released from the bottle serving whoever has last rubbed the polished brass, cannot be escaped. The implication that public relations is some kind of "magic" and serves no higher truth than the present owner's wishes is all too prevalent both in the organizations Jackall studied and in our society.

In the beginning of his chapter on the magic lantern, Jackall claims that public relations "serves many different functions, some of them overlapping" (p. 162). He identifies those he sees as most important as follows:

1. the systematic promotion of institutional goals, products, images, and ideologies that is colloquially called "hype," a word probably derived from hyperbole or, perhaps, from hypodermic;

2. the direct or, more often, indirect lobbying of legislators, regulators, special publics, or the public at large to influence the course of legislation;

3. the creation, through a whole variety of techniques, like matchmaking money with art or social science, of a favorable awareness of a corporation to provide a sense of public importance to otherwise anonymous millionaires;

4. and the manufacture and promulgation of official versions of reality or of benign public images that smooth the way for the attainment of corporate goals or, in special circumstances, that help erase the taint of some social stigma affixed to a corporation. (Jackall, 1988, p. 163)

Jackall later abstracts these characteristics to a series of key phrases: "hyping products, influencing legislation, transforming reputations, or erasing stigma" (p. 173).

Jackall found that the promoting, influencing, creating, and promulgation most often involves symbolic manipulation for the purpose of artificially creating meanings. For example:

From the modern beginnings of their occupation, men and women in public relations have been acutely aware that social reality and social reputations are not given but made. (p. 163)

Men and women in public relations are not generally taken in by their own artifice. Rather, the very nature of their work continually reminds them that the world is put together, often in the most arbitrary fashion. (p. 170)

Since any notion of truth is irrelevant or refers at best to what is perceived, persuasion of various sorts becomes everything. (p. 173)

In the organizations Jackall examined (one of which, remember, was a public relations agency), public relations is defined as symbolic manipulation to reach a succinct and preferred interpretation of reality that is subsequently "sold" to a more or less gullible and accepting public.

Equally as disturbing is Jackall's analysis of the public relations people he observed and interviewed during his bureaucratic sojourns. According to Jackall (1988), public relations practitioners "are acutely aware of the often pejorative public views of their profession. Both because they see their own virtues as hazardous and know that others see their profession as suspect, they apply their abilities of inventing better ways of legitimating what has to be done to their own work" (p. 185). Some of these include: (a) identifying wholeheartedly with the client's interest, thereby maintaining organizational loyalty; (b) justifying efforts that they do not wholeheartedly endorse or value as individuals by "appealing to a professional ethos that celebrates the exercise of technical skill separated from any emotional commitment" (p. 185); and (c) highlighting the "social goods that are the by-products of the corporate stories that they fashion" (p. 186), such as patronage of the arts or other worthy nonprofit causes.

The arrogance to which Jackall alludes is grounded in the misunderstanding of the function of public relations to manipulate an organization's publics, including the media. Historically, as Grunig (1989) attested, public relations is "dominated by the presupposition that the purpose of public relations is to manipulate the behavior of publics for the assumed, if not actual, benefit of the manipulated publics as well as the organization" (p. 29). Others have reached similar conclusions about the practice of public relations as a means by which an organization can manipulate and thereby control others in its environment (Bivens, 1989; Kruckeberg & Starck, 1988; Lapierre, 1990a, 1990b). It is worthwhile to note that public relations as manipulation highlights the negative aspects of some of our assumptions that guide this volume. Manipulation, for example, all too easily leads to organizational arrogance (Assumption 6) and decisions that adversely affect stakeholders (Assumption 4).

Manipulation is grounded in the arrogance that arises from using public relations as a technical tool for achieving organizational goals and objectives. Unfortunately, given widely publicized displays of organizational arrogance such as that witnessed from the leaders and managers of the Exxon Corporation following the Exxon Valdez oil spill (Yagoda, 1990), public relations as manipulation is all too often the primary (if not only) perception people have of the public relations function. I turn now to an examination of the arrogance that arises from an overreliance on technical manipulation.

TECHNICALLY DERIVED ARROGANCE

This section begins with an article written almost 30 years ago, "Values in Public Relations," by Albert J. Sullivan (1965). Sullivan framed a discussion of organizational public relations around a system of values he found operative at the time. Sullivan identified three types of value systems for the organizational public relations function: technical values, partisan values, and mutual values.

Technical values are ones involved with the creating and sending of messages. "These are not primarily concerned with the truth of a message's content or with any rights or obligations of sender or receiver" (Sullivan, 1965, p. 412). They are, in Sullivan's scheme amoral means to an end. These are the things public relations practitioners produce. The communication technician role identified by Dozier and Broom (1995) is the epitome of the practitioner engaged in creating and producing messages. Sullivan's technical values are most often concerned with the effectiveness of the message created.

Partisan values "commit public relations to the cause it serves and demand loyalty, trust, and obedience to the persons who represent that cause" (Sullivan, 1965, p. 412). These are the values that bind the organizational public relations person to the organization for which he or she works. Although Sullivan acknowledges that some partisanship is necessary for the public relations function to aid the organization in attaining its goals, he laments that many organizational public relations practitioners are often excessively partisan. As Pearson (1989a) noted, Sullivan "points out that this belief in the essential rightness and completeness of the organization's point of view leads to a belief that the end justifies the means and to a belief that one-way communication is always sufficient" (p. 56). And, as Bivins (1987) added in his discussion of public relations practitioners, "Client loyalty is seen as the paramount concern of the practitioner and his chief role as that of advocate" (p. 196).

Mutual values, according to Sullivan (1965), are ones that balance the "organization-is-always-right" tendency instilled by partisan values. Mutual values instill the necessity for the public relations person to present the organization's obligation to its publics. Given mutual values, "management is considered as but one of the groups to which public relations is responsible" (p. 412). Whereas Sullivan viewed technical values to be amoral and partisan values to be often less than concerned with the truth, mutual values are grounded in the truth: "According to these [mutual values], public relations is more concerned with the truth than with special pleading" (p. 412).

Mutual values are grounded in two interconnected rights Sullivan

(1965) associated with ethical public relations. The first is that all persons, inside and outside the organization, have the right of access to "true information in matters which affect him" (p. 428). Given access to accurate information, Sullivan suggested a second, concomitant right, that is, "each person has the right to participate in decisions which affect him" (p. 428). The organization's obligation, through the public relations function, is to provide accurate and timely information and facilitate participation.

It is easy to infer that the interaction of amoral technical values and excessive loyalty instilled by partisan values can easily lead to organizational arrogance. The public relations Jackall (1988) discovered in his in-depth study of organizational bureaucracies is one that combines Sullivan's technical and partisan values in an unholy, and potentially damaging, alliance. The brand of public relations practiced by those Jackall interviewed and observed was one of technical manipulation grounded in organizational loyalty. There was little voice given to the implementation of Sullivan's mutual values except as a means of confounding or fooling the public.

Sullivan's description of public relations practice is grounded in "the justification of special pleading, primary responsibility to employer, and lack of concern from objectivity" (Olasky, 1989, p. 93). Its foundation, as Jackall (1988) suggests, is in the technical wizardry of communicating the organization's point of view. Although our conceptual understanding of the role of public relations has grown over time (e.g., the symmetrical two-way model of public relations), the demand for technical proficiency supersedes other considerations. Unfortunately, this demand locks many organizational public relations practitioners into an organizational life grounded in Sullivan's technical and partisan values.

"We Have Met the Enemy and They Is Us!"

The title of this section is a phrase attributed to a cartoon character, Pogo, drawn by the late Walt Kelly. Pogo used the phrase to put blame where blame belonged, which was usually at the feet of whoever was attempting to solve a problem. An environmentalist might use the phrase to suggest that we have become our own worst enemies in creating the deteriorating environment in which we now live because of the household chemicals we flush into the sewer system every day.

I borrow Pogo's expression to insinuate, as much as we might not want to, that the very practice of public relations is partially to blame for the enduringly persistent negative perceptions. Jackall (1988) claimed that public relations practitioners "rationalize" what they do in a number of ways, one of which was the celebration of technical skill. After quoting two public relations executives who extoll the virtues of being a "hired gun," Jackall wrote, "for the most part, hired guns accept the world as it is, without qualms, and *tell stories* for those who can pay the storytellers" (p. 186, italics added). The telling of stories—no matter the plot, characters, or setting—involves the creation and manipulation of symbols. The celebration of the technical wizardry of public relations is the celebration of communicating, more specifically, of writing.

Since the late 1970s, a line of public relations research has focused on the functions or roles public relations practitioners perform (Acharya, 1981; Brody, 1985; Broom & Dozier, 1986; Broom & Smith, 1979; Culbertson, 1985; Johnson & Acharya, 1982). This research indicates there are two major public relations roles: communication technician and communication manager. The existence of these two broad areas of responsibility and function, technician and manager, are indicative of the historical past and future aspirations of public relations as an organizational profession.

The communication technician role is almost solely related to the creation and dissemination of communication pieces. As Seitel (1987) indicated:

> Most practitioners enter the field in the role of communication technician . . . most practitioners are initially hired on the basis of their communication and journalistic skills—writing and editing the employee newsletter, and writing news releases and feature stories for the media. . . . practitioners are concerned with preparing and producing communications, sometimes without full knowledge of the original motivation and the intended results . . . Practitioners not only begin their careers in this role, but they spend much of their *time* in the technical aspects of communication. (pp. 68–69)

This is the role to which Jackall refers when he claims practitioners fall back on a celebration of technical wizardry. Technical expertise is all about communicating effectively, be it in any of the mediums or channels usually discussed when talking about public relations technicians.

Additional support for the heightened prevalence of communication wizardry in the guise of the communication technician role comes from assessments of what public relations professionals and educators think public relations students should be taught. Culbertson (1985) asked educators to indicate how much emphasis they accorded the public relations roles in their teaching. He concluded that:

> Overall, the communication-technician role, with a focus on writing and producing messages, stood out as quite distinct from other roles . . . [analysis] suggested the existence of two communication-technician roles as viewed by educators. First was a *narrow* position focusing on technical aspects of production but not on writing or liaison (media relations) work. Second, some educators took a *broader* communication technician view, emphasizing writing, publication production, and media relations while still downplaying broader behavioral-science and management related concerns. (pp. 18–19)

The existence of this strong emphasis on the communication technician role in public relations education, particularly the emphasis on writing in its many manifestations, is evident in other similar research (Kalupa & Allen, 1982; Schwartz, Yarbrough, & Shakra, 1992; Wakefield & Cottone, 1987). The overwhelming importance of writing in the public relations profession is evident in research indicating that no matter how old or how many years experience, a public relations practitioner *always* writes (Spicer, 1991).

Bear in mind, I agree that the behaviors and skills associated with the communication technician role, especially writing, are important and should be taught in the undergraduate public relations curriculum. I stress writing of all kinds in my beginning public relations classes. Although the profession has gravitated toward a more fully realized communication management role (e.g., Brody, 1985; Broom & Dozier, 1986; Turk, 1989), we have not yet escaped the overwhelming importance of the communication technician role in the public relations profession.

That the technical wizardry associated with the "magical" manipulation of symbols in the name of writing (or, in a larger sense, communicating) is and will be of primary importance in the field of public relations is evident in the criteria used to hire entry-level public relations people. Eight of 10 "prominent public relations professionals" interviewed about "what background they look for when hiring college graduates," prominently mentioned writing skills (Bahls, 1992, p. 22). Comments such as, "I'd prefer someone with a journalism degree because of the writing skills they develop," or "I'd look for a liberal arts degree with strong evidence of writing ability," or "I would hope for someone with a degree in journalism or public relations, but what I'd really look for is a demonstrated writing ability such as working for the school newspaper or an internship" (Bahls, pp. 22, 31), are typical of most employers of entry-level public relations people. My own emphasis on the skills associated with this role is based more on assuring that our students meet the requirements of their first entry-level position than with our feeling that this is the way public relations should be practiced as a profession or taught as an academic subject.

Finally, I turn to comments by William Ehling, retired director of the public relations program at Syracuse University, practitioner and educator for 50 years, and winner of the PRSA "Outstanding Educator Award" in 1988. Ehling offered his views of the field in a two-part interview in *Tips & Tactics* (a supplement of *PR Reporter*). Ehling "offers strong if distasteful evidence that it is practitioners themselves who are selling the field short" (Lapierre, 1990a, p. 1).

Ehling suggests that practitioners are most likely to say that public relations is: (a) a management function, (b) strategic, (c) not merely a marketing tool, and (d) not just publicity. That is what practitioners *say* public relations is or is what they do. From his vantage point after 50 years of practice, teaching, and research, Ehling argues that what practitioners actually do while supposedly doing public relations is: (a) a technical support function, (b) tactical, (c) marketing is the primary task, and (d) media is the highest value. Ehling continued:

> Practitioners have been all too willing to fulfil the role of product publicist within a sales promotion program. The result is a *self-fulfilling prophecy*. Since top executives with a marketing mentality tend to see "public relations" in product publicity terms, they, in turn, encourage the hiring of journalistically-oriented individuals whose primary forte is a rhetorical presentation of written material in a form usable in product publicity and sales promotion. (Lapierre, 1990a, p. 1)

In the second installment of the interview, Ehling laments the abuse associated with the very words "public relations:"

> It's [public relations] been abused, so perhaps it's time to come up with a different name. I'm not endorsing the idea, but I'm considering it. PR has come to mean publicity for unsavory purposes. *Serious practitioners find themselves constantly trying to explain that they are not publicists.* They are handicapped rather than helped by the label. (Lapierre, 1990b, p. 2)

It is disconcerting to read that one of the first proponents of public relations as a management function is still lamenting the overwhelming evidence linking public relations to publicity and marketing-oriented communication activities. Although he stresses the potential power of public relations to "do good" in our society, Ehling does not sound overly optimistic for the short term in Lapierre's written summary of her interview.

The overreliance on the technical and partisan values (often to the virtual exclusion of mutual values) leads to an overemphasis on the importance of media relations. Technical wizardry finds its greatest expression in dealing with members of the media. It has led, as shown in the next section, to arrogance and antagonism between newsworkers (e.g., journalists and editors) and public relations practitioners.

PUBLIC RELATIONS AND THE MEDIA

"When many people consider the function of public relations, their first thought is: 'Those are the folks who deal with the media' " (Baskin & Aronoff, 1992, p. 203). The relationship between public relations practitioners and the media is often the most visible aspect of the organizational public relations function, to audiences in the organization as well as those outside of it. It is a relationship characterized by a strong, symbiotic mutual interdependence (Pavlik, 1987). Like the symbiotic relationship between pilot fish and great white sharks, public relations practitioners and media reporters "feed" on one another. Unfortunately, the relationship is not always as benign as that enjoyed by the pilot fish and the shark. It is ultimately a relationship forged in technical and partisan values—communication techniques used loyally to aid and abet the organization.

PR Practitioner and Journalist Attitudes Toward One Another

The *Public Relations Journal* "Seventh Annual Salary Survey" (Jacobson & Tortorello, 1992) included a number of questions tapping into public relations practitioners' perceptions of how the field is perceived and valued by other groups. One of the statements the 2,019 survey respondents were asked to agree or disagree with was: "Public relations is more respected by the media now than it was five years ago." Sixty-eight percent of the respondents agreed with that statement, indicating that they thought journalists had a more enlightened and more positive awareness of public relations and public relations practitioners. As the data presented suggests, the opinions of these practitioners might be little more than wishful thinking than actual practice.

Research on the attitudes of journalists toward public relations and public relations practitioners indicates an ongoing (and far from resolved) antagonistic attitude between the two professions (Aronoff, 1975; Cline, 1982; Kopenhaver, 1985; Pincus, Rimer, Rayfield, & Cropp, 1991; Ryan & Martinson, 1988). All offer intriguing insights into the paradoxical dilemma faced by public relations practitioners.

The antagonism toward public relations on the part of journalists is most evident in the relatively low opinion journalists hold of the status of public relations as a profession. This less than positive opinion is both historically consistent as well as currently held (see Table 2.1). Kopenhaver (1985) found that 74% of daily newspaper editors dis-agreed with the statement that "public relations is a profession equal in status to journalism" (p. 40). When asked to rank order the status of 16 occupations and professions, the same editors ranked public relations practitioners next to the bottom, between lawyers at the 14th position and politicians at 16th.

Although, the Kopenhaver study is more than 5 years old, (keeping in mind the question from the Jacobson and Tortorello (1992) study asking if public relations is more respected than it was 5 years ago) the results presage the findings in later studies. Seventy-five percent of the public relations practitioners responding in a more recent study felt that the journalists' animosity is partially explained because journalists value their work as being more important to society than the work done by public relations practitioners (Ryan & Martinson, 1988). Belz, Talbott, and Starck (1989) discovered that journalists perceived their own societal role positively and the role of public relations practition-ers negatively, whereas public relations practitioners were more likely to perceive both roles positively. Pincus, Rimer, Rayfield, and

TABLE 2.1
Perceptions of Status of Occupations and Professions

Occupation	Editors		Public Relations Practitioners	
	Rank	Mean	Rank	Mean
Journalist	1	4.35	9	8.42
Physician	2	5.16	1	4.37
Clergyman	3	5.84	2	6.29
Farmer	4	5.93	10	8.92
Architect	5	7.00	8	8.40
High school teacher	6	7.26	11	8.98
Engineer	7	7.65	5	7.83
Artist	8	8.14	13	10.10
University professor	9	8.33	3	6.85
Corporative executive	10	9.05	6	7.94
Carpenter	11	9.33	15	11.89
Barber	12	9.91	14	10.64
Policeman	13	10.05	7	8.35
Lawyer	14	10.96	12	9.50
Public relations practitioner	15	13.02	4	6.92
Politician	16	14.61	16	14.62

*From Kopenhauer (1985). Reprinted with permission.

Cropp (1991), found that 73% of California newspaper editors surveyed were either neutral or *disagreed* with the statement that "PR is equal in status to journalism" (p. 31). Clearly, research over the years indicates that the negative attitudes journalists hold toward public relations have abated little, if at all.

The results of a survey of 118 public relations practitioners (Ryan & Martinson, 1988) are helpful in isolating the source of negative and antagonistic views. Ryan and Martinson (1988) asked public relations practitioners to respond (using a strongly agree–strongly disagree Likert scale) to two statements about their personal views of journalists' antagonism to public relations. The first was: "Journalists think more highly of the individual public relations persons they know than they do of the public relations profession in general" (p. 136). All of the respondents, 100%, either strongly agreed or agreed with the statement. The practitioners appear to be responding based on their interpersonal contacts with journalists they personally know. Obviously, the public relations practitioners feel that these individual journalists show a reciprocating respect for the public relations practitioner they, in turn, know as an individual.

The second statement is somewhat more revealing and serves to compound the "purity" of the overwhelming favorable response to the statement about journalists respecting individual public relations practitioners. Respondents were asked to agree or disagree with the statement, "The negative views many journalists express in surveys toward public relations are consistent with the views held by journalists I know" (p. 136). Almost 45% of the respondents agreed or strongly agreed with this statement whereas almost 47% disagreed or disagreed strongly that journalists' negative views are consistent with the journalists they know. Although individual relationships between reporters and practitioners might be characterized as respectful and positive, public relations practitioners feel that the press, when viewed as an entity, is far from favorable in its views of public relations as an organizational function.

Given their research, Ryan and Martinson (1988) concluded that the hostility that exists on the part of journalists toward public relations is "firmly embedded in journalistic culture, and that the antagonism influences the mass communication process" (p. 139). This conclusion implies that journalistic behavior—what Tuchman (1978) called news-work—is adversely affected by the negative attitudes newsworkers hold toward public relations. If Ryan and Martinson are right, the ways in which journalists portray public relations in the stories they write will be unduly skewed toward negative connotations. This aspect of the dilemma—the influence on the communication process—is even more troubling than the attitudes themselves, for it is through their reporting that the attitudes of journalists become part of the public domain. A recent interview with Morley Safer, co-editor of television's *60 Minutes*, is indicative of many journalists' perceptions (see Exhibit 2.1).

"Public Relations" as a Term Used in the Written Media

A reporter's word choices function as an ongoing cultural dictionary of a society's language. In their book, *Theories of Mass Communication*, DeFleur and Ball-Rokeach (1989) claimed that "as mass communications becomes a larger and larger proportion of our entire communication process, it can also be anticipated that they will have an increasing influence on vocabulary—the symbols we use, *the meanings we associate with those symbols, and the conventions we agree upon to link the two*" (p. 266, italics added). DeFleur and Ball-Rokeach suggest that the media influence our language in four intertwined ways. The media: (a) present new words for public consumption, (b) amplify the meaning of existing words, (c) suggest new meanings for existing symbols, and (d) reinforce the culturally understood meaning of many words.

There is plenty of anecdotal data supporting the assumption that a reporter's bias against public relations influences the connotative presentation of the profession in the press (Banks, 1991; Olasky, 1989). Two empirical research studies (Bishop, 1988; Spicer, 1993) have examined the ways in which public relations is presented in the news. Both are interesting for the light they shed on how public relations practitioners and activities are viewed by reporters and editors in the print media.

Bishop (1988) conducted an electronic content analysis of three American newspapers for a 1-month period in June 1987. He searched for any use of what he termed "public relations activities." These activities were inferred from the newspapers' use of the terms "public relations, press relations, PR, public information, government information, press officer, spokesperson, and publicity" (p. 50). Bishop discovered that the term "PR" was used only three times and in only one newspaper (*The Seattle Times*); two of the usages were in sports stories.

Bishop's search did yield 121 occurrences of "publicity," which he further analyzed. He found that 53% of mentions that included "publicity" were favorable to society at large and 57% were favorable

EXHIBIT 2.1
Morley Safer Versus Public Relations

Morley Safer doesn't think much of the public relations industry. And, judging by the sharp words being lobbed during a recent panel discussion, practitioners don't think much of him, either.

Responding to one panelist's condemnations of "gotcha" journalism, Safer bellowed, "If you think we like hanging around outside somebody's house to get him to talk, you're wrong." He said that such tactics are often necessary, however, because sources clam up even when they are offered opportunities to respond.

The venerable co-editor of *60 Minutes* squared off against four top practitioners at the first Harland W. Warner Seminar of Ethics in Public Relations, presented by the Center for Communications in New York City on May 4. The seminar was sponsored by PRSA and Manning Selvage & Lee.

During the free-for-all, several practitioners insisted that "no comment" is an appropriate response in many situations. William O'Neill, director of public affairs for General Motors North American Operations, said that employees should be informed about changes affecting them before the information is released to the media. In addition, organizations need not legitimize speculative or unbalanced stories by responding to reporters' queries, said Patrick Jackson, APR, Fellow PRSA, senior counsel at Jackson Jackson & Wagner.

"We in public relations have to be a lot more strategic about where information falls before we get into the trap of laying it on the line," said Jackson.

Safer, for his part, wasn't having any of it. "The reason organizations don't talk is not because we're going to manipulate what they say or use only the best part of it. It's because they know we're onto a damn good story," he said.

One "damn good story" that received much discussion during the seminar was the rigged crash tests of General Motors pickup trucks on "Dateline NBC" in 1992. The network later admitted it had attached ignition devices to the vehicle to ensure it would catch fire if the gas tank was punctured. The network issued an on-air apology.

GM's O'Neill said that the report, although proven false, did irreparable damage to the company's reputations. "It bothers me that the American public's perceptions of those pickup trucks is not colored by 11.5 million vehicles that have been in the hands of people for 20 years . . . but by people who lied," he said.

Safer joined the other panelists in censuring NBC's action, calling the networks apology "a coup for public relations." However, he defended the journalism profession, saying that "60 Minutes" is more than fair in its product testing.

As an example, he cited tests that "60 Minutes" did several years ago on American Motors' Jeep. The tests revealed that vehicle was prone to rolling over. After taping 10 test runs, "60 Minutes" producers gave the tape to American Motors and asked to repeat the test on the company's driver, but at the same speeds "60 Minutes" used. American Motors refused, said Safer. Instead, the company offered to film the test themselves and send the tape to "60 Minutes."

"I don't know if they doctored it or if they cheated on speed but they sent it to us. And we ran it," he said.

Another controversial topic debated at the seminar was Hill & Knowlton's activities on behalf of Citizens for a Free Kuwait. Safer blasted H&K for not identifying Nayirah al-Sabah, a witness appearing before a Congressional committee in October 1990, as the daughter of Kuwait's U.S. ambassador. In her testimony, she said that Iraqi soldiers were slaughtering Kuwaiti babies by taking them from incubators.

Safer also lit into H&K for denying that it represented the Kuwaiti government when nearly all of the funding for Citizens for a Free Kuwait was supplied by the government. In addition, Safer had harsh words for H&K's use of video news releases during the affair. "You guys sent out newsreel after expensive newsreel to stations all over the country without saying where they came from, knowing full well that small, hungry stations would have run anything in those weeks that came out of Kuwait," he charged.

Robert Dilenschneider, head of H&K until late 1991 and now president of The Dilenschneider Group, offered little comment on Safer's accusations about Kuwait. He did, however, respond to Safer's comments on video news releases. "If television stations don't want to take these releases or if there should be some kind of stricture passed to say where those releases came from, let's do it," he said.

The evening's debate concluded with Safer characteristically having the last word. He offered this comment on the public relations industry: "My biggest problem with public relations is its determination to get between us and what really happened."—B.W.

to the individual who was the subject of the publicity. Bishop (1988) concluded that:

As far as this sample goes, public relations is equated solely with publicity. There is no mention of planning, research, evaluation, counselling, or the myriad other things which go into the practice of public relations.

This is not surprising, given the limitations of the study and the fact that our contact with the media almost always involves publicity. But *the lack of recognition for other areas of expertise may account for the distorted view which many have of the field.* (p. 51, italics added)

Obviously, the implied denotative definition of "public relations" as publicity uncovered by Bishop is limited, especially given the aspirations of those defining public relations as a management function.

Spicer (1993) replicated and extended Bishop's (1988) study seeking to: (a) understand how the terms "public relations" and "PR" are subjectively defined as embedded in the print media, and (b) determine if the negative attitudes expressed by journalists toward the public relations profession are evident in their use of the terms public relations and PR.

Spicer analyzed 84 examples of the terms public relations or PR used in newspaper stories, headlines, magazine articles, editorials, and cartoons, far more than the three reported by Bishop. Spicer found that when the placement of the terms was examined, 68% of the examples appeared in the story as the reporter's words, 17% were attributable to a source quoted by the reporter, and 12% appeared in a headline. In two thirds of the examples, the reporter used the words public relations or PR in the story as a noun or modifier. The words were used for a reason.

Spicer's thematic analysis of the 84 terms yielded seven categories or themes by which the terms public relations and PR are given subjective meaning in the print media. These are briefly defined and discussed in the following paragraphs. Remember, these themes show the ways in which newsworkers connotatively use the terms in their stories, as shown in Exhibit 2.2.

In discussing the seven themes pertaining to the connotative meanings attached to the words public relations and PR, Spicer (1993) concluded that the majority of examples taken from the print media reinforce the negative stereotype of public relations. Indeed, he concluded that approximately 80% of the examples were either outright negative in tone (disaster, distraction, and merely) or were used in a manner that was not favorable (schmooze, hype, and war). "Admittedly," as Bivins (1987) wrote, "the stain of a number of unsavory acts performed by frequently well-known practitioners has left the public with a bitter taste in its mouth concerning the term 'PR' " (p. 196).

Summary

It is probably healthy for both reporters and public relations practitioners to approach their shared interests with a questioning (we could say skeptical) attitude. It is not our intent to catalog the history of

EXHIBIT 2.2
Images of Public Relations in the News

Twenty years of research indicates that journalists often hold a negative, antagonistic attitude toward the public relations field and public relations practitioners (Banks, 1991; Pincus, Rimmer, Rayfield & Cropp, 1991; Ryan & Martinson, 1988). Eighty-four examples containing the words "public relations" or "PR" published in the print media were examined to better understand how the newsworkers' attitudes influence their connotative use of the terms. Qualitative analysis resulted in seven themes:

1. *Distraction*—The terms often used to indicate that someone is trying to obfuscate an issue or event, or deflect the reporter's interest in the issue.

    Example: "Did the Kennedy administration disguise a lackluster performance behind brilliant *public relations*?" [Associated Press story about John Kennedy's legend].

2. *Disaster*—The terms used to suggest that a decision was made (or almost made) or an action taken (or almost taken) that is perceived to be unwise, foolish, or a mistake.

    Example: "The contest, in which hundreds or even thousands of people won the grand prize of a $17,000 Dodge van, was a *public relations* disaster" [story about a failed promotional campaign].

3. *Challenge*—Referring to genuine public relations difficulties in which the person or organization is not trying to distract or deflect but is seen as honestly trying to fairly deal with the communication aspects related to the issue or event.

    Example: "But the mayor acknowledged she's starting her second year in office with a mighty *public relations* problem. She conceded she has been too quick to criticize . . . and she vowed to change" [article about the first term of the mayor of a medium-sized city].

4. *Hype*—Used in a way that connotes a positive but relatively meaningless action on the part of a person or organization, or to create artificial excitement.

    Example—"And it always seems calculated to be just one more *public relations* maneuver: Madonna the actress playing Madonna the pop star with her hair down" [review of Madonna's film "Truth and Dare"].

5. *Merely*—Suggesting that the action is just or only public relations as opposed to any real idea or program.

    Example: "Schools must drop their 'education by *PR*' campaigns. Substance, Not Fluff" [headline from an opinion piece on educational reform].

6. *War*—Using the terms in conjunction with other descriptors suggesting a battle or fight.

Example: "I've been waiting for it to go to court for months because this can't be won in *public relations* wars" [article about the continuing legal woes of a public agency].

7. *Schmooze*—The stereotypical, glad-handing, smooth talking, personally charming frontman or woman.

Example: "Atlantic Street [a restaurant], overwhelmed by the voluble presence of its owner, oozes *PR* the way its Garlic Gulch Express Pizza exhales garlic [restaurant review].

The analysis indicated that in over 80% of the cases, the journalist used the terms public relations or PR in a negative context.

From Spicer (1993). Image of public relations in the news. *Journal of Public Relations Research, 5,* 47–61. Reprinted with permission.

---

abuses—both real and perceived—suffered by either party to the symbiotic relationship. The point is not how reporters use information provided by organizational public relations practitioners or whether that information is always accurate and responsive. These are important issues and are addressed later in this volume. The point is that the negative stereotypes and perceptions that often seem to envelope the term public relations are fostered by the ways the public relations function and process is portrayed linguistically in the media. The predominant image of public relations provided through the media reinforces the public's perception of organizational arrogance (as well as incompetence, ineptness, and amorality).

CONCLUSION

This chapter began by suggesting that the seeds for organizational arrogance are inherent in a technically oriented managerial mindset or worldview. We examined Jackall's (1988) case study of bureaucratic public relations; the overemphasis of technical values in both public relations practice and education; and the ongoing antagonistic relationship between public relations practitioners and newsworkers. Admittedly, each of these areas is different and we do not want to be accused of comparing apples, oranges, and kumquats. There is, however, a common theme that runs through each of these disparate examples, a theme with which I want to conclude this chapter.

The common theme running through the examples presented is found in the ways in which organizations interact with other groups or stakeholders in their environments. Indeed, as discussed in later chapters, organizational/environmental interaction is the very heart of the organizational public relations function. Public relations exists to facilitate the interactions between organizations and other groups.

The common theme is characterized by the way in which communication is used in each of the three areas. There is an implied definition of communication in Jackall's study of bureaucratic public relations, in the advance of technical values in support or defense of partisan ones, and in the reasons behind the antagonism between newsworkers and public relations practitioners. This inferred definition might be capsulized as being one-way, organization-to-public manipulation for the purpose of achieving organizational goals. It is a definition that as operationally practiced in the previous examples overemphasizes the word "publics" to the virtual exclusion of the word "relations." It is a form of communication that, as just witnessed, all too often leads to organizational arrogance.

If we are to overcome the ways in which organizational public relations historically has been conceptualized and put into practice, we need to better understand the link between the organization's needs and the potential of the public relations function in clarifying and meeting those needs. We need to learn ways in which we can move from a primarily technically oriented support staff function (Mintzberg, 1983) to one in which our counsel and advice are sought in the application of Sullivan's mutual values. We need, in effect, a primer on organizational power and politics. It is to this topic that I turn in the next chapter.

Practitioner Response to Chapter 2: The Bumpy Road to a Fair and Accurate Account of Events

Carol Bowers, Independent Reporter
Towson, Maryland

The relationship between reporters and public relations professionals is adversarial by its very nature. Reporters seek facts. Public relations professionals practice "spin control."

Having worked on both sides of the fence, as the saying goes, experience tells me that each side's expectations of the other does sometimes influence what is published or broadcast. Reporters are typically viewed by public relations professionals as people trying to get the facts at all costs, costs that are usually damaging to the organization. Public relations professionals, on the other hand, are paid to tout the corporate line or stall—at least that is how the job is perceived by both reporters and frequently, the corporate executives for whom the public relations person works.

Reality lies somewhere in between. A good reporter should strive above all for accuracy, trying by all ethical means to obtain all the facts and present them fairly in a story. A good public relations professional can best do his or her job by working to educate the reporter about the subject at hand because providing accurate information will best ensure fair coverage.

What frequently prevents either side from doing a good job, however, is the "corporate arrogance" described in the previous chapter. Corporate executives tend to expect positive coverage—stories that will make their company look good and perhaps even increase its stock value. They are quick to label stories that reveal unflattering information about their company as negative, regardless of whether the statements made by the media are true. Often, they ignore the advice of the very professionals they hire to tell them how to handle such situations, effectively tying the public relations professional's hands.

A case in point involves the Anne Arundel County (Maryland) school system. Three years ago, a veteran high school teacher was arrested and charged with having sex with one of his students. The teacher later admitted on national television that he'd been having sex with female students for more than 20 years—nearly his entire tenure at that high school.

Embarrassed, the county's school board members refused to comment on the arrest or prosecution, saying only that personnel matters should be handled confidentially.

Reporters, however, continued to investigate, and learned that the school system had repeatedly been told about the teacher's exploits, but had done nothing to stop him. It also was revealed that in most cases in which a teacher was accused of having sex with a student, the teacher was encouraged to resign, teaching certificate intact, to save the school system embarrassment.

The state school superintendent and parents were outraged by the revelations of the reporters and by those in a subsequent state-ordered investigation.

Throughout the ordeal, which dragged on for 2 years and was compounded by the prosecution of three other teachers on similar charges, the school board members remained silent. Despite the urging of the school system's public information officer, the board members refused to issue statements, or even say as little as that child abuse is a terrible thing or to reassure parents that their children were safe in school.

The damage was considerable. Distrust of the school board grew; parents staged pickets and protests, and the school system's name was repeatedly in the news. In short, the public information officer's predictions of what would happen if the board members ignored her advice came true in nearly every case. And although the board members acknowledged this, they continued to ignore the advice at every future opportunity.

How then to achieve what everyone wants—a fair and accurate account of events?

Unfortunately, the responsiblity falls on the shoulders of the public relations professional, who must not only educate reporters about facts, but educate corporate executives about the value of comment, and best of all truthful comment, as well. The quintessential example of how telling the truth can save a company's reputation is the case of Tylenol product tampering discussed in most beginning public relations texts.

Ultimately, the public relations professional needs to be truthful with his or her bosses, as well as reporters, at all times. Creating a climate of trust through truth-telling is essential if the relationship between the organization and press is to be mutually beneficial. Telling the truth to all parties, even when it's most damning, will earn you everyone's respect.

CHAPTER 3

Establishing the Organizational Setting: Systems Theory and Beyond

Think about including asymmetrical and symmetrical models of pr. Perhaps in general part.

In chapter 2, I presented a picture of the dark side of organizational public relations. Although the causes for the negative cultural connotations are many, one of the root sources is the inability of the public relations profession to adequately define what it does (Bivins, 1989; Kruckeberg & Starck, 1988). "Symptomatic of the inadequacies of any understanding of the role and function of public relations today is the problem of its definition. What is public relations? What does it do? What is it supposed to do? Is it doing what it is supposed to do?" (Kruckeberg & Starck, 1988, p. 11). In this chapter, I begin to answer Kruckeberg and Starck's questions. This chapter (a) deconstructs a typical definition of organizational public relations, (b) isolates the primary assumptions public relations practitioners make about organizations when they describe the public relations function of organizations, (c) establishes the historical significance of Grunig and Hunt's (1984) two-way asymmetrical and symmetrical models of public relations, and (d) identifies the strengths and weaknesses of the systems approach to the study of organizations and organizational public relations.

At the end of this chapter, I move to a more elaborated model and discussion of organizational processes, of which public relations is but one.

he will book at part of whe I need.

THE DECONSTRUCTION OF PUBLIC RELATIONS

A good definition should focus our attention on the salient characteristics of the object or phenomena being defined. Most definitions of public relations share certain characteristics (Kruckeberg & Starck, 1988), characteristics aptly illustrated in Long and Hazleton, Jr.'s (1987) definition. By dissecting a definition of public relations, we also uncover the assumptions public relations professionals make about the organizations in which they practice. The organizational emphasis is important in letting us more fully and critically examine the perceived role of the public relations function in light of organizational and management theory and research.

The Process Model of Public Relations

So, this can be added in lit review after general defs of roles.

Long and Hazleton, Jr. (1987) defined public relations as "a communication function of management through which organizations adapt to, alter, or maintain their environment for the purpose of achieving organizational goals" (p. 6). They discuss six definitional elements, each of which is now briefly described:

1. *Communication Function*—"Functions are natural and inevitable consequences of a process. Communication is the natural and inevitable result of the production and consumption of messages by human beings. . . . Specifically, public relations practitioners communicate in order to assist organizations in managing information exchange, identifying and solving problems, managing conflicts, and managing behaviors" (p. 7).

2. *Management*—"PR is rarely successful without company-wide cooperation and formal recognition. . . In American organizations, the level of responsibility for decisionmaking is diffused from the top of the hierarchy downward" (p. 7).

3. *Organization*—"Organization may be viewed as structure and as process. Organization as structure is concerned with specification of organizational membership, legal incorporation, common goals, boundary definition, roles, and functional relationships. These constructs vary as a function of organizational process, i.e., input, transformation, and output" (p. 7).

4. *Adaptation, Alteration, and Maintenance*—"Adaptation refers to a change in the organization. Alteration is concerned with environmental change. Maintenance underscores the importance of nurturing functional or satisfying relations with the environment" (pp. 7–8).

5. *Environment*—"Organizations receive energy from their environment; they output energy to the environment" (p. 8).

6. *Goals*—"Organizational and public relations goals are reciprocally related. Public relations goals are the consequences of organizational goals, not the reverse. As such, public relations programs focus

on complementing organizational productivity, efficiency, member and client satisfaction, adaptation, development, and survival through communication management activities'' (p. 8).

The six elements of their definition are incorporated into "an open systems model, consisting of a multi-dimensional environment and three subsystems" (p. 8) as shown in Fig. 3.1. The environmental supersystem provides inputs to the organizational, communication, and target audience subsystems. In this model, the environmental supersystem *also* receives input from the organization through the public relations process. Each subsystem contains an input, transformation, and output mechanism. That is, energy or matter is brought into the system, something is done to it (the "work" of the organization), and the result of that work is output into the next system in their model or the environment.

The transformation process includes what we often think of as the public relations problem-solving process (e.g., research, action, communication, evaluation). The authors note that public relations "begins" when there is a discrepancy between organizational goals and events in the environment or organization that necessitates communication. If the discrepancy is linked directly to *symbolic resource management* then the "successful implementation of a solution requiring communication is a public relations activity" (p. 10). The public relations plan or program becomes the output for the organizational subsystem and the input for the communication subsystem.

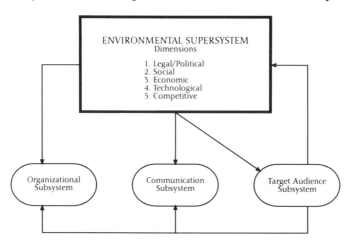

FIG. 3.1. Process model of public relations. From Long, L. W., & Hazleton, Jr., V. (1987). Public relations: A theoretical and practical response. *Public Relations Review, 13,* 3–13. Reprinted with permission of Public Relations Review.

Long and Hazleton Jr., (1987) perceived the communication subsystem as fulfilling a boundary-spanning function between organization and target audience subsystem. Most importantly, they claim the "function of the boundary-spanning role is *production (or encoding) and delivery of messages*" (p. 11, italics added). The messages produced during this cycle become the input for the target audience subsystem. Communication, they assume, is the "inevitable result of the production and sending of messages to the target audience subsystem" (p. 7).

Although they do not explicitly do so, Long and Hazleton Jr. allude to the distinction Sproule (1989) made between public and private organizational communication. Sproule (1989) suggested that organizations "straddle the private and public spheres" (p. 258). In one sense, the decision-making communication necessary in the modern organization is private in that there are often very few people involved in the decision, it is not always communicated to the entire membership, and outside intervention is often not sought and, when offered, rejected. At the same time there is a public sphere for organization communication existing of both the entire organization (e.g., the organizational culture) as well as the larger environment in which the organization exists (e.g., external stakeholders).

When Long and Hazleton Jr. (1987) wrote about the organizational subsystem, they are implicitly discussing the organization's private sphere. When they discuss the audience subsystem, they allude to the more public sphere. Their placement of the communication subsystem in the middle is a visual reminder of the boundary-spanning role of public relations. The organizational public relations function is situated betwixt and between the organization's private and public spheres, an idea that is continually returned to in later chapters.

Summary.   The Long and Hazleton Jr. definition and most others (e.g., Baskin & Aronoff, 1992; Grunig & Hunt, 1984) highlight similar aspects of the organizational public relations process. These include:

1. Communication function (persuasion and understanding, advocacy and consensus building).
2. Organization (as an entity with purpose, goals).
3. Environment (events, issues, publics, or stakeholders).
4. Management (strategic decision making, attempted control).
5. Alignment (with other forces in the environment that have the capability to affect the organization's autonomy).

The fifth, alignment with the environment (through communication), is generally implied as the raison d'etre of public relations, helping the organization align itself (by altering, adapting, or maintaining) with its environment thereby enhancing its autonomy. Each of the five characteristics is essential in understanding what the public relations function does (or should do) for an organization. I turn now to a look at what definitions of public relations tell us about the assumptions the definition makers hold about the organizations.

ASSUMPTIONS ABOUT ORGANIZATIONS: SYSTEMS THEORY REIGNS

Given the characteristics of public relations definitions as a beginning point, what can we deduce about how public relations people perceive organizations? First and foremost, modern definitions of public relations emanate, intentionally or not, from a systems perspective. A *system* is generally defined as "a set of interdependent units which work together to adapt to a changing environment" (Infante, Rancor, & Womack, 1993, p. 81). We might very easily transform this definition of system into one about public relations as follows: Public relations is an organizational function that helps a set of interdependent organizational units work together to adapt to a changing environment. Systems theory is important to the study of organizational public relations for three reasons.

First, The application of systems theory to the study of organizations is credited with shifting the locus of organizational study from one that focused largely on the internal workings of the organization to one focused on the interdependence of an organization and its environment (Conrad, 1990; Euske & Roberts, 1987; Kast & Rosenzweig, 1972; Ruben, 1972; Scott, 1981, 1992). One of the first distinctions systems theorists made was that between open and closed systems. *Open systems* are those that exchange energy, material, and information with other systems in their environments through a permeable boundary. *Closed systems*, such as a windup clock, are ones that have sealed boundaries and therefore do not exchange energy with their environment; the clock eventually runs out of energy and stops. Today, we find this to be a pretty simplistic distinction, one that even my son used in the fifth grade to study ecological systems. In the late 1950s and early 1960s, however, the idea of connectedness was a revelation, and worked to largely refocus our thinking about the study of organizations. Organizations were suddenly characterized as being open systems (Hage, 1980; Katz & Kahn, 1966; Lawrence & Lorsch, 1967), ones that took some type of energy from the environment (input), transformed that energy in some manner (throughput), gave something back to the environment (output), and maintained some kind of "communication" with the environment (feedback) that led to equilibrium.

Second, Kuhn (1970) argued that paradigms, overarching understandings of how things work, guide research and theorizing in scientific communities. At this point in time, research and theorizing in the public relations field is heavily influenced, if not dominated, by the systems paradigm (Grunig & White, 1992; Pavlik, 1987; Toth & Heath, 1992). At the conclusion of his review of public relations research, Pavlik (1987) concluded that, "understanding public relations is aided by an emerging organizational view of the field—general system theory" (p. 126). The use of systems theory tenets is both obviously visible in much writing about public relations (cf., Broom 1986; Grunig, 1989; Pavlik, 1987) as well as more or less implied or inferred in other studies (cf., Lauzen & Dozier, 1992). Many of our most cherished and useful concepts (e.g., public relations as a boundary-spanning activity, adapting to environmental uncertainty) reflect a general systems theory approach to public relations.

Third, systems theory is important to the study of organizational public relations because it serves a useful heuristic tool in helping us conceptualize (especially for us visual learners) the often overwhelming complexities of organizational interdependencies. As Ruben (1972) pointed out, "general system theory is not so much a set of neat propositions as it is a way of thinking about things" (p. 121). The tenets of systems theory help us think about things that are important for understanding organizational public relations decision making and, ultimately, effectiveness. Indeed, in their book *The Unbounded Mind: Breaking the Chains of Traditional Business Thinking*, Mitroff and Linstone (1993) proposed the idea that managers need to adopt unbounded systems thinking to understand the world as an interconnected whole.

This is not to say that systems theory is conceptually perfect or without its critics. Neither is the case. McFarland (1986) suggested that "we are only beginning to realize the potential of systems theory, and much disagreement exists among systems theorists and managers about its nature, its extent, and its possible consequences" (p. 122). Systems theory has been criticized from both an organizational standpoint (Burrell & Morgan, 1979; Infante et al., 1993; McFarland, 1986; Morgan, 1986) as well as more specifically from a public relations viewpoint (Coombs, 1993; Creedon, 1993; Euske & Roberts, 1987; Toth, 1992). Given its historical predominance, we need to seek a better understanding of what systems theory directs us to examine as well as a better understanding of its inherent weaknesses, especially given the communication function of public relations. I address some of the pertinent criticisms at the conclusion of this chapter. First, though, I continue with the assumptions about organizations inherently evident in the definitions of public relations.

A second assumption evident in all definitions of public relations is that organizations are goal-oriented, which means that they have some purpose or reason for their existence. These goals are accomplished through continual interaction with the environment. The accomplishment of organizational goals, vis-à-vis environmental opportunities and constraints, links public relations to the strategic decision-making apparatus of the organization. Grunig (1992), for example, "defined excellent public relations departments as departments that manage communication with strategic publics, publics that threaten or enhance the ability of the organization to pursue its goals" (p. 22).

Definitions of public relations seek to position the public relations function in the management system of the organization. As such, these definitions infer a managerial focus on control, the attempted allocation of resources to meet real and perceived threats to the organization's autonomy. As discussed in chapter 7, this focus emphasizes that the public relations function is generally perceived from a resource dependency model of organizational/environmental interaction (Pfeffer & Salancik, 1978). The public relations function is charged with managing the symbolic environment of the organization, an environment that might not be as amenable to control as the product development or sales environment. Indeed, the issue of control and what it implies in a managerial sense should be of central concern to public relations practitioners.

Underlying all of the definitions is an assumption about the need to enhance organizational autonomy. The end result of managing the organizational/environmental exchange thereby insuring the achievement of organizational goals is to increase the organization's ability to go about its affairs as it best sees fit. The public relations boundary-spanning role might be likened to the drawbridge that is lowered and raised over the moat that surrounds medieval castles. The moat, a circle of water separating the castle from the world, valiantly assures the castle's autonomy from the dangers and intrusions of its environment. The drawbridge, raised and lowered as needed, both links and separates the castle from its environment. This is, of course, a coarse description of the paradoxical autonomy enhancing and environmental bridging function of organizational public relations, but it is one that exists nonetheless.

Finally, most definitions of public relations point to the presumption of disagreement or conflict between the organization and other elements in its environment. Long and Hazleton Jr. (1987) wrote that "public relations practitioners communicate in order to assist organizations in . . . *managing conflicts*" (p. 7, italics added) among other symbolic arenas requiring communication management. That the public relations function is responsible for managing issues (Heath & Nelson, 1986), "defined as a contemporary situation with a likelihood of disagreement" (Cooper, 1989, p. 6), squarely places the public relations function in situations in which the achievement of the organization's goals are in some manner thought to be imperilled. Others have also stressed the importance of managing conflict in relation to organization/environment interaction (Ehling, 1989; Pearson, 1989a).

Our examination of the Long and Hazleton, Jr. definition emphasized that public relations seeks to align the organization with its environment, seeks to maintain an appropriate "fit" as it were, thereby buffering the organization from environmental intrusions. Others echo the importance of the public relations role in aligning the organization to its environment. Wright (1983) noted that by maintaining open communication, the public relations function ensures "the organization's ability to respond and adjust to change as required by societal and environment conditions" (p. 3). And, as Grunig (1992) wrote: "If organizations choose the most appropriate public relations strategies for communication with strategic publics, then that strategy will help the organization manage critical environmental interdependencies and make the organization more effective" (p. 25). Wright's use of the phrase, "as required" and Grunig's choice of the phrase "most appropriate," both speak to the importance of the organizational/environmental fit.

In organizational theory, seeking an appropriate "fit" or alignment between the organization system and the larger environment is most extensively developed in contingency or congruence theories of organizations (Aldrich & Mindlin, 1978; Burrell & Morgan, 1979; Greening & Gray, 1994; Nadler & Tushman, 1980). Contingency theories "seem to dominate modern organizational theory and organizational communication theory" (Conrad, 1994, p. 230). In a review of contingency theory studies, Bluedorn (1993) concluded that the contingency model "has maintained its ability to stimulate research and theoretical inquiries; and as this research has progressed, new questions are being addressed" (p. 168). Given the continued conceptual vigor of contingency theory in organizational studies, it behooves us to examine the contributions of recent contingency theories in order to better understand public relations effectiveness, particularly in relation to strategic management (Bluedorn, Johnson, Cartwright, & Barringer, 1994).

As Scott (1981) succinctly noted, "contingency theory is guided by the general orienting hypothesis that organizations whose internal features best match demands of their environments will achieve the best adaptation'' (p. 144) to those environments. In other words, contingency theory posits that organizations are most successful if they align their internal structures and processes with the demands of their environment. To date, contingency theories have been used with only minimal success in relating models of public relations and organizational effectiveness (Grunig & Grunig, 1989b; Leichty & Springston, 1993). There are a variety of reasons for this limited success in describing differences in an organization's public relations response to its environment. Each of the three principal organizational "players" involved in the Intel Pentium chip case described in Exhibit 3.1 responded differently to the same environmental stimuli.

One of the goals of this book is to suggest ways in which we can better understand the linkages of the internal organizational processes to external environmental events. Understanding how organizational politics, for example, influence the ways in which the public relations function is performed enhances our understanding of the ways in which organizational public relations is effective in aligning with their environment.

The findings of public relations research suggest that differences in the organization's environment, differences in publics or stakeholders, should lead the organization to adopt multiple models of organizational public relations (Ice, 1991; Springston, Keyton, Leichty, & Metzger, 1992). In that the public relations function is founded on the premise that it will represent the organization to other entities in the environment, a contingency model is applicable in understanding the varying environmental demands on the organization's communication and symbol creation systems. Chapter 4 examines a particular contingency model and I expand on the relationship of contingency models to the public relations function in chapter 7.

I turn now to the strengths and weaknesses of the reliance on systems theory as a fundamental conceptual building block of organizational public relations. In order to fully appreciate the recent critiques of systems theory as applied to organizational public relations, we need to examine perhaps the most elegant and elaborated use of systems theory in public relations to date, Grunig and Hunt's (1984) asymmetrical and symmetrical models of public relations. These two models address a fundamental tension in the public relations practice, that is, the tension between advocacy and consensus.

GRUNIG AND HUNT'S MODELS OF PUBLIC RELATIONS

Grunig and Hunt (1984) proposed four models of public relations: Press agentry/publicity, public information, two-way asymmetrical,

EXHIBIT 3.1
"No-Tell" Intel Learns Silence Isn't Golden

Fraser P. Seitel

To Intel Chairman Andy Grove, IBM Chairman Lou Gerstner is clearly "the grinch who stole Christmas." Gerstner is the primary reason that Grove has a far greater understanding today of the importance of "positive public relations" than he did prior to Dec. 12, 1994.

That was the day that IBM announced that it would halt shipments of its highest-powered PCs, containing Intel's flawed Pentium chip, because it was revealed that Intel had "significantly" underestimated Pentium's potential for errors. IBM's shocking news release made the front page of every newspaper in the country.

It also forced Intel to deal with what some labeled the "biggest public relations nightmare since the Exxon Valdez."

Intel snuffed out the crisis on Dec. 21, when it ran full-page newspaper ads apologizing for its poor job in handling consumer complaints. The company also announced that it would offer customers a free replacement Pentium upon request with no questions asked. "It was the right thing to do, both morally and ethically." Grove told *The New York Times.* "Our earlier policy seemed arrogant and uncaring."

IBM's public relations offensive, Intel's initial public relations reluctance, and the more muted response of other Pentium users such as Dell Computer Corp., created the kind of public relations conundrum from which college case studies are born.

Each of these major companies took a separate public relations route in dealing with the crisis. Their responses are instructive to all practitioners faced with profound product-related problems.

IBM's High Profile

Intel's problems began 6 months before IBM went public. In June, a Lynchburg (VA), College math professor discovered the numbers on his Pentium computer simply didn't compute. Intel advised the professor that he was one of two million Pentium users at the time to report the "obscure problem." The professor told some of his friends, who posted the news on Internet, the global computer network of 20 million to 30 million people.

Despite its unwanted Internet publicity, Intel concluded that the flaw would impact "a typical spreadsheet user once every 27,000 years." Consequently, Intel decided not to notify customers or offer a recall. Growing consumer grumbling notwithstanding, Intel may have "gotten away" with its stonewalling had IBM not blown the whistle.

The tidal wave of negative publicity following IBM's announcement stunned Intel.

"We had no choice but to go public," says Michael Ryder, media relations officer in the IBM personal compute area. "Once our research concluded the likelihood of error using the chip, we owed it to our customers to let them know."

IBM's research determined that the flow would create inaccuracies in mathematical calculations 90 times more frequently than Intel has said. IBM's Gerstner reportedly personally approved going public after reviewing the research.

Industry competitors, however, question the "public-spirited" motivation of IBM, where only 5% of computers sold are Pentium-based machines.

"IBM's public relations broadside was obvious," says a public relations official at a competing company. "Their future is in the chip business. They did this to further their own position and weaken Intel's. Period."

In fact, IBM's PowerPC chip, developed with Motorola and Apple Computer, is a direct competitor of the Pentium chip. Nonetheless, IBM defends its high-profile position.

"The question is, 'What do we owe our customers?" says Ryder. "If we had done the research and then announced nothing—how would that have been perceived?"

Dell's Low Profile

Dell Computer, Intel's largest Pentium client, adopted a more moderate course in the wake of the chip problem. Its public relations initiatives were confined first, to working with Intel to learn how its customers might be affected and second, to notifying customers about the problem and working with them directly to deal with it. In contrast to IBM, Dell made no public announcement.

"We decided early on that we didn't want to be the Pentium 'poster child' splashed prominently in the headlines at war with Intel," says Dell public relations manager Roger Rydell.

Dell concluded that the Pentium problem would most likely impact clients involved with sophisticated calculations and high-end statistics— aerospace industry engineers, for example, or doctors and mathematicians. Dell contacted these customers and worked with them, either to seek replacement chips or work around the problem.

"We know our customers very well," says Rydell. "We want them to be delighted with our products and will do whatever it takes to satisfy them. Being in the public limelight isn't really our highest priority."

Intel's No Profile

As for Intel, the Pentium problem proved not to be the company's finest public relations moment. Indeed, the company stumbled from the get-go.

(Continued)

In June when the problem was first reported, Intel chose to downplay its significance. In October, leaks became more intense about Intel's problem and its failure to disclose more details. Nonetheless, the company insisted that anyone who wanted a replacement chip "must prove that the new chip was needed."

At the same time, Intel chose not to throttle down its prominent $80 million "Intel Inside" ad campaign, designed to make its corporate name and its Pentium chip the "quality standards" of the computer industry.

By the time IBM's public bombshell hit in December, Intel was ripe for a fall.

"What you think are the consumer's perceptions of you and what the consumer actually perceives may be two different things," says Susan W. Cole, principal of Cole Communications of Bronxville, NY, who specializes in consumer and technology clients. "Right or wrong, the consumer is right, because he makes the ultimate purchase decision."

In Intel's case, until its public apology, the company and its chairman remained tight-lipped, save for lashing back at the IBM announcement and starting a corporate "war of words." (An inquiry from *Tactics* about the company's public relations strategy, for example, was bucked by the chairman's office to the public affairs director's office to the media relations director's voice mail. *Tactics* did not get a return phone call.)

"Intel isn't used to dealing directly with end-users, and frankly this caught them by surprise," says one competitor. "I suspect that management didn't deal the public relations people a fair hand in this case, and made them look bad. Maybe they've learned a lesson about how aggressively you have to act up front, when a product proves faulty."

Product public relations experts say Intel's "lesson may not only prove costly but also long-lasting."

"The bottom line is that consumers now place Intel and 'defective' in the same sentence" says Cole. "And unfortunately, many also add the word, 'unresponsive' as well."

From Seitel, F. P.(1995). No-tell Intel learns silence isn't golden. *Public Relations Tactics*, 2(1), p. 1. Reprinted with permission.

and two-way symmetrical. Briefly, the *press agentry/publicity model* uses communication techniques for propaganda purposes most attuned to seeking media attention. The *public information model* is most often thought of as the journalist-in-residence who disseminates information to various publics. Whereas these first two models rely on a one-way model of communication, the *asymmetrical* and *symmetrical* models rely on two-way communication between organization and environment.

Grunig's various use and elaborations of the distinctions between these approaches to public relations are central to our understanding of the range of options available to organizations when they face a public relations dilemma. Grunig identified the presuppositions he believes are part of both the asymmetrical (pragmatic and conservative) and symmetrical (idealistic) worldviews. As Grunig (1989) forthrightly admitted, "I studied and accepted most of the presuppositions of the systems approach to organizations and communication" (p. 37). His presuppositions are shown in Table 3.1.

We can characterize the set of asymmetrical presuppositions as highlighting the achievement of organizational goals, encouraging organizational ethnocentrism, prizing efficiency and production at the expense of innovation, and sublimating the individual to the will of the organization. If we think in terms of communication, we might conclude that communication in an organization characterized by asymmetry will be oriented toward advocacy persuasion or presenting the organization's claims.

Grunig's second set of presuppositions most notably places people and their ideas (both in and out of the organization) above the reified organization itself, looks to incorporate diverse views thereby breaking down organizational ethnocentrism, encourages innovation and continual discovery, and builds community. The communication function in a symmetrical organization is genuinely two-way, dialogic, and seeks to expand participation in the meaning creation process (Pearson, 1989b). Effectiveness will be judged less in solely achieving the organization's ends than it will in creating an atmosphere of give-and-take in which all parties seek to achieve consensus or collaboration.

Given the reality that organizations often employ more than one model of public relations, Grunig and others have recently proposed a mixed-motive model of public relations (Grunig & Grunig, 1992; Hellweg, 1989; Leichty & Springston, 1993; Murphy, 1991). This new model is shown in Figure 3.2 and is based on a distinction between craft and professional public relations.

Practitioners of craft public relations are communication technicians who "seem to believe that their job consists solely of the application of communication techniques . . . to get publicity or information into the media or other channels of communication" (Grunig & Grunig, 1992, p. 312). Those who practice professional public relations are communication managers and "see public relations as having a strategic purpose for an organization: to manage conflict and build relationships with strategic publics that limit the autonomy of the organization" (Grunig & Grunig, 1992, p. 312).

This reconceptualization is grounded in the understanding that under certain conditions, one model might be more appropriate than another model. As Leichty and Springston (1993) noted:

TABLE 3.1
Presuppositions of Two World Views

Internal Orientation Outsiders. Members of the organization look out from the organization and do not see the organization as outsiders see it.	*Equality.* People should be treated as equals and respected as fellow human beings. Anyone, regardless of education or background may provide valuable input into an organization.
Closed system. Information flows out from the organization and not into it.	*Autonomy.* People are more innovative, constructive, and self-fulfilled when they have autonomy to influence their own behavior, rather than having it controlled by others. Autonomy maximizes employee satisfaction inside the organization and cooperation outside the organization.
Efficiency. Efficiency and control of costs are more important than innovation.	*Innovation.* New ideas and flexible thinking should be stressed rather than tradition and efficiency.
Elitism. Leaders of the organization know best. They have more knowledge than members of public.	*Decentralization of management.* Management should be collective, managers should coordinate rather than dictate. Decentralization increases autonomy, employee satisfaction, and innovation.
Conservatism. Change is undesirable. Outside efforts to change the organization should be resisted; pressure for change should be considered subversive.	*Responsibility.* People and organizations must be concerned with the consequences of their behaviors on others and attempt to eliminate adverse consequences.
Tradition. Tradition provides an organization with stability and helps maintain its culture.	*Conflict resolution.* Conflict should be resolved through negotiation, communication, and compromise and not through force, manipulation, coercion, or violence.
Central authority. Power should be concentrated in the hands of a few top managers. Employees should have little autonomy. Organizations should be managed as autocracies.	*Interest group liberalism.* Interest group liberalism views the political system as a mechanism for open competition between interest or issue groups. Interest group liberalism looks to citizen groups to ''champion interests of ordinary people against unresponsive government and corporate structures (Boyte, 1980, p. 7).

Note. From Grunig (1989). Reprinted with permission.

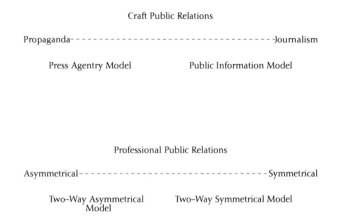

Craft Public Relations

Propaganda- -Journalism

Press Agentry Model   Public Information Model

Professional Public Relations

Asymmetrical- -Symmetrical

Two-Way Asymmetrical   Two-Way Symmetrical Model
        Model

FIG. 3.2.   Craft and professional dimensions of public relations models. From Grunig (1992). Reprinted with permission.

We expect that an organization differentiates between publics and interacts with each of them somewhat differently. The approach that is taken toward any particular public should partially depend upon how that public is perceived within the categories of the predominant organizational culture . . . the direct perceptions of each public should better predict an organization's public relations orientation in a partic-ular instance than global assessments of the organization's environment [e.g., contingency models]. (p. 333)

Grunig and Gruing (1992) agreed that those who practice professional public relations use both "asymmetrical (compliance-gaining) tactics and symmetrical (problem-solving) tactics" (p. 312). I would go even further and suggest that professional public relations probably use (or make use of) all four models depending on their perception of the public relations situation and the internal decision-making process of their organization.

As many in the field recognize and applaud (Creedon, 1993; Leichty & Springston, 1993; Pearson, 1990a), the two-way symmetrical model, although an ideal, has gone a long way in at least conceptually combatting many of the negative aspects of public relations noted in chapter 2. With its emphasis on mutually influential interaction and influence between an organization system and other systems in its environment, the two-way symmetrical model offers a means of cor-recting many of the potentially negative aspects of the overreliance on the two-way asymmetrical model.

CRITIQUE OF SYSTEMS THEORY AS THE DOMINANT PR PARADIGM

Throughout this chapter, I have discussed how the systems paradigm is considered dominant in the public relations theoretical/research sphere (Botan, 1993; Coombs, 1993; Creedon, 1993; Heath, 1993). Through their critiques of the systems-oriented model of public relations, however, these authors make more meaningful our understanding and application of the systems paradigm to organizational public relations. In particular, the critics argue that even the idealistic, systems-based, two-way symmetrical model of public relations ignores or does not adequately address issues of organizational power, the linchpin of organizational success.

In his discussion of the infusion of the pluralist paradigm in public relations, Coombs (1993) suggested that the system paradigm fails to adequately "address the power advantages possessed by corporations" (p. 116). The pluralist paradigm "is the *ideal* type of government where all parties have equal access to and equal power in the policy making process" (Coombs, 1993, p. 112). Grunig and Hunt's (1984) two-way symmetrical model, most particularly Grunig's (1989) inclusion of liberal group activism, is an articulation of the pluralist paradigm.

Based on the work of Jordan (1990) and Smith (1990), among others, Coombs (1993) suggested that the two-way symmetrical model still incorporates power disadvantages that are not overcome simply through dialogue and mutual exchange. As he noted, the "burden and control over whether or not a dialogue develops" (p. 116) rests with the organization. The organization can refuse (at its possible peril, of course) to engage with a stakeholder group. Or, in that the organization often controls access to necessary information, it can refuse to divulge or share with a stakeholder group.

This criticism is particularly acute if we remember that public relations seeks to help the organization achieve its goals by aligning itself with others in the environment. Although the two-way symmetrical model is admirable in the ideal, Coombs (1993) reminded us that we need to remember that it is still used in service to the organization, in achieving the "self-interests which they can and do pursue" (p. 116). The focus on power and its balance or imbalance is more than appropriate and one that is discussed extensively in chapters 7 and 8.

Others have also criticized systems theory in relation to the dimension of organizational power and privilege (Creedon, 1993; Murphy, 1991; Pearson, 1990a). Pearson (1990a) proposed that systems theory has an inherent managerial bias that inadvertently excludes both employees and stakeholder groups. Murphy (1991) argued that because symmetry is implemented on the behalf of management and because it seeks to minimize differences in a search for consensus it "tends to discourage innovation and encourage custom and tradition" (p. 124).

Finally, Creedon (1993) suggested that the functional perspective implied by systems theory inhibits the examination of the "foundation of institutional values or norms that determine an organization's response to changes in its environment" (p. 160), or the *infrastructure*. In that the characteristics of the infrastructure are often unseen (what others have labeled "deep structure"), they need to be brought to the surface and examined.

These critiques of the dominant paradigm are welcome in that they indicate the maturing of the study of public relations as a discipline (Botan, 1993; Hollahan, 1993). The history of the practice of public relations suggests that the discipline will always be concerned with the interaction between organization and environment. This interaction is conducted at least in part because the organization seeks a degree of autonomy from environmental forces. As we move from purely craft or technical public relations to professional or managerial public relations, we expect to find more and more discussion of the societal role of public relations in relation to other stakeholders in the environment. The critiques just examined seem to suggest that organizational public relations must reach beyond the organizational and managerial bias inherent in all current models and strive for a more inclusive interactive base from which to operate. Indeed, the critiques suggest that at least one function of public relations might be to allow the organization to be less autonomous and more interconnected with its environment, a radical idea at best.

SUMMARY

Central to our discussion to this point is the idea that the primary function of organizational public relations is to continually align the organization with elements in its environment. As Long and Hazleton Jr. (1987) suggested, to "adapt to, alter, or maintain their environment for the purpose of achieving organizational goals" (p. 6). The public relations functions seek to maintain a degree of homeostasis between events and forces in the environment and the organization. A continual, moving equilibrium is sought, one that allows the organization to respond in a manner consistent with its goals (whatever those might be).

Two aspects of this focus are intriguing and important given the criticisms of the systems-based, two-way symmetrical model of public relations. The first is the apparent self-centered focus of the alignment process. The process of alignment—of adapting, maintaining, or altering the environment—to achieve organizational goals emphasizes the importance of the organization relative to the rest of the components of its environment. Given this organizationally centered approach, a key question that is asked is "How is this (issue, event, etc.) good, bad, or indifferent for the organization?" In essence, the approach highlights the needs of the organization over the needs of the entire system structure. Although a degree of advocacy is certainly necessary, advocacy by itself does not lead to a concern for the other or a dialectic that seeks to arrive at the best consensual response.

The second aspect of the organizational/environmental alignment approach is that adaptation, alteration, and maintenance imply a sought-after degree of control. Various writers and theorists posit that advocacy is not necessarily control oriented (e.g., Cheney and Vibbert, 1987; Miller, 1989), that it seeks to influence, rather than control. These semantic distinctions are often lost in everyday practice. All too often, advocacy becomes a one-way communicative exercise that seeks to neutralize and control other stakeholder groups in the organization's environment. All too often, advocacy leads to perceptions of public relations as distraction or deception, to perceptions of organizational arrogance.

Do these critiques of system theory mean that it no longer serves as an adequate means for understanding organizational public relations? I think not. The criticisms do, however, point out the areas in which systems theory is perhaps most useful and those areas in which some other framework needs to be incorporated. Systems theory concepts and conceptualization help us understand the complexity of interaction between organizational components. It has helped immensely in directing our attention to the overwhelming diversity and complexity of external components with which an organization might have to attend. The concepts of homeostasis, equifinality, and interdependence have added to our fundamental understanding of what public relations should do. That systems theory led Grunig and Hunt (1984) to propose the distinctions between two-way asymmetrical and two-way symmetrical models of public relations is evidence enough of its heuristic power.

System theory, then, helps us better understand the ways in which components and processes are interconnected, helps us understand organizational/environmental linkages. It is functional (Burrell & Morgan, 1979; Trujillo & Toth, 1987) in the sense that it helps us describe how things work (or how they are supposed to work). Systems theory does not, however, tell us much about the meanings people create for the components or interdependencies or definitions of homeostasis. It does not inform us of how communication works in helping us bring about changes in perceptions or understanding. It does not help us understand how the intricacies of the interdependencies are created, changed, exacerbated, nurtured, elaborated, eliminated, and so on. For these understandings, grounded in the meanings people attach to communication, we need another framework. As Creedon (1993) pointed out "to the extent that systems theory can be reconfigured by public relations theorists [to include currently ignored stakeholders and social relationships], it could provide a basis for the development of a revisionary paradigm" (p. 163). We will do as Coombs (1993) suggested and, by drawing from both systems theory and rhetorical/ critical theory, *complicate ourselves.*

Pearson (1990a) offered one way of "complicating ourselves" in an article subtitled, "The Two Faces of Systems Theory." Pearson suggests that the public relations discipline use systems theory in two ways, as strategy and as ethics. Pearson argued that those who use systems theory to better understand strategic linkages between the organization and its environment do so in a traditional functional sense (cf., Burrell & Morgan, 1979; Hage, 1972). From this perspective, organizational (and public relations theorists) are concerned with the ability of the organization system to maintain homeostasis or equilibrium with other elements of its environment through maintenance, alteration, and adaptation.

Pearson (1990a) extended our understanding of systems theory as applied to organizational public relations by suggesting a second framework, one that focuses less on the variables themselves and more on the interdependent linkages or couplings between the variables. Using systems theory in this sense moves us away from attempts to balance the various system components and toward a more elaborate understanding of the ways in which those attempts are mutually accomplished. A focus on the interdependencies between organization and stakeholder is one that is ultimately concerned with a question of ethical interaction and communication as the organization attempts to maintain, alter, and adapt (as examined more fully in chapter 12).

By way of concluding this initial attempt to identify the strengths and weaknesses of systems thinking on our understanding of organizational public relations, I conclude with a list of some important considerations for managers who wish to understand social systems theory proposed by McFarland (1986):

1. The critical elements in systems thinking are philosophical and emotional.
2. Systems do not provide an easy or automatic way to spectacular success. Still . . . the systems approach is not a bad idea, although it can be confusing as well as enlightening.
3. There are no experts in the systems approach, only learners and ordinary human beings.
4. New systems mean new and special problems.
5. Systems contain the seeds of their own destruction. . . . Systems sometimes act in opposition to their proper or intended functions.
6. Any change in a system produces unintended as well as intended consequences.
7. People in systems do not always do what the system says they should do.
8. People can become excessively enraptured by a system, especially one that seems to work. Outside reality may pale and disappear. The system remains more attractive to locals than to cosmopolitans, which paves the way for stagnation.
9. Systems have a fierce will to live, to endure, to persist, even if change is needed to accomplish this.
10. Among all possible philosophical problems implied by systems, ethics is one of the most challenging. (pp. 140–141)

If we think back to the three case studies in chapter 1, we find that McFarland's list of considerations is most appropriate to organizational public relations. Seafirst Bank found, for example, that change produces unintended as well as intended consequences. Circle K grappled with the philosophical problem of pragmatic ethics. Kid's Place Hospital discovered the emotional element of the most well-intentioned and seemingly rational systems thinking.

Systems thinking provides a conceptual framework for understanding the structures and processes of organizations and the public relations function. Having sprung from systems theory, contingency theories of organizations likewise provide a conceptual framework for at least beginning to understand the emphasis on alignment common to most definitions of public relations. It is notoriously difficult to assess the effectiveness of contingency theories, in part because of the very number of things that need to be taken into account (although we are getting much better at it as we see in the next chapter). The idea behind contingency theories, however, remains viable in helping us conceptualize the challenges facing the organizational public relations function.

TOWARD OTHER PERSPECTIVES

Bolman and Deal (1991) proposed four frames or perspectives for analyzing and understanding organizations: structural, human resource, political, and symbolic. The structural and human resource frames are consistent with Burrell and Morgan's (1979) functionalist paradigm, the political included in the radical paradigm, and the symbolic an approach subsumed under the interpretive paradigm. Bolman and Deal (1991) suggested that each frame "describes a set of phenomena that are present in any human system, but each is likely to be more salient and illuminating in some circumstances than in others" (p. 314).

Based on the salient conditions, Bolman and Deal propose that one frame might be more instructive or useful than another (although they are quick to point out that all four frames need to be used in order to truly understand the nature of the organizational beast). During times of moderate to high *ambiguity, scare resources,* and moderate to high *conflict* and *diversity,* Bolman and Deal (1991) suggested that the political and symbolic frames are most appropriate. Given my contention that the public relations function is most crucial during time of *perceived or engaged organizational/environment conflict* (Assumption 8), what Pearson (1989b) called the "the point where competing interests collide" (p. 67), I propose that both the political and symbolic frames help us better understand the organizational public relations function.

Ultimately, by incorporating a variety of frameworks or approaches to the study of both organizations and public relations, we are better able to indicate the parameters of the public relations function. Indeed, by "complicating our understanding" we are more able to identify when a particular approach to public relations will be most effective. There are times when an organization needs to do nothing more than publicize something; there are other times when a collaborative exchange is necessary. We need to be able to tell when one might serve better than another. To that eventual end, we examine the crucial linkage between internal organizational processes and external demands. In the next chapter, I turn to the complexity of internal organizational structure, processes, and, most importantly, meanings.

Practitioner Response to Chapter 3:
Caught in the Act of Doing Good

Frank R. Stansberry, APR, Manager (retired)
Media Relations and Guest Affairs
Coca-Cola Company
Walt Disney World, Lake Buena Vista, Florida

For as long as I can remember, any discussion about public relations has gotten stuck in the differences between what PR does verses how it's done. Because public relations is a process, the end result of which is better relationships, sorting through the definitions and approaches gets sticky.

Let's look at some definitions. Some are simple, end-result oriented such as that from Mitch Kozikowski who said "public relations is the discipline which manages an organization's relationships with its constituents." Another, in place for years at The Coca-Cola Company, is even more simplified: "Getting caught in the act of doing good."

Other definitions look more to the process of doing public relations. Edward L. Bernays once said public relations is "the application of behavioral science techniques to determine which prosocial actions will lead to a merger of public and private interests." This is a good working definition because it speaks to the research–action–communication–evaluation model we all preach and use.

In a similar vein, Art Stevens said public relations is the "shaping, of perceptions, through communication, to achieve positive goals." Here, again, is the process—understanding extant perceptions, communicating messages to shape those perceptions, with the end result being positive behavior.

Inherent in any discussion of public relations systems is the need to recognize that public relations theory has grown measurably in the last few years. Twenty-five years ago we looked to communication as the end product of our efforts. Clippings were counted, weighed, measured, or otherwise quantified to prove the success and value of our services. Some even determined the advertising value of the net column inches and said our work was worth so many dollars to our bosses.

Today, of course, we know that's not true. In the words of Pat Jackson, we have moved "beyond communication to behavior." That's why the two-way systems model posited by Grunig and Hunt is so critical to the profession today. Establishing a dialog with constituents in today's competitive and hostile environment is critical. As we have seen, communication (as represented in the press-agentry and public information models) does not drive behavior. Such communication might create awareness, but awareness alone is not enough.

Recent surveys by Porter/Novelli show that among the factors that influence buying decisions are (of course) product quality, but also such "relationship" issues as how the company handles complaints, hiring policies, environmental record, and crisis responses. Thus, the communication-as-an-end-to-itself model or even two-way asymmetrical communication won't work in today's world, if it ever did. The wise organization will talk to its stakeholders about what is important to them—and act on what they say. At the same time, the stakeholders must have a clear understanding about what is important to the organization. After all, their fates are inexorably linked—the organization and its publics.

So if we are to drive positive behavior—and that is what should be demanded of us in the profession—then we need to establish corporate trust first, so that relationship can be the foundation from which positive behavior results. Right now, it appears the two-way symmetrical model is the key to building positive relationships that result in positive behavior.

Of course, this model is not restricted to public relations. Highly successful companies have stepped back and looked at how they are relating, to their primary public—the customer. At The Coca-Cola Company, for example, the business has forever been organized around how the product was delivered to the ultimate consumer: cans/bottles or fountain. In many instances, however, a customer was both a bottle/can and a fountain customer. Thus, two different divisions in the company called on this customer, and much confusion frequently resulted.

In the past couple of years, the company has begun to look at a customer as "a customer," irrespective of whether the customer uses bottles, cans, or cups. Now, there is a customer-focused approach that looks first at what is good for the customer—not what is easier to manage at corporate headquarters. The result is higher overall sales and deeper relationships with customers who are wise enough to realize this major supplier cares enough about what is important to the customer to change a fundamental business procedure that had been in place for decades.

That's good public relations—listen and respond—and wait for the positive behavior to ensue.

CHAPTER 4

Organizational Complexities

INTRODUCTION

In 1972, Studs Terkel, a Chicago radio talk show host, published a book entitled *Working: People Talk About What They Do All Day and How They Feel About What They Do*. For more than 400 pages, Americans talked about the work they did and, more informatively, how they felt about their work and working. In his introduction Terkel wrote:

> This book, being about work, is by its very nature, about violence—to the spirit as well as to the body. It is about ulcers as well as accidents, about shouting matches as well as fistfights, about nervous breakdowns as well as kicking the dog around. It is above all (or beneath all), about daily humiliations. To survive the day is triumph enough for the walking wounded among the great many of us. . . .
>
> It is about a search, too, for daily meaning as well as daily bread, for recognition as well as cash, for astonishment rather than torpor; in short, for a sort of life rather than a Monday through Friday sort of dying. Perhaps immortality, too, is part of the quest. To be remembered was the wish, spoken and unspoken, of the heroes and heroines of this book. (pp. xi–xii)

This overriding sense of work-related violence, of something more than just everyday discontent, is aptly captured in a quote Terkel attributes to William Faulkner: "You can't eat for eight hours a day nor drink for eight hours a day nor make love for eight hours a day—all you can do for eight hours is work. Which is the reason why man makes himself and everybody else so miserable and unhappy" (Terkel, 1972, p. ix).

My personal experiences in organizations, my reading, and the stories my friends and colleagues tell lead me to believe that Terkel's contention is all too accurate, work can be violent—physically, emotionally, and psychologically. All too many of the selections in the book *Organizational Reality: Reports from the Firing Line* (Frost, Mitchell, & Nord, 1992) attest to the prevalence of violence associated with working. Although there are innumerable causes of this violence (and Terkel gives dramatic voice to many of them), one recurring theme is that workplace violence is often the result of working in an organization. Terkel's dismay with organizational life is echoed by management consultant Tom Peters who, in a weekly column, wrote: "By their very nature, organizations run roughshod over people. They produce powerlessness and humiliation for most participants" (Peters, 1989, p. B5).

We find results like those reported in a survey of 1,115 working people (Kanter & Mirvis, 1990), in which 72% of the respondents agreed that "management will take advantage of you if you let them," and 59% felt that "management is more interested in profits than people" (p. 58). Summarizing interviews with more than 4,000 managers and professionals in Fortune 500 companies, Halper (cited in Johnson, 1989) reported that almost 60% of her respondents found their lives relatively meaningless after devoting their time to organizational goals and their own careers. Organizations perpetuate and inflict a variety of "violences" against their members. Often these are inflicted unwittingly or unknowingly; often they are perpetuated with knowledge and, to some extent, malicious forethought and intent. Violence is often the illegitimate offspring of organized human activity, much of it resulting from an elemental paradox of organizational life pitting the individual against the organization.

AUTONOMY VERSUS CONTROL: PARADOXICAL CONSEQUENCES OF ORGANIZATION

The observation that violence is often an unfortunate consequence of organizational life is, in part, grounded in the fundamental underlying paradox of organizations. This paradox or dilemma is often stated as follows: Organizations seek to insure and promote individual autonomy and creativity while, at the same time, attempt to limit that autonomy and creativity through the perceived need for organizational control and coordination. The issue at hand is one of organizational control versus individual independence and is as old as the study of human organizations (Conrad, 1992; Mumby, 1988; Peters & Waterman, 1982; Tompkins & Cheney, 1985).

This paradox or dilemma is at the crux of much of the history of organizational theory and research. In an article on the future of organizational communication research, Mumby (1993a) suggested that

> most organizational research is control-oriented . . . in the sense that almost without exception organization theory and research is concerned, either implicitly or explicitly, with increasing the levels of control that organizations exercise over their members. From scientific management to the study of corporate culture, theorists have focused on ways to resolve the inherent tensions between individual values, choices, and goals on the one hand, and organizational values and goals on the other. *Invariably, such tension is resolved by subordinating the former to the latter* (p. 21, italics added).

It is in the resolution of this tension, in the attempts to subordinate individual values, choices, and goals to the organization that Terkel's violence often occurs., as illustrated in Exhibit 4.1.

Does this violence happen to public relations practitioners working in organizations? You bet it does. The following case comes from an interview conducted with a vice president and director of public affairs. In order to insure anonymity and confidentiality, the specifics of the case have been disguised, although the "facts" of the story happened as reported by our interviewee.

CASE STUDY 4.1: VIOLENCE AND THE PUBLIC RELATIONS PRACTITIONER

Paula M. (a pseudonym) is vice president and director of public relations at a medium-sized financial institution. She was hired for the position 4 years ago. During her tenure, she has been amply praised by her superiors and the board, receiving good raises and bonuses. The public relations department has also received numerous awards and commendations from the community served and public relations peers in the area (e.g., won a Silver Anvil Award). All in all, Paula is well-respected in and out of her organization.

The public relations department has two major community-oriented programs. During the Thanksgiving and Christmas holidays, the organ-

EXHIBIT 4.1
Concerned Teacher Flunks Controversy

Thomas Shapley
Seattle Post-Intelligencer

I'll bet that when he was a child, Larry Wagle wasn't much at staying between the lines in a coloring book.

And as a 58-year-old high school teacher, Wagle still doesn't seem very interested in staying between the lines. Which probably makes him one of the better teachers at Longview High School, and generally makes for good teachers anywhere.

Wagle wound up in the headlines the other day—and in hot water. And we're told it's not the first time, either.

You see, institutions don't much like people who don't stay between the lines. And the public school is the institution defined.

Wagle walked right into trouble this time. You get the feeling it was less a matter of Wagle looking for trouble than it was of just not looking where he was going; or giving much of a damn, either.

His ninth-grade history class was studying the Roman Empire. One day the discussion of history flowed into a discussion of a current newspaper story. The story was about a rash of condom shoplifting incidents. The crimes were attributed to teen-agers' shyness about buying condoms.

The bottom line was that for many teens swiping a box of condoms and risking shoplifting charges was less scary than facing a store clerk, especially—God forbid!—a store clerk of the opposite sex, to buy those condoms.

All but the most brazen—or perhaps perfectly well-adjusted—among us will sympathize, not with the larceny but with the anxiety. When I was in high school it was hard enough to get up the nerve to ask a girl out. To muster the towering nerve to ask a dour drug store clerk for a package of sexual prophylactics would have been out of question. Fortunately (I didn't see it fortunate at the time, of course) my high school courting activities never demanded such protection.

Buying condoms surely becomes easier with maturity—like eating avocados, driving within the speed limit and going to work every morning—but it's still not easy, even for 40-something men.

The problem may lie in the unvarnished, right-out-there notion of intent associated with such a purchase. You are going to do something with those things, the clerk knows. And the clerk knows just what you're going to do with those things. And somehow that makes the purchase uncomfortable.

But why just condoms? When you buy a bottle of booze, the clerk knows you're going to drink it. When you rent some brain-dead jiggle fest or blood bath at the video store, the clerk knows you're going to go home and watch the stuff. When you buy a hunting rifle, the clerk knows you're going to go out and kill something with it.

Which brings us back to Larry Wagle's class and teens shoplifting condoms. There is, after all, a great deal of debate over condom use and availability, especially for teens. By the time I needed them it was to avoid pregnancy. Nowadays it's to avoid death. Why make them available in schools, goes one argument, since a kid can buy them at just about any grocery store? But can he—or she—really? Or are kids, even '90s liberated, desensitized kids, too embarrassed to make the purchase?

So Wagle proferred a bit of a dare, in the form of an extra credit exercise. Go to a store, buy some condoms from a clerk of the opposite sex. Take a witness and bring back a receipt. But first, get your parents' permission to do the project.

Three kids volunteered to take on the project. That only three out of the whole class should in itself made the point. But the parents of some of the other students objected, angrily. Why would they object to some other folks' kids buying some condoms for extra credit is beyond me. Perhaps they were worried about the impact on the grading curve.

But when angry parents call, principals quail. School officials demanded to know what Wagle was up to. With a disrespect for authority I can't help but respect, Wagle wouldn't discuss it with them. Something about his academic freedom.

A hearing was held. Wagle was found guilty of serious disregard for authority, insubordination and rudeness. Washington state law clearly defines how—and apparently when and where and by whom—AIDS awareness is to be taught in Washington public schools. History class is not the place.

Testifying in Wagle's favor was Clark Geer, AIDS–HIV coordinator for the Cowlitz County Health District. Geer pointed out that the county had produced nine new HIV-positive cases in the past seven months, several of them young people. The county has the state's highest incidences of sexually transmitted diseases. About 54 percent of the high school students are sexually active and teen pregnancy is "rampant," according to news reports of his testimony.

"We are something like accessories to manslaughter when we do not educate about condom use," Wagle told the hearing examiner.

It was to no avail. While even the hearing examiner himself said, "I honor this teacher," and that many of Wagle's methods were "in the finest tradition" of helping students learn personal responsibility, he said Wagle was "guilty of insubordination. . . . "

Wagle was reprimanded and suspended for two weeks without pay.

Wagle was outside the lines again.

ization sponsors numerous events for families and children in need. These events get widespread coverage in the local media and are cosponsored by other highly visible organizations in the area. The second program is a year-round campaign devoted to a particular issue important to the community at large. One year, for example, it involved cleaning up a local lake. The theme for the coming year (1994) concerned the declining economy and job market. The proposed program included the sponsorship of public service announcements about job availabilities, workshops and seminars for families who might be struggling economically, talks to high school classes about applying for jobs and money management, and so on.

Paula began planning for the 1994 campaign during the summer of 1993. She met with the heads of all relevant departments, soliciting ideas from more than 20 people throughout the organization. During the planning process, she also solicited input about budget needs (e.g., printing brochures, arranging for travel compensation, an educational video). All of the people who would eventually be involved with the 1994 campaign agreed to Paula's final proposal and, more importantly, her budget request. With the backing of her colleagues and the concurrence of her superiors, Paula submitted a total 1994 public relations budget for $300,000, of which $80,000 was for the 1994 public relations outreach program.

It is important to note that, during her time as vice president, Paula had created and submitted four budgets. The organization's budget process worked like that in many organizations. Each department makes a request to a central budgetary authority; the request is returned with a demand that it be reduced by a certain percentage; the department does so; and the budget is approved. One year, for example, Paula requested $260,000 and was told to cut 7% from her request, which she did and went about the business of public relations for that year. Paula followed the identical procedures she previously used in submitting her 1994 budget request. She turned in her request on October 10, 1993.

During the succeeding months, Paula asked her boss (the president of the organization) about her budget. She was told that the executive committee was reviewing everyone's budget request, but that she should just go ahead with her planned campaign. The first phase of the plan went into effect in January 1994 and required the hiring of an outside graphic designer (an expense included in the proposed budget). The designer did her work and submitted a bill. During the first week of February, Paula requested, through appropriate channels, that the designer be paid. The head of the finance department returned her request noting that there was no money budgeted for such an expense.

When Paula called the director of finance, he informed her that, more than just no money for this one request, her budget submission had been cut by 57%!

The president of the organization, Paula's direct supervisor, was out of town. A few phone calls later, Paula learned that the organization's budget had been finalized and approved the *previous November* and that, indeed, the executive committee had cut her request by 57%. Paula called one of the executive committee members, a friend of hers, who told her that he had known about the budget cuts since November. When she asked why he had not confided in her, her friend said that he, "didn't feel it was in my place to tell you. I'm not your manager."

Not only was her budget request cut a whopping 57%, but the cuts were made in particular line items. Two years ago, for example, public relations published an internal newsletter every 2 weeks. Given previous budget cuts, the employee newsletter was published once a month during 1993. On the 1994 request, the executive committee cut the newsletter to once every 2 months. This was a line item cut about which the organizational member responsible had absolutely no say.

Paula reported that there were two issues at stake. The first involved the lack of communication between her boss and the rest of senior management and herself. As she said, this action showed "a lack of respect for me. It was a slap in the face. I felt insulted, disrespected, humiliated, and taken advantage of. I only learned about this through a fluke. How long would they have waited to tell me? How many people knew about this, people I trusted and respected, and didn't tell me. It really pisses me off."

The second issue concerned the status of the 1994 program, a program that had been approved at all appropriate organizational levels, a program that was already underway, with her superior's blessing. What was she to do with a program the budget for which effectively no longer existed?

After a long meeting with her boss on his return, the public relations budget was revised and approved with a 35% cut to the proposed 1994 program and a much lesser cut to the department as a whole. During the meeting, Paula took great pains to show how the lack of communication affected her. She asked many questions, among them: "How do you think I feel knowing that my budget was finalized in November and I hear about it in February?" and "How do you think I feel about the fact that the people who made cuts to the public relations budget had no clue what those numbers represented?"

Paula is still the vice president and director of public relations for this organization. As she herself said of her experience, "This was my worst nightmare about what could happen in an organization." Paula experienced violence, a violence to her self-worth and dignity, a violence to her professionalism, and a violence to the status of her department.

Why did Paula have to suffer through what she did? Indeed, in the best of worlds, we would hope that Paula would never again experience such a degrading workplace episode. But, organizations are often not "the best of worlds." They are merely manifestations of the people who inhabit them, especially the people who manage them (Deetz, 1992; Scott & Hart, 1989). Because organizations are the creations of people, they are, as Bolman and Deal (1991) reminded us, complex, surprising, deceptive, and ambiguous. The violence Terkel (1972) found lurking in most work and organizations, the violence Paula experienced, is found in the complexity, surprise, deception and ambiguity characteristic of all organizations.

Research indicates that the tension experienced by Paula, the tension between real and perceived autonomy and organizational control or constraints, is relatively widespread among public relations practitioners. Ryan (1987a) found that public relations practitioners working in organizations felt constrained in their access to the dominant decision-making coalitions (especially board rooms), were not free to debate corporate policy, and often felt vulnerable to the whims of the organization hierarchy. He also found that practitioners felt constrained "by limitations on their *freedom to disseminate timely, accurate information*" (p. 480, italics added). These are constraints on the professionalism of the public relations practitioner, constraints that limit his or her autonomy in light of organizational control.

In her study of the degree of job satisfaction experienced by organizational public relations professionals, L. Grunig (1990a) found that "autonomy was consistently cited as a source of satisfaction; constraints—whether imposed by oppressive bosses, overwhelming responsibilities, or small budgets—frequently were mentioned as causes for dissatisfaction" (pp. 369-370). Public relations practitioners continually struggle to find a balance between autonomy and constraints, between accepted professionalism and organizational controls.

The autonomy–control paradox inherent in modern organizational life is acerbated by the simple fact that organizations are complex institutions inhabited by people. Organizational complexity arises from the myriad of interactions among the organization's structures and its processes and it is to a model of those structures and processes that we now turn.

A CONGRUENCE MODEL OF ORGANIZATION

All organizations have rules and procedures, some type of division of labor, a communication system, budgets, equipment, and so on. They also have people who meet in the hallways and gossip, people who do not like one another, people who get sick, people who become good friends, people who see each other outside the organization. Organizations have people who tell other people what to do, they have people who offer advice and suggestions, they have people who get angry and yell, they have people who shut their doors and hide, they have people others turn to for advice. They have ways of doing things, as in "that's how we do it around here." They have bosses and the bossed, traditionalists and rebels, the excited and the bored, those who hunger for the new and those who live with the tried and true.

Organizations are systems of structures and processes, systems of actions and meanings. In that the actions differ from organization to organization, so to do the meanings attributed to those actions. All organizations, however, share a least some basic characteristics, characteristics that are both necessary and sufficient for the "beast" to be recognized as an organization. The splendid variety of ways in which these characteristics are joined from organization to organization lead to the infinite variety of organizational action and meaning systems we know and experience.

These characteristics are often captured in definitions of the term "organization." Meyer and Rowan (1992), for example, suggested that "formal organizations are generally understood to be systems of coordinated and controlled activities that arise when work is embedded in complex networks of technical relations and boundary-spanning exchanges" (p. 21). After reading a sentence like this, we understand, at least to some degree, what the authors mean and tacitly accept both the definition as written and our interpretation of its meaning. On closer inspection, it might be both fair and prudent to ask what Meyer and Rowan mean by "systems," "coordinated and controlled activities," "work," "complex networks," "technical relations," and "boundary-spanning exchanges." The words, simple in and of themselves, give rise to any variety of philosophical and operational definitions, applications, assumptions, research, and theory.

A definition that better captures the "fuzziness" of organization is offered by Miles (1980):

An organization is defined as a coalition of interest groups, sharing a common resource base, paying homage to a common mission, and depending upon a larger context for its legitimacy and development. (p. 5)

Miles (1980) used the term "coalition of interest groups" to underscore both the interdependence that comes from the division of work as well as that which comes from "the fact that they must share, and negotiate for portions of, a common resource base" (p. 6). As we saw in Paula's case, the public relations function can easily be stymied if not undercut by a lack of power in negotiating for appropriate portions of the common resource base, that is, money.

I particularly like Miles' (1980) use of the phrase "pay homage to a common mission," which implies that "while they [coalitions] must publicly acknowledge identification with some overall organizational mission or purpose, they frequently displace this common mission with goals more particular to their own interests" (p. 6). This displacement, as well as the negotiation for resources, speaks to the need for understanding the organization in terms of a political metaphor, an approach examined in relation to the public relations function in chapters 5 and 6. As Morgan (1989) aptly pointed out, definitions of people banding together to accomplish a common goal, "eliminates almost all the interesting features of organizations in practice. They are rarely so rational and so united" (p. 30).

Finally, Miles' (1980) use of the "larger context" addresses the importance of the organization's interaction with other stakeholders in its environment "to continue operations, to grow, and to develop" (p. 6). This larger context is the realm of public relations with which we are most interested and to which I turn to later in this volume.

In the last chapter, I noted that definitions of public relations

exemplify a concern for the client being allowed to exist and prosper within the client's environment. This, perhaps more than anything else, justifies a highly pragmatic manner contemporary public relations practice (Kruckeberg & Starck, 1988, p. 16).

Our examination of the Long and Hazleton Jr. (1987) definition showed that a major premise of organizational public relations is to enhance organizational autonomy vis-à-vis the organization's environment. The historical emphasis on organizational autonomy forces us to inadvertently overemphasize some elements of organization and ignore others, often to the organization's eventual detriment.

Given our examination of the characteristics implicit in definitions of organizational public relations discussed in chapter 3, I suggested that most public relations practitioners implicitly proceed from a contingency model of organization. "Contingency theory researchers stipulate that organizations must adapt their internal structure and processes to the conditions that exist in their environment" (Bluedorn,

Johnson, Cartwright, & Barringer, 1994, p. 242). Contingency models are firmly grounded in open systems theory, giving undue precedence to the interaction between internal organizational structures and processes and challenges and opportunities in the larger environment (Child, 1972; Conrad, 1994).

In order to more fully understand contingency theory, especially the dynamics of internal organizational interactions, I will examine a contingency model of organizational development proposed by Kotter (1978). I elected to include Kotter's model because the elements he incorporates are readily applicable to our understanding of organizational public relations. The elements selected by Kotter are also found in one form or another in other contingency models (Burrell & Morgan, 1979; Galbraith, 1977; Greening & Gray, 1994; Scott, 1981). Additionally, Kotter (1978) proposed numerous questions about the seven elements included in his model, questions that lend a more applied and pragmatic slant to the usefulness of his model.

Kotter's Seven Elements of Organizations

Based on his research in 26 organizations, Kotter (1978) identified seven elements essential to all organizations, as illustrated in Fig. 4.1:

1. Key Organizational Processes—"the major information-gathering, communication, decision-making, matter/energy transporting, and matter/energy converting actions of the organization's employees and machines. . . . Taken together, these processes make up what many people would refer to as the behavior of a formal organization" (p. 3).
2. The External Environment—composed of the task environment made up of "all possible suppliers (or labor, information, money, materials, and so on), markets, competitors, regulators, and associations that are relevant in light of the organization's current products," and the wider environment composed of "public attitudes, the state of technological development, the economy, the occupational system, the political system, the demographic characteristics of people and organizations, the society's social structure, current price levels, laws, and so on" (pp. 3–4).
3. Employees an Other Tangible Assets—"the size (or number) and internal characteristics of an organization's employees, plant and offices, equipment and tools, land, inventories, and money" (p. 5).
4. Formal Organizational Arrangements—"all formal systems that have been explicitly designed to regulate the actions of an organization's employees (and machines). These . . . include structure (job

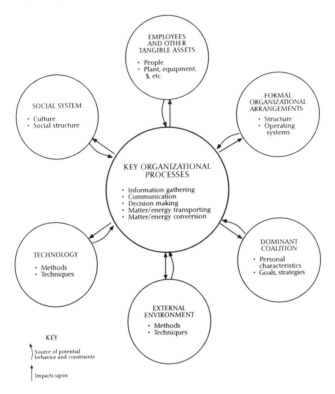

FIG. 4.1. Congruence model of organizational dynamics. From Kotter, J. P. *Organizational dynamics*, © 1978. Addison-Wesley Publishing Company, Inc. Reprinted by permission of Addison-Wesley Publishing Company, Inc.

design, departmentalization, a reporting hierarchy, rules and plans, teams and task forces) and operating systems (resource allocation system, planning systems, measurement and reward systems, hiring and development systems.)'' (pp. 5–6).

5. The Internal Social System—made up of the culture, defined as ''those organizationally relevant norms and values shared by most employees (or subgroups of employees),'' and social structure, defined ''as the relationships that exist among employees in terms of such variables as power, affiliation, and trust'' (p. 6).

6. The Organization's Technology—''the major techniques that are used by an organization's employees while engaging in organizational processes.'' This includes ''the craft of glass blowing, methods for doing market research, and techniques for making steel'' (p. 7).

7. The Dominant Coalition—''the objectives and strategies (for the organization), the personal characteristics, and the internal relation-

ships of that minimum group of cooperating employees who oversee the organization as a whole and control its basic policy making'' (p. 8).

We can begin to analyze Paula's troubles by using Kotter's seven elements. Paula's role in the key organizational processes was important in that this organization supposedly valued community participation. Service to the community, meeting community needs, is stressed throughout the organization's mission statement. Given this external focus, Paula's position definitely involved interaction with stakeholders in the organization's external environment. As noted in the case study, Paula was a valued and often rewarded and praised employee during her 4 years with the firm. The new ideas about externally oriented community service projects Paula initiated speaks to her implementation of new communication technology designed to enhance the organization's commitment and service to its external community.

If we ended our analysis of Paula's case with the five elements from Kotter's model noted in the previous paragraph, we would conclude that Paula was doing what she was hired to do, was doing that job well, and was contributing to the organization's goal of increased service to the community. When we look at her relation to the dominant coalition and the internal social system, however, we need to revise our initial assessment. Although imbued with the title vice president, Paula was not, in this instance, included as a member of the dominant coalition. The dominant coalition (the decision makers including Paula's direct supervisor) decided, for whatever reasons, to cut Paula's budget without informing her of their actions. The members of her internal social system, the other vice presidents who knew of this cut but did not tell her also did not involve or inform her about these decisions. The message Paula received, whether intentionally sent or not, was that the dominant coalition devalued her, her professional contribution, and the organization's commitment to her public relations function.

Indeed, what Paula experienced was a lack of alignment between several of the elements of Kotter's model. Based on her previous experiences with the budget process, the members of the dominant coalition, and the internal social system, Paula proceeded in what would be considered a rational manner. She planned, she talked with people, she made decisions on what could be accomplished, and she created a budget proposal that she submitted as per previously established organizational procedure. Paula aligned the elements in a way that fit her conception or understanding of the organizational task called ''budgeting for the coming year.'' When the dominant coalition responded in the way it did, Paula M. had to question and revise her understanding of her conception of the fit between the elements necessary for budgeting. The rules of the game, as is so often the case, changed. Unfortunately, not all of the players were told of the changes.

Kotter like other contingency-based theorists, is less interested in the elements themselves than he is in their potential interaction with one another. It is through the interactions that organizational dynamics occur, that meanings are created and sustained, that organizational life occurs. The reciprocal impact of the organization's process element and its six structural ones results in eventual success or failure, or, as Kotter labels them, *alignments* and *nonalignments*. These alignments are the key to understanding the explanatory goal of contingency theories .

Aligned relationships occur when the various elements fit together, thereby producing an effective and productive organization. "Performance is not assured by any particular organizational design, but is contingent on an appropriate match between contextual variables (such as task demands) and organizational arrangements (such as communication structures and media)" (Rice, 1992, p. 476). In an article bemusedly entitled, "Fit, Failure and the Hall of Fame," Miles and Snow (1984) wrote:

> Fit is a process as well as a state—a dynamic search that seeks to *align* the organization with its environment and to arrange resources internally in support of that alignment. In practical terms, the basic alignment mechanism is *strategy*, and the internal arrangements are *organization structure* and *management processes*. (p. 11)

Interestingly, Miles and Snow include IBM in their Hall of Fame of organizations that have achieved tight or excellent fit. In chapter 2, we learned that IBM had lost its luster, in part because the ideal of fit is often fleeting and is especially difficult to achieve in the face of organizational arrogance.

A recent empirical study of the economic performances of companies in two manufacturing industries (wooden upholstered furniture and women's dresses), indicated that "some organizational alignments generate supernormal profits to the firm, and constitute an important source of competitive advantage" (Powell, 1992, p. 128). Powell (1992) concluded his study of economic performance with the suggestion that "the concept of competitive advantage need not be confined to traditional economic variables, but may be extended to such nontraditional variables as organizational alignment" (p. 129).

When the relationships are out of whack, or nonaligned, the organization suffers. In a study of hospitals in one northwest state, Boeker and Goodstein (1991) concluded that fewer patients and declining revenues "signal managers that the structure of an organization, including the composition of its board, may not match the requirements of the existing environment" (p. 821). Subsequent changes in the organization's structure are undertaken to "cope with changes in potential sources of environmental threat and uncertainty" (p. 821), thereby enhancing performance.

What constitutes appropriate alignment is much of what is at the very heart of organizational decision making (Child, 1972), especially strategic decision making (Bluedorn, 1993; Bluedorn et al., 1994). The basic precept of contingency theory is that organizations must continually align and realign Kotter's seven elements, searching for congruence, or the best fit. Kotter (1978) suggested that realignments most commonly occur in response to changes in the external environment. Changes in the environment create

> a nonalignment between that element and one or more of the other structural elements. Economic recessions, new technological developments, changes in consumer tastes, competitive product developments, and new federal and state legislation quite often create nonalignments for contemporary organizations. (p. 43)

Not so coincidentally, the emphasis on aligning the organization with its environment lies at the heart of definitions of public relations.

Summary

In chapter 3, I dissected a common definition of public relations thereby isolating the essential characteristics of such definitions. This dissection led us to identify the conceptual precedents public relations professionals hold about the organizations in which they work. I discovered that most definitions of public relations are driven by at least some incorporation of systems theory concepts. More specifically, given the focus on organizational/environmental alignment, I concluded that most definitions of organizational public relations emanate from a contingency-based model of organizations. To this point in chapter 4, I have examined a contingency model of organizational dynamics to remind us of the complexity of organizational interactions.

ORGANIZATIONS ARE COMPLEX

To say that the world is more complex than it used to be is a simple truism that warrants little argument. Driskill and Goldstein (1986) aptly noted that "complexity and change have been heralded as the most salient features of the business world today" (p. 41). In a chapter ironically entitled, "A Bright Future for Complexity," Bennis (1989) wrote that "there are too many predicaments, too many grievances, too many ironies, polarities, dichotomies, dualities, ambivalences, paradoxes, contradictions, confusions, complexities, and messes" (p. 112). And yet, as Bennis (1989) suggested, "sooner or later, each of us has to accept the fact that complexity is here to stay and that order begins in chaos" (p. 113).

Bolman and Deal (1991) suggested two causes of organizational complexity. The first is that complexity occurs because "the interactions among the different individuals, groups, and organizations can be extremely complicated" (p. 25). This source of complexity I call *systems complexity* for the obvious reason that it involves the actual real-world interaction between the components of any organizational system, the seven elements of Kotter's model of organizational dynamics, for example. The use of the term *real world* does not imply that our interpretive understanding of actions, events, and issues is any less real than the actions, events, or issues themselves. Indeed, our understanding of real-world complexity is compounded by our inability to consistently arrive at consensually shared interpretations of real-world events.

The second cause of organizational complexity is that organizations are inhabited by people and "our ability to understand and predict human behavior is still very limited" (Bolman & Deal, 1991, p. 25). This second source of organizational complexity, that related to the complexity of people, is most observable in the different ways in which we experience and interpret our world. I call this source of complexity *interpretive complexity*. This human complexity arising from differing perceptions and interpretations is referred to as "multiple realities" (Mitroff & Linstone, 1993; Moch & Bartunek, 1990) and "multiple schemas" (Conlon & Stone, 1992; Smiley, 1992). This type of complexity is captured in the following statement made by a friend of a baseball player who died of a drug overdose: "[He] had always done everything passionately. There was no halfway about him. That's why he accomplished so much in such a short time. But he was so *complex* that, as much as I knew him, as tight as we were, I still could never get at the bottom of what his real struggle was" (Wilstein, 1993, p. D2, italics added).

The distinction between systems and interpretive complexity is highlighted in Habermas' (1973) distinction between physical and symbolic organizational disruptions. *Physical elements* are those tangible personnel, structures, technologies or the like that can be physically disrupted or altered. *Symbolic disruptions*, on the other hand, are those grounded in the interpretations and meanings "that inform and direct actions, such as the routines of an organization that provide a sense of identity for the members" (Pauchant & Mitroff, 1992, p. 12). For those in organizational public relations, the major concern is that increased systems complexity so often leads to multiple, and often conflicting, symbolic complexities. The work of public relations, the management of symbolic creation and generation of meaning, links the problems arising from systems complexity with those of interpretive complexity.

Systems Complexity: The Coupling of Organizational Interdependencies

A number of recent organizational tragedies graphically illustrate the dilemmas of our increasingly complex technological world and our inability to fully understand the interdependencies that arise from that complexity. We have only to think of the Challenger explosion, the Union Carbide Bhopal plant disaster, and the Chicago sewer system breakdown that flooded buildings and electrical systems to understand that our technology is complex to the point of running amok. These "normal accidents," as Perrow (1984) called them, come about because the technological systems we build are so vastly complex they are prone to breaking down in ways that we cannot even begin to fathom or imagine.

"*Complex systems* are those of unfamiliar sequences, or unplanned and unexpected sequences, and either not visible or not immediately comprehensible" (Perrow, 1984, p. 78). Or, as Bolman and Deal (1992) suggested, "the permutations produce complex, causal knots that are very hard to disentangle" (p. 25). The interactions between the nine stakeholders in the 1984 Bhopal crisis graphically illustrate Daft and Wiginton's (1979) contention that "as the complexity of a system increases, our ability to make precise yet significant statements about its behavior diminishes" (p. 182).

The Bhopal crisis "began" with the leak of a highly toxic gas from the Union Carbide of India, Ltd. (UCIL) chemical plant. But the leak itself was only the precipitating event in a long series of complex interactions.

For example, a contextual vicious circle can be seen in the Indian government's encouragement of industrial development in Bhopal, which influenced the government's reluctance to impose strict safety standards, which contributed to the increase of production by UCIL and its attraction of new workers, which further influenced the Indian government to maintain its initial encouragement (Pauchant & Mitroff, 1992, p. 41).

All of which, in turn, led to more people living closer to a plant that was poorly managed and unsafe. The relatively "minor" physical failure that resulted in a disastrous leak of toxic gas was an unfortunate "incident" embedded in a complex system of stakeholders; chemical processes; legal requirements; economic concerns; pipes, valves, and holding tanks as well as roads, houses, and cities; and people with different needs and aspirations.

The difficulty, of course, is knowing what is happening when and what to do about it. Is the system more open or closed? Is the event one that can be dealt with deliberately and rationally, or is it one that is more spontaneous and indeterminate? Which components of the organizational systems are affected? All are intriguing questions and all are subject to a variety of interpretations by the organization's members and external stakeholders. Understanding systems complexity and accounting for its influence on organizational life occurs on several levels from individual to organizational. The study of systems complexity fails to capture higher human capacities such as shared meaning and belief systems, self awareness, and human emotion that make human organizations unique (Daft & Wiginton, 1979, p. 180). The examination of systems complexity as I have defined it fails to account for the complexity of people, which I have labeled interpretive complexity.

Interpretive Complexity

In order to understand interpretive complexity we need to accept one relatively straightforward proposition about organizational life, that is, the members of any organization interpret and give meaning to their organizational experiences based on their previous individual and collective experiences (Daft & Weick, 1984; Kennedy & Deal, 1980; Krone, Jablin, & Putnam, 1987; Louis, 1980; Smircich, 1983; Weick, 1979). This interpretive approach was introduced in chapter 3, when I discussed Burrell and Morgan's (1979) typology of organizational theories. Individuals accomplish this interpretive process through the use of schemata (Fiske & Taylor, 1984). Schemata are generally defined as knowledge structures that "guide interpretation of novel stimuli" (Dodge, 1993, p. 574). Or, as Bartunek and Moch (1987) suggested, schemata are "templates, that when pressed against experience, give it form and meaning" (p. 484). Schemata are our interpreters, the translators, of our experiences.

Individual schemata "guide and give meaning to behavior: They suggest implications of particular actions, make events meaningful in terms of what participants seek and seek to avoid, and enable people to act intentionally—to identify goals and behave in ways consistent with goal achievement" (Moch, 1990, p. 5). Figure 4.2 shows a simplified model of individual problem solving from a schemata-derived understanding of human choice adapted from Moch and Bartunek (1990).

The model suggests that individuals assign meaning to their experiences using individually held schema. This assignment of meaning can lead to the identification of purpose (desirable conditions), which in turn leads to the identification of the ways in which those purposes can be attained (means). The means themselves are translated into behaviors (actions), which result in an outcome. The outcome may or may not be what was intended through the implementation of the "desirable conditions—means—actions" process. As Moch and Bartunek (1990) noted, feedback from the outcomes can influence the individual to alter his or her actions, means, desired conditions, or, in some instances, their schema.

We might examine Paula's experiences using the simplified model in Fig. 4.2. At the beginning of the budget cycle, Paula understood her task in terms of what we call her "budgeting schema." This schema represents her previous experiences in creating acceptable budgets, both in her current organization as well as others. She identified desirable conditions (e.g., a budget that would allow her department to accomplish its yearly project); considered various means (e.g., involving all parties early in the decision-making process); and she acted

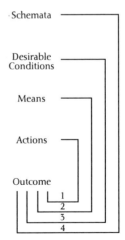

FIG. 4.2. Simplified model of problem solving. From "Simplified model of problem solving" in Creating Alternative Realities at Work by Michael K. Moch and Jean M. Bartunek. Copyright © 199 by Harper Business. Reprinted by permission of Harper Collins Publishers, Inc.

Schemata

Desirable Conditions

Means

Actions

Outcome

1
2
3
4

(e.g., submitted her budget on time to the appropriate person). The outcome was, to say the least, surprising. The initial outcome, the 57% budget slash that she was never told of, caused Paula to question not only her "budgeting schemata" but the schemata that guided her understanding of her relationship with her boss. Indeed, the outcome forced Paula to examine any number of individually held schema about her relationship with her organization. As became evident to Paula, many of the other key players in the organization had schemata that differed from hers. These differences in individual schemata lead to organizational interpretive complexity that, in turn, can foster uncertainty, ambiguity, confusion, dissonance, and harm.

Organizations create organizational schemata that are "schemata shared among significant numbers of organization members" (Moch & Bartunek, 1990, p. 8). Organizational schemata are shared interpretive schemes accessible to numerous organizational members. This approach originally found its voice and acceptance in writings about the creation and maintenance of organizational cultures. The concept of organizational culture was popularized in the early 1980s by Deal and Kennedy (1982) and Peters and Waterman (1982). Their research reinforced a notion that every organization has a unifying culture that is at least partially observable and potentially manageable. Deal and Kennedy (1982), for example, divided the organizational world into four kinds of organizational cultures: tough-guy/macho culture, work hard/play hard culture, bet-your-company culture, and process culture. Peters and Waterman (1982) wrote of "strong cultures," organizations that maintained individual creativity and organizational control through a shared value system.

Although both works were important in helping managers think of their organizations in new ways, they were both misleading in the sense that most organizations are composed of multiple cultures (Meyerson & Martin, 1987; Moussavi & Evans, 1993; Riley, 1983; Smircich, 1983). These multiple organizational cultures are the source of "multiple, or alternative, 'realities' " (Moch & Bartunek, 1990, p. 2). In other words, different individuals and groups in an organization create different interpretations and understandings of their organizational world, forming an organization that might be more accurately likened to the United Nations than to a single country. "Every organizational situation is likely to be filled with multiple and frequently conflicting interpretations and meanings" (Prasad, 1993, p. 1404).

Miles' (1980) use of the phrase, "pay homage to a common mission," in his definition of organization is indicative of an organizational schemata. The common mission is the organizational schemata that links, however loosely, the various coalitions in the organization. The schemata known as "a liberal arts education," for example, links a wide variety (and often highly competitive) group of academic disciplines under the organizational umbrella, or mission. The various academic departments, indeed, individual faculty members in departments, are rarely so united as to be unanimous in their schemata. In any liberal arts university, there are a plethora of what Prasad (1993) called "multiple and frequently conflicting interpretations and meanings" (p. 1404).

The idea of organizational schemata extends to the ways in which the public relations function is valued and implemented. In some senses, we have already discussed the variety of organizational schema operating to define the public relations function. In Jackall's (1988) experience, public relations was understood from a schema that prized manipulation and technical wizardry to insure organizational autonomy. In the Long and Hazleton Jr. (1987) definition, we might describe the schema as being grounded in the understanding of management function of organizational resources. Lauzen (1992) suggested that a powerful organizational public relations schema was one characterized by specialized education and expertise, one in which the public relations function is thought to be nonsubstitutable by other organizational functions.

Most importantly, we need to recognize that organizational schemata are created through the interactions of those in the dominant coalition or top management team. (Daft & Weick, 1984; Finkelstein, 1992; Grunig, 1992; Moussavi & Evans, 1993, Robbins, 1987).

> Systems of shared meanings are created and maintained by members of the top management team. Members of the top management team interpret issues and make judgments relevant to strategic decision making, and they possess the power necessary for implementing the choices derived from those judgements. Thus, although other organizational participants may share interpretive schemes, the top management team is responsible for providing formal interpretations and responsible choices for the organization (Ginsberg, 1990, p. 520).

The members of the dominant coalition, then, are the principal architects of the organizational schemata. Our concern should be how these schemata are created and implemented by the dominant coalition, especially in relation to the organization's worldview on external communication with its stakeholders.

Daft and Weick (1984) suggested that because managers basically think alike, they are more likely to interpret their environment similarly, thereby leading to a relatively shared group schema. Although appealing in its simplicity, research by Moussavi and Evans (1993) indicated that "a shared schema is a *necessary but not sufficient* condition for convergence of interpretations" (p. 92), into an organizationally shared schemata. Moussavi and Evans (1993) argued that information and environmental complexity and organizational politics among the members of the dominant coalition hinder the creation or implementation of a consensually shared schemata. "The fundamental organizational reality of individual interests manifests itself in the form of contentious biases which hinder convergence or collective biases which may compete with the shared schema" (p. 92). In other words, organizational politics, the negotiation of competing internal interests, power imbalances, and nonrational (indeed, even emotional) decision making hinder first, the achievement of a shared schema, and second, the implementation of that schema in strategic decision making.

This recognition is found in Grunig's power-control model of public relations (see Fig. 4.3).

The box labeled "Choice of PR Models as Strategies" is the focal point of the decision-making process. The models referred to are the four Grunig and Hunt (1984) models discussed in chapter 3: press agentry/publicity, public information, two-way asymmetrical, and two-way symmetrical. The critical linkage, however, is that between the box labeled "Power Holders" and the one immediately to the right labeled "World View for PR in Organization." As Grunig (1992) noted, organizations practice public relations in the way that they do "because the people who have power in an organization choose that behavior. Organizations frequently do not choose the most rational type of communication behavior for their environment because the dominant coalition does not make a rational decision" (p. 23).

We can summarize this chapter by proposing the following: If the public relations function is responsible, at least in part, for the symbolic management of meaning between an organization and its environment; the way in which that communication is perceived is, at least in part, determined by the dominant coalition (of which the public relations practitioner may or may not be a member); and the dominant external communication schemata (i.e., public relations worldview) is at least in part determined by organizational politics between the members of the dominant coalition; then it seems reasonable to suggest that the organizational public relations practitioner better understand organizational politics if he or she is to be effective in implementing a contingency-based (or mixed-motive) public relations philosophy and practice.

Indeed, I argue that the interpretive process is a political one, one in

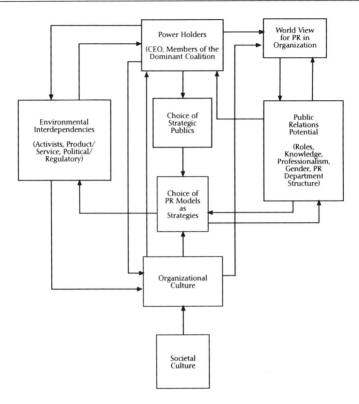

FIG. 4.3.   Power-control model of public relations. From J. E. Grunig (1992).
Reprinted with permission.

which the scarce resource is meaning that ultimately establishes a
context for action. We might want to consider the implications of
transforming Edelman's (1985) classic, *The Symbolic Uses of Politics*,
into "the political uses of symbolism." It is to the study of organizations as political systems and the influence of organizational politics
on the public relations process that we now turn to in chapters 5 and 6.

Practitioner Response to Chapter 4: Practical Lessons from a Theoretical Perspective

Kathleen G. Deakins, APR, Vice-President
Jacobson Ray McLaughlin Fillips
Tacoma, Washington

I found several practical lessons in chapter 4 about how to be a successful public relations practitioner inside an organization:

1. *Seek inclusion over autonomy.* Public relations professionals bring failure on themselves by maintaining a distance, sometimes even arrogance, aimed at others in the organization who are unschooled in public relations. While asserting their superior grasp of communications principles, PR people can be blind to their lack of understanding business fundamentals. They may know how to craft a message but know little about how to craft a widget. But it is widgets, rather than messages, that the organization values more.

2. *Focus on getting results over getting respect.* Respect is earned by getting results. PR programs should be measured against the organization's priorities. If top management's highest priority is boosting sales, the PR program should be measured on how well it paved the way for a sales call, strengthened relationships with existing clients, or increased awareness of new services among referral sources. Public relations contributions should be measured and the results shared with top management. Then the results should be used to make changes that will improve the program.

3. *Apply two-way communications skills internally.* Sometimes PR people are terrible listeners, especially inside their own organizations. PR pros are most effective when they accept the responsibility for understanding and for being understood. Using these skills serves as a

reality check to assure PR goals and programs are in alignment with the organization's mission and current priorities.

Top managers, too, can find useful lessons in chapter 4 about how to get the most out of the public relations function for their organization:

1. *Accept responsibility for the quality of your organization's public relations.* PR doesn't happen in a void. Like any other resource, it can be used or squandered. The mission top management articulates, the priorities it sets, the results it rewards, the resources it allocates, and the degree to which it includes the PR practitioner in decision making determines the PR program's ability to succeed on behalf of the organization.

2. *Reward results.* Successful senior managers should work with their PR staffs to define the results important to the organization, commit the necessary resources to achieve them, and build measurement into the PR program. Pointing out PR's contribution to the management team, including PR pros more fully in strategic planning and decision making, and devoting more resources to PR programs all are ways of rewarding and motivating PR pros.

Organizations are certainly complex and are so in so many different ways. The PR pro needs to understand the "rhyme and reason," the local organizational logic, that drives decision making in his or her organization. Once that is understood, public relations people can truly work professionally for the good of both their organization and the community.

CHAPTER 5

Organizations as Political Systems

> Knowledge without power is of remarkably little use. And
> power without the skill to employ it effectively is likely to
> be wasted.
> —Pfeffer (1992, p. 47)

> Simply stated, politics is what takes place in the space
> between the perfect workings of the rational model (effi-
> ciency) and the messiness of human interaction.
> —Ferris and King (1991, p. 60)

Most of us know the Red Cross as a first-on-the-scene disaster relief
agency, lending a hand during floods, earthquakes, and hurricanes.
The Red Cross also provides less dramatic, ongoing services to local
communities in the form of programs such as those that aid the victims
of single-family disasters, provide lifeguard training, provide medical
help for the homeless, or offer classes in baby-sitting. The following
case study, from the public affairs director of a Red Cross agency,
vividly illustrates the quotes at the beginning of this chapter.

CASE STUDY 5.1: WHAT YOU NEED TO KNOW TO GET THE JOB DONE

Like many charitable organizations, the Red Cross is a national
organization that has a national office and numerous local and regional

ones. The national offices of such groups lobby in Washington, DC, raise and distribute funds, and set policy and priorities. In 1988, the national Red Cross office began an in-depth analysis of the mission and services provided by the approximately 2,700 local chapters called, "Services Delivery in the 21st Century," or "SD21." The driving force behind the national review was the increasingly tight economic environment in which the Red Cross operates. Rising costs and diminishing funding increasingly constrained the expanding scope of the Red Cross's mission. A task force was convened to conduct the analysis and make recommendations.

Survey data gathered from the local chapters led the SD21 task force to conclude that the Red Cross must refocus its energies, given the advent of continuing budgetary constraints. The task force identified three categories of services offered by local Red Cross agencies:

1. MUST—services demanded by the charter (e.g., disaster relief, helping military families).
2. SHOULD—services that are deemed necessary in the local community if there is money and the services identified as "musts" are being met.
3. MAY—services that are added to the commitment of the local chapter (e.g., a language bank that provides translators for immigrants).

After the initial review, word came from the national office that all local organizations needed to review their services with an eye to eliminating programs, especially those under the "may" category.

Local Red Cross chapters are composed of a paid staff as well as volunteers. Volunteer committees mirror the functions provided by the paid staff. There is, for example, a volunteer public affairs committee that exists to aid the paid public affairs staff. The local chapter from which this case study is taken created a task force comprised of the volunteer chairman of the board, volunteer chairman of strategic planning, the paid executive director, and some others, but not the paid staff director of public affairs. This group examined the services offered by the local chapter, analyzed the cost of each service, and assessed which services could be provided by other agencies in the area. In December 1992, based on the recommendations of the local task force, the executive committee voted to delete five programs from the "may" category. Simple, rational organizational decision making, right? Not quite.

The seemingly straightforward process of review was complicated by two factors. In July 1992, as the task force was beginning its work, eight positions were eliminated at the local chapter as a cost-cutting measure. The elimination of eight paid staff caused a great deal of concern and uncertainty in the office, especially with the threat of the program review.

The second complicating factor occurred in October when the director of public affairs went to Miami to help with the recovery efforts in the aftermath of Hurricane Andrew. During the month that she was gone, the national office provided a replacement from another chapter. October just happened to be a crucial month in the review process because the final decisions were being shaped by the task force. Before leaving for Miami, the permanent director created a communications plan to make sure the appropriate staff, volunteers, affected service providers and agencies, and press were effectively notified of the board's eventual decisions. As this plan was left with the temporary replacement, he had, to use Pfeffer's (1992) word, "knowledge." His knowledge was in the form of his previous experiences at his local chapter and the particular plan left to him by the permanent staff public affairs person.

The dilemma. One of the five services eliminated by the task force was supported (to the tune of $35,000) by a local newspaper's holiday fund drive. According to the communications plan left by the permanent director, the volunteer chairman of the board of the local chapter was to call the newspaper publisher and tell him of the changes, encouraging him to continue donating the money to the Red Cross to support other "may" category services. When the permanent director returned from Miami, she called the woman in charge of the newspaper fund drive to give an update on the transition. The director of the newspaper's campaign drive knew nothing of the change in services, nothing of the deletion of the program, and nothing of the spin-off of the five agencies. Not only did she know nothing, she was irked that money she was raising was not going to be used for the Red Cross program. Indeed, the communication mishap resulted in the local Red Cross chapter losing the $35,000 from the newspaper fund drive.

What happened? According to the permanent director, "What happened was that the temporary replacement knew Red Cross policies but didn't know this chapter. He didn't know the intricacies of getting things done, didn't know the players. He didn't know the ins and outs of the politics." The chairman of the board, a volunteer, who was supposed to call the newspaper publisher, did not think the situation called for as extensive a communication commitment as the one offered in the original plan. Although he apparently tried to call the publisher, he did not get through and did not implement any of the other aspects of the communications plan. "This resulted in severe questioning of my credibility and the credibility of the local chapter by the newspaper people and others in the affected agencies and the media," said the permanent director (personal communication).

Immediately on her return, the director began to repair the damage caused by the miscommunication between the Red Cross board chairman and her temporary replacement. She did so by using her political knowledge of the organization. The director believed that her message would have more credence with the chairman if it was delivered by a board member on her behalf. Accordingly, she confidentially asked the volunteer board member who chaired the public affairs committee to deliver her plea for more open and direct communication. The director's surrogate

> spoke my piece about the importance of communication. My replacement, a talented and committed man, didn't know that he needed a leadership volunteer to present his case to the chairman because the chairman listened more attentively to the volunteer board than to the staff. Politics, nothing but politics. Knowing whose buttons you need to push in order to get things done. (personal communication)

The director of public affairs certainly understood Pfeffer's maxim. Her knowledge of how to communicate and with whom was at least initially wasted, however, because she was not at the agency during a critical period. Although her replacement had the *knowledge* to create a comparable plan, he did not possess the *power or skill* to employ it effectively in his temporary assignment. He did not know the ins and outs of the organizational politics necessary to carry out the communications plan. It is to power and skill that I now turn to in this and later chapters.

In chapter 4, I identified seven elements all organizations accomplish during the process of organizing, stressing the alignment of the elements with internal and external events. I also suggested that the interpretive process, the creation of organizational schemata, are political in nature. For us to better understand the consequences of organizing, we need to examine organizations from an analytic screen that helps account for competing interests, unequal power distributions, and the birth and management of conflict. The political system metaphor provides such a screen.

Viewing organizations from a political metaphor is particularly apt given the organizational public relations function. In that the public relations function often is called on to manage the symbolic resources of the organization during episodes of organizational/environmental distress, the political metaphor is uniquely helpful in understanding the whys and wherefores of organizational decision making. It is especially useful for understanding decisions made during "messy situations" or "ill-defined" episodes (Mintzberg, Raisinghani, & Theoret, 1976; Mitroff & Emshoff, 1979; Nutt, 1984) that are characterized by both systems and interpretive complexity as discussed in chapter 4.

In this chapter, I (a) discuss the use of metaphors in understanding organizations and the process of organizing, (b) differentiate between organizations as political systems and organizational politics, and (c) examine the three primary aspects of the political metaphor: interests, power, and coalitions.

As with succeeding chapters, we are building a framework with which to better understand how public relations works in organizational settings. Understanding organizations from a political metaphor gives us one more tool for building that framework. I begin with a brief discussion of organizational metaphors.

ORGANIZATIONAL METAPHORS

Krefting and Frost (1985) defined metaphor "as an explanation of one thing, the topic, in terms of another, the vehicle, where the topic and vehicle share some characteristics (the ground) but not others (the tension)" (p. 158). In their book, *Metaphors We Live By*, Lakoff and Johnson (1980) argued that "our ordinary conceptual system, in terms of which we both think and act, is fundamentally metaphorical in nature" (p. 3). As Morgan (1986) suggested, the "use of metaphor implies *a way of thinking* and *a way of seeing* that pervade how we understand our world generally" (p. 12). Using metaphors allows us to understand one thing or experience in terms of another. As shown in Exhibit 5.1, Lakoff and Johnson provide a telling analysis of how we in the American culture conceptualize time (hours, days) using money as a metaphor.

Interpretive approaches to thinking about organizations have advocated the use and analysis of metaphors (Pondy, Frost, Morgan, & Dandridge, 1983; Putnam & Pacanowsky, 1983; Smircich, 1983). Organizational theorists use metaphors and metaphorical analysis to better understand and explain how organizations, as a class of social phenomena, "work" (Morgan, 1986; Smircich, 1983). Morgan (1986), for example, identified eight metaphors organizational theorists have used in their research: machines, organisms, the brain, cultures, political systems, psychic prisons, flux, and instruments of domination.

In a more applied frame, Weick (1979) observed that the world of

---

EXHIBIT 5.1
Metaphorical Concept of "Time is Money"

You're *wasting* my time.
This gadget will *save* you hours.
I don't *have* the time to *give* you.
How do you *spend* your time these days?
That flat tire *cost* me an hour.
I've *invested* a lot of time in her.
I don't *have* enough time to *spare* for that.
You're *running out* of time.
You need to *budget* your time.
Put aside some time for ping pong.
Is that *worth your while*?
Do you *have* much time *left*?
He's living on *borrowed* time.
You don't *use* your time *profitably*.
I *lost* a lot of time when I got sick.
Thank you for your time.

Reprinted with permission from Lakoff and Johnson (1980).

---

business and organizations is dominated by a reliance on a military metaphor (an observation echoed by Peters & Waterman, 1982). The explanation of life in a business organization (the topic) is understood using expressions from the military and war (the vehicle). For example, organizations "have a staff, line, and chain of command. They develop strategy and tactics. Organizations give people marching orders, pass muster, attack competitors, recruit MBAs, conduct basic training, confer with the brass at headquarters, wage campaigns," (Weick, 1979, p. 49). Implicit in the military metaphor are the notions of open conflict, aggression, adversaries, prisoners, and battlefields.

Reliance on the military (or any one metaphor) deprives us of more creative and possibly useful solutions to both everyday and unusual organizational dilemmas. How differently might we think of organizational processes if we thought of our organization through the vehicle of dance (e.g., waltz, line-dancing, square dancing, ballet). I often ask students in my organizational communication class to conceive of an organization using dance as a metaphor. Invariably, I gain a new insight into organizing from their extended descriptions linking the salient characteristics of dance (e.g., ballet, country western line dancing, waltz) to their understanding of organization, particularly organizational communication, coordination, and control.

We need to keep in mind both the expanded understanding and

limitations or constraints of seeing organizations through any one-frame (Bolman & Deal, 1991; Gioia & Pitre, 1990). The political metaphor guides us to examine certain critical aspects of organizational life that other metaphors exclude, most notably, power and conflict. In that these attributes are important for understanding the creation of the symbolic environment, the political metaphor is one way of seeing that is useful to public relations practitioners. The remainder of this chapter explores the implications of the political metaphor for understanding organizations.

THERE ARE POLITICAL SYSTEMS AND THERE IS POLITICS

To say that organizations are political systems is not the same as saying that all organizations experience organizational politics. Using politics as a metaphor for analyzing and understanding organizations, particularly organizational behavior, provides a conceptual framework for seeing organizational life in terms of political life. The political metaphor is based on the underlying premise that organizations are composed of a variety of groups that compete for relatively scarce resources (Zaleznik, 1970).

The political metaphor is based on our understanding of government, be it democracy, monarchy, autocracy, or some other form, as a means of coming together for the common good; a means by which order is created or imposed over disparate groups and divergent views. The political metaphor of organizations draws upon our knowledge of the political system of government. As Morgan (1986) wrote:

> By recognizing that organization is intrinsically political, in the sense that ways must be found to create order and direction among people with potentially diverse and conflicting interests, much can be learned about the problems and legitimacy of management as a process of government, and about the relations between organization and society. (p. 142)

The whys and wherefores of politics provides a useful means of understanding what happens both within organizations and between the organization and other stakeholders in its environment during times of uncertainty, decreasing resources, radical change in mission, and so on.

By itself, the use of the political metaphor does not result in judgments about the relative "good" or "bad" we associate with everyday organizational politics. Organizational politics is often viewed as detrimental to the organization (Bolman & Deal, 1991; Ferris

& Kaemar, 1992; Kanter, 1977; Mintzberg, 1983). In both research and everyday organizational life, organizational politics is perceived to be a force that is perhaps necessary but unsavory. In a way, using the political metaphor provides a macro view of the organization from a political perspective, whereas looking at organizational politics provides a more micro analysis of individual and group behavior in organizations. Both views, organizations as political systems and organizational politics, are important because they are linked by certain assumptions about organizational life. This chapter sketches the macro view of organizations as political systems. Chapter 6 turns to the micro examination of organizational politics as behavior.

ORGANIZATIONS AS POLITICAL SYSTEMS

Most writers who approach organizations from a political perspective note that such a focus highlights three aspects of organizational life: interests, power, and conflict (Lucas, 1987; Mintzberg, 1983; Pfeffer, 1982, 1992; Tushman, 1977). *Interests* include the ends desired by various groups in the organization. The negotiating and bargaining between interest groups is advanced and constrained by that elusive and ephemeral concept of *power*. Finally, a focus on *conflict* recognizes that interests may not always be compatible and that not all interests can be attained. The political metaphor helps us understand the interrelationships between these three realities of organizational life.

Bolman and Deal (1991) suggested five dimensions of the political frame that aptly summarize the focus of the political metaphor:

1. Organizations are *coalitions* composed of varied individuals and interest groups.
2. There are *enduring differences* among individuals and groups in their values, preferences, beliefs, information, and perception of reality.
3. Most of the important decisions in organizations involve the *allocation of scarce resources*: they are decisions about who gets what.
4. Because of scarce resources and enduring differences, *conflict* is central to organizational dynamics, and *power* is the most important resource.
5. Organizational goals and decisions emerge from bargaining, negotiation, and jockeying for position among members of different coalitions (p. 186).

The interplay between these dimensions results in politics as we commonly understand the term as exemplified in Pfeffer's (1982) model shown in Fig. 5.1.

Pfeffer's Model of Power and Politics

In what I consider one of the more parsimonious models, Pfeffer (1982) described the conditions producing the use of political power in organizational decision making as shown in Fig. 5.1.

Pfeffer begins his discussion of the conditions by noting two sources of potential dilemma of all organizations: Internal differentiation and the external environment. Organizations, as noted in our discussion of contingency models, are composed of a variety of functions or subunits (e.g., sales, production, marketing, public relations). These subunits are often only loosely connected to one another in that they are often in competition with one another, ignore one another, ambivalent toward one another, or cooperative with one another. Differentiation speaks to Bolman and Deal's (1991) first dimension of coalitions composed of varied individuals and interest groups.

At the same time, the environment exerts numerous pressures on the organization and its constituent subsystems. Although environmental aspects of scarcity and munificence affect the organization as an entity (see chapter 7), they also often affect subunits in the organization differently. There may be some subunits that are particularly hard hit by the a scarcity of some resources. In many cases of organizational downsizing, for example, support staff positions, of which public

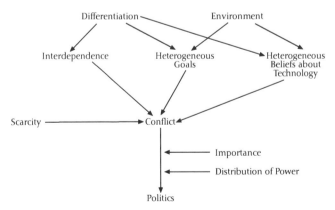

FIG. 5.1.   A model of the conditions producing the use of power and politics in organizational decision making. From Pfeffer (1981). *Power in organizations.* Reprinted with permission of Pitman Publishing.

relations is one, are often the first to be trimmed. Recent external upheavals in the hospital industry caused a major shift in the external communication programs of many hospitals. Given rising costs and decreasing patients, many hospitals switched from a public relations orientation designed to serve the community to a marketing focus designed to woo doctors and patients (Spicer, 1988).

The subgroups of the organization are, to at least some extent, interdependent, the first condition for the use of power. If the subunits were completely independent, they would each have a source of resources independent of the others, therefore eliminating the need to compete for shared resources. Interdependent, differentiated subunits share at least some common pool of resources.

The second condition identified by Pfeffer (1982) is the existence of heterogeneous goals and/or heterogeneous beliefs about the relationship between decisions and outcomes. The subunits have differing goals or interests, ones that are not always consistent with those of the other subunits. Likewise, different groups might assess different alternative courses of action and link them differently to perceived outcomes. Heterogeneity of goals and beliefs about what is necessary to succeed reinforces Bolman and Deal's (1991) suggestion of enduring differences.

The spark for fanning smoldering differences into the flames of conflict is the existence of scarce resources available to the interdependent subunits in the organization. The argument goes something like this: When times are flush, when the organization is awash in resources, there is little conflict because every subsystem gets enough of what it needs. When resources become scarce, however, subunits find they must compete with other units for their fair share of a shrinking pie. Scarce resources, Bolman and Deal's "who gets what," are the precursor to organizational conflict.

Pfeffer (1982) added that there are still two more conditions that are necessary if organizational politics are to occur: importance and power distribution. If the issue is not important, has little salience for some of the subunits, then decisions will be made without resorting to the political arena. Politics occurs when the issue is important to more than one competing group. Likewise, if power is not at least partially dispersed throughout the organization, if it is centralized such that one person or unit makes all decisions, then there is no need for political activity. Bolman and Deal (1991) alluded to this aspect of power dispersion in their fourth dimension, "power is the most important resource," and the fifth one in which they suggest that subunits bargain, negotiate, and jockey for position.

The following case study suggests the ways in which a political metaphor helps us analyze organizational decision making, especially in times of environmentally induced stress.

CASE STUDY 5.2: THE UNIVERSITY BUDGET CRISIS

ABC University is a medium-sized, private, liberal arts university established in the late 1800s. The school has been, and continues to be, a university devoted to teaching. Excellence in teaching is noted in the university's mission statement, is the first listed criterion for faculty tenure and promotion, and is the major activity of faculty. ABC has been characterized as a family, one in which faculty, staff, and students live and work together in a supportive and communal manner. As used by the members of the university community, it implied a warm, loving, caring place where everyone lived and worked. Indeed, the family metaphor so permeated the university's culture that until recently it was prominently incorporated in all university publications and marketing communications. On an administrative level, it implied a somewhat patriarchal management style, with major decisions made by the president and board of Regents with modest input from faculty, staff, and students.

The family metaphor was so strongly encouraged that the president of the university often used it as a structuring device in his formal speeches to the academic community. The president was fond of introducing his topic by referring to his own family, either his birth family from days of his youth or his immediate family of wife and children. He would tell a humorous and generally self-deprecating story and then draw three principles from it that he would apply to life at ABC University. The president's public pronouncements reinforced for the academic community the ideal of the family metaphor.

Like all universities, ABC has a structure through which the peoples' activities are organized. ABC is comprised of a college of arts and sciences (humanities, natural sciences, social sciences) and five professional schools (business, physical education, education, nursing, and arts). There are 29 academic departments such as music, philosophy, and chemistry. Most of these are relatively small, with as few as three faculty and as many as 16 full- and part-time faculty. As with most universities, there is an administrative hierarchy composed of a board of Regents, a president, provost (chief academic officer), a number of vice-presidents (e.g., finance, admissions), deans, and department chairs.

When people speak of the university, they most often speak of three groups: students, faculty, and staff. Students include both full- and part-time and, contrary to popular belief, more than 30% of the student body is over 25. Faculty includes all teaching faculty, both full- and part-time. The most important thing to remember about the faculty is their independence based on the age-old concept of academic freedom. For the most part, faculty have absolute say in their classrooms as far as what and how they teach. The most diverse group is that labeled staff. This group includes everyone from the groundskeepers to the computer whizzes as well as everyone in administration (the registrar's office, financial aid, counseling, public relations).

There is a faculty assembly that meets once a month, various faculty committees that oversee the work of the academic side of the university, various staff committees that oversee the administrative side of the university, a student governing body, a resident hall (dorms) council, and other overlapping committees and groups. In short, ABC is a typical university organization.

Over the years, and especially throughout the 1980s, ABC experienced tremendous growth. The student body grew from 2,800 students in 1979 to more than 4,000 students in 1989. Because ABC is a private organization, the money to run the university comes from private sources, most notably, from tuition. Approximately 75% of ABC's income is derived from student tuition. Obviously, a simple equation states that the more students who attend ABC, the more money the university has. Such was the case during the growth years of the 1980s. More students generated more money that was, in turn, spent creating new programs, hiring additional faculty, and expanding the range of student services. The university's budget grew from $28 million in 1979 to $50 million in 1988.

Like all good things, however, the growth years at ABC came to a screeching halt in 1989, the year of the budget crisis. In June of that year, the vice-president of admissions admitted that enrollment projections for the coming fall semester were lower than anticipated. Indeed, they were 20% lower than expected. ABC went from a high of more than 4,000 students to 3,200 in a year's time. Such a drastic drop in enrollment meant a corresponding drastic drop in operating revenues. Indeed, over the course of the 1989–1990 academic year, ABC cut its budget by roughly 20%. The university made do with no new equipment and far fewer supplies. Travel was curtailed, all unnecessary purchases were put off, maintenance was postponed. Hiring new faculty and staff positions, even those already approved, was frozen. No one got a salary increase. ABC found itself in an organizational crisis.

The budget shortfall resulted in huge tensions between the faculty and the administration, and, to a somewhat lesser degree, the administration and students. Everyone wanted to know how the university got into this mess, and no one seemed willing or able to tell how it happened. The university was not a happy place to be working. These tensions were made evident and acted on in a variety of ways. A coalition composed of the chairpeople and deans of the humanities and arts departments began meeting regularly to address the situation. Memos and letters questioning the administration's decision-making process were exchanged, chiefly between the president and various faculty committees. The budget process was called into question, faculty and students demanding a greater say in its creation. Ad hoc task forces and committees were appointed to examine a range of issues, from current levels of staffing to early retirement. A "super committee" composed of representatives from the various schools and committees was established to make recommendations to the president about reducing the size of the university.

One of the most striking aspects of the years of turmoil following the initial announcement of the budget shortfall was the rapid change in metaphor used to describe ABC University. The trust generated by a warm and caring "family" was replaced by skepticism and downright hostility.

Indeed, as the crisis worsened and as relationships between faculty and administration became more strained, people began to question the validity of the family metaphor. As more than one wag commented, the ABC family seemed less like those depicted on the happy, shining days of television sitcoms and more like a real-world, 90s dysfunctional one. A new metaphor, one dependent on the idea of 'community' rather than family, was introduced in public discussion, in large part by the provost and some key faculty. ABC University as a community was much different than ABC University as a family. The highlights of the community metaphor and the differences between it and the family one are still being defined and implemented.

Eventually, ABC weathered the immediate crisis. After dipping even further, enrollments stabilized at roughly 3,200 students. The size of the administrative staff was reduced, especially in the areas of maintenance. An attractive early retirement package enticed enough faculty to retire that faculty cuts were not necessary, although hiring was frozen and a number of unfilled positions were lost. After 2 years of numbing crisis, ABC seems to have survived, albeit as a smaller school than it was before.

The experience at ABC was not an unusual one during the late 1980s. Universities and colleges around the nation were experiencing some of the most drastic budget dilemmas they had ever faced. A number of smaller schools were actually forced to close. Others eliminated departments or programs, reduced faculty and staff, and/or did away with student programs in an effort to remain operational. It was not a good time for most institutions of higher education. Organizational life was tough. The ABC experience is particularly instructive when viewed from a political metaphor analysis.

ABC University is an organization in that Kotter's seven elements—key organizational process, external environment, employees, formal organizational arrangements, informal social system, technology, and a dominant coalition—are all evident. The seven elements combined in ways that can be analyzed using Pfeffer's conditions for political decision making and Bolman and Deal's five dimensions of the political metaphor.

First, the *environment* was the source of *scarcity*. The primary monetary resource of ABC is students and the tuition they pay for the opportunity to attend the university. The 20% drop in "natural" resources faced by the university qualified as an environmental jolt (Meyer, 1982). The university was *differentiated* into a number of different subsystems. Faculty, staff, and students each comprised a subsystem. Another subsystem analysis might focus on the departmental differentiation, especially between the departments of the College of Arts and Sciences and the professional schools.

Each department had its own interests and *heterogeneous goals*. Departments differed in their relationship to students. Some departments, communication for example, had many student majors. Others, such as philosophy, had few majors but served the liberal arts core of the university in that all students were required to take a philosophy course. Different subunits had different ideas about the connection between decision and result, or *heterogeneous beliefs about technology*. This was most apparent in the tensions that developed between faculty and staff. Faculty, arguing that teaching was the most important technology of the university, tried to put themselves first, arguing for cuts elsewhere in the university, especially among staff. As might be expected, these arguments were not particularly well-received by members of the university staff.

The different interests, the heterogeneous goals and decision assumptions, and the increased interdependence forced by the scarcity of resources led to *conflict* in the university. In that the scarcity was serious enough to call into question the justification for departments and programs, the conflict had great *importance* or *salience*. Although patriarchal in that ultimate decision-making authority rested with the president and the board of Regents, the various committees asked to review options, especially the super committee, gained a measure of power. Indeed, the informal groups that began meeting and proposing solutions began to influence the formal decision-making process.

Pfeffer's conditions for politics in organizational decision-making existed. Groups with differing interests coalesced to present their case, decisions were continually made to distribute the scarce resources (or allow the university to respond to the need to eliminate costs to meet the constraints of scarcity), bargaining, and negotiating and jockeying took place among the various constituencies and coalitions. The political metaphor presented by Bolman and Deal (1991) and Pfeffer (1982) as well as by others (Edelman, 1985; Morgan, 1986) is intrinsically dependent on the management of differences. It is to a greater understanding of this pluralist view of politics that I conclude this chapter.

PLURALISM AND COALITIONS

Politics and the political metaphor of organizations recognize that each subgroup also has its own mission, vision, or agenda. This view is best summarized in what is called the *pluralist* view of organizations (Bacharach & Lawler, 1980; Lucas, 1987). Morgan (1986) captured the ideal of the pluralist view of government when he wrote:

> The pluralist vision is of a society where different groups bargain and compete for a share in the balance of power and use their influence to realize Aristotle's ideal of politics: a negotiated order that creates unity out of diversity. (p. 185)

As Lucas (1987) noted, the relationships among interest groups in an organization play a large part in determining the organization's work and the structuring of that work.

The pluralist view is often contrasted with two other views of government or political systems: unitary and radical. In terms of interests, the unitary view sees the organization as relatively homogeneous in that it assumes the members are most likely to share relevent interests (cf., Riley, 1983). The radical view sees interests to be in direct competition, often based on divisive contradictions and class. Key aspects of all three are presented in Table 5.1.

It is important to note that what we understand as "politics" in the political metaphor of organizations is closely linked to what Mansbridge (1980) described as adversary democracy. *Adversary democracy* is based on self-interests that conflict with others' self-interests. The

TABLE 5.1
Unitary, Pluralist, and Radical Frames of Reference

Organizations can be understood as mini-states where the relationship between individual and society is paralleled by the relationship between individual and organization. The unitary, pluralist, and radical views of organization can be characterized in the following terms:

	Unitary	Pluralist	Radical
Interests	Places emphasis on the achievement of common objectives. The organization is viewed as being united under the umbrella of common goals and striving towards their achievement in the manner of a well-integrated team.	Places emphasis on the diversity of individual and group interests. The organization is regarded as a loose coalition which has just a passing interest in the formal goals of the organization.	Places emphasis on the oppositional nature of contradictory "class" interests. Organization is viewed as a battleground where rival forces (e.g., management and unions), strive for the achievement of largely incompatible ends.
Conflict	Regards conflict as a rare and transient phenomenon that can be removed through appropriate managerial action. Where it does arise, it is usually attributed to the activities of deviants and troublemakers.	Regards conflict as an inherent and ineradicable characteristic of organizational affairs and stresses its potentially positive or functional aspects.	Regards organizational conflict as inevitable and as part of a wider class conflict that will eventually change the whole structure of society. It is recognized that conflict may be suppressed and thus often exists as a latent rather than manifest characteristic of both organizations and society.
Power	Largely ignores the role of power in organizational life. Concepts such as authority, leadership, and control tend to be preferred means of describing the managerial prerogative of guiding the organization towards the achievement of common interests.	Regards power as a crucial variable. Power is the medium through which conflicts of interest are alleviated and resolved. The organization is viewed as plurality of power holders drawing their power from a plurality of sources.	Regards power as a key feature of organization, but a phenomenon that is unequally distributed and follows class divisions. Power relations in organizations are viewed as reflections of power relations in society at large, and as closely linked to wider processes of social control (e.g., control of economic power, the legal system, and education).

Note. From Morgan (1986). Reprinted with permission.

resolution to these interests is accomplished by some type of majority rule, either through direct democratic participation (e.g., faculty meeting at which all faculty have a single vote) or a representative model at which an elected or appointed official represents a particular constituency (e.g., House of Representatives). Mansbridge (1980) compared adversary democracy, which she suggests heightens our awareness of differences in a win/lose fashion, to unitary democracy founded on common as opposed to conflicting interests. The first, adversary democracy, is based on a perception of conflicting interests, majority rule to resolve disputes, and secret voting. The second, unitary democracy, assumes common interests, seeks equal respect for all parties, resolves disputes by face-to-face consensus-seeking communication. The pluralistic model used in most discussions of organizations from a political perspective adopts, as a matter of course, an adversarial model of democracy.

This adversarial model of democracy is intimately linked to the Grunig and Hunt two-way asymmetrical model of public relations. It is communication that is persuasive in nature and, as such, often conflict-escalating rather than conflict-reducing. It is a model of democracy that pits various coalitions or interest groups against one another in the struggle for limited and finite resources.

Meyerson and Martin (1987) suggested that organizational cultures can be viewed in ways that are similar in scope to the three types of political views just presented. Meyerson and Martin identify three views in understanding organizational cultures: integration, differentiation, and ambiguity. The first, *integration* highlights organizational-wide consensus and homogeneity, while denying or neglecting ambiguity in meaning or process. It assumes that "almost all members share the same taken-for-granted interpretations" (Aldrich, 1992, p. 23) and that these interpretations are most often provided by the organization's leaders or dominant coalition. It is clearly akin to the unitary model of politics.

Like the pluralist view of politics, the second view of organizational culture, *differentiation*, focuses attention on the differences between organizational units. This view highlights the lack of consensus, the ambiguity that arises because of differing interpretations of events and issues, and the ways in which subunits create their own discrete subcultures. These subcultures are often at odds with the so-called dominant culture as evident in the integrated approach.

Finally, the *ambiguity* view of organizational culture suggests that "irreconcilable interpretations are simultaneously entertained; paradoxes are embraced" (Meyerson & Martin, 1987, p. 637). Or, as Meyerson and Martin (1987) wrote: "Individuals share some viewpoints, disagree about some, and are ignorant of or indifferent to others. Consensus, dissensus, and confusion coexist, making it difficult to draw cultural and subcultural boundaries" (p. 637). Whereas the integration approach seeks to negate or control ambiguity, and the differentiation approach channels ambiguity into the organization's political decision-making process, this third approach celebrates the existence, indeed, the creation of ambiguity. The ambiguity view is most clearly aligned with the radical view of politics, one in which creative anarchy is prized. Although some of us might wish for such an organizational state, we are most likely existing in an organization characterized by pluralist political systems and differentiated organizational cultures. Both stress the coalescence of divergent or competing interests for the good of the whole.

To get a better handle on the ways in which interests coalesce in the pluralist organizational framework, I use Bacharach and Lawler's (1980) suggestion that there are three types of groups important in any organization:

> Work groups may be based on departmental differences, differences in departmental work activity, or differences prescribed by the organizational hierarchy. Interest groups may be defined as groups of actors who are aware of the commonality of their goals and the commonality of their fate beyond simply interdependence with regard to the conduct of work. A coalition is defined as a grouping of interest groups who are committed to achieving a common goal. They are based on the joint action of two or more interest groups against other interest groups. (p. 8)

In many ways, work groups are predetermined by the structuring mechanisms of the organization, what work needs to done and how the organization elects to divide the work. In the example of ABC University, the university is divided into a number of academic departments (e.g., English, chemistry) that comprise one form of work group. The administrative staff is also divided into work groups (e.g., registrar's office, student life) that comprise another set.

Interest groups may be composed of members from a variety of work groups. As the budget crisis became public and worsened, faculty members began talking about their perceptions of the crisis. When faculty met at lunch or in the faculty club at the end of the day, the budget crisis was a major topic of conversation. In a short time, it became obvious that faculty members differed in their understanding of the crisis, their perception regarding what steps needed to be taken to alleviate the crisis, and their support of the administration. There was, for example, a group of "radicals" who blamed the administration for the crisis and wanted more power in the budget process. Another group was much more willing to absolve the administration of blame and let the president and his officers work the university out of the crisis as they best saw fit. However, these differences only existed during faculty discussions, formal or informal, as part of the ongoing daily life at ABC University.

Eventually, as the crisis deepened and it became obvious that drastic measures would be required to balance the budget, coalitions formed pitting one set of interest groups against another set. The most obvious was a coalition of the vocal "radical" faculty, the editors of the student newspaper, some of the officers of the student government, and a few members of certain administrative departments, all of whom demanded a greater voice in the governing of the university.

The political metaphor of organizations emphasizes the importance of the formation of coalitions within organizations. The term coalition, as Stevenson, Pearce, and Porter (1985) noted, has been variously defined and used throughout its relatively brief conceptual life. It was first introduced by Cyert and March (1963) as a way to understand the organization as a system of subunits (employees, managers, stockholders) working together for some minimal common good but with goals that may be conflicting and change over time.

Stevenson et al. (1985) attempted to distinguish organizational coalitions from other types of organizational groups, such as stakeholders. They suggest using the term "coalition" to refer to a "particular type of subset of organizational members" (p. 258) that meets eight defining characteristics:

1. *An interacting group of individuals*—consists of "members who communicate with one another about coalition issue(s) and potential coalition action" (p. 261).
2. *Deliberately constructed*—"explicitly created by their members for a specific purpose" (p. 261)
3. *Independent of the formal structure*—is not a part of a formally designated work group. Coalitions form as extracurricular groupings outside any formal structure.
4. *Lacking its own internal formal structure*—do not have a formal mechanism for coordination or control such as a hierarchy. Coalitions are temporary.
5. *Consisting of mutually perceived membership*—members have a pretty good idea of who else is a member of the coalition even though there are no formal requirements for membership and support for the coalition will vary in strength from member to member.

6. *Issue oriented*—"formed to advance the purposes of their members. When their members cease to interact around these issues, the group no longer exists as a coalition" (p. 262).
7. *Focused on goal(s) external to the coalition*—the coalition forms to influence another organizational entity (individual decision maker, management group). They can be proactive or reactive.
8. *Requiring concerted member action*—the members "must act as a group, either through a group action—for example, a jointly signed memorandum—or through orchestrated member action—for example, dividing tasks" (p. 262).

Stevenson et al. (1985) pointed out that coalitions might share some of the eight characteristics with other kinds of organizational groups. Interest groups, for example, might be independent of the organization's formal structure, lack any coherent internal structure, be issue oriented, recognize membership, and have an external focus. The group will not become a coalition until the members elect to interact around the issue, deliberately construct a group, and actively work as a group. The authors use the example of women in management as often comprising an interest group (interested, for example, in equity issues) but not a coalition unless some of them come together and meet the eight criteria.

Although Stevenson et al. did not elaborate on their example of women in management, the following case study illustrates just such a coalition.

CASE STUDY 5.3: THE EQUAL PAY COALITION

Zylex is a medium-sized high-tech computer software company of 3,500 employees. Approximately 800 emloyees are women. Although the majority of the women work in so-called "pink collar" positions (e.g., clerical), an increasing number of women are in technical line positions and managerial positions. The public relations department consists of five people, four of whom are women. The director of the department, Joan, holds the title of assistant vice-president of public relations.

Joan has worked for Zylex for 3 years and makes what she thinks is a reasonable and respectable salary. As any good public relations director might, Joan makes a concerted effort to meet other people in the company and learn what they do. Over time, she has developed a routine of having lunch once a week with five or six other women managers in the company cafeteria. As with any lunch group, the topics of conversation vary from the personal, such as family matters, to the professional, such as what's happening at work. This group of women have been meeting pretty faithfully for the better part of a year, even referring to themselves as the "Thursday Lunch Bunch."

One Thursday, one of the women, the group leader of a small research team, comes to the table in an agitated state. When asked what's wrong, she says that she just discovered that one of her male peers makes 20% more than she does for the same job. After talking about this throughout the entire lunch period, the women agree to seek out information regarding their own salaries in relation to their male counterparts. They also agree to query other women they know in the organization about their salary status.

The following Thursday, the women meet again but this time each of them has invited another female colleague to join the Bunch to tell her story about working conditions and perceived pay discrepancies. The group has swelled to 12 women gathered around two round tables pushed together. As the women share their experiences, it becomes apparent to all that there seem to be inequities in a variety of working conditions, especially pay scales. The women informally agreed to seek out more information by interviewing the heads of personnel, finance, human resources, research and development, production, and sales to learn more from an official organizational standpoint. It should be noted that all but the head of human resources are males.

The next Thursday the group met and shared the findings of their research. Two items stood out. One was the fact that there did indeed appear to be pay inequities. Second, the administrators to whom the women talked appeared to be reluctant to disclose relevent information. Indeed, a few of them were characterized as being uncooperative, bordering on patronizingly hostile. The women decide that they will not learn any more unless they bring the issue into the open. One member suggests that they draft a memo with all their questions and send it to the president of the company. All the women at lunch that day agree to sign the memo.

Here we have an informal group that became a coalition. There is an *interacting group of individuals, independent of the formal structure, and lacking in formal structure.* Although not originally created for a specific purpose, once the Lunch Bunch members invited other women to share their stories, they became a *deliberately constructed group.* Similarly, as the group became more activated *membership became mutually perceived* as women in managerial positions who felt organizationally disadvantaged. The informal sharing at a lunch about one woman's discovery of a pay inequality led to a focus on a *particular issue* and on a roughly stated *external goal* (i.e., bring the inequities to the attention of the organization). Finally, the sending of the memo *required concerted member action.* A coalition was born with which the management of Zylex had to contend.

SUMMARY

Organizations, as Miles (1980) reminded us, "are coalitions of interests groups who share a collective resource base, are allied at least in some degree to a common mission and strive for legitimacy and growth in a competitive environment" (p. 5). Miles certainly thinks of organizations as being pluralist in nature, where interests are diverse, conflict is inherent, useful, and power is the lifeblood of the organizational decision-making process. In that interests change, conflicts are resolved, and power shifts, pluralist organizations are, in a sense, continually redefining themselves, continually recasting the relationships between Kotter's seven elements.

Although we might wish that organizations were more rational decision-making machines, bound by appropriate and sensitive rules and regulations that guided the allocation of resources, we know they are not. The bureaucratic paradigm of rules, procedures, regulations, and fixed-decision criteria are appropriate for only the most routine types of decision contexts, for "simple phenomena that managers typically can follow an objective computational procedure to resolve problems" (Daft & Lengel, 1984, p. 198). Or, as Fiedler and Garcia (1987) alternately suggested, "many jobs do not provide much structure" (p. 56), thereby paving the way for multiple interpretations of how to best accomplish the unstructured task.

Public relations is faced, more often than not, with unstructured situations, "issues that are difficult, hard to analyze, perhaps emotion laden, and unpredictable" (Daft & Lengel, 1984, pp. 198–199). This is especially true for many of the external boundary-spanning activities in which the public relations function engages. The variety of systems and interpretive complexity discussed in chapter 4 is often incredibly diverse. The idea of "adapting, altering, or maintaining" (Long & Hazleton Jr., 1987) with other stakeholders in the larger environment is fraught with competing interests, conflict, and differences in power distributions.

Recall the Kid's Place example presented in chapter 1. The apparently simple (deceptively simple, we might say) job of building a concrete slab to serve as a helipad became a difficult, emotional, and unpredictable issue with neighborhood stakeholder groups. There were competing interests that led to conflict between the organization and some of its stakeholders. Kid's Place Hospital is a prime example of a pluralist organization dependent on the external environment for both growth (building the helipad) and legitimacy (being seen as a concerned corporate neighbor). With its focus on divergent interest, conflict, and power, the political metaphor of organizations is apt in examining the role of public relations in the Kid's Place debacle as well as most organizational/environment situations in which the management of symbolic resources is critical.

This chapter has examined the macro view of using the political metaphor to examine organizations. The metaphor, grounded in our knowledge of political systems, points us toward the study of interests, conflict, and power. The metaphor also points us to the inevitable conclusion that it is people inside and outside of the organization whose interests conflict and who use power to assure that their interests receive due consideration. The aspect of people operating in a political context leads us to the micro analysis of organizational political behavior: How do people act politically? It is to the issue of organizational politics that we now turn, with particular emphasis on organizational public relations practitioners.

Practitioner Response to Chapter 5: Politics Redux

Dan Voelpel, Community Relations Officer
City of Tacoma
Tacoma, Washington

Do you want the ultimate public relations challenge? Then try your hand doing PR for a local government. If the political metaphor applies to public relations in general, then how do you think the political metaphor applies to public relations for a political organization like a city government? The politics increases exponentially. It's not just political PR. It's political PR × political PR = political PR^2.

How so? Consider this: You have no bottom line to drive you. Unlike a private company, you can't point to profit as the prime objective for everyone in the organization. So, the most creative publicity or promotional campaign won't bring in more money, get you a bigger staff, or provide you with more power.

You don't have a single product or related product line on which to focus your public relations. Instead, you have a plethora of unrelated public services, each with its own constituency—police, fire, street maintenance, libraries, parks, social programs—all fighting for limited resources.

You have elected overseers who have their own political prime objective—either get re-elected or become electable to a higher office. This often manifests itself in decisions that appease a minor, vocal constituency at the expense of more honorable, community-wide goals.

You have a bureaucratic structure often concerned more with self-preservation than public service whenever faced with a decision between the two.

You operate in the fiery crucible of coverage by local media who tend to disbelieve pronouncements from a city government, no matter how true, and give weight to rantings of any vociferous citizen, no matter how false.

You face a public relations paradox. You would think that, by its nature, everything a public agency does it should do in public and keep the public informed each step of the way. But the organization tends to withhold information from its workers and its citizens until deals are done and decisions are made.

Local government most resembles Spicer's description of the "differentiation" view of an organizational culture, in which you will find many different warring factions. So much so, that you'll feel more at home in local government public relations if you understand the principles of Sun Tzu's "The Art of War" than Tom Peters' "The Pursuit of Wow!"

So, what can a public relations practitioner do about it? You have three choices:

1. Fight back.
2. Go along.
3. Get out.

Just like any investment strategy, each approach has its own degree of risk:

1. Fight back, and you could lose big (by big, I mean your job).
2. Go along, and you could lose your spirit and self-respect (yet probably still keep your job).
3. Get out, and you could lose the chance to change the organizational culture, to really make a difference for a community (and you may or may not have your spirit, self-respect, or a new job).

Some people describe the PR practitioner as the "conscience" of an organization. In local government, you must be that and more. You must be the conscience, advocating that the organization do the right thing over doing the politically right thing. You must be the invincible Terminator, able to bear any bombshell better than Arnold Schwarzenegger. You must develop more stamina than the Marathon Man, display more grace than Miss Manners, employ more logic than Mr. Spock, and dispense more compassion than Mother Theresa. To the public relations student thinking about a career in public relations in the public sector, all this may sound like that roadside sign encountered by the Scarecrow, Tin Man, and Lion when they headed off to rescue Dorothy from the Wicked Witch of the West—"I'd turn back if I were you!" it read.

Au contraire. Isn't the ultimate success for a PR practitioner in a local government to cut through the diversions and rhetoric so people can see the truth? Then think how much more rewarding it is to cut through those diversions and rhetoric for the people inside your own organization.

Besides, everyone roots for the underdog. Even in the *Wizard of Oz,* it took Toto, a canine PR practitioner, to pull back the curtain and reveal the truth about the Wizard.

CHAPTER 6

Organizational Politics: Political Behavior and Public Relations Practitioners

> Here I am partial to a Russian saying: power is like a high, steep cliff, only eagles and reptiles may ascend to it.
> —Furst (1991, p. 393)

> He was one of those never interested in the choreography of power.
> —Ondaatje (1992, p. 195)

Chapter 5 examined how a political metaphor of organization focuses our attention on interests, power, and conflict. Our examination indicated that the political metaphor with which we are most innately familiar is one characterized by adversarial, pluralist democracy. Pfeffer's (1982) model highlighted the preconditions necessary for organizational politics to occur: heterogeneous goals and values, differentiation, and scarcity which, in combination, lead to conflict. If the conflict is salient to more than one group and these groups have a degree of dispersed power, politics will occur.

As a response to conflicting demands, politics is more than just a neat metaphor for understanding the workings of organizations. Politics is behavior. Politics is people confronting, cajoling, castigating, compromising, comforting, and creating. It is intimately linked with our interests and our power, our understanding of self as well as the organization. It is uniquely personal as well as often little more than a game to be played (Baddeley & James, 1986; Cobb, 1986; Dobos, Bahniuk, & Hill, 1987).

Drory and Beaty (1991) suggested that organizational politics is increasingly recognized as the vehicle through which individuals and groups achieve their goals and needs. Politics, as Conrad (1994) succinctly reminded us, is "the overt communication of power" (p. 283). Or, as Pfeffer (1981b) also more than aptly noted, "Power is the property of the system at rest; politics is the study of power in action" (p. 7). In that power and politics go hand-in-glove, it is necessary to first come to an understanding of the notion of organizational power before turning our attention to politics and the public relations function.

Until recently, both the concepts of power and politics have been treated as conceptual lepers by scholars of organizational theory, management, and communication. Bolman and Deal (1991) wrote that it is "extremely disquieting to see political forces corrupting organizational decision making" (p. 185). Organizational politics, as Morgan (1986) noted, "is seen as a dirty word" (p. 142). And, power, Kanter (1979) suggested, "is America's last dirty word. It is easier to talk about money—and much easier to talk about sex—than it is to talk about power" (p. 65).

However distasteful organizational politics is as a theoretical concept or a practical experience, organizational politics exists and influences how power is used to make decisions. The results of a survey of manager's perceptions about workplace politics (Gandz & Murray, 1980, and Table 6.1) indicated that 93.2% of their respondents agreed with the statement that "*the existence of workplace politics is common to most organizations*" (italics added). Fully 89% of the managers agreed that "*successful executives must be good politicians.*" And, 69.8% of the respondents agreed that "*you have to be political to get ahead in organizations*" (from Gandz & Murray; Table 6.1). The overwhelming evidence of research on managerial perceptions and experiences confirms the magnitude of Gandz and Murray's (1980) findings (Ferris & Kaemar, 1992; Madison, Allen, Porter, Renwick, & Mayes, 1980; Zahra, 1989).

A similar survey conducted with organizational public relations practitioners (Spicer, 1994) confirmed the impressions about organizational politics reported by Gandz and Murray (1980). Organizational public relations practitioners identified through the Public Relations Society of America (PRSA) responded to the same items used by Gandz and Murray (1980). The responses of these public relations practitioners are shown in the second column of Table 6.1.

The data in Table 6.1 show that perceptions about the perceived presence of organizational politics have not abated over the years since the Gandz and Murray study. If anything, the perception that politics

TABLE 6.1
Comparisons to Gandz and Murray (1980) Results

Item[a]	Gandz and Murray	Public Relations
1. Workplace politics is common to most organizations.	93.2% (1.59)	98.3% (1.29)
2. Successful executives must be good politicians.	89.0% (1.75)	92.4% (1.56)
3. Politics in organizations are detrimental to efficiency.	55.1% (2.57)	48.3% (2.59)
4. The higher you go in organizations the more political the climate becomes.	76.2% (1.99)	74.8% (1.99)
5. Only organizationally weak people play politics.[b]	68.5% (2.21)	89.8% (1.82)
6. Top management should try to get rid of politics within the organization.	48.6% (2.67)	41.5% (2.81)
7. Organizations free of politics are happier than those where there is a lot of politics.	59.1% (2.34)	39.7% (2.74)
8. Powerful executives don't act politically.[b]	15.7% (3.87)	10.9% (3.94)
9. You have to be political to get ahead in organizations.	69.8% (2.37)	69.5% (2.31)
10. Politics help organizations function effectively.[b]	42.1% (2.76)	35.3% (2.96)

[a]The percentages reported show the percentage of respondents who selected either "strongly agree" or "agree" as a response to the item. Mean scores are shown in the parentheses. The lower the score, the more agreement with the statement.

[b]Items are reversed. In other words, 88.3% of the public relations respondents either "strongly disagreed" or "disagreed" with the statement, "Only organizationally weak people play politics."

is common to organizations (Item 1) has increased from 93.2% of the Gandz and Murray (1980) respondents to 98.3% of today's public relations practitioners. This perception of increased politics is supported in the differences in responses to the statement, "only organizationally weak people play politics." Gandz and Murray (1980) found that 68.5% of their respondents disagreed with this statement, whereas 89.8% of the public relations practitioners disagreed. Almost 93% of the public relations respondents perceived that "successful executives must be good politicians." Politics, it appears, is "alive and well" in the random selection of organizations Spicer surveyed.

There are two possible explanations for the differences noted between the Gandz and Murray (1980) study of managers in general and Spicer's (1994) study of public relations practitioners. One is that public relations practitioners are more likely to experience organizational politics or perhaps be more vulnerable to organizational politics (Ryan, 1987a). Given the nature of the public relations function (a communication function of management that seeks to align the organization with various stakeholders), public relations practitioners may often find themselves in situations demanding the use of influence, that is, situations that are political in nature. Additional support for this explanation is found in the analysis of responses to another item included in the Spicer (1994) survey: "The public relations function is perceived as being political." Fifty-two percent of the respondents strongly agreed or agreed with this statement while only 27.8% disagreed or strongly disagreed. Almost twice as many public relations practitioners feel that the public relations function is perceived as being political, a strong indication that power and influence issues are linked to the public relations function.

A second explanation for the perception of increased organizational politics is found in research that indicates a growing cynicism in the American workplace. Kanter and Mirvis (1991) reported survey results indicating an increase in cynicism among workers between 1980 and 1990. Sixty-six percent of the workers polled in 1990 thought people "will tell a lie if they can gain from it" compared with 60% in 1980. Other data indicate a growing mistrust of management itself. Seventy-two percent of the respondents agreed with the statement, "management will take advantage of you if you let them" (p. 58). In that our first impressions or perceptions of organizational politics are often negative, it seems reasonable to suggest that growing workplace cynicism, especially about management, is at least partially related to the increases in perceived organizational politics.

There are, as discussed in this chapter, some special reasons for the organizational public relations practitioners to perceive the existence of organizational politics. Research indicates that organizational politics is more likely to occur under certain conditions, conditions strikingly similar to those encountered by the organizational public relations practitioner. The purpose of this chapter is to examine the phenomenon of organizational politics, paying particular attention to the influence of politics on the organizational public relations practitioner. The following sections: (a) identify the various sources of power within an organization, (b) define organizational politics, (c) discuss the conditions under which organizational politics is most likely to occur, (d) examine how those conditions relate to an understanding of the organizational public relations function, and (e) elaborate on the ways in which organizational public relations practitioners characterize and use organizational politics.

ORGANIZATIONAL POWER BASES

In a telling comment about the difficulty of legally defining obscenity, former United States Supreme Court Justice Stewart, in a concurring opinion to *Jacobellis v. State of Ohio*, 378 U.S. 184 (1964) said, "I may not be able to define obscenity, but I know it when I see it." The same feeling applies, I think, to most discussions of organizational power. We might not be able to definitively define it but we sure know it when we see it.

Organizational power can be as overt as behavior that is physically humiliating or as covert and hidden as the cultural hegemony that exists in most organizations. The rawness with which power was used to demean and belittle Paula in the case study presented in chapter 4 is a good example of an overt use of power. The perception that organizations are still male-oriented in a way that is detrimental to women employees, especially professionals, is an example of the hidden or covert power that comes from organizational hegemony (Marshall, 1993; Mumby & Putnam, 1992).

This section examines some of the ways in which power is discussed in the literature. Like others (Clegg, 1983; Kanter, 1977; Mintzberg, 1983; Pfeffer, 1981b), I am far less interested in coming to a definitive conceptual definition of organizational power than I am in identifying the aspects of organizational power that should be of particular interest to public relations practitioners working in (or for) organizations.

In some ways, to speak of the sources or bases of power is a misnomer. Power, most often defined as the ability to influence, is found in the interactions *between* people. It is a phenomena that arises in our attempts to coordinate our activities with other people inside and outside the organization. It is relatively meaningless to speak of power without speaking of interaction (Hickson, Astley, Butler & Wilson, 1981). It is also, given the discussion of competing interests and scarce resources, almost impossible to talk about power and organizational politics without talking about intent. Organizational players use power intentionally to achieve an end. This examination of power and politics begins with a look at the sources of organizational power.

The most widely used typology of the sources of power comes from the work of French and Raven (1959). French and Raven identified five sources or bases of power available to the members of organizations. They are:

1. *Legitimate or authoritative power*, which comes from the position a person occupies in the organizational hierarchy.

2. *Reward power,* which is inherent in the fact that certain people in the organization control the rewards others seek and receive.
3. *Expert power,* which comes from possessing crucial knowledge and information that the organization needs that others do not have.
4. *Referent power,* which is defined in terms of personal attractiveness to others such that others will want to defer or emulate.
5. *Coercive power,* which is based on the ability to negatively sanction or punish others in the organization.

French and Raven (1959) argued that all power accrued by individuals within an organization emanates from one or more of these five bases.

Mintzberg (1983) also proposed five sources of power available to organizational members. According to his scheme, power results from the control of (a) a resource, (b) a technical skill, or (c) knowledge. Power is also derived from (d) legal prerogative inherent with the position in the organization's hierarchy. Finally, power is gained by (e) access to those who have one of the first four. The first three become bases of individual or group power in the organization only if the organization is dependent on one or all of them. If the resource, skill, or knowledge is essential to the organization; is in short supply or concentrated; and is irreplaceable, then it can be used as a springboard for organizational power. The overwhelming influx of computer technology in organizations made the expertise provided by computer systems managers in short supply and irreplaceable, and therefore powerful.

The source of power connected with Mintzberg's legal prerogative is synonymous with French and Raven's legitimate power. It might also include French and Raven's reward power because the person occupying a legitimate position in the organization is also generally able to access a wide variety of rewards (e.g., money for raises or bonuses, preferred work times and schedules). French and Raven's referent power is akin to what Mintzberg called, ''access to those who have another source'' (p. 24).

To these five sources, Mintzberg (1983) added a condition, the ''will and skill'' to use one of the five sources (p. 25). Organizational members must exert energy to put into use one or more of the sources available to them. Not only must they exert the energy, they must also have the competence or skill to do so. We all know people in organizations who are bright, have a source of power, will exert energy to use that power, but who are considered klutzes when it comes to using that power effectively. The Red Cross director in Case Study 5.1

is a good example of an organizational player having a power base (knowledge/expertise), the will (expending the energy to talk with the volunteer chair of the public affairs board), and the skill (knowing that she needed this person to present her case for her). That she was ultimately successful in belatedly getting her communications plan approved is testimony to her political power.

In numerous writings, Mintzberg (1983, 1985) expanded on his analysis of organizational power, especially in relation to the external and internal organizational coalitions. The external coalition is composed of owners, associates (suppliers, customers, competitors), employee associations (trade unions, professional groups), various publics (government, stakeholder groups), and the board of directors. The internal coalition is composed of six groups including the CEO, operators (workers who make the product), managers, analysts of the technostructure (staff concerned with the design of systems for the operators), support staff ("the mailroom staff, the chef in the cafeteria, the researchers, the public relations officers," p. 28), and the ideology or organizational culture. For this discussion of power and politics, it is very important to understand that public relations is included in the support staff group.

Mintzberg (1983) expanded his discussion of power by proposing that at least in the internal coalition there are four systems of influence: authority, ideology, expertise, and politics. Of these, Mintzberg views authority (the legitimate basis of rational organizational power), ideology (the values, beliefs, myths, stories, and traditions that comprise the power of the culture), and expertise (necessary knowledge and skills) as being legitimate sources of internal influence. By legitimate, he suggests that these three sources are sanctioned by the organization in such a way as to make them positive sources of influence. If we look back at the sources of power previewed earlier, we find that these three systems of influence are based on legal/authoritative, technical skill and knowledge, resource control, and ideology.

In Mintzberg's view of the organizational world, the public relations function is subsumed under the internal coalition composed of professional support staffers. As part of this group, the public relations practitioner finds his or her source of power in the system of expertise. If we define expertise as having special knowledge and skill in the discipline of public relations, then recent calls for public relations education certainly support Mintzberg's contention (Lapierre, 1992; Public Relations Journal, 1992). Lauzen (1992), for example, found that a powerful public relations schema included "formal professional training," and "specialized educational preparation and job training" (p. 72). It is accurate to summarize recent writings on the role of the organizational public relations professional as follows: Greater inclusion in the decision-making coalition of the organization rests on the practitioner's expertise in something we call public relations. This call for more professional recognition is often connected with a call for increased practitioner autonomy (Dozier, 1990; L. Grunig, 1990b; Ryan, 1987b; Serini, 1993). But, Mintzberg (1983) had some very interesting observations about the supposed autonomy of support staffers, observations that seem to fly in the face of recent public relations writings. Mintzberg suggests that because professional support staffers "work in small, fractionated groups offering rather vulnerable services to the organization (because these can usually be bought externally), it is in their interest *not to pressure for autonomy* but rather the reverse—to encourage their involvement in decision processes. Collaboration is important to the professional support staff" (p. 138, bold in original, italics added).

The need to encourage involvement is also evident in research on organizational politics and support staff reported by Allen, Madison, Porter, Renwick and Mayes (1979). Three levels of management (CEO, staff managers, and supervisors) described the personal characteristics of effective political actors. Staff managers agreed that

> the successful political actor must be articulate. . . . The politician must be socially adept, must understand the social norms of the organization and behave so as to be perceived by influential others as 'fitting in well,' not as a 'rebel' or 'trouble maker.' Staff managers, as contrasted to the other two groups, said it is important for the politician to be logical and inoffensively clever. Successful politics, they said, requires competence and, agreeing with the chief executive officers, sensitivity to others and varying situations. (p. 81)

Many of these characteristics are evident in the ways in which public relations practitioners describe the politically astute person. This is shown later in this chapter.

The necessity for collaboration among organizational members brings us to the fourth system of internal influence: the system of politics. Mintzberg approaches organizational politics with a somewhat bemused and skeptical view. On the one hand, he acknowledges its importance and place in the organization's decision-making structure. On the other hand, though, he decries its existence. Mintzberg (1985) ruefully summarized an article on the political arena of organizations:

> While this author is not personally enthusiastic about organizational politics—and has no desire to live in the Political Arena, even the kind he

has described as functional—he does accept, and hopes he has convinced the reader to accept, its purpose in a society of organizations. Organizational politics may irritate us, but it also serves us. Hopefully we can learn more about this paradoxical phenomenon. (p. 152)

It is apparent in his writings that Mintzberg would feel much better about organizational life if it were more likely lived in the three legitimate systems of influence: authority, ideology, and expertise.

The word "legitimate" is crucial in understanding the way in which Mintzberg and others (Baum, 1989; Drory & Romm, 1990; Tushman, 1977; Vredenburgh & Maurer, 1984) approach organizational politics. Mayes and Allen (1977) argued that the organization "provides each member of the organization with a description of duties that specifies the organizationally desired job outcome and the limits of discretionary behavior acceptable in attaining those outcomes" (p. 675), known as *sanctioned behaviors*. They conclude that behaviors in these boundaries are nonpolitical in that they are expected (sanctioned by formal rules or accepted standards) by the organization. Mayes and Allen (1977) defined organizational politics as "the management of influence to obtain ends not sanctioned by the organization or to obtain sanctioned ends through non-sanctioned influence means" (p. 675).

Other definitions similar to the one offered by Mayes and Allen focus on the discretionary aspects of political behaviors, but are more insistent that political behaviors promote or protect self-interests at the expense of others in the organization (Drory & Beaty,1991; Porter, Allen, & Angle, 1981). It is this view that is most clearly dependent on or responsible for the overwhelming negative meanings attached to organizational politics promoting the "dog eat dog" adage of organizational life often portrayed in works of fiction.

Several authors, however, suggest that organizational politics can be a positive force in the organization. Frost and Egri (1991), for example, proposed that innovations and change—new products, new ideas— only come about through the process of organizational politics. Pfeffer (1992) argued that "power and political processes in organizations can be used to accomplish great things" (p. 35). Survey studies of workplace managers also attest to the existence of a positive side of organizational politics. Madison et al. (1980) concluded that organizational politics is perceived as being both helpful and harmful to the individual and the organization. Ferris and Kaemar (1992) reported that "politics can be positive as well [as negative], for organizations and for individuals" (p. 113).

In a pluralist organization, politics is inevitable. If we accept organizational politics as a given, we need to ascertain under what conditions it is most likely to be the system of influence chosen by organizational members. It is to those conditions that we now turn.

Conditions Under Which Organizational Politics Occurs

Although there are numerous conditions and variables influencing the prevalence and use of organizational politics, I have elected to examine three most closely related to current work in the public relations discipline: uncertainty, conflict, and managerial level.

Uncertainty. One of the most consistent findings in the organizational politics literature is that the more uncertainty surrounding a decision, the more likely it is that politics will become a vehicle of potential influence (Ferris & King, 1991; Ferris, Fedor, Chachere, & Pondy, 1989). Riley (1983) noted, "the more grey, the more politics" (p. 429). Gandz and Murray (1980) found that MBA graduates working in organizations perceived politics to be most likely in those situations in which "there are usually few established rules or standards and criteria tend to be 'fuzzy' or open to great subjectivity" (p. 241). Sixty-eight percent of Gandz and Murray's respondents identified interdepartmental coordination as the organizational situation most likely to be political. These situations are often fraught with uncertainty because there are few rules or procedures to guide the coordination between departments, especially on nonroutine matters. Given that the public relations practitioner is often involved with projects requiring interdepartmental coordination, we might expect that he or she will experience organizational politics.

Madison et al. (1980) found that reorganization changes were identified as the organizational situation most likely to be influenced by politics, followed by personnel changes and budget allocations. They concluded that "the groups or departments engaged in absorbing uncertainty are seen as relatively more political, while the groups engaged in functions shielded from uncertainty are seen as less political" (p. 95). Respondents to their survey identified the marketing function as involving the highest level of political activity, followed by the board of directors and sales (public relations was not provided as a choice among the ten functions respondents were asked to rate). Given that the marketing and public relations functions are often perceived as being similar (especially in 1980 at the time of the Madison et al. study), it seems reasonable to suggest that the public relations function might also be perceived as one of the most political. As boundary-spanning functions, both public relations and marketing perform as uncertainty absorbing buffers for the organization.

Conflict. Organizational politics is more likely to occur in situations in which there is the potential for conflict (Feldman, 1990; Mintzberg, 1985; Morgan, 1986). In their survey of the literature on organizational politics, Drory and Romm (1990) concluded that "when the definition elements are considered together, two major common characteristics emerge, namely, a divergence from the formal organization and underlying assumption of potential conflict" (p. 1146). Bourgeois and Singh (1983) examined the political behavior of the members of top management teams during times of decision making. They reported that although the members of top management teams arrived at goal consensus, this process is characterized by a great deal of conflict and coalition formation. Feldman (1990) showed how politics arises in the context of organizational stories told about the conflicts surrounding the selection of a new senior level manager.

Managerial level. Research consistently indicates that organizational members perceive politics more likely occurring at the higher levels of management (Bourgeois & Singh, 1983; Gandz & Murray, 1980; Madison et al. 1980). More than 90% of three levels of management hierarchy (CEO, highest level staff officer, lowest level task area manager) thought politics was more likely to be found in the upper reaches of the organization. Mintzberg (1985) proposed that "senior managers often use politics to gain acceptance for their decisions . . . in the preparation stage of decision-making, the making of decisions themselves, and the execution of such decisions" (p. 150).

Paradoxically, much of the same research indicates that people at the lower levels of an organization perceive that the organization is more political than those at the upper levels of management. Gandz and Murray (1980) found that the senior level managers who responded to their survey about organizational politics "viewed the climates at each managerial level (top, middle, lower) to be less political than did less senior and nonmanagerial respondents" (p. 243). This finding was supported by the results of another survey about the perceptions of organizational politics by organization members (Drory & Romm, 1988). These results are explained by the fact that those in the upper levels of the decision-making hierarchy are so used to initiating and receiving informal influence attempts (i.e., politics) that they no longer think of them as something out of the norm. They are the initiators as well as the recipients of political behaviors whereas those at lower levels of management or those not involved in managerial decision making are more likely to be only the recipients of political behaviors. In summary, organizational politics is most likely to occur during times of organizational uncertainty that might lead to potential conflict. This conflict can be either internal (e.g., interdepartmental coordinating between marketing and sales) or external (e.g., the organization and an environmental group). Additionally, organizational politics is thought to be most often used in upper levels of management although those in lower levels or nonmanagement positions are more likely to perceive their organizational environment as being political.

Each of these conditions under which organizational politics is thought to be most prevalent is evident in recent research about the organizational public relations function. First, organizational public relations practitioners often work with situations marked by ambiguity and uncertainty (Murphy, 1991). As discussed in chapter 3, public relations is "a communication function of management through which organizations adapt to, alter, or maintain their environment for the purpose of achieving organizational goals" (Long & Hazleton Jr., 1987, p. 6). In that public relations practitioners perform the roles of organizational gatekeepers or boundary spanners (Baskin & Aronoff, 1992), they are involved with assessing environmental uncertainty (At-Twaijri & Montanari, 1987; Leifer & Delbecq, 1978; Perry & Angle, 1979). As Cheney and Dionisopoulos (1989) suggested, "the ambiguities of organizations and environments can be and are managed through corporate public communications" (p. 146).

Functions such as issues management, environmental scanning, or community liaison address the role of public relations in searching for information that will help the organization reduce uncertainty or ambiguity about the environment it seeks to adapt to, alter, or maintain. Studies confirm the uncertainty reduction aspects of the public relations position (Acharya, 1985; Schneider, 1985).

Second, Ehling (1992) argued that "the primary purpose of public relations management is the 'resolution of conflict' between a specific organization and other organizations or stakeholders. . . . Hence, to have a 'public relations situation,' an organization must be placed in a situation that manifests actual or potential conflict" (p. 624). The existence of conflict is implied in the Long and Hazleton Jr. definition in the idea that there are those in the environment to whom the organization must respond if it is to achieve its goals—namely, stakeholders with different goals, perceptions, and influences. Or, as Dozier (1990) noted, "public relations programs are implemented proactively to avoid conflicts that reduce autonomy" (p. 9).

Third, as a management function, public relations practitioners are often included in the higher levels of an organization's management structure (L. Grunig, 1990a). Although the degree of their autonomy and power differs from organization to organization and is sometimes limited, these practitioners are nonetheless considered members of the management level most likely to experience organizational politics. The informal nature of organizational politics and the public relations process was evident in Serini's (1993) study of organizational public relations practitioners. Serini found that practitioners negotiated informally for changes in the organization's newsletter purpose and content with other managers. As Serini (1993) wrote, "at its essence, power is used here to refer to the ability to evoke change and to resist forced change through negotiation" (p. 4).

It is important to note that, although the practitioners' behaviors might be thought of as managerial ones, the situation described by Serini is a technical one, the purpose and content of a newsletter. A reinterpretation of her results suggests a dilemma facing much research on the public relations function, that is, adequately distinguishing between communication technicians and communication managers. This dilemma is compounded by research that indicates that public relations practitioners at all levels of organizational hierarchy spend considerable time engaging in communication technician activities such as writing (Spicer, 1991). It is difficult, then, to conclude that simply because a public relations practitioner is in the dominant coalition or holds a senior management position that he or she is truly a communication manager. As L. Grunig (1990b) noted, the public relations practitioner's power is often limited to technical decisions "rather than to the managerial role of counseling, planning, evaluating, and decision making" (p. 495). A better indicator of the role of public relations in the organization, no matter what the hierarchical level, is the perceived use top management makes of the public relations function (Lauzen & Dozier, 1992).

Results of research by Spicer (1994) confirm the paradoxical findings that public relations technicians perceive more organizational politics in their organization than do public relations managers. Technicians were more likely to feel that the public relations function was political than were managers; more likely to feel that organizational politics was detrimental to the effectiveness of the organization; more likely to perceive the existence of political cliques; and less likely to feel encouraged to speak out.

In summary, organizational politics appears to be a way of life for organizational public relations practitioners. The organizational public relations function often deals with environmental uncertainty, addresses potential and actual conflicts between stakeholders, and coordinates communication efforts across departments, hierarchical levels, and organizational boundaries. As such, public relations practitioners should be attuned to the presence of organizational politics. Research indicates that public relations practitioners working in organizations are aware of politics and, to a large extent, perceive the public relations function as being political. I turn now to a more in-depth examination of how organizational public relations practitioners actually define organizational politics and characterize those who are politically astute.

Public Relations Practitioners and Organizational Politics

We can summarize the discussion of power and politics to date by ascertaining the elemental characteristics of both concepts. *Power* is the ability to affect organizational ends, to influence the decision-making process. Power is found in the interactions between organizational members and is used to influence others. Power can be used from legitimate, sanctioned organizational bases, such as those that formally come with any position or accrue through perceived expertise.

Politics is one way in which power is expressed and used. Although there is disagreement about the negative consequences of power, we can conclude (for the sake of this argument) that politics is characterized as being informal, is related to the decision-making process, and is often perceived as being self-serving, either for the individual or a particular group or subunit in the organization. Politics is treated as being neither legitimate or nonlegitimate. As already noted, in a pluralistic conception of organization, both internal and external, politics is often used to resolve the conflicts arising from competing interests.

If, as is apparently the case from research, organizational public relations practitioners agree that their organizations are political and, to a somewhat lesser degree, that the public relations function is perceived of as political, then it behooves us to learn more about what makes a politically astute public relations practitioner. What does he or she need to know and do—Mintzberg's "will and skill"—in order to succeed in the political arena in which he or she must function. In this section, I present the results of research on organizational politics and public relations practitioners conducted for this chapter.

PUBLIC RELATIONS PRACTITIONERS DEFINITIONS OF ORGANIZATIONAL POLITICS

During a series of interviews and through survey research, I asked organizational public relations practitioners to define organizational politics and to describe the characteristics of the politically astute organizational player in their organizations. The results of those interviews and surveys are summarized here. Although there were certainly differences in the ways in which the various practitioners defined both organizational politics and political astuteness, the similarities of responses across organizations and hierarchical levels were striking. The content analysis of the definitions of organizational politics are presented in Table 6.2, showing the label describing the category group as well as two representative descriptors from the data.

The responses of the public relations practitioners indicated a very astute understanding of the system of organizational politics. As one respondent wrote, "Organizational politics is the assertive interaction of power clusters within an organization that establishes influence priorities among competing coalitions." Another wrote that organizational politics is the "unsanctioned method of communication by

TABLE 6.2
Public Relations Practitioners' Definitions of Organizational Politics

Unwritten
"Unspoken, not-in-the-job-description to get a job done or a situation resolved in unorthodox ways."
"Set of unwritten rules, seldom discussed but widely understood."
Gaining support for decisions
"Obtaining approval or support of various groups before being allowed to move forward on a project or proposal."
"Act of persuading others to adopt or support your view."
Interaction-based
"People dynamic by which an organization is run outside of and regardless of functional responsibility."
"Internal infrastructure based on human dynamics."
Alternative structure
"Sometimes completely deviates from the organizational chart."
"Cooperation that can cut through problems or sidestep problem people to get a job done."
Ingratiating behavior
"Posturing necessary by managers to please upper level executives."
"Going out of my way to stroke people in power."
Separate from expertise
"Has nothing to do with knowledge required to perform public relations."
"Favoritism overrides skill and ability."

which individuals within an organization parlay ideas and alliances into power bases.'' These two respondents clearly link organizational politics to power, interaction, coalitions among organizational members, and competition for influence. The use of the word ''assertive'' by the first respondent and ''parlay'' by the second indicate a pragmatic realization of Mintzberg's ncessary condition of ''will and skill.''

Other respondents focused on the accomplishment of the organization's mission. One wrote that organizational politics was found in ''the ways in which groups change as competing interests are synthesized to become part of the organization's mission.'' Another suggested that organizational politics is the ''interpersonal activity that may be related to the mission of the organization but does not bear directly on the successful accomplishment of that mission.'' Both of these comments echo Miles' (1980) definition of organization, especially regarding the competition between coalitions in the organization and the idea of allegiance to some overall mission.

Quite clearly, the public relations practitioners articulated a view of organizational politics representative of that found in the organizational and management literature. Interestingly, although the respondents occasionally identified negative consequences of organizational politics, most responded with a benign if not slightly positive view. One respondent wrote that organizational politics was a ''surprisingly efficient way of getting your objectives accomplished.'' Another suggested that it ''is a fact of human nature and can be beneficial to the organization if it involves beneficial interpersonal exchanges.'' The definitions, examples, and comments by those interviewed and surveyed serve to confirm the results reported earlier in this chapter that 98% of the respondents to a survey feel that ''the existence of workplace politics is common to most organizations'' (Spicer, 1994).

PUBLIC RELATIONS PRACTITIONERS PERCEPTIONS OF POLITICAL ASTUTENESS

The more negative side of organizational politics became apparent when respondents were asked to define what it meant to be *politically astute*. The characteristics described in Table 6.2 indicate the ways in which public relations practitioners symbolize organizational politics from their perspective in the organization. The data presented in Table 6.3 show how organizational politics is practiced or used in the organization, at least as observed by the public relations practitioners interviewed and surveyed.

TABLE 6.3
Characteristics of the Astute Political Player

Identifying the players
"Knowing which players belong to which camps."
"Knowing who holds the power if not the title."
Analyzing the players
"Know the personalities of the management committee."
"Be aware of others' 'hot buttons' and degree of territoriality."
"Awareness of the working relationships between people and departments."
Supervisors are most important
"Understands his or her supervisor's goals and how (or whether) they relate to the organization's goals."
"Aware of the strategies his or her supervisor is comfortable with and acts accordingly."
"Identifies and uses the ideas, feelings, and opinions held by his or her supervisor."
Quid pro quo
"Being able to trade favors for the good of the organization."
"Being able to play forces off one another for personal gain or to get the work done."
Strategic interaction
"Understand what makes them (key players) respond in a positive manner and gear your approach to obtain what you want."
"Understand what people want (their self-interest) and being able to give it to them."
"Knowing how to negotiate through the organization's chain of comand to get what you want or need when you need it."

The most striking assessment of the responses to the astuteness query was the overwhelming agreement that political astuteness is not particularly about *what* you know but about *who* you know and, more critically, *what you know about them*. The politically astute organizational member has knowledge of the formal and informal decision-making process; he or she knows how to use the system to his or her advantage. Knowledge of the process of decision making is grounded in being able to identify the key players and knowing their strengths, weaknesses, penchants, hidden agendas, personal likes and dislikes, and their degree of political astuteness. Political astuteness demands that one be aware of human nature, of the strengths and weaknesses of those with whom one interacts.

This analysis is particularly important given the immediate supervisor. One respondent wrote,

In my organization, for example, the public relations executive who has risen to the top of the function avoids professional conflict at all costs—

to the extent that he admits he has yet to fight for any proposal that has encountered any resistance from above. Such an example of working strictly within the bias of management is a good personal strategy that probably doesn't serve the company well.

Another (coincidentally echoing the avoiding conflict theme) wrote:

> You need to understand what makes them respond in a positive manner and gear your approach to obtain what you want. For example, if you know your director does not like confrontation, you develop a method of delivering news or critiquing opinions that does not arouse her anger. Or, if you want her to know what the public is thinking and she doesn't agree with your analysis, you devise ways the public can share their opinions with her so she can understand that your evaluations are accurate

"Selling" the supervisor is an important attribute of political astuteness.

This emphasis on understanding the supervisor in a political/behavioral framework is supported by an analysis of the dimensions of organizational politics perceptions (Ferris & Kaemar, 1992). Factor analysis of scale data similar to that reported earlier in this chapter (see Table 6.1) revealed three sources of political perceptions: supervisor behavior, coworker and clique behavior, and organizational policies and practices. Ferris and Kaemar (1992) found that perceptions originating with behaviors associated with one's supervisor accounted for far more of the total variance (30% of total variance) than the other two.

The overall assessment of the open-ended interview and survey data indicated very little difference between male and female public relations practitioners. One minor but interesting difference was observed in the responses to the astuteness query. A number of female respondents indicated that political astuteness, as one respondent wrote, was related to "knowing what battles you want to win and which ones are not worth fighting for." There seemed to be a greater perception on the part of the female respondents that engaging in organizational politics is conflictual and demands that whatever power is brought to the fray is precious and needs to be used sparingly. Given recent trends showing an increasing number of women entering the public relations field, this chapter concludes with data showing how women and men feel about organizational politics.

FEMALE AND MALE PR PRACTITIONERS PERCEPTIONS OF ORGANIZATIONAL POLITICS

The data reported in this section are part of a larger survey I conducted with a national sample of organizational public relations practitioners.

Data were collected using a mailed survey questionnaire to public relations practitioners throughout the U.S. The questionnaire included the 10 items Gandz and Murray (1980) used to measure managers' perceptions about workplace politics (see Table 6.1) and four items from Ferris and Kaemar (1992):

1. Favoritism rather than merit determines who gets ahead.
2. There are cliques or in-groups that hinder the effectiveness around here.
3. Employees are encouraged to speak out frankly even when they are critical of well established ideas.
4. There is no place for yes-people around here; good ideas are desired even when it means disagreeing with your supervisor.

An additional item assessing the perceptions about whether men or women were more likely to be political was included as was one other item assessing the organization's encouragement of organizational politics ("My organization encourages organizational politics").

The respondents were asked to agree or disagree to the various statements using a 5-point Likert-type scale (ranging from 1 (strongly agree) to 5 (strongly disagree). The lower a respondent's score, the more he or she agreed with the sentiment expressed in the statement. Respondents were also asked to provide demographic data about their management level, number of people supervised, and length of time with the organization.

A pretest mailing of 30 questionnaires indicated that the respondents understood the research objectives and could respond to the demands of the questionnaire. Three hundred questionnaires were mailed to potential respondents. Recipients were selected from the Public Relations Society of America membership list. A total of 130 surveys were returned for a 43.3% response rate. Of those returned, 120 were usable for a final response rate of 40%. Data were analyzed using statistical programs from Nie, Hull, Jenkins, Steinbrenner, and Bent (1975). Whenever tests of significance were conducted, a .05 level of confidence was used to determine significance.

The 14 items from Gandz and Murray (1980) and Ferris and Kaemer (1992) were totalled to produce an organizational politics score. The scale had an alpha reliability coefficient of .70, which was judged appropriate for this research. There were no statistically significant differences in the total scores for women, x = 33.5, and men, x = 35.9. There were, however, differences in the perceptions of the respondents about who is more likely to be political. A t-test showed that men, x =

1.8, were perceived to be significantly more political than women, $x = 2.8$; $t = 3.43$, $df = 26.22$, $p < .01$.

Although there were no overall differences in the political scores of the women and men, there were statistically significant differences on four items. Women thought organizational politics was more common to most organizations than did men. Women were more likely to agree with the statement that "you have to be political to get ahead in organizations." Women were also more likely to agree with the statement that "there are cliques or in-groups that hinder the effectiveness around here." And last, women were far more likely than men were to agree with the statement that "my organization encourages organizational politics."

It is especially interesting to note that women were more likely to perceive that their organizations were more likely to have cliques that hindered effectiveness. This perception is particularly interesting in light of the responses to another item from a different scale completed by the same sample of public relations practitioners. In a series of questions about the role of public relations, female public relations practitioners were more likely than their male counterparts to feel that the public relations function in their organization *did not* have a "great deal of freedom in designing and implementing programs."

In summary, there are inklings of differences that might be masked by the overall totalling of the items used to assess perceptions of organizational politics. Although there were no statistically significant differences in the scores of women and men for the entire scale, they differed on enough items to warrant further investigation.

SUMMARY

In chapter 5, we began looking at organizations from a political metaphor. We concluded that organizations are pluralistic in nature and as such are characterized by competition among competing interest groups. This is not to say that every issue or decision in a pluralistic organization is one that results in conflict. Many times the various subgroups in the organization work in relative peace and harmony toward what Miles (1980) termed the "common mission" (p. 5).

Using Pfeffer's (1982) model, we determined that politics was more likely to occur when there are interdependent subgroups who hold heterogeneous goals or beliefs about what the organization should do. Situations that might result in these conditions leading to politics are most often characterized by a lack of resources. In the ABC University case study, we saw how political behavior increased as the budget crisis forced staffing and program cuts. Pfeffer added two final conditions, the distribution of power and importance or salience of the issue. This chapter began by examining sources of organizational power proposed by French and Raven (1959) as well as Mintzberg (1983, 1985). We determined that, as a staff function, the public relations unit of an organization should seek to collaborate with others in the organization as opposed to seeking autonomy. The basis for the collaboration, the source of power accorded to the public relations function, is that of expertise. Public relations practitioners should be expert in the symbolic management process, particularly that which occurs between the organization and external stakeholders.

We also saw that organizational political behaviors are more likely to occur during times of uncertainty, competing interests, and conflict among organizational constituents. The source of expert power is, in and of itself, not enough to always ensure that the best or most effective public relations decision is made by the organization's dominant coalition. Therefore, public relations practitioners must be politically cognizant and astute if they are to succeed in enhancing their opportunities for organizational collaboration.

That public relations practitioners do recognize the existence of organizational politics and are able to use the system of politics was brought out in the interview and survey research presented in the last part of this chapter. Based on the sample of practitioners who took part in the author's research, we can conclude that public relations people are aware of the strategic possibilities of using the organizations system of politics to their organization's and function's advantage. Indeed, the responses indicated a high degree of sophistication on the part of the public relations practitioners.

We are now at the end of the first part of this book, which examined the internal workings of organizations. Throughout these 6 chapters, I alluded to the importance of the organization's environment and, most particularly, the importance of the public relations function in helping to manage the organization's interactions with that environment. In the second part of this book, I turn to a greater elaboration of the environment and the ways in which the public relations function operates as a symbolic management boundary-spanning function.

Practitioner Response to Chapter 6: The Power of Performance

Joseph C. Allen, Director
Communications
Borg-Warner Corporation
Chicago, Illinois

The sources of power in organizations identified by French and Raven in the 1960s and by Mintzberg in the 1980s are still being tapped. But an additional power base has solidified in the 1990s: the power of performance.

This power base usually relies on successive achievement and can be amassed at any level in an organization. A sales representative who perennially exceeds his or her quota creates a potentially influential power base, as does a manager with the ability to quickly fix ailing operations. These star performers are extremely valuable to the organization because of their skills, productivity, and profit contribution. Their power and reputation are enhanced with each professional success.

Performance-based power also can be established with a single major achievement. Examples include a corporate lawyer who wins a multi-million dollar settlement, or an acquisition specialist who masterminds a wildly successful leveraged buyout during a merger. However, the power base of one-time achievers tends to wane if not supported by subsequent successes. Over time, observers begin to question whether the achievement resulted from expertise or simply fortunate circumstances.

The power of performance has grown in tandem with the adoption of "pay for performance" programs by an increasing number of organizations. (No one needs to conduct research to validate the direct correlation between pay and power.) The percentage of employee compensation tied to performance varies among organizations, and is not necessarily based solely on financial performance. Many organizations place a high value on measures such as productivity, quality, customer satisfaction and/or safety performance, and reward employees accordingly. But all of those performance measures are deemed important because of their ultimate impact on the bottom line.

Top management, particularly those of publicly held companies, are under intense pressure to produce steadily increasing profits every quarter, and can be punished with precipitous declines in stock prices if reported earnings are even slightly below analyst expectations. Boards of directors are becoming increasingly active in exercising their fiduciary responsibilities, including replacing top management when performance and investor returns lag.

For these reasons, employees who can be counted on to consistently meet or exceed profit or other important performance targets often cut a wide swath in organizations. Management tends to allow these top performers more latitude in decision making and often are more lenient in supervising those employees. If the star performer has an outsized ego and an inflated sense of business prowess, he or she may even disregard corporate initiatives with impunity.

All this affects the public relations manager's efforts to gain buy-in and consensus among employees and employee groups. Those who wield power gained through performance tend to be opinion leaders among peers, and may not readily identified, because their power is not necessarily institutionalized by position or responsibility.

The most effective way for public relations managers to avoid being out-powered by others in the organization is to also build a power base through performance. Public relations objectives should always mesh with those of the organization. Always look for ways to objectively document the results of public relations initiatives. Benchmark and identify the "best practices" of other organizations, public relations departments.

Finally, do not align the public relations function or yourself too closely with any individual, including the top executive, whose power is derived through performance. Exemplary performance often is the result of favorable circumstances and circumstances can change quickly.

CHAPTER 7

Organizational Environments: Uncertainty Abounds

The everyday life and work of the typical organizational public relations practitioner is filled with time spent linking the organization with its larger environment. This is done under a variety of rubrics including:

1. media relations, which link the organization to general and trade media in the organization's symbolic environment,
2. community relations, which anchor the organization in its immediate physical environment,
3. investor relations, which link the organization with important players in the organization's institutional environment,
4. issues management, which monitor the social, competitive, regulatory environment for opportunities and threats,
5. marketing communications, which enhance the connections between the organization's products or services and the stakeholder groups known as clients or prospective clients.

Each of these activities is part of a larger organizational role, one subsumed under the concept of boundary spanning. Organizational public relations practitioners fulfill (or should be fulfilling) the organizational role of boundary spanner in those instances in which communication with some portion of the larger environment is necessary.

The boundary-spanning concept comes directly from the application of open systems theory to organizational theory (At-Twaijri & Montanari, 1987; Leifer & Delbecq, 1978; Lysonski, 1985). In the organizational literature, the concept emphasizes the relative interconnectedness and degree of openness of one organization with other groups or organizations in its environment. In that the concept labeled "environment" is ubiquitous in definitions, models, and theories of public relations, we might expect that the concept is a well-defined and conceptualized one. "One difficulty, however, is that in the public relations literature, environment remains a largely undifferentiated concept. As an explanatory construct, environment has limited utility as an undifferentiated concept" (Hazleton & Cutbirth, 1992, p. 188). This difficulty is not limited to the public relations discipline's use of environment. Addressing the concept in the organizational and management literature, McCabe (1990) noted, "Unfortunately, there has been considerable disagreement concerning both the conceptualization and measurement of the environment construct" (p. 1204). One means of focusing the discussion of organizational environment is to highlight the obvious implication that communication occurs between an organization and the stakeholders in that organization's environment.

Public relations is a communication function. *Communication* is a process through which entities (e.g., individuals, groups, organizations) are linked and presumed interdependent. As already discussed and examine further in chapters 8, 9, 10, there are a number of approaches to the organizational/environment communication process. What is important for public relations practitioners to remember is that, no matter how defined, the communication process implies the existence of a source and a receiver, in this case, an organization and its stakeholders. Like Kreiner and Bhambri (1991), I conceive of "an organization's environment as consisting of various *stakeholder groups*" (p. 5, italics added).

My emphasis on stakeholders in no way rules out the existence of other types of information out there in the organizational environment. There is a multitude of information, data, surveys, opinion polls, issues, policy statements, interpretations, meanings, accounts, and other bits and pieces of our world we label "information." It is crucial, however, to remember the relations function of the public relations communication process. We do not form relationships with information or data or issues. We form relationships (through the communication process) with stakeholders, with people, who create and use the bits and pieces of information available in our world. Thus, from a public relations' perspective, our examination of the organization's environment should focus on our knowledge of, perceptions about, history with, and expectations for the various stakeholders in that environment. We need to maintain an emphasis on the stakeholders.

This chapter examines a number of complementary ways in which organizational environments are conceptualized, particularly in regard to a better understanding of organizational stakeholders. Equally important, we need to learn how the linkages to the environment influence organizational perceptions of the value and structure (e.g., worldview) of the public relations function. Given the precepts of organizational contingency theories, we also need to better understand *how* the choice of public relations strategies (i.e., communication) is influenced by the organization's perceptions of the stakeholders in the environment. To that end, the goals of this chapter are (a) to identify the important dimensions of organizational environments and discuss how they have been operationally defined in the organizational and management literature, (b) to examine the distinctions between objective and perceived environments, suggesting that each portends a different role for public relations, (c) to better distinguish between types of environmental uncertainty, especially in light of organizational stakeholders, and (d) to describe the contributions of both resource dependency and institutional theories to our understanding of stakeholder influence.

Chapters 8 and 9 examine two types of strategic approaches to communicating with external organizational stakeholders. However, here I begin with a discussion of how organizational environments are characterized or described in the organizational and management literature.

ENVIRONMENTAL DIMENSIONS

Recall that the Long and Hazleton Jr. (1987) process model of public relations identified five dimensions of environment: social, legal/political, competitive, economic, and technological. In his discussion of the external environment, Kotter (1978) suggested that every organization exists in both a task environment and a wider environment. These are also referred to as the technical environment and the cultural environment of the organization. Although Long and Hazleton Jr. (1987) did not distinguish between types of environments in their model, they allude to the distinction proposed by Kotter. The social and legal/political dimensions are most clearly a part of Kotter's *wider* environment, whereas the competitive, economic, and technological dimensions are more closely related to the *task* environment. The organizational public relations function often finds itself engaged in both types of environments, environments that often create conflicting demands for the boundary-spanning function.

External forces located in both the task and the general environment influence the ways in which the organization seeks to maintain a degree of autonomy. One of the first distinctions I make about the boundary-spanning activities of public relations practitioners is that they link stakeholders in both types of environments to the organization. There is relevant information to be gleaned from both the task and the general environment. Recall the case studies in chapter 1—the selling of a piece of corporate art, the building of a hospital helipad, and the creation of a new policy on open restrooms. Each of these cases illustrates the complexity of connections between the task environment and the larger general environment.

The selling of the artwork, for example, began as a simple transaction between the bank and the purchasers of its former office building, a task environment transaction. All too quickly, as the bank learned to its dismay, the transaction evolved into one that became embedded in public attitudes associated with the general environment. How the bank's dominant coalition perceived and interpreted the external conditions surrounding the sale differed vastly from those of external art-oriented stakeholders.

At this point, we should briefly recall Grunig's power-control model of public relations presented in chapter 4. Grunig (1992), and certainly others (e.g., Lauzen & Dozier, 1992; Long & Hazleton Jr., 1987), posited a reciprocal relationship between the influences of external stakeholders and the internal decision-making process of the organization. This reciprocal relationship is evident in the ways in which the arrows in Fig. 4.4 "flow" from environment to dominant coalition to worldview for public relations to choice of public relations and back to the environment. At the same time, however, there is an arrow from the dominant coalition to the environment suggesting that the dominant coalition both interprets events in the environment and attempts to control them to at least some extent (e.g., contingency theory as well as definitions of public relations). This reality/perception cycle is illustrated in Fig. 7.1.

The reciprocal relationship between organization (i.e., dominant coalition) and the environmental interdependencies influences the choice of public relations worldview. Environmental influences, filtered through the dominant coalition's organizational schemata, dictate (at least in part) the structure of the public relations function. This external influence on the internal workings of the organization is appropriately conceptualized in contingency models of organization. It is dependent on both reality and our interpretations of that reality, a dependency to which we now turn.

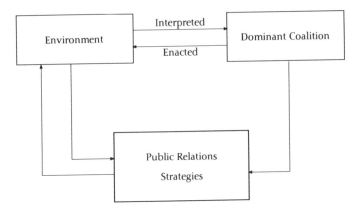

FIG. 7.1.   Environment/dominant coalition interdependence. From J. E. Grunig (1992). Reprinted with permission.

Resources and Information: Objective Versus Interpreted Reality

The following excerpt from an article on the sales and earnings of a publicly traded company illustrates our concerns in this section:

> Whether Esterline, a collection of a dozen industrial equipment and electronic instrumentation companies, can sustain that performance [up 73 percent] *depends in large measure on what occurs in the economy*. . . . Wendell Hurlbut, Esterline's chairman and chief executive officer, said the first quarter of last year was hampered by customers holding back on spending *until they figured out what was going on* in the economy. 'The really big question is *how do our customers perceive the economy*,' Hurlbut said, adding that for the moment they seem willing to spend. (Virgin, 1995, B6, italics added)

The author of the article alludes to what occurs in the economy, or, in other words, what happens in Esterline's environment. By using the phrase "until they figured out what was going on," the CEO is indicating that what occurs in the economy (in reality) is not always easily known or understood. And, finally, most tellingly, the CEO of the company notes that his company's success rests on "how our customers perceive the economy," thereby addressing the crucial link between environmental reality and the organization's collective perception of that reality.

One of the primary dilemmas facing those who study organizational environments is distinguishing between real-world events or actions and our *interpretations* of those events or actions. This dilemma was alluded to in chapter 4 in the discussion of both *systems* and *interpretive* complexity with which organizations must contend. There is real-world complexity associated with the interactions between the organization's internal components, external stakeholders, market forces, societal changes, and disruptive natural events, such as the 1995 earthquake in Kobe, Japan. These real events influence how effective the organization's alignment is with those influencing forces in its external environment.

The events are real. At the same time, however, the organization's response to these events is largely dependent on how the members interpret and understand these events (Daft & Weick, 1984). Our interpretations of environmental reality, the meanings we ascribe to the events we witness, become a source for additional information as well as a source for potential bias and confounding. The potential donor pool of eligible high school graduates available for ABC University steadily declined during the 1980s. The dominant coalition of ABC University, for whatever reasons, did not perceive this decline to be a threat to the continued growth and health of the organization. Unfortunately, the dominant coalition's perception of the external reality was eventually shown to be faulty and negatively impacted the university.

Any discussion of organizational environments needs to contend with the simple truth that organizations exist in both an objective and a perceived environment. Organizational environments consist of both a stock of available resources and a source of information (Dess & Origer, 1987). Indeed, given what we know about shared organizational schemata and organizational politics, we might go further and suggest that there could easily exist (and usually does) more than one perception of the objective environment (Daft & Weick, 1984; Jauch & Kraft, 1986, Moussavi & Evans, 1993). On seeing a decline in sales for a particular company, one stockbroker might perceive this as a great time to buy the stock because the price is going down, whereas another might perceive the decline as indication that it is time to sell. Identical data grounded in a real event is given different meanings and thus results in different actions. It is to the link between environment reality (resources) and environmental uncertainty (information) that we now turn.

Dimensions of Environmental Uncertainty

Resource dependency theories of organizational environments focus attention primarily on the organization's *task* or *technical* environment

(Oliver, 1991; Pfeffer & Salanick, 1978; Scott, 1992). Resource dependency theories are grounded in the assumption that organizations exist in an environment of potential resources and competitors for those resources (Aldrich & Mindlin, 1978; Bluedorn, 1993; Huber & Daft, 1987; Jauch & Kraft, 1986; McCabe, 1990). A supplier goes out of business, an employee group files an injunction against the organization, a newly negotiated labor contract increases the starting wage at the company by $.75 an hour, or a competitor drastically lowers its prices. All of these events happen in real time and are often perceived as causal events that necessitate a response from the organization. The role of management in resource dependency theory is to strategically manage these external dependencies to their organization's advantage, thereby moderating the power of the external forces to influence the organization's autonomy (Greening & Gray, 1994; Herbeniak & Joyce, 1985; Kreiner & Bhambri, 1991; Pfeffer & Salancik, 1978)

Resource dependency theories describe variations in organizational environments using primarily three variables: complexity, munificence, and dynamism (Bluedorn 1993; Dess & Origer, 1987). These three variables have been the focus of much environment/organization research, especially that from contingency theory approaches. Other variables have been added to the primary trinity such as domain consensus and organizational similarity (cf., Aldrich, 1979), but complexity, munificence, and dynamism have remained the key variables in most descriptions of an organization's environment.

Complexity speaks to the number, diversity, and degree of interdependence among the elements of the environment (Huber & Daft, 1987). Environmental complexity is associated with the degree to which the relevant elements of the task environment are increasing in number, differences, and linkages. Most major urban school districts, for example, are facing increasing complexity in that they are serving a more divergent number of invested stakeholder groups and students (e.g., multiple ethnicities, greater disparities between socioeconomic levels). A good example of complexity is demonstrated in the Union Carbide example presented in chapter 4. In public relations research, complexity is often defined as the number of stakeholders with which the organization must be concerned (Cox, 1984; Lauzen & Dozier, 1992).

Munificence refers to the availability of resources in the environment; the amount of critical resources available to the target organization and other organizations operating in the same or similar sphere. In general, scarce resources lead to increased competition for limited resources whereas abundant resources lead to either relative organizational stability or new competitors entering the environment (Castrogiovanni, 1991). ABC University faced a scarcity of high school graduates, which led to increased competition from universities and colleges in the area. There was a lack of munificence in the university's most critical resource. All too often scarce resources have (at least in the past) been detrimental to the organizational public relations function in that public relations is often one of the first staff functions eliminated during times of scarcity.

Dynamism or turbulence, according to Huber and Daft (1987), incorporates both instability and randomness. By instability, they mean the frequency of change and by randomness the "unpredictability of both the frequency and direction of change" (p. 135). Turbulence refers to the unpredictability of the rate and direction of change in the environment. In essence, turbulence speaks to the both the degree of complexity (interconnectedness) and the rate at which that complexity is becoming more complex. As a boundary-spanning function, organizational public relations often attempts to balance the demands of competing organizational stakeholders (e.g., activist groups versus stockholders).

These three characteristics or dimensions—complexity, munificence, turbulence—apply, not to the organization itself, but to the organization's environment. Environments vary in the degree to which they are characterized by the three dimensions. At the same time, although all three dimensions are evident in every environment, not every dimension will be accorded equal importance or weight by the organization. The dimensions of complexity, munificence, and turbulence are ones that contingency theorists suggest the organization must take into account if the organizational structures and processes are going to effectively fit the demands of the environment. They are also the source of much uncertainty about the organization's environment.

In his review of research on organizational size and environment from 1980–1992, Bluedorn (1993) succinctly summarized contingency theory research in relation to the three variables associated with resource dependency models and managerial interpretation:

> The task environment consists of three variables: complexity, dynamism, and munificence that affected an omnibus perception of the environment: uncertainty. Although the literature referred to this concept as environmental uncertainty, this phrase was really a misnomer because the uncertainty was not in the environment. It was, of course, in the perceptions and minds of the managers in terms of their ability to predict future environmental states. (p. 166)

The perceptions of the managers leads us to the second way in which organizational environments are conceptualized in the organizational and management literature, a conception grounded in the perceptions of organizational managers. The *perceived* model of the environment is different from the *objective* model in that it is based on interpretations of the events, actions, people, and other organizations in the real environment. Information processing approaches to the environment are grounded in the organization's perceptions of its resource environment. They focus our attention "on the processes through which the environment influences an organization's structure and processes, especially its communications. More generally this perspective focuses on the fact that organizations extract, process, and act on information from their environment" (Huber & Daft, 1987, p. 132). This perspective, and the interpretative similarities and differences in organizations, was noted in chapter 4 when we discussed multiple organizational schemata.

In all cases, one of the primary attributes of organizational environments is the degree of certitude with which organizational members can accurately know and predict the various variations evident in their environment (Driskill & Goldstein, 1986; Gerloff, Muir, & Bodensteiner, 1991; Milliken, 1987). This concept is best known as *environmental uncertainty*. Uncertainty refers to the degree with which future events, actions, issues, or trends are predictable. By predictable, we simply mean known, the degree to which the future is known or knowable. Environmental uncertainty suggests that the source of the inability to accurately predict is found in the environment, not in the organization itself (Milliken, 1987). The dilemma we encounter when we try to assess environmental uncertainty is the inability of most people to disassociate their perceptions of reality from reality. Uncertainty exists in both the objective and perceived environment, but which is which and which is most important are often confused conceptually and pragmatically. Someone in the organization, or many someones, are continually interpreting data about the organization's objective environment, which ultimately leads to a reliance on perceptions, the assignment of meaning.

My view of environmental uncertainty rests on the assumption that every organization has an objective environment that is perceived by organizational decision makers. Both reality and the sense-making of that reality are important to the organization (McCabe, 1990). This combination is similar to that proposed by Bourgeois (1980):

> Every firm has an objective environment that places constraints on the way it operates—e.g., an industry group has certain technical characteristics that must be attended to. At issue is whether a manager's perceptions of volatility or variability induce uncertainty and whether these

subjective impressions override the objective situation when critical decisions are made. My position is that the objective task environment is "real," measurable, and external to the organization, and that perceptions of the environment are also real events taking place within the organization. Additionally, and of central importance, when held by the dominant coalition or top management team, these perceptions are considered to be crucial inputs to the strategy-making process. (p. 35)

This combination is illustrated in Jauch and Kraft's (1986) "Revisionist Model of Environmental Uncertainty" displayed in Fig. 7.2. Jauch and Kraft (1986) proposed that their model "can be best understood by viewing it as representing the decision sequence of a strategist" (p. 784). Their revisionist model shows the impact of the objective environment on both perceived environmental uncertainty as well as actual organizational outcomes. That reality and perceptions of reality might differ was graphically illustrated in the ABC University

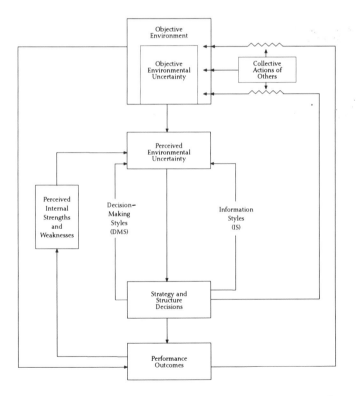

FIG. 7.2.   A revisionist model of environmental uncertainty. From Jauch, L., & Kraft, K. (1986). Strategic management of uncertainty. *Academy of Management Review*, 11, 777–790. Reprinted with permission of the Academy of Management.

case presented in chapter 5. Recall that, although the number of high school graduates declined during the 1980s (the objective reality), the ABC University dominant coalition did not perceive this to be particularly problematic (perceived environmental uncertainty).

The Jauch and Kraft model also indicates that the organizational outcomes are ameliorated by the actions of other stakeholders (e.g., competitors, regulators) in the environment (collective actions of others). Again, using the ABC University example, during the time of financial crisis brought on by decreasing enrollments, a large public institution in the region decided to open a branch campus in ABC's area. Although it is still too soon to predict the real outcomes of this action, the opening has created both objective environmental uncertainty as well as a great amount of perceived environmental uncertainty in ABC University.

Ultimately, organizational decision makers, influenced by both their information-gathering and interpreting styles (IS), as well as their individual and collective decision-making styles (DMS), must arrive at decisions based on their perceptions of environmental uncertainty. It is the perceptions of uncertainty that guide the decisions about strategy and choice. Reality, the objective environment, comes into play only as a yardstick by which to measure the eventual success or failure of the strategic decisions. Perceived environmental uncertainty, then, is a primary precondition of all strategic decision making.

One of the most enlightening discussions of perceived environmental uncertainty is that by Milliken (1987) who proposed that there are three types of perceived uncertainty about the environment: state, effect, and response.

1. *State uncertainty.* Milliken argues that what she labels "state" uncertainty most closely resembles what others have traditionally labeled perceived environmental uncertainty. This state uncertainty arises when "one does not understand how components of the environment might be changing . . . [or] may involve an incomplete understanding of the interrelationships between elements in the environment" (Milliken, 1987, p. 136). State uncertainty involves an inability to understand the complexity dimension of the environment.

2. *Effect uncertainty.* Milliken gives the example of knowing that a hurricane is headed for your town and house does not necessarily mean that you will be able to predict how that hurricane will possibly damage your house. We might know and understand changes in the complexity of our environment very well, but not be able to predict how those changes will influence our organization. To whit, Milliken (1987) defined effect uncertainty as "an inability to predict what the

nature of the impact of a future state of the environment or environmental change will be on the organization'' (p. 137). She suggested that ''if state uncertainty involves uncertainty about the future state of the world, then effect uncertainty involves uncertainty about the implications of a given state of events in terms of its likely impact on the organization's ability to function in that future state'' (p. 137).

3. *Response uncertainty.* We may well be in the situation of the hurricane approaching our house and, given previous experiences with strong storms, understand that we have several options available to protect the house and contents. We might want, for example, to put plywood over the windows, move cars to a safer location, take down the children's play set, fix the garage door so that it closes and locks, bring everything up from the basement in case of flooding, and so on. Given the limited time available to us, however, we might be uncertain as to which action to take first. Response uncertainty is defined ''as a lack of knowledge of response options and/or an inability to predict the likely consequences of a response choice'' (Milliken, 1987, p. 137). This type of uncertainty, related to state and effect uncertainty, is ''experienced in the context of a need to make an immediate decision'' (p. 138).

Milliken (1987) summarized her distinctions by assessing the types of information that organizational decision makers might be lacking in each situation:

In the case of state uncertainty, administrators lack information about the nature of the environment. The experience of effect uncertainty, on the other hand, does not necessarily involve a lack of information about environmental conditions (in fact, the administrator may have all he/she can handle); rather, the shortage of critical information is in knowledge of how environmental events, changes, or sets of changes will *affect* the particular organization, if at all. Finally, in the case of response uncertainty, there is a perceived lack of information about what the organization's response options are and/or about the value or utility of each course of action in terms of achieving desired organizational outcomes. (p. 138)

An exploratory analysis (Gerloff et al., 1991) indicated that project managers can, indeed, identify the three types of perceived environmental uncertainty.

Intel Corporation's recent difficulties surrounding a flaw in its widely touted Pentium computer chip help to clarify the distinctions and usefulness of Milliken's three types of uncertainty.

CASE STUDY 7.1: UNCERTAINTY ABOUT THE INTERNET: THE PENTIUM CHIP WARS

[This article is printed verbatim from a forthcoming issue of Knowledge Tools News, an electronic newsletter of Omegacom, Inc. James Baar (jimbar@omegacom.com) is president/managing consultant. Theodore Baar (tedbar@omegacom.com) is vice president/chief technologist.]

Back in June, Intel and some of its customers already knew about the bug that was preventing the new Pentium microprocessors to divide accurately out to more than nine or 10 decimal places in some cases. Intel did not publish the information. If any messages about the bug appeared here and there in various newsgroups on the Internet for the next few months, they initially attracted little attention.

This was not the kind of consumer problem that causes a lot of excitement at your neighborhood 24-hour store. But this bug was of interest—and in some cases importance—to parts of the world technical community engaged in major mathematical calculations: This is a community that also appreciates that such a flaw is not the first nor will be the last in the increasing complexity of computer components and software; exalts technical openness; recognizes quickly when it is being stonewalled; and has a biting specialized sense of outrage and humor.

Professor Thomas Nicely of Lynchburg College reports that when he began running into a potential flaw in the Pentium in June he started a three month effort to determine whether the problem was the Pentium or something else. For example, his own calculations; or possibly known bugs in other hardware such as the Borland C Compiler. And in Copenhagen mathematicians developed a T-shirt satirizing the Intel chip logo "Intel Inside" as "No Intelligence Inside" and published memos saying "We knew about it early in June. . . ."

Intel managed to downplay and contain word of the bug for the most part through the next three months. Any callers were told at first that a fix was underway and that the bug affected only very special situations.

Then, on Oct. 30, Dr. Nicely posted a message to "whom it may concern" on the Internet, reporting his findings and his frustrations with getting Intel to pay serious attention to him. In the succeeding weeks, the war between Intel and its users exploded. Each day there were more reports about the bug and Intel's truculence.

The number of the strings of messages on the Internet increased and grew longer as users at universities, laboratories and corporations around the world reported the same bug and its potential variations;

discussed their research for possibly more bugs; and reported on their unsatisfactory and frustrating phone calls to Intel.

And here was where the war was really fought.

Intel treated each caller as an individual, linear event to be dealt with in isolation; turned around or at least mollified. Intel's position was that this was a routine bug that was being taken care of and was of no major importance to most of its customers. The Intel position essentially remained that there was no need for a general replacement on demand; that the problem was relatively minor; that if a user was engaged in the kind of heavy mathematics that could be affected by the bug then Intel, if it agreed, would replace a Pentium.

Meantime, Intel and its commercial allies continued to promote and sell Pentiums. More than four million Pentiums were reported sold.

The words "greedy" and "arrogance" became popular on the Internet among customers describing Intel's position. The Internet discussion was highly technical and profane. It also included useful suggestions for broadening the discussion. For example, participants were provided with the fax number of The New York Times. And more and more of the callers to Intel shared their mostly frustrating experiences on the Internet with a worldwide audience of customers. An angry mob—slowly recognized as a threat by Intel—began to assemble in cyberspace.

Intel CEO Andrew Grove issued a statement on the Internet Nov. 27 seeking to quiet the mob. Instead the roar in cyberspace increased. Intel's Software Lab Technology Lab Director Richard Wirt on Dec. 8 issued a statement on the Internet describing Intel plans to provide a fix for the flaw. The roar continued and spread and Intel's weakening protests were increasingly drowned out as the users reinforced each other with new data and complaints around the clock around the world.

It was at this point on Dec. 12 that IBM—a reported minor player in the sales of Pentiums, but the developer of a competitive chip, the PowerPC—decided to announce both on the Internet and to the major national media the halting of its shipments of Pentium-based IBM PCs.

The war was now spread to the major national media where the problem was easily confused with various consumer product recalls and the Internet where IBM's move was both discounted as self-serving and used simultaneously to pummel Intel further.

By Dec. 20 Intel had had enough. It agreed to a general recall and apologized for not doing so sooner.

The public relations lessons are clear.

People—particularly customers—are no longer isolated waiting to learn sooner or later what is happening through the third party media screen and, in turn, relying on the third party media to screen and sooner or later report their reaction. Even when the third party media is accurate this process can take many days.

Through the Internet, people—particularly consumers—can tell a corporation or organization exactly what they think and why they share that simultaneously and instantaneously with all concerned around the world. The Internet returns the world to the agora where everyone hears what was said; and everyone hears all comments and reactions; everyone knows who is talking and can make credibility judgments.

The first Intel error was not to spot the issue stirring on the Internet months ago when the commentary was helpful and understanding. At that time and for several months later, Internet commentators could have been embraced and thanked for their efforts; immediate plans for a work-around fix could have been disclosed; and work on a permanent fix could have been described: all in cyberspace among sophisticated customers who well understand the complex nature of the technology.

Intel's second error was not to recognize that because of the Internet it no longer could reason at least semi-privately with customers and advance rational technical arguments. In pre-cyberspace days, that could be effective: the customer is grudgingly mollified until the issue is eventually resolved. But in this case, as its customers shared both their problems and experiences with each other in real time, they fed each others frustrations; were empowered as a group to demand better treatment; and built mutual strength with each day for new battles to come.

Intel's third error was not to go directly online with its customers and deal with the issue interactively. Instead, Intel pursued the classic static public relations mode of issuing statements and news releases. These were turned into blackened ruins by Internet flame messages in a matter of hours.

Meantime, IBM by its announcement, uncorked the Law of Unanticipated Consequences. The Internet mob really understood the issue; the general public for the most part did not. IBM, with motives already under suspicion, opened the bottle labeled ''Doubt about Technology'' to the overall potential future detriment of the Information Technology Industry in general.

As more people around the world join the millions already using the Internet for communications, corporations and government will be forced, if they wish to succeed, to function within the new realities of cyberspace: information is shared and sifted by thousands of knowledgeable people; time is collapsed; facts are quickly checked; loss of credibility can be instantaneous; second chances are rare and harder to effect; grandstand plays better be perfect; and the playing off of one audience against another is far more easily detected.

In this case study we find all three types of Milliken's (1987) uncertainty. First, we can surmise that Intel Corporation did not fully grasp the ways in which its environment had changed, given the popular advent of the Internet, and Intel did not have a complete understanding of the complexity and swiftness of the interrelationships forged by Internet connections (i.e., state uncertainty). Second, even after it recognized that the flaw in the chip might be of concern to more than just sophisticated computer users, Intel apparently did not understand the implications of finding itself the target of exchange by Internet users (i.e., effect uncertainty). Intel did not fully comprehend the magnitude of the effect the Internet had on its operations. Third, at least as portrayed by the authors of the case study, Intel suffered severe lapses in response, first trying one tactic and then another, unsure which would effectively limit the damage to its reputation (i.e., response uncertainty). Uncertainty—state, effect, and response— played a major role in Intel's inability to control its environment. This inability led many to question the public relations response of Intel to the increasingly public furor over the Pentium chip's flaw.

The originators of contingency theories based on resource dependency models of organization and environment interdependencies presumed that managers had a fairly wide degree of latitude when selecting ways in which to respond to the demands of task environments (Child, 1972; Lawrence & Lorsch, 1967). This discretion was seen as crucial in aligning the organization to the demands of its environment. Over time, however, research indicated that the theorized degree of discretion was often much less than that exhibited in practice. Factors other than managerial decision making about the organization's alignment with its task environment were equally important in accounting for the success or failure of an organization. In the late 1970s, these alternate explanations led to the *institutional approach* to organizational environments (Meyer & Rowan, 1977). These institutional forces are alluded to in Jauch and Kraft's (1986) model in the box labeled ''collective actions of others.'' These collective actions influence the objective environment as well as the success or failure of the organization's strategy and structure decisions and the organization's performance outcomes. The collective actions include both those attributed to stakeholders ''fighting'' for the scarce resources described in the technical environment, (e.g., competitors), as well as those stakeholders not directly engaged in the struggle for resources, but those who can influence the legitimacy of the organiza-

tion's quest. These legitimizing stakeholders are currently conceptualized to be part of the organization's institutional environment.

Institutional Theory

Institutional approaches to organizational environments focused on
the larger cultural and societal environments in which groups of
similar organizations exist (Aldrich, 1992; Gordon, 1991; Greening &
Gray, 1994; Meyer & Scott, 1992; Oliver, 1991; Powell & DiMaggio,
1991). As Meyer and Scott (1992) wrote in the preface to the updated
version of their seminal work on institutionalism, "Environments are
more than stocks of resources and energy flows; they are cultural
systems, defining and legitimating organizational structures and thus
aiding in their creation and maintenance" (p. 1).

Institutions can best be thought of as meta-organizational groupings
that can influence individual organizations in that group. Institutions
are most often defined as:

> regulatory structures, governmental agencies, laws, courts, and profes-
> sions . . . institutional constituents that exert pressures and expectations
> include not only the state and professions, as institutions, but also
> interest groups and public opinion. (Oliver, 1991, p. 147, italics added)

Institutions "specify rules, procedures, and structures for organizations as a condition of giving legitimacy and support" (Greening &
Gray, 1994, pp. 470–471). Given the traditional function of public
relations in maintaining the symbolic environment of the organization,
often captured in the phrase "organizational image," the institutional
conceptualization of legitimacy looms large (Dunbar & Ahlstrom,
1995).

Symbolic legitimacy, as opposed to a more legalistic legitimacy, is at
the core of many public relations situations. The legitimacy of Seafirst
Bank as a responsible corporate citizen was called into question by
institutional "interests groups and public opinion" (Oliver, 1991, p.
147), who questioned the bank's perceived "right" to sell the sculpture. The power of symbolic legitimacy is evident in the simple fact
that the bank certainly had a legal right to sell its solely owned artwork
to whomever it pleased. Interest group pressure coalesced public
opinion to the point that the bank was perceived as losing its symbolic
legitimacy in the community.

ABC University, for example, is an accredited university; it is
provided legitimacy through periodic reviews by an external agency.

This accrediting body specifies that the university must meet certain requirements in order to maintain accreditation, or legitmacy. In addition to general accreditation, there are more specific accrediting bodies for specific programs in the university that affect the structure of the university. The School of Business, for example, is accredited by a business school accrediting body. One requirement of this external stakeholder is that each full-time School of Business faculty member be actively engaged in research. This demand from an external legiti- mating body has resulted in School of Business faculty receiving course release time not readily available to faculty members in other disciplines. An external institutional "force" that in essence dictates at least a portion of the university's structure and process.

Institutional theorists have taken a relatively deterministic view of the effect of environments on organizational structure and process (Bluedorn et al., 1994). Aldrich (1992), commenting on an article about institutional environments by Scott (1987), noted that "most of the verbs used to describe organization-environment relations carry the connotation that environments dominate or overpower organizations . . . organizational structures may be: imposed, authorized, induced, acquired, imprinted, and incorporated" (pp. 21–22). Unfortunately for most managers, this determi·nistic view left little leeway for the role of managerial choice and discretion.

Fortunately, reconceptualizations of institutional and resource de-pendency theories have attempted, via contingency theory approaches, to reconcile the two, especially in conjunction with the degree of managerial discretion to guide the organization (DiMaggio; 1988; Greening & Gray, 1994; Herbiniak & Joyce, 1985; Kreiner & Bhambri, 1991; Oliver, 1991; Powell, 1988). Indeed, Herbiniak and Joyce (1985) suggested that even in the most deterministic of organizational envi- ronments (e.g., highly regulated industries), "organizational choice nonetheless exists as a separate, independent variable important to the development of a dynamic equilibrium with the external environ- ment" (p. 338). These models and the research they spawned are interesting in light of the public relations function because they so often incorporate issues generally subsumed under the public relations function (e.g., issues management). They also attempt to relate ex- ternal stakeholder power to the ways in which the organization structures certain information-seeking activities, again, a public rela- tions function.

Attributed Stakeholder Power

In a study of the attributed power of external stakeholders, Kreiner and Bhambri (1991) assessed the relative importance of institutional and technical stakeholders. The researchers were particularly interested in how the power attributed to various stakeholders influenced the organization's information-seeking behaviors surrounding public policy issues. The authors were looking at the ways in which the perceived external stakeholder power influenced the structure and process used by the organization to gather information about either the stakeholder or the policy issue related to that stakeholder.

Kreiner and Bhambri (1991) identified nine major stakeholders associated with the insurance industry. Although Kreiner and Bhambri cautioned that it is "difficult to draw a sharp distinction between technical and institutional environments," (p. 13), they categorized the nine stakeholders as being *institutional*, *technical*, or *quasi-institutional* (stakeholders whose very nature qualifies them as having the potential impact of institutional groups) as shown in the following list:

1. agent's associations—quasi-institutional
2. consumer interest groups—technical
3. federal agencies and actors—institutional
4. industry trade associations—quasi-institutional
5. media representatives—technical
6. National Association of Insurance Commissioners (NAIC)—institutional
7. other insurance companies—quasi-institutional
8. state insurance commissioners/departments—institutional
9. state legislators—institutional

Interestingly, Kreiner and Bhambri (1991) categorized the media as being technical. Their argument is that the

> activities of Consumer Interest Groups and Media Representatives importantly impact the awareness of customers and potential customers. . . . Because they are not actually charged with elaborating rules and requirements, we consider them mainly to be part of the technical environment. (p. 13)

The Kreiner and Bhambri Study gathered data from interviews with 73 top managers in the 25 largest insurance companies in the United States. The managers interviewed assessed the stakeholder's attributed power, that is, the power the manager (and his or her company) thought the stakeholder held to either *disrupt* the operations of the company or to *influence* the importance the company assigned to any particular public policy issue. *Attributed power*, then, is conceptualized as consisting of two factors: ability to disrupt and ability to influence.

Results of the data analyses indicated differences in the degree of power attributed to the institutional and technical stakeholder groups. Three institutional stakeholders (federal agencies, state insurance commissioners and departments, state legislatures) and two quasi-institutional groups (agent's associations and other insurance companies) were perceived as having a direct impact on the organization's processes and plans as well as its perceptions of issue importance. In other words, for these groups, attributed power was perceived as being a single force comprised of the ability to disrupt as well as influence.

By contrast, the two technical stakeholders (consumer groups, media representatives), one institutional group (NAIC), and one quasi-institutional group (industry trade association) were perceived as having only an indirect impact on the organization's operations or perceptions of policy importance. Indeed, the potential influence of these four groups came only from their perceived ability to influence one of the five institutional and quasi-institutional stakeholders perceived to have disruptive power.

Kreiner and Bhambri's (1991) analyses of information seeking behaviors by the managers of the insurance companies led them to conclude that

> the information seeking-attributed power relationship was present only among institutional stakeholders. We further found, again, only for the institutional stakeholders, both (1) an association between stakeholder attributed power and perceived organizational nonroutine information generation activities, and (2) a perception by top staff professionals . . . of a higher use of staff professionals in these nonroutine information generation activities. (p. 32)

These findings are important for the organizational public relations function for two reasons. The first is the apparent increase in nonroutine information generation activities associated with only institutional stakeholders. Nonroutine information generation activities are defined as the use of "task forces or special studies by staff professionals, line executives, or both" (Kreiner & Bhambri, 1991, p. 6). Insurance companies were more likely to use task forces, ad hoc committees, or study groups to deal with institutional stakeholders than they were with technical ones. The use of internal support groups in response to perceived institutional stakeholder power is consistent with research reported by Greening and Gray (1994). This suggests that the power attributed to institutional stakeholders should be of primary concern to public relations practitioners who should be involved in task forces or ad hoc groups created to study such stakeholders. The second is the very use of staff professionals in these nonroutine information gathering activities associated with institutional stakeholders. This finding supports Mintzberg's (1985) admonition that support staff most effectively employ their expertise power base by forming coalitions with other organizational members. In this study, the degree of potential environmental determinism of institutional stakeholders is perceived to be high (Herbiniak & Joyce, 1985), leading to an increased need for external monitoring. The public relations function, as a management function, needs to seek avenues of interdepartmental and interorganizational level collaboration. The success of the public relations staff function will be commensurate with the degree to which the public relations practitioners are sought out for inclusion in nonroutine staff task forces or ad hoc committees.

Summary

By way of summary, I want to examine an article by Lauzen and Dozier (1992) that incorporates perceptions of the environment, the public relations manager role, and organizational power. Their research is an excellent example of the way in which public relations practitioners are beginning to expand on our understanding of the organizational/ environment linkage. Lauzen and Dozier (1992) began their article with the following statement:

> In this study, we examined the relationship between the environments of organizations and the consequences that external conditions exert on the public relations function. Specifically, we examined the range and changeability of publics in an organization's environment, positing that environmental challenge creates a demand for enactment of the public relations manager role by the organization's top communicator. Such manager role enactment, in turn, leads to power consequences for the public relations function. . . . The public relations manager role is offered as a critical linkage between environment and internal consequences, as well as a bridging concept between two frameworks in organizational theory [environmental influence and power-control perspective]. (pp. 205–206)

Lauzen and Dozier operationally defined environmental uncertainty in relation to the complexity and turbulence surrounding organizational stakeholders. Respondents to their survey assessed the importance of a list of stakeholders and then judged how changeable those stakeholders were perceived to be.

Lauzen and Dozier found that, as both the range (complexity) and changeability (turbulence) of stakeholders in the organization's environment increased, the more likely the public relations practitioner was to enact the public relations manager role. In other words, perceived differences in the organization's pantheon of stakeholders, led to the structural implementation of a public relations role grounded more in a management function than in a technical function. Lauzen and Dozier's findings lend support to the contingency interpretation of the linkage between organizational stakeholders and the structure of the public relations function.

Future research in this area might do well to incorporate the concepts presented in this chapter, especially those related to apparent differences in organizational responses to institutional and technical stakeholders. The stakeholders listed by Lauzen and Dozier (1992) included "top management, staff/employees, government regulators, consumers, society/local community, environmental groups, investors/creditors, union officials, special interest groups, and the media" (p. 213). It is instructive to note that, of the 10 stakeholders, 8 are external. Following Kreiner and Bhambri's (1991) lead, we might classify government regulators, investors/creditors, and union officials as institutional stakeholders in that they distinctly have the power to influence (indeed, disrupt) the organization's functions. Consumers, society/local community, special interest groups, environmental groups, and the media are more likely to be technical stakeholders in that their influence is indirect. Interestingly, Lauzen and Dozier have not included what Kreiner and Bhambri (1991) labeled quasi-institutional stakeholders, competitors, or trade associations. Knowing that a stakeholder is part of the organization's institutional environment might well lead the public relations practitioner to propose a communication strategy, different from one proposed for a technical stakeholder group.

Jauch and Kraft's (1986) strategy and structure decisions component and Milliken's (1987) response uncertainty lead us to the key link between an organization's environment and the organization's response: the development and implementation of strategic responses. We have proposed that the public relations function is a necessary function of contingency models of organization. As such, the public relations function seeks ways in which the organization and environment can be better aligned. The seeking of alignment—adapting, altering, or maintaining (Long & Hazleton Jr., 1987)—implies the necessity of strategic choice on the part of the public relations practitioner. Certainly, all definitions of public relations with which I am familiar include some aspect of strategic choice, the ability to choose among alternative actions and implement that action (or those actions) selected, thereby influencing the organization's environment on behalf of the organization. It is to the dilemma of choice in regard to interactions with the environment that we now turn.

Practitioner Response to Chapter 7: Changing Environment Offers PR Challenges

Hope Tuttle, Director
Marketing and Community Relations
Overlake Hospital
Bellvue, Washington

I recently changed jobs, moving to a nonprofit, nontax-supported community hospital. On the surface level in my new position, I have had to put a fair amount of energy into just learning a "new language," figuring out who does what, and even finding my way around a complex building. Overlying this, and primary to the marketing and public relations function, is the "redesign" of our operations, on which the hospital has just embarked. Our external environment is changing drastically. We have to work smarter if we want to survive.

We have been, and are, perceived by our stakeholders as delivering quality care in a cost-effective manner. We also rate high in staff, volunteer, physician, and patient satisfaction. But to survive, we must at least maintain our quality and satisfaction while significantly cutting our costs. Hospital management could have been mired in the deterministic view of our environment and felt there was nothing that could be done. But, that's not what has happened. With involvement of the stakeholders, we are making decisions on *how* we operate.

Who the stakeholders are has basically stayed the same but the power balance has changed. Our messages to the audiences have changed as has the method and frequency of communication with them.

A prime factor in the hospital's approach has been its commitment to its internal audiences. Steven Covey in his book *The 7 Habits of Highly Effective People* reminds us that in order to have a product, we must take care of those who produce the product. The producers have the heart and minds to assure the finances and physical assets. Without support of the producers (the staff), the product (service) can remain at the previously high level in the short term, but this cannot be maintained in the long run.

Management is very open with what needs to be done. Costs have to be cut—people will be laid off. But, the commitment to quality and satisfaction is prime also. The graphic of the redesign project shows three intertwined circles—quality, cost, and satisfaction—the visual representation of these commitments.

Employees, volunteers, and physicians at the hospital have been an integral part of revising the support processes and the method of delivery of patient care. Representatives of those groups have analyzed the current situation, looked at ways to improve the way we work, and are implementing new practices. Throughout the process communications have been a paramount concern. Communication efforts must be constant even when the final answers aren't known at a particular time and must always be open and honest. The regular weekly internal newsletter has contained short updates, special newsletters are produced when major events occur, input is given by e-mail and voice mail, and regular, small forums with management are held in order to strengthen communication.

Also of prime consideration is the process that people must go through when change occurs, particularly when the changes are so inclusive and far-reaching. It is like the grieving process. First is the loss of what people are used to, followed by a time of unrest when uncertainity reigns. People need to experience and deal with, these steps before they can even begin to build a new structure. Training managers to deal with their own turmoil and then assist their staff has already started. Again, communication is so important. People need to know that it is normal and okay to feel unsettled and perhaps even angry and depressed. They need to know how to move through these phases and how to recognize when they may need additional help.

So, how does this affect me as the primary marketing and public relations person? Some of the effects had occured before I started. As often happens when resources are limited, the department staff was cut from six to two. The emphasis of the work of the department, because of the limited staff, had been technical rather than strategic. Then you add me—an unknown to those I work with. I am having to learn quickly who the key players are, what their perceptions are of the situation and the capabilities of the department/function, and what the politics are. It is working-things are changing. I am becoming part of the strategic planning group.

CHAPTER 8

Communication From an Advocacy Frame

The object of oratory is not truth, but pursuasion.
(sic, from a fortune cookie I got at Chinese restaurant while writing this chapter)

INTRODUCTION

"Communication," Gibson (1991) reminded us, "lies at the heart of public relations practice; certainly, no thoughtful observer would deny this truism" (p. 176). In considering the disciplinary locus of public relations education, Heath (1991) also noted that "consideration of the functions that public relations perform for organizations and society at large demonstrates its extensive reliance on communication. At its foundation, public relations is a communication discipline" (p. 186). Few will quibble with the assertion that organizational public relations is, at heart, a communication process. This is especially evident in the public relations interactions between organizations and stakeholder groups, as evident in chapter 7.

In that the public relations discipline defines public relations in terms of communication (e.g., a communication function of management), how we subsequently define communication is critical in understanding the organizational public relations function. It is critical to distinguish the public relations function from other organizational functions that also rely on communication, such as marketing, human resources, and training and development. It is critical because so many facets of organizational life that ultimately influence public relations effectiveness, such as control and coordination, organizational politics, and conflict negotiation, are accomplished through communication (or, are communicatively accomplished). It is critical in that how we define communication is intimately linked to our definition or worldview of public relations. The schema we hold for organizational public relations will dictate, at least in part, our ability to effectively employ the communication process.

We use the word communication in everyday life to imply some kind of attempt to exchange understanding with others. This everyday experientially based definition is evident in comments we frequently make or hear, such as "I just can't communicate with him," or "We have a communication problem," or "We don't have time to really communicate." As illustrated in Exhibit 8.1, we share general cultural assumptions about what it means to communicate in our everyday world, assumptions that, for the most part, go unspoken (Katriel & Philipsen, 1981).

But, do these unspoken assumptions, or tacit agreements, provide enough of an understanding of communication for us to be able to say that public relations is a communication function? I think not. Indeed, if we continue to define public relations as a communication process (which I think is appropriate), then we need to consider seriously what we mean when we say that public relations is a communication function. Very simply, what we mean by communication necessarily dictates what we do when we do public relations.

In chapter 2, I suggested that a certain amount of organizational arrogance can be attributed to the misuse of the public relations (as a communication) function. We concluded that the technical emphasis on persuasive communication obscures the need for other, more inclusive, communication. We continued this line of thought in chapter 3 by introducing Grunig and Hunt's (1984) two-way asymmetrical and symmetrical models of public relations. Although both models are used to enhance the organization's autonomy vis-à-vis the demands from its environment, we concluded that the asymmetrical model fostered a more control-seeking, persuasion-based form of communication than did the two-way symmetrical model.

In our discussion of the political metaphor in chapter 5, we examined the relative power differential that implicitly exists in the pluralist model of organizations, again implying that a persuasive form of organizational public relations communication predominates. This was reinforced by Mansbridge's (1980) discussion of our cultural understanding of democracy from a pluralist framework as being adversarial in nature, one that demands active advocacy for one's

EXHIBIT 8.1
What We Need Is Communication

Using several different sources, including in-depth individual case studies and the Phil Donahue show, Katriel and Phillipsen (1981) analyzed the ways in which Americans use the term "communication" in their everyday life. In their analysis, the authors found evidence of two clusters of terms referring to communication. The first cluster includes terms like "real communication," "really talking," "supportive communication," and "open communication." The second set or cluster is composed of phrases such as "small talk," "normal chit-chat," and "mere talk." Katriel and Phillipsen suggest that the two clusters are differentiated on three semantic dimensions: close/distant, supportive/neutral, and flexible/rigid.

The first dimension, close/distant, implies a spatial metaphor in that the kind of communication suggested in the first cluster, real communication, is based on proximity, similarity, and the degree of penetration. The degree of penetration refers to how likely the communicators are to penetrate "psychological boundaries and barriers." When people use the first type of communication they are, in effect, offering something of their self to the other person or persons with whom they are speaking. They are opening up, allowing others to become communicatively close. "Mere talk," as the authors point out, "is talk in and through which one 'keeps his distance' or 'stays at arm's length' from another" (p. 308).

The supportive/neutral dimension "refers to the degree in which each [communicator] is committed to providing positive evaluations of the other's self" (p. 308). This should not be understood as necessarily agreeing with or approving everything the other speaker says or does. It does mean, however, that each speaker is committed to the communication episode or event as well as to the other speaker. When a speaker is really communicating, he or she approaches the other with positive regard for the other. "Mere talk," on the other hand, is not negative but rather neutral. We can take it or leave it; it does not greatly affect our self-centered well being.

Finally, the third dimension, flexible/rigid, refers to degree to which a person is willing "to listen to and acknowledge the other's presentation of self, to listen to and actively try to understand the other's evaluation of oneself, and . . . to consider changing one's perception of self or other contingent upon the meanings which emerge in the speech event. This is speech of emergent realities, of negotiated selves and the negotiated relationship" (p. 308). In contrast, "mere talk," is governed by a set of rules of interaction, of guidelines for what is appropriate and what is not in any given situation.

Although Katriel and Phillipsen studied communication use in inter-

(Continued)

> personal situations, the dimensions they suggest—close/distant, suppor-
> tive/neutral, and flexible/rigid—are important ones in understanding the
> ways in which public relations is and should be a communication
> function. Like Heath (1991) I think that there are many ways to improve
> the communication between an organization and its stakeholders by
> attending to ideas first broached in research on interpersonal communi-
> cation. As we continue our discussion of communication, the usefulness
> of many of the ideas presented here will become more readily apparent.
>
> Reprinted with permission from Katriel and Philipsen (1981).

position in the face of competing voices and positions. In summary, to
this point we have been playing with the competing ideas of advocacy
and consensus, ideas definitely integral to the organizational public
relations function.

Advocacy Versus Consensus Building

Our previous allusions to the paradoxes and dilemmas faced by the
public relations profession finds practical voice in the ongoing debate
about the appropriate role of public relations. Readers of the December
1992 *Public Relations Journal* were given the opportunity to respond to
the following question: "Are practitioners advocates, consensus builders, both or other? Please explain your answer" (Katzman, 1993, p. 11).
Of the 84 readers who responded, 57% indicated that public relations
practitioners were both advocates and consensus builders, 21% felt
that practitioners were advocates, 7% said that practitioners were
consensus builders, and 14% thought public relations people did
something else.

A sampling of arguments from those who see public relations as
advocacy, consensus building, and both is included in Exhibit 8.2. Of
those who thought public relations included both advocacy and
consensus building (a view I personally endorse), "some commented
their role was to gain or strengthen support for ideas, programs or
products, or work on behalf of some interest. Others wrote "they
establish mutuality, reconcile conflicting interests through better understanding, bring parties from opposing sides together, build understanding and support, mediate, and serve as a liaison" (p. 11). In these
comments we see evidence that the struggle between partisan and
mutual values Sullivan identified 30 years ago is still with us.

The distinctions between advocacy and consensus building, like the
distinctions between the asymmetrical and symmetrical models, are
indicative of competing ways in which an organization communicates

---

EXHIBIT 8.2
What's the Role of Public Relations?
Profession Searches for Its Identity

Statements from Advocates:

"Clients and employers expect their PR advisors to be dedicated to the realization of corporate goals through persuasive and constructive management of communication channels."

"We are advocates of our client, for our client. They can get consensus from their mothers. If you don't believe your client or their product can solve a problem or address a need, why bother with them? If they do meet a need, advocate for them."

"Practitioners need to be zealous advocates on behalf of their clients. There are times when conciliation and compromise are called for, however, our primary role and function should be to advance the client's interests. To do less is to emasculate the role of the PR professional."

Statements From Consensus Builders:

"PR people manage opinion by listening carefully to divergent or unaware audiences and creating a message. That process is intended to develop consensus—to 'crystallize' opinion."

"We lose sight of the altruistic and high standards of our profession when we focus on advocacy. We should refrain from advocacy—one of the reasons our profession is sullied."

"Advocates typically present only one side of an issue. While that may be necessary under certain circumstances, our job is to gain mutual trust and understanding. That means listening, negotiating, and actively responding to key publics through issues management, communication programs and special projects."

Statements From Consensus Builders and Advocates:

"It depends on the situation. PR practitioners are ultimately hired guns whose job it is to serve their employers. Sometimes hired guns do evil, sometimes good works—sometimes both. But they are always hired guns, accountable to their bosses."

"Practitioners must have passion about their subjects in order to represent them properly and convincingly. That passion works to build consensus as well as advocate a position."

"We should strive to be consensus builders first since our primary role should be to reconcile conflicting interests to establish mutuality. We can also be advocates when the public interest is well-served."

From, J. B. Katzman (1993). What's the role of public relations? Profession searches for its identity. *Public Relations Journal*, 48(4), pp. 11–15. Copyright April 1993. Reprinted by permission of *Public Relations Journal*, published by the Public Relations Society of America, New York, NY.

with stakeholders in its environment. Like Grunig (1992), I propose that the ways in which organizational public relations is framed influence the ways in which communication is defined and, subsequently used, during the organizational/environment interaction. I compare communication that is grounded in and arises from an advocacy frame with communication grounded in and arising from a consensus-building frame. This dichotomy or duality of human interaction (advocacy vs. consensus-building) is found in any number of sources from a wide variety of disciplines. Weiser (1988) distinguished between *rhetoric* and *responsibility*; Bailey (1983) proposed a *rhetoric of assertion* and a *rhetoric of compromise*; and we already noted that Mansbridge (1980) spoke of *adversary democracy* and *unitary democracy*. The purpose of chapters 8, 9, and 10 is to explore how the dimensions of the communication process are situated and implemented, depending on how the public relations function is framed from either an advocacy approach or a consensus-building approach.

THE POWER AND PAUCITY OF FRAMES

Framing is about the "organization of experience" (Goffman, 1974, p. 13). It "essentially involves *selection* and *salience*" (Entman, 1993, p. 52). As Bolman and Deal (1991) proposed, "Frames are both windows on the world and lenses that bring the world into focus. Frames filter out some things while allowing others to pass through easily. Frames help us to order experience and decide what action to take" (p. 11). Frames allow us to define problems, diagnose causes, suggest remedies, and make moral judgments (Entman, 1993).

Perhaps most importantly, frames highlight certain aspects of our experience of reality "which logically means that frames simultaneously *direct attention away from other aspects*" (Entman, 1993, p. 54, italics added). We are captured and constrained by the characteristics of our frame. We see, in essence, what we want to see or want we are guided to see, but have difficulty seeing the same situation or reality from another frame. The following case study from Baxter (1993), although not a public relations case, provides an excellent example of the power and paucity of communication frames, especially during times of competing interests, or conflict.

CASE STUDY 8.1: THE UNIVERSITY OVERHAUL

Baxter (1993) extensively studied the communication interactions at a small, private university in the United States. The Board of Trustees of this university mandated that the university overhaul its governance procedures and policies, "with the twin goals of codifying all governance practices and increasing formal coordination among the schools" (p. 315). For more than 2 years, Baxter participated and observed the communication interactions between members of two groups, the faculty and the administration, as they sought to comply with the wishes of the university's governing board.

Baxter (1993) uncovered two communication codes that framed the issue for the faculty and the administrators. For the most part, faculty members were much more likely to frame the discussion through a code based on the openness of ongoing oral interaction, labeled *the code of collegiality*. Administrators were much more likely to prefer to frame the issue through a code based on the written word, labeled *the code of professional management*. Briefly, those adopting a code of collegiality sought to implement a university decision-making system that relied most heavily on open debate and oral communication, with relatively few written prescriptions or rules. Those adopting a code of professional management sought the opposite, a governance system that was largely codified in writing with rules and procedures that were [supposedly] unambiguous and impartial. These two frames "are mirror opposites of one another with respect to three underlying themes: models of personhood; models of social relations; and beliefs about channel effectiveness and efficiency" (p. 316).

Models of Personhood

Those favoring a code of collegiality placed great faith in the individuality of the person, whether faculty or administrator. "Faith in the ability of people to 'talk things through' displayed 'trust and respect' for the capacity of the individual to bring good sense and honesty to bear in resolving problems as they occurred" (p. 317). Seen from this frame, written communication indicates a basic mistrust of the individual's integrity and autonomy.

Those favoring a frame of professional management were more likely to think of people in terms of groups or categories (e.g., assistant professors, females, deans) than as individuals. They argued that informal, face-to-face communication "potentially jeopardized people's rights through the bias of personalized responses" (p. 318). Advocates of the professional management frame believed that "written codification of records, policies, and procedures provided maximum protection for the rights of people" (p. 318).

Opposing Models of Social Relations

The university members who framed the discussion from a code of collegiality thought that social interactions, relationships between people, were based on equality, democracy, and community. They believed individuals were generally equal in what they could add to any decision-making event; approved of a democratic approach to talking things through and reaching the best decision for all; and felt that the university should highlight commonalties rather than differences.

Those who viewed the world from a professional management frame felt that the university's members would be empowered by a written code through which "everyone was fully informed of their position-based rights and responsibility" (p. 322). They felt that informal, face-to-face communication created information disparities in that not everyone would be privy to all such conversations. These people argued that "social relations should be based on impersonal interaction between occupants of organizational positions" and that personal feelings "had no place in organizational functioning" (pp. 320–321).

Channel Effectiveness and Efficiency

The collegial frame provided a basis for arguing that the oral tradition was more efficient than any written codification. Written policies and procedures could only address the most general of cases, whereas face-to-face interaction allowed members to directly deal with the specifics of various situations. These proponents "favored a short, written document of governance that basically would articulate a philosophy of 'collegiality' and thereby serve as 'enabling legislation' for interpersonal problem-solving and decision-making on as as-needed basis" (p. 322).

Members of the professional management frame believed that written communication: (a) identified "clear guidelines and parameters for action;" (b) provided the greatest flow of complete information both up and down the hierarchy; and (c) "protected the organization against external forces" (p. 323). In essence, those who approached the problem from a professional management frame argued that putting it in writing made for a more rational and effective system of management.

Baxter (1993) concluded that the existence of the two frames resulted in a discourse that was filled with assertions and counterassertions. The participants in this discourse "proclaimed the superiority of their own governance model and caricatured members of the competing

code community through a variety of negative dispositional attributes''
(p. 324).

The administrators and faculty in Baxter's example had a problem
for which a solution was needed. The frame each group used to
understand the situation, professional management or collegiality,
influenced how the problem was defined, influenced the understanding of underlying causes related to human action, influenced the
remedies suggested by each group, and, finally, influenced the moral
judgments each group made about the other's suggestions. Perhaps
more fundamentally, the frames each group used to ''see'' the situation
resulted in competing visions of what it means to be a person in an
organization.

The examples Baxter provides are instructive, given our attempt to
delineate between communication that occurs in an advocacy frame
and that which occurs in a consensus-seeking frame. Although Baxter
reports that the final governance procedure proposed to the Board of
Trustees was remarkably similar to the one already in existence, the
frames adopted by both groups during the struggle to redefine the
university appear to be rooted in advocacy. As Baxter points out, the
advocacy inherent in adopting either the code of collegiality or the
code of professional management resulted in the hardening of adversarial positions. Baxter (1983) wrote:

> The themes that characterized the ''collegiality'' and ''professional
> management'' codes were mirror opposites of one another, thereby
> ensuring that one code community would reject what the other code
> community regarded as a logical premise upon which to build a well-
> reasoned and persuasive argument . . . emotive assertions of moral
> superiority designed less to promote reasoned dialogue with competing
> factions and more to bolster the ''true believers'' of one's own faction. (p.
> 324)

Ultimately, as shown in this chapter and also in chapter 9, the process
of communication is vastly different depending on the frame adopted.

One last note on Baxter's study is interesting for those in public
relations. Baxter (1993) concluded that ''talking and writing are not
merely neutral technologies of information transmission and exchange
but powerful symbolic forces that articulate broader themes including
models of personhood and sociability'' (p. 325). Here is the beginning
of another frame, one that directly influences how public relations
activities are perceived and implemented. We might call this the
beginning of the ''technical frame.'' The emphasis public relations
practitioners place on writing serves as a frame by which public

relations practitioners experience and respond to their communicative world. This frame of writing is rooted in the advocacy frame of public relations and guides much of what is done in the name of public relations. It is an idea I return to in chapter 10.

The remainder of this chapter examines the way in which communication is defined and used in the advocacy frame of organizational public relations. The sources included in chapters 8, 9, and 10 present the two frames, advocacy and consensus-building, as dichotomous or polarized. That is, the characteristics of one are presented and contrasted with the characteristics of the other. I might, for example, argue that communication from an advocacy frame is encased in *monologue,* wheras communication from a consensus frame is grounded in *dialogue.* These contrasts are useful in that they allow us to tease out distinctions that we might ordinarily miss or not think about. I do not intend to imply, however, that one frame is, by necessity, "better" than another frame. As stated at the end of chapter 3, both frames exist, both are useful, and both should be available to public relations practitioners. We should be thinking of advocacy *and* collaboration, rather than advocacy *versus* collaboration. What we want to do in these last chapters is to determine under what conditions each frame is optimal.

One final author's note before going forward. I firmly believe in the mixed motives model of public relations (Grunig, 1992; Lichty & Springsten, 1993). One reason for writing this book was to determine how the models—two-way asymmetrical and two-way symmetrical—could be better construed, given the demands of various organizational and environment interactions. At the same time, if it has not been apparent to this point, I now confess: I have a great concern about the tendency for organizations to turn immediately to the asymmetrical model (or variations thereof) as their predominant public relations response, be it proactive or reactive. Advocacy, as the respondents to the *Journal of Public Relations* survey overwhelmingly indicated, is part and parcel of public relations. And, I agree it should be. My concern is that unbridled advocacy, by either the organization or stakeholder group, so often exacerbates unnecessary polarization between the two, thereby obscuring any reasonable chance for negotiating shared understandings or meanings.

This polarization is especially likely when we metaphorically view the organizational life world from the military metaphor (Weick, 1979). Crushing the enemy becomes the goal rather than negotiating a nonviolent course of reasonable action. With this confession out of the way, we turn to an examination of the potentially less than positive consequences of unbridled advocacy.

EFFECTIVENESS VERSUS PARTICIPATION

As a starting point in better understanding how communication grounded in the frames of advocacy and consensus differs, we turn to Deetz's (1992) discussion of participation and effectiveness as two fundamental goals of communication. Deetz (1992) argued that all definitions of communication share a "dual concern with *participation* and with *effective presentation*" (p. 94). How each definition defines and incorporates the concerns for effectiveness and participation is fundamental in understanding the communication worldview or frame inherent in the definition.

Participation, according to Deetz (1992), "deals with who in society or a group has a right to contribute to the formation of meaning and the decisions of the group—which individuals have access to the various systems and structures of communication and can they articulate their own needs and desires within them" (p. 94). All theories of communication explicitly, or more often implicitly, speak to the issue of participation by either limiting participation or by enhancing participation in the symbol/meaning process. In a very simple sense, traditional one-way models of communication that focus on the speaker focus on the speaker's ability to create meaning and articulate his or her desires. One-way, speaker-centered models of communication grant the right of participation to the speaker and much less to the receiver or the listener.

Another example of communication participation (or the lack thereof) was witnessed in the Senate Judiciary Committee Hearings for the confirmation of Clarence Thomas as a Supreme Court Justice. The hearings gained widespread attention when Anita Hill, a law professor and former aid to Mr. Thomas, accused him of sexual harassment. Her accusation led to 2 riveting days of nationally televised testimony before the Senate Judiciary Committee by Thomas and his supporters and Hill and her supporters. The Committee, and ultimately the Senate, voted to confirm Thomas even after hearing Hill's allegations. One hypothesized explanation for their decision was found in the fact that the Committee was comprised of 15 White males. The argument put forth in any number of analyses and editorials was that 15 White males could not understand what a woman experienced when she experienced harassment. Although they listened to her testimony, the senators did not allow Anita Hill to participate in the creation of meaning surrounding the volatile issue of sexual harassment.

I recently experienced an example of communication used to increase participation. During the time I began this book, I attended a drug prevention workshop for children and teenagers. The workshop leaders focused on the need for family meetings designed to include all family members in the decision-making process, or, in Deetz's (1992) terms, the *meaning creation process*. So, what it means for a movie to be rated "R" beyond the simple phrases "some nudity," "language," or "adult themes," changed as the decision-making process opened up to include the family members under the age of 17.

Deetz (1992) argued that communication can be used to enhance participation in the creation of meaning, to enhance access to the communication mechanisms. At the same time, communication can be used to limit, if not stifle, participation and access to the meaning creation process. When the organization carefully guards access to the meaning generation process, it does so with the intention of maximizing its autonomy from others in its environment (or, indeed, others in the organization itself).

Effective presentation "concerns the value of communicative acts as a means to accomplish ends—how meaning is transferred and how control through communication is accomplished" (Deetz, 1992, p. 94). In its simplest expression, effectiveness asks the question, "Did the speaker accomplish what he or she set out to do?" Certainly, much of our public speaking education is devoted to the teaching of appropriate methods or scripts to enhance the likelihood that the speaker will be effective.

The expression of the effectiveness of communication as a means to an end is most significantly noticeable in the conception of rhetoric. Deetz (1992) argued that the Roman appropriation of Aristotle's ideas about rhetoric, an appropriation that ignored the participatory culture of Athens, fostered a rhetoric concerned with "personal gain and political control rather than the participatory emergence of truth" (p. 96). Rhetoric, at least those conceptualizations defined as all available means of persuasion employed to influence an audience to a predetermined point of view, speaks to the perceived need to accomplish ends by controlling meaning.

We can use the Baxter (1993) case study presented earlier as an example. Baxter found that the faculty members who adopted a collegial frame sought to initiate procedures that enhanced or increased participation in the decision-making process. In their view, greater participation leads to greater effectiveness. Those adopting a professional management frame tended to emphasize effectiveness as communication efficiency at the expense of greater or more enhanced participation. In their view, written communication, which limits available participation in the creation of meaning, was the more effective vehicle for university governance.

We turn now to an examination of the characteristics of communication grounded in an advocacy frame beginning with a discussion of the *conduit metaphor* of communication. This metaphor drives so much organizational communication and management research, let alone public relations research, that we might say it acts as a paradigm for our understanding of the public relations process. The conduit metaphor is akin to the mystical saying that drove Kevin Costner's character to build his baseball field in the middle of a cornfield in the movie "Field of Dreams": If you "build it, they will come."

THE CONDUIT METAPHOR OF COMMUNICATION

Recall that Long and Hazleton Jr. (1987) defined communication as "the natural and inevitable result of the production and consumption of messages by human beings" (p. 7). Their definition of communication is one that is message production-oriented. It implies that the production of a proper message delivered through an appropriate channel will result in desired consequences. As Long and Hazleton Jr. wrote, "The function of the boundary-spanning role [the communication subsystem] is *production* (or encoding) and *delivery* of messages" (p. 11, italics added). This definition is characteristic of what Reddy (1979) labeled the *conduit* or *container metaphor* of communication. It is also characteristic of communication firmly grounded in an advocacy frame, one based on relatively one-way persuasion.

In his analysis of how English speakers talk about communication, Reddy (1979) discovered that they most often do so as if they were talking about a pipeline or a conduit. He asserted that one or more of the following assumptions are present in most sayings we use about speaking or writing: "1) language transfers thoughts and feelings from person to person; 2) speakers and writers insert thoughts and feelings into words; 3) words contain the thoughts and feelings; and 4) listeners or readers extract the thoughts and feelings from the words" (Axley, 1984, p. 429). In other words, the conduit metaphor presents a model of communication that emphasizes the person creating and sending the message rather than the receiver of the message.

As Axley (1984) only somewhat facetiously suggested:

The only tricky part, implicit in the metaphor, is packaging or inserting the content for the transfer. Once the communicator finds the right words to accomplish the transfer, then the fidelity between intended meaning and received meaning becomes almost guaranteed, even routine. All the listener or reader needs to do is extract or unpack the thoughts from the words. (p. 433)

Does this sound at all familiar? It should in that it is often what we as public relations professionals all too often find ourselves doing: packaging messages for an intended audience. Indeed, it is not too far-fetched to argue that the packaging of messages, however useful and necessary, is at the very heart of much public relations research and practice. Our research journals and practitioner resources are full of metaphorically conduit research and tips. The authors of a recent study on using cognitive response analysis to better enable communicators to tailor messages (Slater, Chipman, Auld, Keefe, & Kendall, 1992) for example, concluded that

> situational theory and cognitive response approaches may be usefully combined to study a variety of dimensions of attention to messages. Such a combination may also serve to better inform message strategy in communication campaigns by providing a conceptually rigorous approach to conducting message tests. (p. 189)

We have, to date, focused far more attention on the creation and packaging of messages from a conduit frame, to the exclusion of attention to the relationship development aspects of public *relations* (Leichty & Springston, 1993). This leads to what Reddy (1979) labeled the "success-without-effort" notion, because the conduit metaphor suggests that communication is viewed as being relatively easy, requiring little effort.

But the conduit metaphor is not only found in our everyday life or in public relations practice. As Axley (1984) pointed out, it is the dominant metaphor used to describe the process of organizational management communication. Axley found, for example, that the conduit metaphor dominated definitions of communication in 21 management textbooks (e.g., "This second process, communication, requires the sender to package the idea in an understandable manner").

Axley suggests several interesting implicit lessons organizational managers learn from their reliance on the conduit metaphor. These include: (a) a self-inflated complacency about one's own abilities as a communicator (a packager of messages); (b) justification for spending little time and effort on communication in that the packaging is relatively easy; and (c) the notion that communication, because it is so easy and inevitable, is often "among the last of the possible causes seriously considered when real mis-communication difficulties inevitably arise among organizational members" (Axley, 1984, p. 435).

Extrapolating from Axley's arguments (by way of Reddy, 1979), I suggest that the organizational public relations function is often bedeviled by a double-edged sword. On one hand, many in the profession (Long and Hazleton Jr., 1987, for example) define communication in terms of the conduit metaphor, perhaps (and I do emphasize perhaps) leading to an inflated notion of the ease with which success can be achieved. On the other hand, as Axley suggests, managers in organizations apparently rely on a conduit-based metaphor of organizational communication, which again reinforces the apparent "success-without-effort" notion of the nature of public relations as communication.

In terms more familiar to public relations students, professionals, and educators, the Long and Hazleton Jr. (1987) definition is one that Grunig and Hunt (1984) labeled asymmetric. It is one that is persuasion-based, and, although two-way in that feedback is sought, the feedback is only about the success of the message as opposed to the mutual creation of the meaning intended by the message. The definition does not offer much in the way of understanding how meaning is created between the organization and various aspects of its environment.

Persuasion As Control

The persuasion-based model of public relations is dominant in today's public relations world. Indeed, public relations is often equated with persuasion, the two considered more or less synonymous (Cheney & Vibbert, 1987; Miller, 1989). The underlying assumption of this view is the necessity for the organization to engage with the other components of its environment to fulfill its mission or reach its goals. In their review of the history of corporate public relations, Cheney and Vibbert (1987) claimed that the field has entered a phase in which organizations "began to adopt a stance that would go far beyond their relatively reactive position of the past. The new position, in fact, explicitly recognizes the creative power of large organizations in shaping their 'environment' " (p. 173).

The argument goes something like this: If the successful completion of the organization's goals is dependent on stakeholders in the larger environment, then those stakeholders need to be "brought on board," or persuaded to the organization's point of view. "Corporate public persuasion attempts to control the terms under which such [public] discussions take place . . . to control the ways internal and external environments discuss such key concepts as values, issues, images, and identities" (Cheney & Vibbert, 1987, p. 173). Or, as Miller (1989) suggested in his article, "Persuasion and Public Relations: Two 'Ps' in a Pod," public relations "serves as a definitional label for the process of attempting to exert symbolic control over the evaluative predispositions ('attitudes,' 'images,' etc.) and subsequent behaviors of relevant publics or clienteles" (p. 47).

In their review of the state of persuasion research, Miller and Burgoon (1978) concluded that most persuasion research is based on a passive reception model. Although they do not label it as such, the passive reception model is what Reddy (1979) identified as one based on the conduit metaphor. To wit, "the persuader, who is the primary symbolizing agent, encodes and transmits a message to a relatively passive audience . . . as a unidirectional process where the persuader *acts* and the persuadees are *acted upon*" (Miller, 1989, p. 53). The pervasiveness of the conduit metaphor of communication, especially communication as persuasion, is especially prevalent in what Sproule (1988) called "the new managerial rhetoric."

Sproule's "New Managerial Rhetoric"

Sproule (1988) argued that there was a significant shift in rhetorical practice after 1900 that is only now being fully addressed by those who study rhetoric (cf. Haynes, 1988). The shift was one from a traditional rhetoric that focused on the individual speaker and his or her message to new persuasions and propagandas employed by institutions, both corporate and government. This argument is extended by Deetz (1992) who argued that the public sphere of rhetoric has been captured by institutionalized corporate interests that are often at odds with the larger societal good.

Sproule's (1988) historical analysis of the new managerial rhetoric is especially interesting to those in the public relations field because he proposed that the shift began with the successes enjoyed by that public relations pioneer, Ivy Lee, "a pivotal figure in the development of institutional propaganda" (p. 468). Sproule wrote that Lee's ability to radically alter the public perception of John D. Rockefeller, from a "reviled symbol of monopoly capitalism into a grandfatherly folk figure of industrial America" led to corporate public relations in "its now familiar status as institutional persuasion often symbolized by key spokespersons" (p. 469). This form of corporate public relations is alluded to by Long and Hazleton Jr. (1987) when they wrote that "Lee Iacocca, for example, is as much a symbolic resource as a human resource for Chrysler Corporation" (p. 10).

A second feature Sproule identifies with the new managerial rhetoric is its reliance on the media to reach a mass audience. Sproule suggests that the significance of this move is found less in the simple fact that media can reach a large audience of listeners or viewers and more in the nature of the direction of social influence. In short, Sproule suggests (without saying it quite so bluntly) that the media pander to the nature of the crowd, the so-called lowest common denominator. He wrote, "However important may be the function of opinion leaders in digesting communications relative to particular issues, the discursive public remains caught between the institutional persuaders, who frame discussion, and the crowd, whose beliefs and attitudes figure in the preparation of managerial messages" (p. 472).

Sproule offers seven key ways in which the new managerial rhetoric differs from traditional studies of persuasion. In that Sproule's explanation of the new managerial rhetoric is descriptive of public relations as advocacy persuasion, we need to briefly examine his seven characteristics. Sproule proposes that the new managerial rhetoric differs from the old rhetoric in the following ways:

1. The new managerial rhetoric provides people with prepackaged conclusions, what Sproule called "packaged ideology." The old rhetoric pays much more attention to the development of reasons whereby people can or should be persuaded.
2. The staples of the new rhetoric are found in self-contained slogans that speak for themselves. The old rhetoric, by contrast, is based on the logic and reason provided by the enthymeme.
3. In that the new rhetoric is based on images, there is less call for or room for discussion of the prepackaged conclusions and slogans. The old rhetoric, founded on the presentation of and debate about ideas, fosters means whereby the receiver can offer counterarguments.
4. The new rhetoric emphasizes the importance of interpersonal attraction and identification as a means of persuasion. The credibility of the old rhetoric is defined by expertise gained through experience and reflection.
5. Whereas arguments framed in the old rhetoric are built on empiricism and facts, the new rhetoric is just as likely to create its own facts through pseudoevents.
6. Entertainment is a primary staple of presentation in the new rhetoric. In the old rhetoric, entertainment is viewed as a supporting form or avenue of presentation.
7. The old rhetoric seeks to address (and in a sense create) a holistic audience. The new rhetoric seeks to segment the audience for individual attention (pp. 472–474).

A recent study of competing environmental and forestry interests in the Northwest by Lange (1993) provided an excellent analysis of the results of a persuasion-based, argumentation grounded framework for public communication. Lange's analysis is important in understanding some of the ways in which an advocacy frame guides our use of communication. Key aspects of Sproule's definitional characteristics of the new managerial rhetoric are presented in the next case study.

CASE STUDY 8.2: OLD GROWTH TIMBER AND THE SPOTTED OWL

Lange immersed himself in the controversy surrounding the spotted owl rulings in the Pacific Northwest, rulings that have pitted environmentalists against loggers. Although not in the strictest sense a public relations study, Lange reviewed "hundreds of local newsletters, press releases and miscellaneous publications written by representatives of each side" (p. 242). In other words, he examined the communication artifacts produced by and for organizations trying to "adapt to, alter, or maintain their environment for the purpose of achieving organizational goals" (Long & Hazleton Jr., 1987).

Lange's analysis is based on a study of the *interactive logics* of the two sides' information campaigns. As he wrote, when participants

> in a communication system address each other, intending to influence each other, their utterances evoke—almost force—specific types of responses, while delegitimating or even disallowing others. . . . As with other disputes, both environmentalists and industry representatives choose strategies that are dependent on and responsive to their antagonist. (p. 241)

In this particular case, the strategies selected by one side mirror and match the strategies chosen by the other side in a reciprocally negative spiral.

Matching communication strategies are ones that copy the strategies of the other party. Strategies that mirror are ones that "duplicate the other party's tactics by presenting antithetical, polar or 'mirror image' information" (p. 245). It is helpful to remember that when we look into a mirror we see the exact opposite image of ourselves. When competing interest groups mirror a strategy, they present opposite information or interpretations.

Lange identified five major strategies used by both environmental groups and timber representatives, each of which is briefly described:

1. *Frame and Reframe*—Each side seeks to define the central aspects of the issue in its own terms and to its own advantage. The environ-

mentalists, for example, argue that old growth forests are a finite resource, that overcutting and poor planning are more to blame for the downturn in timber than the spotted owl restrictions, and that the timber workforce has been rapidly dwindling due to other market forces. The timber advocates, on the other hand, attempt to make jobs the primary issue at every juncture. Trees are portrayed as a renewable resource, that it is the lack of harvestable logs that has closed mills, and loggers have families to feed.

2. *Select High/Select Low*—Each side seeks out and presents information, "facts," that contradict the other sides. The anticipated loss of timber industry jobs is a good example. Timber industry public relations presented figures of 102,000–147,000 jobs at risk, whereas the environmentalists suggest between 12,000–14,000 that might be lost.

3. *Vilify/Enoble*—Communication strategies of this type seek to cast one group as the good guys and the opposing group as the bad guys. Lange's analysis led him to write that "the majority of workers and owner-operators now view environmentalists as 'radical preservationists' who want to 'lock up the forests' preventing their 'wise use' " (p. 248). Environmentalists are depicted as "wealthy, highly organized, outside 'obstructionists" or "East Coast carpetbaggers" (p. 248). Environmental groups counterargue by saying that the timber industry is run, not by small family owned mills, but giant corporations, "industry beasts" out to "take every last possible stick while the taking is still good" (p. 249).

4. *Simplify and Dramatize*—In order to make their messages palatable to the public-at-large, each side has grossly oversimplified a hugely complex environmental, economic, social, political, and technological issue. The timber industry, according to Lange (1993), has "at least partially succeeding in creating an 'owls versus people' scenario in the media" (p. 250). Lange quoted *The Wall Street Journal* as writing that the issue "sets about 1500 pairs of spotted owls against the people who make their living cutting down trees in the Pacific Northwest" (Lange, 1993, p. 250).

The most simplistic and dramatic slogans, however, appear on the bumper stickers of the loggers' pickups and the environmentalists' Volkswagon buses. "Save a Logger, Eat an Owl" was countered with "Save an Owl, Educate a Logger."

5. *Lobby and Litigate*—"Both groups believe that the most serious theaters for the conflict are in the courts and Washington, D.C." (Lange, p. 252). Lange noted that "while litigation used to be the sole province of environmental groups, recently, lumber companies and timber associations have matched the strategy, filing appeals that challenge timber inventory accuracy, clarity of guidelines, and even use of indicator species to test the health of a forest" (p. 252).

Through his research, Lange

> finds a logic of duplication and antithesis, a matching and mirroring, more like a synchronous spiral of *non-interaction*, as messages are directed not to each other, but to the public and members of government and government agencies. There is so little face-to-face interaction, one might ordinarily conclude that each group's communicative behavior has little to do with the other, with the obvious exception of preventing the other the other from achieving its goals . . . if one group vilifies the other, it is incumbent on the other to respond, refuting the charge and/or providing one's own. When timber representatives frame the major issue as job loss, environmentalists must attempt to reframe it; otherwise, a fully unfavorable context, from their point of view, would prevail. If one party neglected to lobby or litigate, the other party's practices in these areas would transform the entire conflict. The consequences of not mirroring or matching one's antagonists are untenable. (pp. 253–254).

The characteristics Sproule (1988) ascribed to the new managerial rhetoric are distinctively derived from an advocacy frame of organization/environment public communication. The new managerial rhetoric, grounded in what Sproule called "packaged ideology," (p. 472) most definitely makes use of Reddy's (1979) conduit metaphor. Sproule's elaboration goes beyond the conduit metaphor in that Sproule proposes that the "stuff" of communication carried in the conduit is now reduced to images, pseudoevents, entertainment, and self-contained slogans.

The "spotted owl" case study also highlights an important characteristic of communication grounded in an advocacy frame in relation to effectiveness and participation (Deetz, 1992). Participation, who is allowed to participate in the creation of meaning, problem definition, and potential solutions, is limited to those in the advocating group. There are few, if any, efforts made to encourage and incorporate the participation of those from competing advocacy groups. Effectiveness, then, is gauged in the ability to mirror the other side's message, to respond quickly to other's claims, to refute the other's information and data, to castigate the other's arguments, and to call into question the very worth of the other side. Effectiveness is captured in the ability of communication artifacts to respond to the other, but not include the other. It is the effectiveness of monologue, or as Bailey (1983) proposed the effectiveness of assertion.

Rhetoric of Assertion

In his book, *The tactical uses of passion: An essay on power, reason, and reality*, Bailey (1983) proposed that there exists a rhetoric of assertion, about which it is inappropriate to ask whether an argument advanced in this form of rhetoric is valid or invalid, and to test it by the rules of logic. The proper question to ask about assertive rhetoric concerns *effectiveness*. It is intended to provoke attitudes of approval or disapproval, to compel assent, to bring people over to one's own side. (pp. 135–136, italics added)

Bailey (1983) suggested a number of rhetorical devices or techniques for initiating a rhetoric of assertion among which are the following: (a) presentation of the moral self especially as intertwined with the audience, (b) invocation of authority in the form of a cause or a doctrine, or one's own knowledge and wisdom, (c) invocation of danger by suggesting that something dire will happen if we continue to follow the "enemy's" course of action or will be alleviated if we follow our proposed action, and (d) invocation of moral judgements about the other's motives and desires, indeed about his or her person (pp. 136–141).

In Lange's (1993) analysis of the spotted owl controversy, we find a rhetoric of assertion. Each side seeks to occupy the moral high ground, castigating the other as opposing the very way of life the sides seek to preserve. Knowledge and authority is used in the form of experts as well as anecdotal data from the participants themselves. Certainly, the invocation of danger is present in the dire warnings emanating from either side, either the doom of the species of spotted owl, or the eventual disappearance of the logger's way of life. And, the arguments presented morally judge the other in the form of "tree huggers" or "rednecks." The characteristics of Bailey's (1983) rhetoric of assertion form the backbone of the spotted owl controversy.

Weiser's Rhetorical Versus Responsible

Weiser (1988) wrote of two concepts of communication: the *rhetorical* and the *responsible*. The rhetorical model "is primarily responsive to facts of corporate power. As a result, communication is preoccupied with self-image and loyalty, unduly promoting secrecy, denial, knowledge-hoarding, defensiveness and loyalty-without-exception" (p. 739). The rhetorical model is grounded in Sullivan's (1965) technical and partisan values, values that commit the use of persuasive communication in the maintenance of organizational loyalty.

Not long ago, I became involved in a school district task force examining the delivery of K–12 education for gifted or highly capable students. The task force was composed primarily of concerned parents and teachers. In preparation for a workshop I was to facilitate, I had to interview a member of the school district administration responsible for gifted education. I was seeking information about the history and success of the gifted program currently in place. This person was extremely reluctant to provide me with any concrete information, data, or, for that matter, any direction in which to proceed in a search for the data. At one point during the interview she said, in deflecting my request for something, "Information is power, and in this district only the powerful get anything done." When I asked who else in the district I might talk with, she replied that "You need to know who your friends are and who your enemies are," but she would never tell me who she thought these people were. Clearly, she used what Weiser (1988) called the rhetorical model.

Weiser built an argument that accountability for actions is the most important aspect of any organization, especially in times of crisis and apparent organizational mistake (e.g., Union Carbide in Bhopal, India). Weiser (1988) argued that the responsible model is "not primarily responsive to power . . . but is primarily responsive to clarity, accuracy, legitimacy, truth and significance, responsible communication features traits of openness, admission, information-sharing and self-assurance" (p. 740). Weiser's argument suggests that many modern organizations equate communication effectiveness and success with the rhetorical model, in that the model provides means for distorting or sidestepping accountability by only appearing to accept responsibility. In other words, by limiting participation, to use Deetz's (1992) term, the organization limits complaints against its accountability, thereby "effectively" wrapping the organization in a rhetorical cocoon of invulnerability. Effectiveness is viewed as limiting participation and access in the communication process.

Both Deetz and Weiser presented conceptual understandings of communication that focus on the opposing characteristics of inclusion and exclusion in the communication process. Ultimately, they argued in favor of a more inclusive form of organizational/public communication, one that does not rely solely on one-way organizationally instigated persuasive attempts. They argued for the creation and nurturing of mutually influential relationships between organization and stakeholder groups, mutually influential in determining the meanings of actions. Deetz and Weiser argued that an advocacy frame all too often leads to an adversarial stance that limits, if not denies, the potential positive benefits of the interactions between competing interests. They argued for a more collaborative understanding of organizational/ stakeholder communication, an understanding to which we turn in chapter 9.

Practitioner Response to Chapter 8: Life in the PR Trenches

Susan Hulbert, APR
Public Relations and Marketing Manager
Northwest Trek Wildlife Park
Eatonville, Washington

I am trying to imagine you, the student reader, reading chapter 8. Is there a test tomorrow and are you reading the material for the first time, trying to memorize the main points, hoping in your haste you are not missing a critical point? Are you contemplating, maybe even taking issue with, one or two tantalizing ideas? Are you wondering, as I did in my classroom days, how can this chapter possibly relate to the real world of public relations, or your life in any way?

Amazingly, it *is* the real world of public relations. Although practitioners may communicate the ideas in different words, maybe in one of those convenient packages, chapter 8 accurately describes life in the PR trenches. You communicate, collaborate, advocate, and communicate again, over and over, until you reach your goals.

Advocacy and collaboration both play an important role in public relations strategic plans. Ideally, one seeks a win–win solution to problems, the result of collaboration and consensus-building with concerned parties or targeted audiences. However, in today's adversarial society, collaboration may not be possible with those who vehemently oppose your views, your company, or your product. But, collaboration is an important element in determining your message and your messengers, even when you are facing an outspoken foe. As the old saying goes, collaboration begins at home.

To bring real-world relevance to the previous chapter, look again at Sproule's seven key ways in which the new managerial rhetoric differs from traditional studies of persuasion. The win–win scenario finds you using traditional persuasion inside the company, meeting with the internal stakeholders to reach consensus, preparing your messages, and selecting your channels. It is here that you determine the goals of your communications program. It is important to have what I like to call *layers of goals*, because you will not win every war but you can still advance your cause and that should be recognized. The collaboration in your organization is a critical element in public relations planning, without which your programs are doomed to fail. At times this may be as difficult as facing hostile audiences outside the organization.

You will next use collaboration to seek support from key audiences affiliated with your company and your industry. In the nonprofit world, for instance, you may turn to volunteers, a citizen's advisory council, or affiliated organizations to endorse your viewpoint and lend support.

Now comes the exciting part, you are ready to take your message to the street. If you have a narrowly defined audience reached by reliable channels, go for it. Unfortunately, it is not as easy as some people in the organization think to bundle your messages for the general public. Most are not interested in what you have to say. You may have 20 pages of material to support your position, but the general public's interest in and tolerance for no more than 30 seconds on the evening news is hard to combat. This is where you can employ community relations programs, advertising, and promotions to enhance your position.

Up to this point, your efforts and methods have been collaborative. But you have yet to communicate with "the enemy," those who will listen to your carefully worded messages and analyze your well-planned strategies so they can refute them, or better yet, use them against you. The time has come to advocate. Go ahead, use the self-contained slogans that speak for themselves, paint the images, and plan the events. This is what the media loves and the public (unfortunately) responds to.

Normally, I do not like to communicate from an advocacy frame. It goes against my faith in people as intelligent, rational beings who care about the truth. It panders to a few outspoken critics instead of bringing people together for the good of the majority. You reach your goals by making sure someone else does not meet theirs. But there also comes a time when something vitally important to your organization is threatened. Or there is an issue about which you are passionate. Then you are most fortunate if your targeted audiences want to collaborate with you; most often they will not.

How can you use the information in chapter 8 to be a better public relations practitioner? Start by analyzing what you read, see, and hear. Get more information about the issues that interest you. Do not respond to slogans and pure advocacy messages. Question the writers and speakers; give them an opportunity to delve into the real issues. Make informed decisions. Not only will you have a better understanding of the process you will be using as a practitioner, you will be a better person. What more could you ask of a reading assignment?

CHAPTER 9

Communication From a Collaborative Frame

In chapter 8, we examined some of the characteristics associated with adversarial communication in the two-way asymmetrical, or advocacy, model. Advocacy communication is largely based on a managerial point of view in that it clearly is used as a means of controlling the ways in which situations are defined and given meaning. Organizational advocacy communication is grounded in a combination of Sullivan's (1965) technical and partisan values. As such, communication effectiveness lies with the creation of a persuasive message (via the conduit metaphor) that successfully limits participation in the organization's sphere of influence, or system (Deetz, 1992).

This chapter turns to an alternative view of communication, one that emanates from Grunig's (1992) ideal two-way symmetrical model of public relations. Because this alternative view is often discussed in terms of consensus, I originally intended to title this chapter the rhetoric of consensus. My reading and thinking, though, have moved me beyond the relative notion of consensus as an end-product to the more process-oriented experience of collaboration. As evident throughout this chapter, consensus might be a by-product or result of collaboration, but not necessarily. Collaboration much more clearly delineates the communication distinctions between the two-way symmetrical and two-way asymmetrical models of public relations.

In chapter 8, we examined a case study of the timber/environmental conflict in the northwest that highlighted an advocacy approach to communication between ideological foes. We begin this chapter with a case study that highlights a collaborative approach to communication between foes, foes much more inimical toward one another than even the loggers and environmentalists in Lange's (1993) study. This case study describes the collaboration between two people intimately involved with the political and personal struggle over abortion.

To set the stage for the magnitude of this case study, I quote from two sources, one academic and the other from the mainstream press. The first comes from an examination of vilification strategies used by pro-life and pro-choice advocates that appeared in the *Quarterly Journal of Speech*:

> The contemporary controversy over abortion has revealed glaring differences in American perceptions of life, liberty, and responsibility. The gap between pro-life and pro-choice perspectives has itself become a part of the national political and social consciousness. Clashing arguments over the pregnant woman's relationship with the fetus, the impact of abortion on society, the point at which a fetus becomes a legally protected human life, and whether freedom of choice should be extended to a woman's control over fetal life have been aired extensively in popular and scholarly forums. The values underlying these arguments are so polarized that some scholars have concluded that the abortion dispute is irreconcilable. (Vanderford, 1989, p. 166)

The second comes from a newspaper column in the *Cleveland Plain Dealer*:

> In 10 years of writing about the issue [abortion], I have seen people shove, spit at and curse one another in the name of protecting some all-important *right*. The right to privacy. The right to life. I have also spent enough time with people on each side to know that most arrive at their position out of heart-felt belief and only after much soul-searching. . . . Privately they acknowledge shades of gray. Publicly they talk of black and white: It's the baby-killers vs. the oppressors of women. The idea of sitting down with *those people* strikes most activists as pointless, even repulsive. (Frolik, 1993, p. 1–C)

Adversarial communication in the cause of advocacy has led many to conclude that the abortion dispute is irreconcilable. This conclusion was all too vividly confirmed with the shooting deaths of abortion clinic workers during 1993–1994. Do adversaries, even ones as opposed as those on either side of the abortion issue, have to engage in advocacy that belittles, demeans, polarizes, indeed, causes violence to the soul and the body? I think not, as the following case study illustrates.

CASE 9.1: COMMON GROUND

The major players in this case are Andrew F. Puzder, an attorney formerly from St. Louis, Missouri, who coauthored Missouri's 1986 abortion legislation and B. J. Isacson-Jones, President and Board Chair of the Reproductive Health Services, also in St. Louis, whose organization challenged the legality of the 1986 legislation. The case, *Webster v. Reproductive Health Services*, eventually made its way to the U. S. Supreme Court, where a decision upholding the law and the rights of the state was eventually obtained.

In late 1989, Puzder, a pro-life advocate, wrote an opinion piece published in the *St. Louis Post-Dispatch* newspaper titled, "Common Ground on Abortion." In his commentary, Puzder (1989) wrote that "the abortion debate must escape the strictures of a simple win–lose attitude that lacks perspective and distorts judgement" (p. 3B). He then described statistics showing the extent of children living in poverty with single female-headed households. He used the statistics on poverty to call suggest that "it would seem that those who truly support choice and those who truly support life must realize that these impoverished women and children (whose interests both sides seek to protect) need help and that as two very powerful lobbying groups, we can give it to them" (p. 3B). He concluded his article with a call for joint action:

> While the common ground may be slim, it exists. If we can put aside for a moment our simple win–lose attitudes and approach this issue sensibly and calmly, perhaps we can jointly accomplish some good for those we all seek to protect. (p. 3B)

B. J. Isaacson-Jones was one of the people who read Puzder's proposal. "Still, when I read an opinion piece by pro-life lawyer Andy Puzder in the *St. Louis Post-Dispatch* . . . I knew I had to talk with him" (Isaacson-Jones, 1992, p. 12). Isaacson-Jones invited Puzder to come to the Reproductive Health Services clinic and meet with some of the staff. "A week or so later, we had dinner together and decided to widen our circle . . . it was not long before [we] formed a working group called Common Ground to look into solving some of our shared problems. We began working on some of the issues within the deeper agenda" (Isaacson-Jones, 1992, p. 12).

And so, Common Ground was born. A group of the most unlikely participants came together and accomplished quite a bit toward the ultimate shared goal of reducing the number of abortions performed in Missouri. Reproductive Health Services, for example, added a service that provides adoption placement for women who elect to give birth rather than have an abortion. Other areas were identified and targeted as deserving of the combined efforts of the common ground approach. According to Isaacson-Jones, "It was shockingly easy to identify issues we agree on . . . the need for better prenatal care, and the need to reduce unwanted pregnancy" (Raspberry, 1992, p. 3C).

In a commentary piece in the *St. Louis Post-Dispatch* a year and a half after Puzder's first call for collaboration, the four founders wrote that:

> Of course, this point of view we call "common ground" continues to leave the fundamental conflict intact. Abortion is not a simple issue, and it does not lend itself to compromise. The freedom of individual choice and the right to life seem to be at an ethical impasse in this conflict. . . . Nonetheless, we believe it is possible to maintain respect for each other's right to hold one's position and to work within our political and judicial system without rancor and bitterness. We also believe that talking to one another and listening to one another is the only path to a lasting resolution of the issue. (Isaacson-Jones, Puzder, Wagner, & Cavender, 1991, p. 3B).

Or, as Isaacson-Jones wrote, "We are not trying to mediate a compromise or even find middle ground. We do search for solutions to shared problems, but, foremost, we embrace the process rather than the outcome. We understand that the journey is the destination" (Isaacson-Jones, 1992, p. 12).

The Common Ground case study exemplifies some of the best aspects of a rhetoric of collaboration. These include respect for the other, willingness to lay aside previous polarities, willingness to listen openly, searching for root causes rather than moral absolutes, seeking areas of agreement rather than disagreement, courage, and the necessity to see "the other" as a person rather than an object. In a sense, the collaboration illustrated by the Common Ground case shows a willingness to create together new shared meanings, to create understanding that could not exist in the advocacy framework. As shown in Exhibit 9.1, other traditional adversaries are also coming together in more collaborative frameworks.

In this chapter, I seek to tease out some of the ways in which we might better think about communication as a process by which we seek to create or negotiate shared understandings. The by-product of this negotiation process is a reaffirmation of the other, the reaffirmation of self. The advocacy model presented in chapter 8 all too often seeks to vilify or destroy the other (metaphorically through argument, of

---

EXHIBIT 9.1
Former Foes Team Up to Save Salmon—Tribes and Fishermen Unite

Bob Baum
Associated Press

PORTLAND—Over the past 30 years, Native Americans, environmentalists and commercial fishermen have waged some heated battles over Northwest salmon.

Now they are putting their differences aside and joining forces in an effort to restore dwindling fish runs in the Columbia River system and elsewhere across the region.

Their common targets are the federal government, which they say has failed to address the problem, and the system of hydroelectric dams that has shredded most of the young salmon that try to make it to sea.

These newfound allies plan to combine their knowledge with the clout the Native-American tribes carry because of treaty rights.

"We've got the tomahawk," said Nathan Jim of the Confederated Tribes of Warm Springs. "We need them to show us where to throw it."

About 80 representatives of tribes, environmental groups and fishermen's organizations came together Wednesday for what they called an unprecedented gathering.

Environmentalists and fishermen are coming to appreciate the depth of the Native Americans' feeling toward the salmon.

For years, the tribes, non-Indian fishermen and environmental groups quarreled over salmon harvests. Now, with harvests virtually non-existent off the coast and severely diminished for the tribes, the groups have realized they must fight together.

"Something like this is really amazing because back in the '60s and '70s there were tremendous conflicts, we're talking shooting conflicts, between tribal fishers and others, white people, about allocation of salmon resources," said Dan Rohlf, a Lewis & Clark College law professor and member of the Save Our Wild Salmon coalition.

Among those attending the meeting was Bob Eaton, executive director of Salmon for All, a coalition of Columbia River gillnet fishermen and fish processors.

The commercial salmon-fishing industry is on the verge of collapse, he said, and his organization realizes "the tribes are in a unique position to create the kind of environment where the salmon can recover."

At the heart of the new alliance are the treaty rights signed by Northwest tribes over a century ago. They guarantee salmon forever, the Native Americans say.

But the Native Americans' share has dwindled so that now virtually the entire catch is stored for ceremonial purposes.

Ted Strong, executive director of the Columbia Inter-Tribal Fish Commission, said the rights represent "what was right when the Indians

first met the non-Indians—it is right today, and it will be right forever."
"It's up to the American people to determine whether they have the
will, the strength to abide by what was made as a promise to the Indian
people in the past," he said.

The groups are heartened by last month's federal-court ruling that the
tentative recovery plan for salmon proposed by the National Marine
Fisheries Service is insufficient.

U.S. District Judge Malcolm Marsh ruled that the plan failed to
account for the fact that 90 percent of all Columbia and Snake River
juvenile salmon die on their way to the Pacific because of hydroelectric
dams.

The Columbia River tribes—Warm Springs, Yakima, Umatilla and Nez
Perce—are forming their own recovery plan, and Strong said he hoped
the other groups represented at Wednesday's meeting would help.

The groups had no other specific plans on what they will do with their
newfound unity.

Reprinted by permission of Associated Press, New York, NY.

course), with rhetorical bombs neatly packaged in the container
metaphor. The collaborative model seeks to create relationships that
affirm one another through dialogue.

The emphasis on dialogue is crucial. The participants in the
Common Ground experience "are celebrating the accomplishment of
people of different views having a *dialogue*" (Berns, 1992, p. 3A,
italics added). Dialogue, or dialogic rhetoric, seeks to move communication during times of conflict from

statements designed to convince to statements designed to explore . . .
one's approach may change from accusing and belittling others for their
beliefs, which is motivated by an attitude of exclusivity, to a realization
that both sides are limited by the axioms of their social realities, which is
an attitude of inclusivity. (Freeman, Littlejohn, & Pearce, 1992, p. 322)

The distinctions between dialogue and monologue have been addressed in several ways in the communication and public relations
literature. In our quest for an explication of a rhetoric of collaboration,
we examine two areas: Habermas's (1984, 1991) distinctions between
communicative action and strategic action and recent writings on a
feminist reformulation of organizational communication. Both add
tremendously to a better understanding of the relations part of public
relations.

By way of quick review, I argued in chapter 8 that the two-way
asymmetric model of organizational public relations is founded on a

container metaphor of communication, one that prizes technological significance in creating persuasive messages. Following Deetz's (1992) lead, I suggested that effectiveness in the traditional model is based on the ultimate ability of the contained message to influence the target audience or public to accept the organization's definition of the world. At the same time, the organization seeks to limit participation in the communication process, thereby reserving for itself the ability to assign meaning to issues or events in which it has an interest. The restriction of participation and effectiveness characterized by persuasive success is the means to achieving the organizational end of autonomy in decision making. This autonomy is gained largely through the power of monologue.

When we view communication from a dialogic rhetoric, we need to revise our ideas about effectiveness and participation. Organizations employing a dialogic rhetoric seek to encourage participation from other stakeholders rather than limit it. Participation refers not only to the physical presence of communicators, but also the ability of those communicators to offer their definitions of salient meanings. Participation in the dialogue requires collaboration on the part of the participants, collaboration that is encouraged and rewarded rather than discouraged and stifled. In a list of functions recommended for public relations education, Heath (1991) more than once alluded to the necessity for teaching communication based on dialogue and collaboration:

1. Assessing the terrain to determine whether problems exist and which adjustments are necessary to build harmony between involved parties.
2. Influencing judgment and behavior through information and persuasion with the incentive of achieving agreement and harmony on evaluative perspectives.
3. Exerting and yielding to control in a dialectic of interests.
4. Reducing uncertainty and achieving understanding.
5. Planning and managing interests toward mutually beneficial outcomes (p. 190).

The words "harmony," "exerting and yielding to control," "dialectic," "achieving understanding," and "mutually beneficial outcomes" all speak to a process of negotiation, of dialogue between organization and stakeholders. To address this issue and more fully appreciate the ramifications of a dialogic (as opposed to a monologic) rhetoric, we turn to Habermas.

HABERMAS'S THEORY OF COMMUNICATIVE ACTION

In a series of writings, Habermas (cf. 1970, 1979, 1984, 1991) laid out a theory of communicative action in which he examined the ways in which members of a society use communication to create and maintain reason and rationality. Although any number of his ideas are insightful in our attempt to better understand organizational public relations, I focus on three that I think are most germane to our discussion: (a) the ideal speech situation, (b) distinctions between strategic action and communicative action, and (c) distinctions between cognitive instrumental rationality and communicative rationality. At the very outset of this section, I acknowledge both Deetz (1992) and Pearson (1989a, 1989b) for their explanations and insights.

The Ideal Communication Situation

In Habermas' *ideal speech situation*, "individual speakers possess an equality of speaking chances and they can speak about whatever they wish to call into the play of discussion. Therefore . . . reason itself is grounded in social norms like freedom, equality, and justice" (Meisenhelder, 1989, p. 120). Pearson (1989) suggested that the ideal speech situation occurs when there is "equal freedom among participants to initiate and maintain discourse, to challenge or explain, freedom from manipulation, and equality with respect to power" (p. 73). As Pearson (1989b) and Grunig and White (1992) noted, Habermas's ideal speech situation is one characterized by symmetry between participants.

Habermas's ideal is just that, an ideal that is seldom (if ever) reached in everyday life, especially social interactions between organizations and stakeholders. When symmetry is lacking, when the ideal situation is not realized,

> communication difficulties arise from communication practices that preclude value debate and conflict, that substitute images and imaginary relations for self-presentation and truth claims, that arbitrarily limit access to communication channels and forums, and that then lead to decisions based on arbitrary authority relations. (Deetz, 1992, p. 161)

The key to reaching the ideal is the focus on participation resulting in a shared (or what I am calling a *collaborative*) process toward negotiated meanings. As noted in chapter 8, public relations that proceed from an asymmetric worldview do not allow for consideration of Habermas's ideal.

Strategic Action and Communicative Action. Habermas (1991) suggested that social actors (e.g.., organizations, stakeholders) approach any social interaction with one of two orientations: either toward success or toward reaching understanding. Habermas (1984) termed an orientation toward success *strategic action* and an orientation toward understanding *communicative action.* The underlying distinction between the two is the degree to which the participants share or agree on definitions of the situation and the acceptability of potential outcomes.

In defining success, Habermas focuses on the consequences or outcomes of the actor's actions. "They will try to reach their objectives by influencing their opponent's definition of the situation, and thus his decisions or motives, through external means" (Habermas, 1991, p. 133). In such cases, Habermas proposes that the actors are acting, or using communication, strategically. Strategic action is of two types: open strategic action and concealed strategic action. *Open strategic action* is comprised of those communications that, although based on argument, are presented in an honest effort to persuade. *Concealed, or latent, strategic actions* are based on deceptions that lead to systematically distorted communication or manipulation (depending on whether the concealment is unconscious or conscious, respectively).

An example of conscious deception is outright lying by an organizational member to a stakeholder group. During the Three Mile Island nuclear power plant accident that led to the release of radioactive vapor into the atmosphere and radioactive tainted water into the Susquehanna River, for example, a representative of Consolidated Edison, the plant owner, lied to the media about the releases (Farrell & Goodnight, 1981). Systematically distorted communication is more difficult to ascertain because it is embedded in the dominant value system of organizational life (Mumby, 1988).

In contrast, Habermas (1979) suggested that communicative action is the result of consensual interaction

> in which participants share a tradition and their orientations are normatively integrated to such an extent that they start from the same definition of the situation and do not disagree about the claims to validity that they reciprocally raise. (pp. 208–209)

As Habermas (1991) noted in an essay on "Moral Consciousness and Communicative Action,"

> I speak of *communicative* action when actors are prepared to harmonize their plans of action through internal means, committing themselves to

pursuing their goals only on the condition of an agreement—one that already exists or one to be negotiated—about definitions of the situation and prospective outcomes. (p. 134)

Or, as he wrote in an earlier work (Habermas; 1984),

I shall speak of *communicative* action whenever the actions of the agents involved are coordinated not through egocentric calculations of success but through acts of reaching understanding. In communicative action participants are not primarily oriented to their own individual successes . . . the negotiation of definitions of the situation is an essential element of the interpretive accomplishments required for communicative action. (pp. 285–286)

We could easily argue (and have) that public relations, as most often currently practiced, falls under Habermas's definition of strategic action. Public relations of this type is concerned most often with the effectiveness of presentation. Or, to rephrase Deetz (1992), public relations is most often concerned with the "strategic *reproduction* of meaning" rather than the "*production* of understanding" (p. 160).

Two Types of Rationality

Habermas (1984, 1991) wrote that people use speech for three purposes: (a) the depiction of facts or an *objective world* (about which we are debating a course of action), (b) the production of interpersonal relationships between actors thereby creating a *social world*, and (c) the expression of their individualized experiences with the world, a subjective expression leading to a *subjective world*. Agreement about which of these is admissible and when is paramount in creating consensual communicative action.

As used by Habermas (1984), strategic action is limited to communication about only the first, the objective world. It is grounded in an assumption of *cognitive-instrumental rationality*, which "carries with it connotations of successful self-maintenance made possible by informed disposition over, and intelligent adaptation to, conditions of a contingent environment" (Habermas, 1984, p. 10). Communicative action, on the other hand, is grounded in what Habermas (1984) labeled *communicative rationality*. This alternative view of rationality is found in the linking between the actors' perceptions of the objective world (i.e, the world of observation and fact) and their subjective world (i.e., values) resulting in social interaction. It is a rationality that is created from dialogue between actors acting in a social situation. It is a rationality that allows for differing interpretations of what is real. Through his writings about the theory of communicative action, Habermas distinguished between an objective, effectiveness, monologic-oriented form of interaction and a more subjectively oriented, participation-based, dialogic form. As Pearson (1989b) summarized:

> Habermas is concerned to articulate an alternative kind of rationality that would act as a bulwark against an instrumental rationality . . . like other critical theorists, he is worried about the dehumanizing effects wrought by instrumental reason, of the specter of life administered according to monological rationality. For this reason he would be concerned about an allegiance between public relations theory and asymmetric social scientific technique. He would be concerned that such a relationship would lead to the flourishing of two-way asymmetric public relations. . . . (pp. 74–75)

As we see in the next section, others are also concerned with the emphasis on cognitive instrumental rationality that leads to strategic rather than communicative action on the part of organizational communicators. We turn now to a feminist interpretation of organizational life and its ability to enhance our understanding of a rhetoric of collaboration.

A FEMINIST VIEW OF ORGANIZATIONAL COMMUNICATION

One way of getting at the nuts and bolts of a rhetoric of collaboration is to examine the recent emphasis on feminist critiques of both organization and communication. As a theoretical stance, feminism falls in Burrell and Morgan's (1979) radical/critical perspectives of sociological understandings of organizational theory (cf. Bullis, 1993; Creedon, 1993; Martin, 1989; Mumby, 1993; Witz & Savage, 1992). Feminist scholarship and research offers a means of critiquing the inherent weaknesses of the dominant functional paradigm (i.e., functionalism based on a masculine bias). More importantly for our purposes is the fact that feminist writing is beginning to point to an alternative way of understanding and using communication in (and between) organizations (Ramsay & Parker, 1992). It is a way definitively grounded in a rhetoric of collaboration and thus offers some useful insights for expanding our understanding.

Shepherd (1992) argued that the "dominant tradition of defining communication has exhibited a masculine bias, resulting in a conceptualization of communication as influence" (p. 203). In a brief and admittedly selective history of communication, Shepherd (1992) suggested that

> from humanistic definitions of rhetoric in the 1930's, through social scientific conceptions of communication in the 1960's, to critical considerations of discourse in the 1990's, interaction processes have typically been characterized essentially and primarily in terms of persuasion, influence, and power. (p. 204)

Drawing on a number of sources such as Gilligan (1982) and two recent studies of women's initiations and responses to persuasive attempts (Applegate & Woods, 1991; Hample & Dallinger, 1987), Shepherd (1992) concluded that

> women appear to be more concerned than men with the *relational consequences* of messages in persuasive situations, asserting greater responsibility toward and care for the other in such situations. . . . Men, in contrast are more likely to be concerned with the *persuasive effectiveness* of messages in such situations . . . [resulting in] a masculine view that focuses on communication as influence, and a feminine view that focuses on communication as relational responsibility. (pp. 209–210, italics added)

Taking his conclusion at face value for the moment, we see a masculine emphasis on effectiveness in the form of message construction in a container metaphor and a feminine emphasis on effectiveness as inclusion of the other. Ramsay and Parker (1992) suggested that, although the male ideal type values goal accomplishment and consistency, the "female ideal type values emotional connection and human interaction above a single goal or ideal . . . the latter stresses the process as being as valuable as the final outcome" (pp. 263–264).

This stereotyped male view of the nature of communication emanates from Habermas's (1984) cognitive instrumental rationality and is, subsequently, revealed through an emphasis on strategic communication. The stereotypical mode Shepherd (1992) attributes to women is grounded in Habermas's communicative rationality revealed through communicative action for understanding.

In a similar manner, Marshall (1993) summarized male and female values as follows:

> male values or the male principle can be characterized as self-assertion, separation, independence, control, competition, focused perception,

rationality, analysis, clarity, discrimination, and activity. Underlying themes are a self-assertive tendency, control of the environment, and focus on personal and interpersonal processes. Female values or the female principle can be characterized as interdependence, cooperation, receptivity, merging, acceptance, awareness of patterns, wholes and contexts, emotional tone, personalistic perception, being, intuition, and synthesizing. Underlying themes are openness to the environment, interconnection, and mutual development. (p. 124)

In her essay, Marshall (1993) argued that organizations are dominated by male values to an extent that female values are either ignored, disregarded, treated with contempt, or marginalized. The modern organization is seen as a masculine, patriarchal institution inimical to the needs and desires of women (as well as men; Ferguson, 1984; Pringle, 1988; Savage & Witz, 1992). Through critiques based in a feminist theory of social life, these scholars have indicated many ways in which the dominant organizational phenomena (e.g., hierarchy, power) perpetuate a male domination, however virulent or subtle.

Marshall (1993) suggested a number of "potential human qualities that have been socially devalued in male-dominated cultures" (p. 139) including:

adopting a relational orientation
valuing connection and affiliation
defining identify through relationships
exercising power *with*
adopting task strategies that maintain relationships
facilitating others' development
emphasizing equality and participation
seeking dialogue
personalizing communication
twining speaking and listening as an epistemology (p. 138).

Clearly, the feminist approach to organizational communication list just outlined is much different than the one described in chapter 8. The ultimate importance of this approach to public relations is the focus on relationships, empowerment, and dialogue. A model of public relations based on Marshall's (1993) qualities would be vastly different from a model based on a persuasion-oriented adversarial model that seeks, as its ultimate goal, autonomy. At the very core, a feminist model (at least as outlined here) seeks connection and finds autonomy in those connections.

Marshall's (1993) "potential human qualities" are also ones apparent in the Common Ground case study. Given the descriptions of their process in the articles the Common Ground participants wrote as well as comments made during televised interviews, Puzder and Isaacson-Jones adopted a relational orientation. They valued the connection they made with one another; they redefined at least part of their professional identities as pro-life or pro-choice advocates through their new relationship with one another; they began to exercise power with one another to address shared concerns; they continued to meet, thereby adopting strategies that maintain the relationship; and they apparently emphasized equality and participation. The adoption of the relational orientation led to a continual seeking of dialogue between the two groups.

Indeed, many of Marshall's (1993) qualities are evident in the ground rules established by the Common Ground group in Wisconsin:

1. Listen to each other; restate others' views before stating our own.
2. State our views honestly, without rhetoric or cliches.
3. Commit ourselves to building mutual trust.
4. Judge viewpoints, not people; avoid character assassination.
5. Accept that all participants are entitled to their thoughts and feelings, which may differ from our own.
6. Recognize the power of words and choose them carefully.
7. Keep others' comments within the group confidential (Cage, 1992, p. 10).

In this list of ground rules, we find a blending of reason and emotion, of feelings and thought. We find, a merging of the traditionally (and stereotypically) masculine and feminine.

Organizational Rationality Versus Organizational Emotionality. In an essay entitled, "Habermas and Feminism: The Future of Critical Theory," Meisenhelder (1989) suggested that the "philosophical core of Habermas's critical theory—his notion of reason—is marred by errors characteristic of patriarchal thought" (p. 125). In particular, Meisenhelder (1989) critiqued Habermas's acceptance of "patriarchal rationalism," particularly his "tendency to describe reality as a structure composed of essential dualities or divisions" (p. 125).

> Perhaps the most crucial of these divisions is that between intellect and emotion, head and heart, mind and body. The former, it is supposed, is the realm of knowledge and truth, the latter is described as an unpredictable region characterized by sentimentality, deception, and the absence of reason. . . . It is important to note that in each of these cases

the patriarchal mind not only sees a basic duality but also posits an invidious differentiation where one element of the pair is dominant. . . . (p. 125)

Nowhere is the idea of rationality more crucial or apparent than in the management or administration of organizations (Scott & Hart, 1989). As noted elsewhere, logical empiricism, in the guise of rational decision making, is a linchpin of public relations decision-making models, especially those seeking to match messages to publics or stakeholders. The next section examines Mumby and Putnam's (1992) attempt to compare and contrast traditional organizational rationality with a conception of organizational emotionality.

Mumby and Putnam (1992) provided a feminist reading of bounded rationality, one of the primary concepts in much decision-making literature. "Rationality is typically defined as intentional, reasoned, goal-directed behavior . . . [suggesting] that optimal choice is limited or restricted by organizational actors and their institutional practices" (Mumby & Putnam, 1992, p. 469). Mumby and Putnam (1992) "read" bounded rationality from a feminist perspective and offer what they call *bounded emotionality* as an alternate means of "organizing in which nurturance, caring, community, supportiveness, and interrelatedness are fused with individual responsibility to shape organizational experiences" (p. 474).

Mumby and Putnam (1992) compared bounded rationality with bounded emotionality on six characteristics, three of which are particularly interesting given the study of organizational public relations that incorporates a collaborative rhetoric: tolerance of ambiguity (as opposed to the reduction of ambiguity through satisficing), heterarchy of goals and values (opposed to hierarchy, means–ends chain), and community (opposed to fragmented labor). Mumby and Putnam (1992) proposed that the masculine or patriarchal-bounded rationality is based on a desire to reduce ambiguity, especially that evident in the organization's environment. Rules and systems are created in the hopes of accomplishing just such a reduction in ambiguity (e.g., environmental scanning). A feminist conceptualization of emotionality would do just the opposite. "Tolerance of ambiguity would facilitate the formation of organizational structures that recognize divergent and even contradictory positions" (p. 475). Creedon (1993) suggested the concept of "*dissymmetry* in which the goal is to value various symmetries, rather than to achieve homeostasis by minimizing differences [or reducing ambiguity]" (p. 164).

As expressed by Mumby and Putnam (1992), bounded emotionality would rely on a heterarchy in which goals and values "are flexible, and they alternate unpredictably in a coordinated arrangement'' (p. 164) Mumby and Putnam (1992) quoted Marshall's (1989) use of the child's game paper, stone, and scissors to illustrate the concept of hierarchy:

> The childhood game of paper, stone, and scissors provides a simple illustration: paper wraps stone, stone blunts scissors, scissors cut paper. There is no fixed hierarchy, but each is effective, and recognized in its own realm. (Mumby & Putnam, 1992, p. 475)

The authors, using the Challenger space shuttle disaster as an example, show that "organizations often engage in poor decision making precisely *because* of their inability to transcend hierarchical, boundedly rational forms of behavior" (p. 476). Based on an analysis by Schiappa (1989), Mumby and Putnam suggested that the engineers at Morton Thiokol (the makers of the rocket used to launch the shuttle), who were originally against having the launch due to cold weather, eventually gave way to the hierarchical-based decision-making structure of the company. In essence, they allowed their better judgment to be overruled by hierarchy, rather than by sound evidence (albeit based on a patriarchal notion of technological rationality).

Third, organizations characterized by bounded emotionality celebrate the individual's self-identity through "nurturance and supportiveness" (p. 476). This, in turn, leads to an enhanced sense of community and shared experience rather than the isolation that so often comes from fragmented labor characteristic of many organizations. The idea of enhanced self-identity and community are crucially maintained, not through monologue or strategic action, but through dialogue and communicative action.

As Mumby and Putnam (1992) concluded:

> Rationality, (whether bounded or otherwise) is not bad per se. Rather, the concept of bounded rationality, which objectifies individuals and privileges instrumental process, excludes alternative modes of organizational experience. By shifting rationality to include intersubjective understanding, community, and shared interests, insights into alternative forms of organizing are created. (p. 480)

In essence, Mumby and Putnam (1992) echo Marshall's (1993) understanding that the range of characteristics associated with rationality and emotionality be available to and accepted by all organizational players. "Rather than the exclusive properties of men and women, respectively," Marshall (1993, p. 125) allows that both males and females have access to all values, feminine and masculine.

SUMMARY

In this chapter, I attempted to lay the groundwork for a second view of communication as it relates to organizational public relations. It is a view grounded in the necessity for dialogue among collaborating parties who seek to understand one another first before moving to a problem-solving, solution-oriented framework. It seeks, not to avoid conflict situations or messy dilemmas, but to mitigate debilitating contention based on the sole and single-minded reliance on persuasive control.

Habermas (1984) proposed that communication interaction based on the demands of cognitive instrumental rationality (technical rationality, bounded rationality) leads to strategic action. From a feminist perspective, strategic action is best characterized as arising from predominantly male values. This leads to communication that is patently monologic, designed to control the definition of the situation, and asymmetric. It is a form of communication that seeks to exclude or limit participation at the expense of a cognitive-rational definition of effectiveness as successfully altering the other's attitudes, beliefs, or behavior.

In contrast, Habermas (1984) suggested as an alternative to the concept of communicative rationality, one grounded in the subjective experiences and perceptions of the actors. It is a rationality that prizes the establishment and maintenance of interpersonal relationships that lead to communicative action, which is designed to foster and encourage understanding. From a feminist perspective, communicative action arises from decidedly female values, particularly those emphasizing relationships. This leads to communication that is patently dialogic, designed to build mutual definitions of the situation, and is symmetrical. In addition, the feminist view, particularly of organizational life and communication, endorses the validity of claims arising from emotions and feelings.

In a rhetoric of collaboration, effectiveness is judged by the degree to which participants are able, willing, and encouraged to participate in the communication process. With appropriate apologies to Deetz (1992), who did not diagram his conceptualization, we use the diagram in Fig. 9.1 as a means of summarizing the key issues discussed in chapters 8 and 9.

The horizontal axis in Fig. 9.1 indicates the continuum of participation enrichment or encouragement. The degree of participation in the creation of meaning (the definition of the situation) ranges from low to high. Communicative events falling toward the right side of the horizontal axis indicate those in which participation is invited and

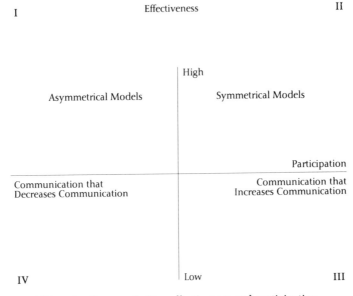

FIG. 9.1.   Communication effectiveness and participation.

encouraged; those falling toward the left are ones in which participation is stifled or ignored. Similarly, the vertical axis indicates the range of effectiveness, illustrating the potential ability of a party to accomplish his or her ends. Effectiveness can also be gauged using a low to high scale, low indicating less likelihood of accomplishing the desired end, and high indicating the opposite.

Two interrelated questions arise from examining Fig. 9.1. The first involves the operational definition of *effectiveness*, or the delineation of the end desired by the organization or its stakeholders. The second concerns the degree to which participation is (or should be) invited in achieving effectiveness. As shown in the figure, if effectiveness is to be judged in relation to the creation of a message, a conduit, then participation in the establishment of meaning is perhaps less crucial. The creation of the message we commonly call an "annual report" is a good example (although many people in the organization might take part, few external stakeholders help create the meanings). Conversely, if effectiveness is considered in terms of relationship, then participation is crucial.

In Fig. 9.1, collaborative rhetoric falls to the right along the horizontal axis. Effective collaborative rhetoric, communication that allows all participants a say in the creation of meaning, is found in Quadrant II: high participation/high effectiveness. In some elemental ways, then, effectiveness is not about control, but rather, about the

TABLE 9.1
Characteristics of Public Relations Frames

Advocacy	Consensus
self-oriented	other-oriented
persuasion	relational
control	sharing
masculine	feminine
presentational	negotiational
effectiveness	participation
autonomy	interconnected
conduit metaphor	conversation metaphor
product	process
arrogance	humility
monologue	dialogue
power over	power with
adversary democracy	unitary democracy
perceptual myopia	perceptual expansion
competition	collaboration
written	oral
assertion	question
timely	lengthy
polarization	inclusions
short-term	long-term

yielding of control. It is about the recognition of the other, the self and the need to include both in any definition of the situation. Effective adversarial rhetoric falls in Quadrant I: low participation/high effectiveness. Again, effectiveness is measured in the ability of the organization to control and disseminate its preferred symbolic meaning.

The distinctions in effectiveness come down to the difference between effectiveness measured as the production of messages that result in a desired effect or effectiveness measured as the production of relationships that result in the sharing of meaning creation power. Or, we might distinguish between effectiveness measured by the success of produced messages and effectiveness judged by the strength of produced relationships.

Finally, at the sake of grossly oversimplifying the dichotomous nature of an advocacy/adversarial frame (high effectiveness and low participation) and the collaborative frame (high effectiveness and high participation), I present the dichotomous terms I associate with each in Table 9.1.

Many of these descriptors come from other writers already cited who address the fundamental dichotomy between advocacy and collaboration. Others come from my own observations and experiences. As I had mentioned in chapter 8, I believe there is a place for both approaches.

The descriptors are offered as a means of summarizing the discussion in chapters 7 and 8 and as a tool for expanding our abilities to think critically about the ends and processes of communication and, consequentially, public relations.

Practitioner Response to Chapter 9: Cooperation Pays Big Dividends

Gay Campbell, APR, ASPR
Coordinator of Community Relations
Everett School District
Everett, Washington

For those of us who work in the public sector, there is no question about whether we will collaborate. To do anything else can be disastrous to the future of our organizations. Our "stockholders" are the people who pay the taxes that support our agencies. They want to be part of our decision-making processes. They are quick to percieve, and have little patience for, techniques that attempt to manipulate them or play mind games with them.

Recently released Roper-Starch research shows a declining confidence in public institutions and in our ability to address the problems we were created to address. That lack of confidence extends not only to state and federal government bodies, but also to public schools and the news media. There is a growing feeling on the part of the public that "They can't do the job. We'll just do it ourselves."

Those who have practiced manipulative public relations techniques rather than open, honest communications have contributed to this disillusionment with public institutions. They have forgotten the most important steps in building an effective, long-term communications program research, analysis, planning, and evaluation.

Effective communications programs are built on research techniques that involve a lot of listening to the target audience of the program and building collaborative, grassroots movements with them. This requires techniques for building long-term relationships based on mutual trust that result in the desired behaviors that support our organizations.

This often requires changing the way the organization approaches decision making and community involvement. Whether we are building a long-term strategic plan, engaging in total quality management, or deciding on the type of program to place in a given neighborhood, we must involve the key influentials to the group(s) affected by the decision from the very beginning of the process.

We can no longer afford to make decisions in a vaccuum and then "sell" those decisions to the public. The public will no longer tolerate an approach that tells them that if they just properly understood the facts, they would agree with us and support our position. Many of our most critical organizations decisions touch on the basic philosophies of those we serve. Telling them they need more facts in order to "buy in" is insulting to them; in effect we are telling them that we are the "experts" and, if they just become as knowlegable as we are, they will see the light and agree with us. In other words, we intimate to them that we are smarter then they are. We are saying, "We will educate you and then you will change your mind." The result is more and more anger on the part of our "customer" and eventually total disengagement with our institution. In disgust, they give up on us, and it is very difficult, sometimes impossible, to get them back.

This is not to say that we should entirely abandon sophisticated public relations techniques that are based on knowledge of how to reach a given audience. We must pay attention to demographics and psychographics combined with our own research in order to deliver messages that will be noticed by the audience. We must search for the common ground that enables us to build collaborative efforts. If we never get the attention of the group we need to work with, the conversation will not occur and the relationship will never be built.

This process is much more time-consuming then the old, manipulative techniques of thinking of a clever way to reach the audience, getting them to do what you want, and then forgetting them until you need them. It requires a belief that all of us are smarter than any one of us alone. It requires the belief in the people we serve. It requires a willingness to contribute our expertise to planning the process, nurturing it, and strategizing the best way to get the job done.

Learning to strategize in this new way pays big dividends in the form of long-term loyal support of our agencies and those they serve.

CHAPTER 10

Managing Ambiguity: Implications for External Communication Choices

In chapters 7, 8, and 9, we explored some of the ways in which organiztions interact with their environments. In chapter 7, we assessed the concept of environmental uncertainty as it related to the organization's stakeholders. Given previous research (Greening & Gray, 1994; Kreiner & Bhambri, 1991) I suggested that stakeholders with the power to confirm or deny legitimacy to the organization, those primarily located in the institutional environment, represent a different set of public relations dilemmas than do those in the organization's technical or resource environment.

In chapters 8 and 9, we examined two frames that characterize (at least in a polarized manner) the ways in which organizations respond to their external stakeholders. The adversarial frame is grounded in the perceived necessity for communicative advocacy on the part of the organization to achieve a measure of control vis-à-vis alternative control attempts initiated by external stakeholders. As we noted, advocacy communication is historically grounded in our pluralistic ideal of adversarial democracy (Mansbridge, 1980). Public relations practiced from an adversarial frame is most closely related to Grunig and Hunt's (1984) two-way asymmetrical model of persuasive, goal-oriented communication. In their discussion of corporate rhetoric, Cheney and Vibbert (1987) captured the essence of this approach:

> Recent reformulations of public relations suggest that organizations can no longer let others control their communicative agenda; hence corporate public persuasion attempts to control the terms under which such

discussions take place. . . . Through public relations communication, corporate actors attempt—admittedly with varying degrees of success— to control the ways internal and external environments discuss such key concepts as values, issues, images, and identities. (p. 173)

Effectiveness, as defined by Deetz (1992), is measured by how successful the organization is in persuading stakeholders to its preferred position. Participation, at least participation in the definition of the situation, is minimized.

The collaborative frame outlined in chapter 9 offers a distinctly different (some might say ideal or altruistic) model of public relations. Like the adversarial frame, the collaborative frame is grounded in the necessity to manage ongoing and potential conflict between the organization and its stakeholders. This frame is based on the metaphysical conundrum that, in order to *gain* control, the organization has to *share* control with others in its environment. In writing about the challenge of managing ambiguity, McCaskey (1988) suggested that "the managers who cope best with the stress of a messy problem [one that creates ambiguity] paradoxically combine a sense of controlling and *not* controlling events" (p. 5). Conflicts between the organization and its stakeholders are resolved through the negotiation of shared definitions and the collaborative assignment of meaning to symbolic acts. As evident in chapter 5, this frame closely resembles what Mansbridge (1980) labeled *unitary democracy*, democracy that functions by way of enhanced individual participation in the process of definition.

The ideas presented up to this point help us understand why the implementation of the organizational public relations function so often occurs from potentially conflicting premises. I have argued that the mixed metaphor model of public relations is an appropriate way to conceptualize the range of available organizational public relations responses, as evident in chapters 8 and 9. If this is accurate, then we need to identify the environmental characteristics that most clearly indicate why a response grounded in one model will have a greater likelihood of success than a response from an alternate model. We need to better understand why an organization might elect to respond to one stakeholder using an asymmetrical model, for example, and to another using a symmetrical model.

In this chapter, I present four ideas that are crucial to better describing and subsequently understanding the public relations and organizational environment linkage. This chapter (a) distinguishes between instrumental and symbolic outcomes of organizational decision-making processes, (b) discusses the distinctions between the discourse perspectives of organizational insiders and outsiders. (c) examines the ways in which the instrumental and symbolic outcomes are often perceived as being only loosely coupled, and (d) proposes that two related concepts—information richness and media richness—offer a means of better understanding appropriate organizational responses to external stakeholders.

Each of these topics informs us of the complexity of the relationship between the public relations communication function and the organization's environment. The conceptual linchpin linking these ideas as a means of better understanding external organizational public relations is the concept of *ambiguity*. Indeed, the four ideas—instrumental/symbolic decision making, insider/outsider perspectives, loose/tight coupling, and information/media richness—are grounded in our often feeble attempts to understand, create, and manage organizational ambiguity. Given its central importance for our discussion, we begin with an examination of organizational ambiguity.

ORGANIZATIONAL AMBIGUITY

Bolman and Deal (1991) claimed that organizations are filled with ambiguity:

> Figuring out what is really happening in businesses, hospitals, schools, or public agencies is difficult. . . . Sometimes, information is incomplete or vague. Sometimes the same information is interpreted in different ways by different people. At other times, ambiguity is deliberately created to hide problems or avoid conflict (p. 27)

In the introduction to their book, *Managing ambiguity and change*, Pondy, Boland, and Thomas (1988) concurred:

> In the manufacturing and service industries, as well as in the professions, the fundamental nature of how we do business, and thus how we must manage, is in transition. Technologies of production, communication, and distribution are changing. Expectations of customers, regulators, and financial markets are volatile and uncertain. Established rules of the game no longer seem to hold. What was once solid ground is now moving under our feet. The situations managers face today are complex, interdependent, and often poorly understood. (p. xiii)

Stakeholder expectations are unknown or at odds with the organization, problems are only partially understood, interdependencies are unclear, change is the only constant, and, consequently, ambiguity abounds (cf, Hennestad, 1990; Jackson & Pippa, 1992; March & Olson, 1979; Nooteboom, 1989). The case study presented in chapter 4 about the violence experienced by Paula illustrates two aspects of ambiguity. Recall that Paula was deceived about her budget, surprised at the enormity of the deception, and subsequently experienced a great deal of ambiguity about her position, her status, her relationships with other members of the senior management team, and, especially, her relationship with her boss. It was difficult for Paula to interpret what the deception meant for her individual existence in the organization as well as what it said about the perceived worth of her department's function. This is the ambiguity Bolman and Deal (1991) and Pondy et al. (1988) wrote about. It is ambiguity that arises from the complexity of the situation or event, or from the decision-making and political systems in the organization. It is ambiguity that is grounded in our inability to adequately define what is going on or ascertain the motivations driving other actors' actions.

Interestingly, a study of the effects of ambiguous organizational policies on the social support provided managers dramatically underscores Paula's experiences (Erera, 1992). Data Erera (1992) gathered from surveys and in-depth interviews indicated that when conflicts arouse because of ambiguous policies (e.g., Paula's budget process), superiors were perceived as "providing inconsistent and insufficient information and for withholding emotional, approval, and tangible support" (p. 247). During these times, the managers' relationships with peers deteriorated and were characterized by competition and mistrust (e.g., Paula's peers did not tell her of the decision). The only source of support available to managers working under ambiguous conditions came from their subordinates (e.g., Paula's staff came to her emotional support).

Although Paula's experience was one internal to the organization, a similar type of ambiguity, an ambiguity resulting from an inability to figure out what is really happening, is equally likely to occur between an organization and its external stakeholders. We might call this the *ambiguity of disparate meanings*. Indeed, much of this book has alluded to the ambiguity that arises from our inability to either understand complexity and change (e.g., state uncertainty) or our inability to forge shared understandings on how best to respond to those complexities and changes (e.g., response uncertainty).

A second aspect of ambiguity exists, however, that is of crucial importance to the public relations function. It is ambiguity resulting from the intentional communication of vagueness. Ambiguity of this type, what Eisenberg (1984) so appropriately labeled *strategic ambigu-*

ity, is the conceptual opposite of message clarity. Ambiguity, as Eisenberg (1984) neatly pointed out, is intimately intertwined with our notions of clarity particularly message clarity. He wrote:

> Clarity, then, is a continuum which reflects the degree to which a source has narrowed the possible interpretations of a message and succeeded in achieving a correspondence between his or her intentions and the interpretation of the receiver. (pp. 229–230)

Clarity is grounded in a message-centered understanding of communication that reinforces Reddy's (1979) conduit metaphor. The criteria for success—correspondence between intentions and interpretation—is the type of success Deetz (1992) isolated as one component of traditional definitions of communication (see chapter 8).

Eisenberg (1984) alternately suggested that people in organizations often use strategic ambiguity to gain a variety of desirable ends, ends that can not be attained with messages designed to enhance clarity or correspondence. He argues that "people in organizations do not always try to promote this correspondence between intent and interpretation" (p. 230), they do not always try for clarity. He argues, in other words, that vagueness has its place. As an example, he discusses the idea that organizational goals are often vaguely stated and open to widespread interpretation. The motto of the university at which I teach is "A Quality Education in a Christian Context." Although an apparently concise statement of mission, after 16 years at this university I can tell you that there are a wide variety of interpretations of the sentiment expressed in the deceptively succinct motto. McCaskey (1988) confirmed the positive role of ambiguity when he wrote that "ambiguity is valuable for protecting options in the future. Decisions, goals, and slogans, if fecundly ambiguous, can be reinterpreted depending upon what the future brings" (p. 15). It is here that ambiguity of perception and ambiguity of communication bump into one another.

Although Eisenberg has a number of interesting things to say about how strategic ambiguity allows for organizational wiggle room in the symbolic interpretation of a variety of organizational communications, the importance of his argument for public relations practitioners lies in his elaboration of a context for the study of strategic ambiguity. Eisenberg (1984) posited two dimensions important for understanding strategic ambiguity: type of audience (internal/external) and level of communication formality (formal/informal). From these dimensions, he creates a two-by-two matrix of areas ripe for the study of organizational strategic ambiguity as shown in Fig. 10.1.

As indicated in the Fig. 10.1, Eisenberg suggests that one area of

		FORMALITY	
		FORMAL	INFORMAL
AUDIENCE	INTERNAL	I goals, missions rules, regulations policies and procedures	II conversation group discussion organizational story-telling
	EXTERNAL	III public relations advertising sales interorganizational agreements	IV informal agreements weak links old boy networks overlapping directorates

FIG. 10.1. Dimensions of communicative context and strategic ambiguity. From Eisenberg, E. M. (1984). Ambiguity as strategy in organizational communication. *Communication Monographs, 51,* 227–242. Reprinted with permission from the Speech Communication Association.

study of strategic ambiguity is in formal communication to external audiences, including public relations. He wrote:

> In Cell 3, formal external communication, the research focus should be on the *preservation of future options* and the *deniability of formal statements* to external audiences. Examples of communication of this type are *public relations campaigns*. . . . (p. 238, italics added)

Cheney (1991) also lauded the value of ambiguity when he wrote, "Organizations, as rhetors, exploit the resource of ambiguity to manage multiple interests and multiple identities" (p. 179). The difficulty with exploiting the resource of ambiguity, especially in the public arena, is that the organization is often perceived as being duplicitous with its stakeholders. This is especially true under the conditions Eisenberg (1984) referred to as "the deniability of formal statements to external audiences" (p. 238). Publicly denying a previous statement or stance is often perceived as being an outright deception rather than a strategic management of communication. Perhaps our world is too cynical to allow for genuine denial through ambiguity. In the world of professional sports, for example, the owner of a losing team who publicly announces support for his or her coach is often perceived by fans and sportswriters as having sealed that coach's demise, usually in a short period of time from the announcement.

Ambiguity functions as a double-edged sword for the organizational public relations function. On one hand, the practitioner might find him or herself creating communications that are intentionally ambiguous. In other instances, the practitioner might discover a strong need to reduce symbolic ambiguity, to clearly define a symbolic interpretation. Symbolic ambiguity is found in the space between intention and action. It is especially evident in the communication between organizational insiders and organizational outsiders, a theme to which we now turn.

DISCOURSE PERSPECTIVES OF INSIDERS AND OUTSIDERS

In chapter 4, we discussed the nature of organizational schemas, the ways in which organizational members organize their perceptions and assign meaning to events. We concluded that there are multiple organizational schematas at work often linked, however tenuously, to a shared organizational mission or vision, a grand schemata. In this section, I want to use the idea of schematas in reference to the ways in which organizational insiders and outsiders perceive one another.

Dunbar and Ahlstrom (1995) suggested that insiders are bounded (and perhaps blinded) by the organizational culture in which they work, particularly during those episodes of conflict with external stakeholders. Insider views

> tend to be pragmatic, reflecting the practices and activities that are pursued by their organization. What is meaningful is linked to the established ways of doing things in a particular organizational context and to the ideals to which the organization aspires. Within this institutionalized context, insiders monitor their performance, seek effective implementation, and select directions in which to make further investments. (p. 173)

We might say that insiders are limited in their ability to appreciate external views precisely because their organizational schemata so often result in "routine ways of doing things" (Dunbar & Ahlstrom, 1995, p. 173).

Outsider perspectives, on the other hand,

> are not bounded by organizational or professional affiliations, but rather they may reflect many different interests in the behavior of a target organization. Outsiders are mainly concerned about whether a target organization seems sensitive and responsive to their specific needs and broader social concerns . . . they seek to compare the target organization's outputs with those available from alternative sources. (p. 173)

Dunbar and Ahlstrom (1995) suggested that outsiders perceive the organization to be a "black box." Because outsiders are not privy to the decision-making systems in the organization, they can only judge the organization on the product or outcome of those decisions. We witnessed this focus on organizational outputs with both the Kid's Place Hospital and Seafirst Bank decisions in chapter 1. Outsiders are forced to assess the validity of the outputs by comparing them to the outputs of other organizations or some broader assessment criteria. Dunbar and Ahlstrom (1995) gave the example of the ways in which those outside the medical profession (e.g., legislators) attempt to assess the effectiveness of alternate treatments for the same condition by using cost effectiveness or the enhancement of quality of life. These two comparative measures are much broader and more difficult to ascertain with objective data than are medical measures grounded in research that compare the success rate of treatment A with that of treatment B. The research comparison is a technical comparison those inside the medical profession might use.

Based on the differences in insider and outsider perspectives, Dunbar and Ahlstrom (1995) proposed that "insiders and outsiders become committed to their knowledge bases, values, associated ways of understanding, and methods of evaluation" (p. 174). Given these schemata, they "approach one another in self-centered ways, making interpretations based on their own understandings rather than on an appreciation of the others' perspective" (p. 175). We saw prime examples of this self-centeredness in the case study presented in chapter 8 about the northwest spotted owl controversy.

This organizational self-centeredness is important to public relations practitioners because Dunbar and Ahlstrom (1995) also suggested that during times of conflict with external stakeholders, insiders "may decide an appropriate response to outsiders is *to work to neutralize, manipulate, or hold them off in whatever way they can* so the established ways of doing things can continue" (p. 175, italics added). This response is one in which organizational control of the issue is paramount. Communication with external stakeholders is designed to control the symbolic definition of the situation as well as aid the implementation of instrumental outcomes favored by the organization (Bettman & Weitz, 1983; Cheney & Vibbert, 1987).

In an interesting study of how internal organizational cognitions were communicated externally, Fiol (1995) compared how organizational issues were presented internally through documents such as planning memos and how those same issues were discussed externally in the letter to the shareholders in the organization's annual reports. Fiol (1995) assessed statements about similar issues or events culled from internal and external documents based on attributions of positive or negative evaluation (i.e., the issue or event is perceived as being good or bad for the corporation) and perceptions of organizational control (i.e., the degree to which the organization's managers felt they controlled the organization's response). She concluded that internal and external statements are consistent only when "internal documents reflected high levels of communicators' perceived internal control over events without an accompanying evaluation of those events as either positive or negative" (p. 533). When managers made some type of evaluative assessment (positive or negative) in their internal documents, external documents appear not to reflect those attributions. Fiol (1995) concluded that, "insiders' frames seem to differ from those communicated to outsiders" (p. 524), especially when they have internally made an evaluative assessment of an event or information. Other research supports Fiol's (1995) conclusions regarding the primary importance of perceptions of control for organizational insiders (Thomas, Clark, & Gioia, 1993).

Keeping in mind the broadly divergent perspectives of insiders and outsiders, and, most importantly for the public relations function, the discrepancies noted by Fiol (1995) in insider communications to outsiders, we turn now to an examination of the instrumental and symbolic results of organizational decision making.

INSTRUMENTAL AND SYMBOLIC DECISION-MAKING OUTCOMES

It has become increasingly evident to speak of organizational decision making as being both instrumental and symbolic (cf, Dutton, Fahey, & Narayanan, 1983; Meindl, 1985; Pfeffer, 1981a). The instrumental or substantive function of decision making refers to the technical work accomplished, the objectively identified choice between alternatives that results in a course of action. Pfeffer (1981a) suggested that substantive dimensions, "profits, sales, profit margins, capital budgets and other allocations . . . are all tangible, real outcomes of organizational activities" (p. 5). The cuts in faculty, staff, and administration that ABC University made after the available money from tuition declined by 20% are examples of instrumental decisions (see Case Study 5.2). These are decisions generally made in the realm of the resource-dependency model of organizational environments.

Instrumental actions are thought to be grounded in a rational approach to organizational decision making based on the identification of an objective reality. That is, a problem is identified, information gathered, alternative options identified and assessed, a decision made, and the results implemented. By objective reality I mean that rational models of decision-making approach environments as real, knowable, factual, and true places where information can be gathered and used in an unbiased manner. The decision to build the helipad in the Kid's Place Hospital presented in the chapter 1 was, on one level, an instrumental decision. The decision incorporated data or information that was translated into a cause of action that ultimately resulted in a tangible concrete landing pad.

This Kid's Place decision also resulted in a symbolic or expressive dimension of organizational decision making that can not be ignored. The process by which the decision was made resulted in multiple interpretations or meanings attached by various stakeholders. Several stakeholders, for example, interpreted the decision as another instance of the arrogance associated with the growing hospital. Other groups, most notably those inside the hospital, attached meanings grounded in saving children's lives. The symbolic aspects of organizational decisions involve the meanings and interpretations attached to the process or products of the decisions. Pfeffer (1981b) suggested that those interested in analyzing organizations must proceed on two levels:

> One level involves the prediction of actions taken within the organization, such as decisions that have observable, substantive outcomes. The second level involves the perception, interpretation, and sentiments which surround these organizational choices. (pp. 183–184)

The analysis of only instrumental decision making often fails to account for the intriguing complexity inherent in many symbolic and expressive aspects of interpreting organizational actions.

This seems to be particularly true if we think about organizational decision making from the perspectives of insiders and outsiders offered by Dunbar and Ahlstrom (1995). Given their bounded perspective on pragmatics and process, insiders make instrumental decisions that they then evaluate using standardized organizational or industry assessment measures (e.g., return on investment). Insider interpretations are, by force of organizational perspective, bounded. This is not always the case for outsider interpretations of the insiders' instrumental decisions. Outsiders are as likely to key in on the symbolic nature of the decisions as they are on the instrumental aspects. Their outlook is not bounded by the organization, is often broader in perspective (or, at the very least, different), and is concerned with issues of equity and fairness. Outsider assessments are much more likely to be emotionally laden responses to symbolic interpretations than to the instrumental decision-making process itself. The selling of the Henry Moore artwork, discussed in chapter 1, for example, quickly went beyond the simple decision of the corporate insiders to one grounded in the organization's symbolic responsibility to the city's aesthetic enhancement for the enjoyment of all.

In their discussion of organizational strategic information management (SIM) systems, Dutton and Ottensmeyer (1987) elaborated on the distinctions between instrumental and symbolic functions in relation to the process and output of the issue management process. Dutton and Ottensmeyer (1987) defined, SIM *processes* as the ways in which organizational members search for and use information from the environment. SIM *outputs* are the results or products of the process. As they suggest, an instrumental focus on outputs results in the presumed generation of "accurate, complete, and efficient identification of strategic issues" (p. 359). An instrumental view often heightens the salience of particular issues in the organization, thereby insuring that the SIM process accords these issues' relevance or primacy. Recent calls for increased diversity in university student populations, for example, have most definitely raised the awareness of the issue in the university's admissions procedures.

At the same time, however, the SIM systems function at a symbolic level in that they allow for multiple interpretations of events and issues, seek consensual understandings among groups, and often control the organization's response to events through managed interpretations. According to Dutton and Ottensmeyer (1987), "the most important outputs of SIM systems are the labels given to strategic issues, not that actions taken to resolve them" (p. 360). The interpretive process, the management of the symbolic environment, is crucial for understanding and, indeed, implementing the instrumental decisions previously discussed. All decisions, then, incorporate to one degree or another, instrumental (technical) and symbolic (interpretive) dimensions available to those affected by the decisions.

These symbolic aspects of the organizational decision-making process (and product), the meanings generated by the organization and its stakeholders, are often the arena in which the organizational public relations function is supposed to most appropriately function. Long and Hazleton, Jr. (1987) spoke of the management of *symbolic resources*. Krippendorf and Eleey (1986) presented a model for monitoring an organization's *symbolic environment*. Unfortunately, for those in public relations, the linkages between the two—instrumental and symbolic—are often forgotten or ignored.

A recent article on two Democratic senators competing for the minority leader position after the 1994 midterm elections, emphasizes this distinction (Kramer, 1994). Kramer wrote that Senator Tom Daschle

> supports the [balanced budget] amendment, apparently with an eye to *public relations rather than policy.* "We Democrats have a perception problem," he argues. "The public thinks we're only about taxing and spending. Supporting the amendment says with an exclamation point that we're for fiscal discipline." (Kramer, 1994, p. 34, italics added)

Senator Daschel's comment is a prime example of the uneasy dilemma of separating substance from symbolism. All too often, the substance of an organizational decision is perceived to be decoupled from the symbolic "take" on the decision. Public relations often finds itself struggling to survive in this organizational tension, a tension created by the degree of coupling, or fit, between the instrumental and symbolic aspects of organizational decisions.

ORGANIZATIONAL COUPLING

Organizational coupling refers to the degree to which components of a system are linked to or with one another, the degree to which they are dependent on one another, or the degree to which one can be said to influence or control another. The strength of the coupling between the components of a system are generally described as being either tightly or loosely coupled. Tight coupling occurs when two components share many variables or directly and consistently impact one another. Loose coupling, as the term implies, is the opposite. Organizations are loosely coupled when their components share few critical variables or do not directly and consistently affect one another (Glassman, 1973; Perrow, 1984; Scott, 1981; Weick, 1979).

The concept of loose coupling came into extensive use after the publication of Karl Weick's (1976) article, "Educational Organizations as Loosely Coupled Systems." Weick's (1976) analysis of educational systems, especially of the control of teaching, highlights the notion of loose coupling. He suggests, for example, that although the curricular goals of a school district are established or defined by the district superintendent and the school board, there is very little direct supervision in individual classrooms that monitors how (or even if) the goals are operationalized through instruction. What the individual teacher does in his or her class, how he or she elects to teach a proscribed topic, is only loosely coupled with the school district's ability to control what happens in the classroom.

Meyer and Rowan (1992) argued that "educational work [instruction] takes place in the isolation of the classroom, removed from organizational controls of a substantive kind" (p. 73), a form of loose coupling. The attachment (coupling) between the teacher's daily task of teaching and the school district's control of curriculum is circumscribed, infrequent, weak in its mutual effects, generally unimportant, and generally slow to respond. A supposedly tightly coupled bureaucratic educational system is indeed only rather loosely coupled at least in terms of the delivery of instruction.

Weick (1982) acknowledged that,

> to talk about a loosely coupled system is not to talk about structural looseness, but about process looseness. *The image is that of a sequence of events that unfolds unevenly, discontinuously, sporadically, or unpredictably, if it unfolds at all.* (p. 381, italics added)

We begin to see loosely coupled relationships between components as more flexible, ambiguous, less time-dependent, less predictable, and perhaps not immediately understandable. Orton and Weick (1990) suggested that every organization "contains interdependent elements that vary in the number and strength of their interdependencies. . . . The resulting image is a system that is simultaneously open and closed, indeterminate and rational, spontaneous and deliberate" (pp. 204–205). Different situations, different configurations of organizational components, are variously loosely or tightly coupled, as is evident in the following case study.

CASE STUDY 2.1: SHOOTING WOLVES AND THE CRUISE SHIP INDUSTRY

In the fall of 1992, the Alaska State Game Board announced a wildlife control program designed to reduce the number of wolves. As outlined, the aerial wolf-hunting program would allow hunters to shoot wolves from airplanes or helicopters. Proponents of the proposal argued that the increasing wolf population was threatening the size of the caribou and moose herds. Reducing the wolf population, the Game Board argued, was one means of insuring healthy herds of caribou and moose. In the press release announcing the aerial wolf-hunting program, the Game Board cited increased populations of caribou and moose as tourist attractions as one of the reasons for implementing the plan.

Meanwhile, back in Seattle, Washington, the Holland America Line-Westours Incorporated staff went about business as usual, preparing for the 1993 cruises to Alaska. Holland America Line-Westour is the largest cruise tour company operating in the very profitable Alaska cruise ship industry. Passengers on these cruises see glaciers and snow covered mountains, not caribou or moose herds being chased down by hungry wolves.

Immediately after the announcement of the aerial wolf-hunting program, environmental and animal rights groups announced the start of a boycott of the Alaska tourism industry. These groups called on tourists to cancel their plans to travel to Alaska until the program was rescinded. The threats of a boycott made the papers, and suddenly, with the threat to the tourist industry, the aerial wolf-hunting program became a concern of the Holland America Line-Westours public relations director. Indeed, the company received 20–25 letters from passengers already booked on upcoming cruises stating their intentions not to go if the aerial hunting program went forward.

On December 15, 1992, Holland America Line-Westours put out a news release calling for the cancellation of the wolf-hunting program. A. K. Kirk Lanterman, President and CEO of Holland America Line-Westours said,

We believe the program should be cancelled immediately and alternative methods sought to control the wolf populations in the affected areas, if, indeed, research substantiates that their numbers need to be reduced at all. . . . We feel that the adverse impact on tourism far outweighs the alleged benefit to supporters of this policy and firmly believe it would be in the best interests of the state to cancel this program permanently. (p. 1)

As the director of public relations said, "the challenges that arise are usually not of your own making. There is the constant challenge of the unknown." Or, as we suggest, Holland America Line-Westours was the surprised recipient of the unintended consequences of someone else's decision.

The process by which the proposed killing of wolves in Alaska was eventually linked to the public relations department of a cruise company is one that is loosely coupled. Or, as Weick (1985) wrote, "much ambiguity occurs because there are events floating around that seem to bear no relation to one another" (p. 128). Certainly, that is the case with the relationship between Alaska's decision to shoot wolves from helicopters and cruise ships transporting tourists to see glaciers and perhaps whales. Cruise ship passengers do not see wolves or caribou and moose herds, at least not from the ships themselves. What is most intriguing for the public relations practitioner is the degree of coupling between the instrumental aspect of decision making and the symbolic results. In the wolf case, the cruise line's instrumental process of decision making was influenced by a loosely connected instrumental change in its environment leading to the need for a symbolic response

As discussed earlier, most definitions of public relations see the public relations practitioner as the manager of the symbolic environment. "The symbolic and instrumental aspects of organizational activity are clearly linked, but at the same time it is likely that the coupling between them is loose" (Pfeffer, 1981a, p. 6). In other words, the "explanation for a decision and the decision itself may be very loosely linked" (Jongbloed & Frost, 1985, p. 104). It would appear that the symbolic response of the cruise company (the news release calling for cancellation) is tightly coupled to the cruise line's mission in that it symbolically links the instrumental decision to call for stopping the program with the adverse impact on tourism.

Pfeffer (1981b) based his argument about the relative loose coupling of instrumental and symbolic decision making on his understanding of the external constraints on managers of organizations and their ability to internally manage meanings through symbols. He suggests that instrumental outcomes are tightly coupled with factors that are external to the organization (e.g., availability of resources) and loosely coupled to managerial control of symbolic action. Conversely, Pfeffer (1981b) suggested that management control derived from symbolic management is only loosely coupled to external events and tightly coupled to internal organizational interpretations.

The difficulty, of course, is knowing what is happening when and what to do about it. Is the system more open or closed? Is the event one that can be dealt with deliberately and rationally or is it one that is more spontaneous and indeterminate? Which components of the organizational systems are affected? Are they more tightly or loosely coupled and what difference does that make anyway? All of these are intriguing questions that are subject to a variety of interpretations by the organization's members. Understanding systems coupling and accounting for its influence on organizational life occurs on a number of levels from individual to organizational. Coupling is also of key concern in determining the appropriate mode of communication to use in responding to various types of issues. It is to the idea of communication choice that we now turn.

INFORMATION AND MEDIA RICHNESS

A line of research has recently explored the ways in which managers select from a variety of available media to respond to the varieties of information situations they face (Daft & Lengel, 1984; Daft & Wiginton, 1979; Lengel, 1983; Rice, 1992; Schmitz & Fulk, 1991; Stork & Sapienza, 1992; Trevino, Lengel, & Daft, 1987; Valacich, Paranka, George, & Nunamaker, Jr., 1993). This research is based on the premise that organizations process information dealing with a range of simple and complex phenomenon using communication media. Simple phenomenon are those everyday events that are considered routine or predictable, ones that do not involve a great deal of creative information search or media use. They are ones for which organizations develop procedures (e.g., opening a checking account in a bank).

Complex phenomenon, on the other hand, are those events or issues that are "difficult, hard to analyze, perhaps emotion laden, and unpredictable" (Daft & Lengel, 1984, p. 199). Complex phenomenon, phenomenon that are often perceived as being quite ambiguous in nature, require different information search procedures than those associated with simple phenomenon. Although there may be organizational protocols that help individuals deal with complex phenomenon (e.g., crisis management plans), the very complexity of the event indicates that each information search and decision sequence will result in different conclusions and actions.

Daft and Lengel (1984) persuasively argued that "organizational success is based on the organization's ability to process information of appropriate richness to reduce uncertainty and clarify ambiguity" (pp. 194–195). Daft and Wiginton (1979) suggested that human communication media, or languages, can be classified on a continuum that ranges from high to low variety. Variety refers to the degree to which alternate interpretations or meanings can be assigned a symbol. Low variety communication media, such as statistics, convey reasonably exact and specific meanings. High variety languages, such as art and music, are extraordinarily subjective in the ways they can be experienced and interpreted. Human language—speech and nonverbals—falls somewhere in between art and statistics in the range of variety. Daft and Wiginton (1979) proposed that low variety languages or mediums are appropriate for communicating about relatively simple and straightforward phenomenon and high variety languages are appropriate for communicating about complex problems and phenomenon.

Daft and Wiginton's (1979) work led Lengel (1983) to propose the concept of information richness, defined as "the potential information-carrying capacity of data" (Daft & Lengel, 1984, p. 196). The richness of the information processed by the organization is determined in large part by the communication media used to gather and process that information. Interpersonal face-to-face communication, for example, is the most information-rich, whereas computer generated numeric data is the least information-rich. Speaking over the telephone would be somewhat less rich than speaking face-to-face in that the participants have less information (i.e., facial expressions) to draw on.

The concept of information richness and media choice relates to both instrumental and symbolic forms of decision making. Stryker and Statham (1985) proposed a distinction that is useful in clarifying the degree of agreement about the meaning of data or information. Building on an understanding of low and high variety, Stryker and Statham (1985) suggested that we need to be cognizant of two types of symbol use in organizations: Symbol *communication* behavior and symbol *creation* behavior. The distinction between the two lies in the agreed-on meanings attached to the symbols being used. During times of symbol communication behavior, managers communicate with symbols whose meaning is agreed on and shared. In most universities, for example, the credit hour is a symbol with which we communicate. The meaning of a credit hour is shared and agreed on. Indeed, departmental effectiveness is often measured in the number of credit hours produced.

Symbolic creation behavior, on the other hand, involves situations in which organizational members must negotiate and create shared meanings about their interpretations or symbols. Symbol creation behavior occurs (or should occur) during times when managers must deal with complex situations, when ambiguity is rife, when uncertainty exists about a course of action, and when emotions are brought into play.

It is possible to use the example of symbol communication behavior—credit hours—to extrapolate a condition requiring symbol creation. Although there is agreement about the meaning of a credit hour, there is generally not nearly as much agreement on the appropriate cost of generating those credit hours. If we take a university department's annual budget and divide that figure by the number of credit hours produced in that department, we arrive at a unit we can call the cost per credit hour generated. This cost varies widely across departments on the university. The cost of generating a nursing credit hour, for example, might be more than $300, whereas the psychology department generates their credit hours for only $80. The meanings attached to the cost per credit hour symbol will not be as easily agreed on by the various groups in university as, say, the cost charged each student per credit hour. The meaning attached to this symbol must be negotiated.

Taking these various ideas into account, Daft and Lengel (1984) proposed that the organization has a "domain of effective information processing" dependent on matching the complexity of organizational phenomena with information richness as shown in Fig. 10.2.

If the phenomenon is relatively simple, then we want to process it using communication media that are relatively low in information richness. This is the realm of Stryker and Statham's (1985) symbol communication behavior. If, on the other hand, the phenomenon is high in complexity then the organization is best served by using a medium that accentuates the richness of information. This is the area of negotiation of meaning captured in Stryker and Statham's (1985) communication creation behavior. Daft and Lengel (1984) suggested that to use a media high in information richness on a simple phenomenon overcomplicates the issue and is time consuming and costly (e.g.,

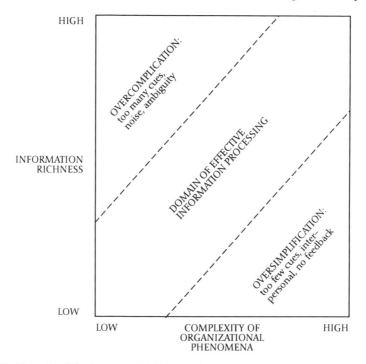

FIG. 10.2.   Model of managerial information processing. From Daft, R. L., & Lengel, R. H. (1984). Information richness: A new approach to managerial behavior and organization design. In B. M. Staw & L. L. Cummings (Eds.), *Research in organizational behavior* (pp. 191–233). JAI Press. Reprinted with permission.

a task force meeting for a simple phenomenon). Using a medium low in information richness on a complex phenomenon will result in over-simplification of the issue, perhaps to the organization's detriment.

SUMMARY

At the end of their article, Daft and Lengel (1984) suggested six directions for future research, all of them applicable to the public relations function: (a) media selection and usage, (b) boundary spanning, (c) interpretation of external events, (d) interdepartmental coordination, (e) equivocality (uncertainty) reduction, and (f) symbolic values attached to media usage.

Interestingly, some of these fall under the communication technician role of the public relations function (e.g., media selection) and others under the communication management role (e.g., interpretation of external events). A useful distinction we might want to observe in discussing the technical and managerial roles of public relations has to do with the distinctions between symbol communication and symbol creation behaviors. Communication technicians most often operate in the realm of symbol communication behaviors. Communication managers are more likely to engage in symbol creation behaviors, especially ones involving external stakeholders during times of uncertainty.

During times of organization–stakeholder interaction, especially that which is conflict-laden, organizations might be better served with a communication medium that allows for rich information exchange. This is true from both instrumental and symbolic perspectives. Daft and Lengel (1984) suggested that, all things being equal, the more information processed during times of complex decision-making incidents, the better the decision that is eventually made. Organizational decision makers need to incorporate a broader view into their instrumental decision making than that afforded by their truncated insider perspective. At the same time, seeking a communication medium that enhances richness symbolizes a willingness to listen to and perhaps engage in dialog with the external stakeholder group. As Pearson (1989b), in a discussion of the conversation metaphor, suggested:

> To promote interaction that is more like dialogue, practitioners might prefer specialized publications with fast feedback loops along with mediating structures or small, "in-between" organizations, membership in which is equally available to representatives of organizations and publics. (p. 83)

Such formats provide the vehicle for the generation of richer information and, hopefully, better informed decisions. They should also promote tighter coupling between the organization's instrumental decision and the symbolic meaning attached to that decision by external groups monitoring the organization's actions from an outsider perspective.

These ideas come together in a case study presented and analyzed in chapter 11.

Practitioner Response to Chapter 10: Embracing Ambiguity

Pamela Katims Steele, PhD
Director of Communication
Northshore School District
Bothell, Washington

By training, I am an educational psychologist. I was taught to listen, help people understand their own and another's perspective, and help them unravel semantic entanglements. I helped people understand the choices they were making and the consequences they were likely to experience. I helped people look at situations from another's viewpoint, put themselves in another's shoes, and figure out ways to communicate so the recipient could/would hear the intended message. These skills have been an asset to me in my work in three very different industries: education, financial services, and the media.

Much of what I perceive as basic communications and public relations skills seems like commonsense, simple logic. External audiences do not have the benefit of the internal knowledge. They ask questions that often seem basic to an insider. They do not understand the language that insiders take for granted. The result is a need for translation. But the translation is lost if there is not a clear definition of what needs to be communicated in the first place.

Managing ambiguity is really another way of talking about managing change. During times of change, everything is in flux; ambiguity reigns. It is the overriding characteristic of the 21st century, in both the public and the private sector. Global economy, fast-paced technological changes, downsizing, rightsizing, the era of public engagement: all of this symbolizes change.

Public relations efforts are very different in the private and the public sector. In the private sector, shareholders share some agreement regarding performance standards and evaluation criteria. Communications with this audience, therefore, tend to be objective. In the public sector, there is no differentiation between stakeholders—investors in the system—and customers of the system. Performance standards and measurements are more subjective and individualized. Issues are often emotionally charged and that heightened sense of emotional urgency needs to be anticipated and addressed in any communication.

PUBLIC SECTOR ENGAGEMENT IS EVOLVING

I am currently working in the public sector as the director of communications in a large school district. The multitude and diversity of customer demands on the school board, administration, and staff is amplified by the emotional investment of people expressing their concern about their child's education. In this era of education reform and increasing public engagement, every stakeholder feels he or she has a right not only to be involved, but also to dictate how a child should be educated. The rules are changing. The old ones do not work and the new ones are just being written. It is a time of great uncertainty. Although school districts recognize the inherent value of both shared decision making and the incorporation of the outsider's perspective as well as the importance of involving the community in the educational process, many of the "old time" educators are resistant.

STANDARDIZED TESTING—AN EXAMPLE

We currently have a number of parents concerned about standardized testing in the district. Who takes various tests? Who does not? Who decides on the exceptions? Whose results are included in the overall district scores? This topic is not only complex and filled with technical issues, but also emotionally charged and ambiguous. Given the number of people expressing concern, the school board decided to hold a public forum on this topic. The administrator in charge of testing and evaluation created an agenda that scripted presentations by numerous staff involved in testing and special education. The public's role was primarily to sit and listen to the district's answers to what they believed were the publics' questions.

I suggested a different approach. Knowing that it is important for parents to feel they have been heard, and that the district has responded to their concerns, I created a questionnaire to solicit their input. What would you like to accomplish in this forum? What specific questions do you have? What are your concerns? On the night of the forum, we will review this list together and allow time for any additions. The district will also have the opportunity to list informational items it believes should be reviewed. Now, an agenda can be developed cooperatively. This approach will enable appropriate district personnel to respond to real questions posed by the audience instead of assuming they *know* what the audience wants to know. There will be room for spontaneity and openness. The district will not look as if it is trying to control the forum. Hopefully, everyone will walk away better-informed, feeling acknowledged and respected. Approaching the forum in this manner requires a willingness to change, and a willingness on the part of the presenters to take some risks.

As public engagement becomes the norm rather than the exception in school districts, stakeholders will accept less and less strategic ambiguity. They will demand clear messages that really help them understand issues that are often complex and emotionally charged. As professionals working in this arena, we must remain flexible in our approach and recognize that there is no *one* formula for success. Public relations is both an art and a science. Much of the activity relates to understanding shifting issues and perspectives, and finding the balanced approach needed to manage ambiguity.

CHAPTER 11

Toward a Collaborative Advocacy Frame

The press must "create that atmosphere of moderation and courtesy in which advocates of contrary views and interests are most likely to listen as well as talk to each other."
—Archibald MacLeish (Bates, 1995)

Many contemporary critics of the media find the sentiments expressed by poet MacLeish in the 1940s to be an ideal that has long since passed us by. Indeed, the first of Sproule's (1988) distinctions between the old rhetoric and the new rhetoric is that the new rhetoric provides people with prepackaged conclusions that *eliminates* the necessity to either listen to or talk with one another. And, to speak of civility in argument seems a quaint nod of the head to social conventions long since vanished as we endured for another presidential election, replete with its barrage of negative advertising.

The case study about Common Ground presented in chapter 9, however, serves as a vivid reminder that the advocates of contrary views can come together and listen as intently as they often only talk. That members of the two opposing sides in our most emotionally charged national debate can find a forum in which to heed the other— to engage in a truly integrative dialogue—is evidence for cautious optimism. That the process of coming together began with an editorial piece published in a newspaper even affirms the sentimentally idealistic role of the press espoused by MacLeish.

What I seek to accomplish in this chapter is to identify some of the ways that the concepts discussed in chapter 10 (i.e., insider/outsider perspectives, symbolic communication behavior and symbolic creation behavior, media richness) help move us toward a more dialectic view of the modern organizational public relations function. At the very beginning of this quest, I will tip my hand and admit that I am arguing for a change in the way that organizational public relations is perceived and implemented, a change in the way that we frame organizational public relations. I am arguing (and I am certainly not the first) for a reframing of the organizational public relations function into one that emanates largely from a communication ombudsman perspective. The concepts from the previous chapter help guide us in the direction of creating a forum for *collaborative advocacy*.

This chapter (a) examines the concern for self and concern for other dichotomy by which conflicts are often framed, (b) examines approaches to stakeholder management that focus on alternative perspectives of concern for self and other, (c) analyzes a case study of organization–stakeholder interaction using the concepts from this chapter and those addressed in chapter 10, and (d) suggests a series of questions organizational public relations managers should begin to address when dealing with organizational–stakeholder conflicts.

WAYS OF CONFLICT

In a commentary on an article about communication altruism in the organization (Browning & Henderson, 1989), Boulding (1989) referred to three interdependent systems from which power is exercised in our society: threat, production and exchange, and integrative. The *threat system* is one in which power is accomplished through coercion in its many guises, often including asymmetrical one-way persuasive communication exchanges. The *production and exchange system* speaks to the economic system, of which public relations is certainly a part. And, finally, the *integrative system* "deals with such matters as respect, legitimacy, community, friendship, affection, love, and of course their opposites, across a broad scale of human relationships and interactions" (Boulding, 1989, pp. 670–671). In the next sentence, Boulding (1989) added:

> in the long run the integrative system is the most dominant of the three . . . without some form of legitimacy, threat is ineffective . . . without legitimacy and some sort of community acceptance, exchange is extremely difficult. And complex communities are impossible without trust and a widespread sense of "belonginness." (p. 671)

It is to the creation of trust and a sense of belonging between organizations and their constituent stakeholder groups that the public relations function as communication ombudsman must be grounded.

The concern for others' frame is certainly not new, especially in the conflict management literature. Conflict, as we have seen throughout this book, is endemic to organizations and organizational life. To again quote Pearson (1989b), "public relations practice is situated at precisely that point where competing interests collide" (p. 67). This collision results in the necessity for organizational responses, responses grounded on a continuum with adversarial advocacy anchoring one end and collaboration advocacy the other.

Competing interests also lead to political theories of organizations as discussed in previous chapters on politics and power. Indeed, organizational politics is defined "as activities undertaken by individuals and groups to obtain desired outcomes in situations where there is disagreement about appropriate choices or conflict (Huff, 1988, p. 80). Conflict occurs when interdependent parties seek incompatible goals. The interdependence necessary for conflict situations has led to a dialectic view of conflict that reinforces the tensions between cooperation and competition (Kolb & Putnam, 1992; Mason & Mitroff, 1981). In other words, we cannot compete with someone unless they are willing to cooperate in the competition. The tensions that arise from this dialectic understanding lead to the notion that I call collaborative advocacy. As I show, it is quite possible to advocate an organizational position while collaborating with external stakeholders.

Recent research on conflict management in a variety of social arenas sheds light on the dialectic between advocacy and collaboration. In their review of negotiation literature, Carnevale and Pruitt (1992) suggested that negotiators come to conflict situations with one of two orientations: individualistic or dual-concern. Those with an individualistic orientation, one based on a high self-interest to the virtual exclusion of others, most often results in contentious behavior, leading to slower concessions and a lack of problem solving. A dual-concern model, one that incorporates concern for the other party's outcomes, results in greater problem solving and satisfaction.

The polarity between concern for self and concern for other is a critical conceptualization in the conflict management and negotiation literature. Thomas (1976, 1977) made use of the polarity in his model of conflict management strategies. Thomas identified five types of strategies used in conflict situations: avoidance, accommodation, competition, compromise, and collaboration (Thomas, 1976, 1977). These strategies are based on an assessment of the organization's desire to satisfy the needs of others as opposed to the organization's desire to satisfy its own needs. Two other dimensions, the degree of cooperation desired and the degree of assertiveness with which the organization pursues its objectives, are included as shown in Fig. 11.1.

Using the five strategies or modes available to conflicting parties, Thomas and Kilman (1975) created a self-assessment instrument for individuals to assess their predominant conflict management modes. In order to briefly describe communication strategies associated with each of the five strategies I selectively quote from their scale.

Avoiding strategies are those in which the actor withdraws from the conflict situation, a strategy captured in the items, "There are times when I let others take responsibility for solving the problem" or "I sometimes avoid taking positions that would create controversy." *Accommodating* strategies are used by those who put the other's concerns ahead of their own, as evidenced in statements like, "I sometimes sacrifice my own wishes for the wishes of the other person," and "If the other person's position seems very important to him, I would try to meet his wishes."

A *compromising* strategy "appears to be a cornerstone of American pragmatism, which emphasizes practicality, realism, workability, expediency, and the search for satisfactory solutions rather than optimal ones" (Thomas, 1977, p. 486). This strategy is evident in statements such as, "I try to find a position that is intermediate between his and mine" and "I will let him have some of his positions if he lets me have some of mine."

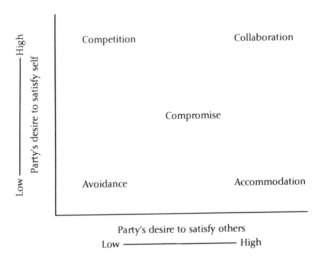

FIG. 11.1.   Orientations to conflict continuum. From Thomas, K. (1976). Conflict and conflict management. In M. Dunnette (Eds.), *Handbook of industrial and organizational psychology* (pp. 889–935). Reprinted with permission of Professor Marvin Dunnette.

Competing strategies are grounded in Boulding's (1989) system of threat, they are designed to coerce the other. On the Thomas and Kilman (1975) instrument, they are verbalized in strategies such as, "I press to get my points made" and "I assert my wishes." And, lastly, collaborating strategies, those often subsumed under the general rubric of problem solving, are evidenced in statements like, "I consistently seek the other's help in working out a solution" and "I attempt to get all concerns and issues immediately out in the open."

One of the reasons I like Thomas's work (1976, 1977) and the scale Thomas and Killman (1975) created is that they do not advocate one conflict management mode as being more appropriate than any of the others as a normative absolute. Instead, they suggest that each of us has a tendency to employ a particular mode (or two) more often than not. More important in translating this interpersonal concept into the realm of organizational/stakeholder exchange, is their admonition that under differing circumstances, a particular style might be better suited than another.

Thomas (1977) interviewed chief executive officers (CEOs) to determine the conditions or situation in which a particular conflict mode was considered appropriate. His findings are included in Table 11.1. The CEOs said that they used collaboration "to find an integrative solution when both sets of concerns are too important to be compromised," "when your objective is to learn," "to merge insights from people with different perspectives," and "to gain commitment by incorporating concerns into a consensus." The situations so described are ones arising from Boulding's (1989) integrative system as a source of power, in this case, collaborative and sharing power. It is instructive, I think, that the CEOs Thomas interviewed do not suggest that one need abandon advocacy when operating in a collaborative framework.

Although there are times when a self-focus (competing mode) is appropriate, one difficulty of an individual or single-concern orientation is that those negotiating from such a framework attach relatively more importance to prospective losses than to prospective gains (Ross & Stillinger, 1991). The negotiation process is conducted to protect against such losses to the eventual disregard to any potential mutually beneficial gain. Ross and Stillinger (1991) suggested that such a loss-aversion mentality leads to suspicion and eventual enmity between parties, enmity between the organization and its stakeholders. Collaborative advocacy is a framework based largely on the search for as-of-yet unknown gains for negotiating both the organization's and the stakeholder's concerns.

TABLE 11.1
Examples of Conflict Modes Used by CEOs

Conflict Mode	Situation	Conflict Mode	Situation
Competing		*Avoiding*	

Competing
1. When quick, decisive action is vital—e.g., emergencies.
2. On important issues where unpopular actions need implementing—e.g., cost cutting, enforcing unpopular rules, discipline.
3. On issues vital to company welfare when you know you're right.
4. Against people who take advantage of non-competitive behavior.

Collaborating
1. To find an integrative solution when both sets of concerns are too important to be compromised.
2. When your objective is to learn.
3. To merge insights from people with different perspectives.
4. To gain commitment by incorporating concerns into a consensus.
5. To work through feelings which have interfered with a relationship.

Compromising
1. When goals are important, but not worth the effort or potential disruption of more assertive modes.
2. When opponents with equal power are committed to mutually exclusive goals.
3. To achieve temporary settlements to complex issues.
4. To arrive at expedient solutions under time pressure.
5. As a backup when collaboration or competition is unsuccessful.

Avoiding
1. When an issue is trivial, or more important issues are pressing.
2. When you perceive no chance of satisfying your concerns.
3. When potential disruption outweighs the benefits of resolution.
4. To let people cool down and regain perspective.
5. When gathering information supercedes immediate decision.
6. When others can resolve the conflict ore effectively.
7. When issues seem tangential or symptomatic of other issues.

Accommodating
1. When you find you are wrong—to allow a better position to be heard, to learn, and to show your reasonableness.
2. When issues are more important to others than yourself—to satisfy others and maintain cooperation.
3. To build social credits for later issues.
4. To minimize loss when you are outmatched and losing.
5. When harmony and stability are especially important.
6. To allow subordinates to develop by learning from mistakes.

Note. Table taken from Thomas (1977). Reprinted with permission.

STAKEHOLDER MANAGEMENT SCHEMES

Organizational stakeholders are those individuals and groups (however conceived) who can affect organizational decisions and actions and/or who are affected by organizational decisions and actions. The stakeholder concept is grounded in the physical act of staking a claim, as gold miners staked their claims in the old west, marking the boundaries of their territory. The phrase, ''I have a stake in that,'' derives from the physical use of stakes to mark boundaries. This sense of stakeholder is grounded in Boulding's (1989) production and exchange system of influence, but one dependent on the integrative system in that all parties have to agree to recognize the legitimacy of another's markers, or stakes.

Not long ago, I watched as two men using stakes and string laid out the coordinates for the foundation of a house. The stakes they used were about 4 feet long. Whenever a stake was needed, one man held the piece of sharpened 2 × 2, while the other man hammered the wood 1 foot or so into the ground. The stakeholder in this case was exhibiting a great deal of trust in the aim of the man with the hammer. A blow from an 8-pound sledge would most definitely hurt even the most hardened stakeholder. This derivation of stakeholder shifts the symbolic meaning from asserting a claim to one of establishing a working relationship built on mutual trust, one definitely grounded in Boulding's integrative system.

A final definition of stakeholder is derived from a definition of stake as "a vertical post to which an offender is bound for execution by burning" (Morris, 1973, p. 1255). In this usage, the stakeholder would be the one who positions the stake and ties the intended offender to it thereby preparing the way for the execution. I think many executives, when faced with challenges from external stakeholders especially the media, probably have this vision of stakeholder in mind, consciously or not. This last usage is certainly grounded in Boulding's (1989) system of threat, a most definite coercion.

The characteristics of stakeholder groups are important determinants in deciding how to most beneficially engage the organizational public relations function. The characteristic most often discussed and used by organizational decision makers is an assessment of the stakeholder's potential power to influence the decisions of the organization. The assessment of potential stakeholder power often takes the form of identifying the degree to which the stakeholder group is hostile to or threatens the organization's will. It is usually based on an assessment of stakeholder power attributed to the organization's dependence on a stakeholder.

In chapter 7, we saw how certain stakeholder groups were more likely connected with the organization's instrumental environment as opposed to its technical environment (cf, Greening & Gray, 1994; Kreiner & Bhambri, 1991; Lauzen & Dozier, 1992). Given existing research, I suggested that these instrumental stakeholders have more direct ability to influence the decisions and actions of organizations than do stakeholder groups in the technical environment. In addition to having at least some minimal power to direct the organization's attention, instrumental stakeholders also have the power to confer symbolic legitimacy on the organization and its actions.

Although the focus of stakeholder analysis often rests on the identification of perceived or real threats, stakeholders also have the potential for cooperation with the organization. "Cooperation," as Savage et al. (1991) suggested, "should be equally emphasized since it allows stakeholder management to go beyond merely defensive or offensive strategies" (p. 63). Based on an analysis of potential threat (high to low) and potential cooperation (high to low), Savage et al. (1991) classified stakeholders into four types—supportive, marginal, nonsupportive, and mixed blessing. The four types and a master strategy for communicating with each are shown in Fig. 11.2.

Savage et al. (1991) suggested that the organization should involve *supportive* stakeholders in the decisions about relevant issues, particularly by "increasing the decision-making participation of these stakeholders" (p. 66). *Marginal* stakeholders need not be communicated with directly but they should be monitored to determine if their orientation toward the organization might change.

Organizations need to institute a defensive communication strategy when dealing with the nonsupportive stakeholder. Savage et al. (1991) noted that "for many large manufacturing organizations, typical non-

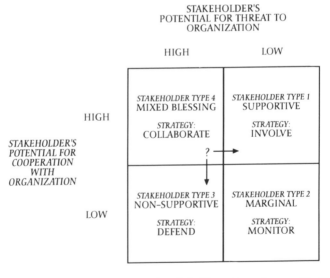

FIG. 11.2. Typology of organizational stakeholders. From Savage, G., Nix, T., Whitehead, C., & Blair, J. (1991). Strategies for assessing and managing organizational stakeholders. *Academy of Management Executives*, 5, 61–75. Reprinted with permission of Academy of Management Executives.

supportive stakeholders include competing organizations, employee unions, the federal government (and possibly local and state governments) and sometimes the news media'' (p. 66). It is instructive to note that using the guidelines set forth by Kreiner and Bhambri (1991), we can classify governments and employee unions as belonging to the institutional environment, competing organizations as quasi-institutional, and only the news media as technical.

Finally, Savage et al. (1991) recommended that the organization initiate a communicative strategy grounded in collaboration for the mixed blessing stakeholder. "Stakeholders of the mixed blessing type would include employees who are in short supply, clients or customers, and organizations with complementary products or services'' (Savage et al., 1991, p. 67). Again, using Kreiner and Bhambri's (1991) scheme we can classify employees, clients, and customers as belonging to the technical environment, and other organizations as being quasi-institutional. Quite clearly, Savage et al. (1991) anticipated the most communicative difficulty with institutional stakeholders as evident in their description of the nonsupportive stakeholder, those high in ability to threaten and low in potential for cooperation.

Daft and Lengel (1984) offered a framework for assessing the interdependence between an organization and its stakeholders as well as the degree of difference between them on any given issue as shown in Fig. 11.3. Daft and Lengel (1984) operated from the premise that organizational departments exchange information for two crucial reasons: "reducing equivocality and providing a sufficient amount of information for task performance'' (p. 214). Equivocality is akin to uncertainty as discussed in chapter 7. Cues, especially ones from external sources, are often equivocal in that they are not easily interpreted or might have ambiguous meanings. The organization needs to provide a means of reducing this equivocality in information in order to process and use the information. Situations high in difference require media high in richness to reduce the equivocality. Low-rich media are appropriate for situations in which there is little difference or equivocality.

Interdependence is equivalent to the degree of coupling discussed in chapter 10. High interdependence generally means that the stakeholder and organization are tightly coupled for at least some decisions or they are dependent on one another for at least some actions. Low interdependence, on the other hand, means that the organization and stakeholder share little on a particular issue or are only loosely coupled. Differences between stakeholders and organization are the result of differences in frames of reference about an issue, event, or decision process. When differences are great and interdependence is

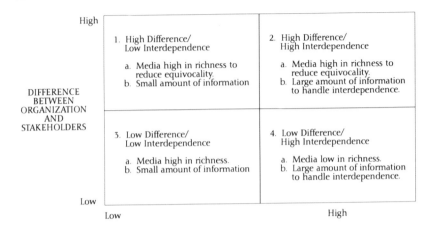

FIG. 11.3.   Difference and interdependence between the organization and the stakeholders. From Daft, R. L., & Lengel, R. H. (1984). Information richness: A new approach to managerial behavior and organization design. In B. M. Staw and L. L. Cummings (Eds.), *Research in organizational behavior* (pp. 191–233). Reprinted with permission of JAI Press.

high, members of the stakeholder group and the organization "must meet face-to-face, discuss their assumptions, goals, and needs, and develop a common language and framework with which to solve problems" (Daft & Lengel, 1984, p. 215).

Given that conflict is characterized by parties who are interdependent yet seek to pursue incompatible goals, situations described by Daft and Lengel (1984) as high interdependence and high difference are inherently conflict-laden. We can roughly equate the degree of interdependence to Savage et al.'s (1991) potential for cooperation between stakeholder and organization. As cooperation increases, as the units are more tightly connected, interdependence increases. Interdependence is enhanced, at least temporarily, by cooperation. We can likewise equate Daft and Lengel's (1984) degree of difference to Savage et al.'s potential for threat in that threat comes about because of differences in frames of references, differences in goals and assumptions.

The following case study illustrates the frustration and benefit of stakeholder inclusion in organizational decision making. The case example is based on my experiences with an urban school district's attempts to "manage" a particularly vocal stakeholder group, the parents of children in a program for gifted students.

CASE STUDY 11.1: EDUCATING THE HIGHLY CAPABLE
STUDENT

City School District (CSD) serves approximately 42,500 students from an increasingly varied ethnic population. As with most large public school districts, the CSD is a traditional bureaucratic behemoth. A seven member elected school board is supposed to guide policy, but all too often strays into the day-to-day operations of the district. The superintendent of schools is the titular head of the school district bureaucracy, aided by three assistant directors who are responsible for operations and any number of administrators centrally located in district headquarters. There are almost 90 schools in the district, so there are 90 principals, more than 2,000 teachers, and an untold number of parents. In addition, school officials must also deal with the teachers' union, staff union, parent/teacher organizations, a mayor with a publicly voiced commitment to education, various business leaders stirring the pot, and ethnic groups seeking to foster increased understanding of their heritages (21% of City's students come from families in which English, when spoken at all, is a second language). There are also state legislators from the City who recently funded a highly critical independent review of the school board/school district administration, parents of affluent children leaving for private schools or the suburbs, and increasing numbers of single-parent families. In short, a typical, highly politicized, revenue-strapped urban school district.

In this hodgepodge of organizational stakeholders are the supporters of a program for highly capable children known as the Horizon program. The Horizon program was originally put in place in the mid-1970s as a magnet program to help with City's voluntary desegregation plan. A handful of elementary schools scattered throughout the four subdivisions of the district were designated Horizon schools and maintained at least one classroom at each grade level for "gifted" children (by definition, those who scored in the top 5% on standardized achievement tests, were nominated by a teacher, and successfully completed an admissions procedure).

Although successful, both academically and as a magnet, there was a strong perception among parents of Horizon students and some Horizon teachers that the program never had much full-fledged support at the district level. Indeed, it has often been left to wither from benign neglect, if not outright administrative hostility. The benign neglect is structurally rooted in state mandates and bureaucratic reporting procedures. The state mandates and financially supports an Advanced Placement Program (APP) devoted to students who score in the top 1%-2% on standardized achievement tests. This program is located in a single school to which eligible students from around the district are bused. Bureaucratically, the Horizon program and the APP program are lumped together into one office. The director of this program, as well as the directors of 20 other programs (e.g., textbook adoption, library media, health services, special education), report to the assistant superintendent for curriculum and instructional support.

Much of the hostility stemmed from the fact that the vast majority of the Horizon students were White and from the northern, more economically affluent part of the city. Horizon programs in that area were bursting at the seams. One of the most persistent complaints from parents was that eligible students were waitlisted at what they considered their neighborhood school; there was as strong feeling that all eligible students should be provided a space at the nearest elementary school with a program. Horizon programs in schools located in the more economically strapped and minority-laden areas of the city had a more difficult time attracting the minimum number of students needed to maintain an effective program. Some of the less attractive schools combined grades (e.g., third and fourth) just to meet the minimum number of students necessary to warrant a teacher.

The historical administrative ambivalence came to a head in the fall of 1991 when a small group of parents of Horizon students perceived that the school district was going to discontinue the program in the 1992-1993 school year. Consequently, through the efforts of a few concerned and committed parents, 200 irate, articulate, and vocal parents supportive of the program met to discuss the situation and force the attention of the school district. The result of this initial agitation by a stakeholder group resulted in the formation of a district-sponsored task force composed of parents, teachers, and two district administrators. The charge given the task force by the superintendent was to recommend to the superintendent of the City Public Schools the most effective service delivery model for meeting the needs of highly capable children, within the context of district-wide restructuring and the unique nature of [City] as an urban school district. The organization, the City School District, sought input for internal decisions regarding program development from the constituent stakeholders.

Over the course of 2 years, members of the task force met almost weekly (sometimes even more frequently) and struggled with the issue of highly capable education. As the process unfolded, the task force also struggled with the City School District bureaucracy as well as the individual agendas of both task force members and school district administrators. The issue is complicated because many task force members and CSD administrators were not convinced that the 5%

benchmark on standardized tests was a sound means of determining giftedness. The members of the task force spent much of the first 6 months engaged in research about gifted education, compiling summaries of existing research as well as completing an interview-based research project of their own with principals and teachers in the district.

At the same time that the task force struggled with the necessity to create an appropriate and inclusive definition, the assignment of meaning, they also came head-to-head with a variety of administrators openly hostile to the very idea of a separate program for gifted education. Still another group of administrators was less overtly hostile but still ambivalent because resources given the Horizon program were ones they thought should be better used on other programs, programs they championed. Three major programs appeared to compete with the perceived need for a special program for the highly capable: (a) an early education model grounded in individualized student assessment and classroom instruction, whose proponents claimed achieved the needs of highly capable students in "regular" classrooms, thereby eliminating the need for separate classrooms for the gifted; (b) a budding move toward site-based management of individual schools by parents, teachers and community members, many of whom perceived the Horizon program to be elitist and one that should be available for all students, regardless of intellectual capability however defined; and (c) increasing efforts to mainstream disabled students into the classroom, supported by a very vocal stakeholder group as well as state and federal regulations. In addition, the district had just inaugurated, with much public fanfare, a strategic plan that did not have any specific reference to highly capable students.

The three programs identified in the previous paragraph were often called into play as a way of legitimizing administrative reluctance to accept a proposal from the task force. In response to the first draft of the program that was eventually accepted, an administrator (in charge of one of the other 20 programs reporting to the assistant superintendent for curriculum and instructional support) wrote:

> It seems to me that much of what is indicated in the recommendations is contrary to our stated belief in equity, pluralism, and inclusiveness. There seem to be many references to HCL's in terms of exclusivity. That is, their right to be separated from their age mates for a program that only meets their unique needs (personal communication).

Time and again, the task force faced opposition grounded in defense of already existing programs.

The members of the task force were often at odds with one another as

well as with administrators of the CSD. Some members wanted to see
the program stay as it was including separate classrooms for the highly
capable. Others sought to expand the definition of highly capable by
drawing on research outside the sphere of cognitive ability. Others had
a vested interest in making the program more ethnically diverse.
Tactically, some wanted to confront the administration, forcing its
hand in publicly announcing support for the program. Others wanted
to low-key the potential conflicts, seeking to work for areas of mutual
agreement. Meetings, especially those of the executive committee,
were often emotionally charged. Indeed, throughout the 2 years,
several members left the task force in disgust or frustration, returning
at a later date to take up the challenge.

After 2 years of work, the task force recommended a program to the
school district, a program that maintained much of the original
Horizon concept yet allowed for more variation from school to school.
This new program, Spectrum, was accepted by the district, eventually
presented to the school board, and implemented.

It seems fair to ask if this case represents a public relations dilemma.
Public relations is "a communication function of management through
which organizations adapt to, alter, or maintain their environment for
the purpose of achieving organizational goals" (Long and Hazleton Jr.,
1987, p. 6). At the start, the creation of the task force occurred in
response to stakeholder agitation, an unsettling force in the CSD
environment. The organization, the CSD, was forced to take action in
face of this agitation. Although there was disagreement as to the motive
behind the formation of the task force, the most positive view is that the
CSD seriously wanted input by which the school district could adapt to
demands from its environment. A more negative and Machiavellian
view held by some task force members regarded the formation as
nothing more than symbolic window dressing, designed to quiet
dissent in the long process of fact finding and analysis, thereby
maintaining the status quo if not altering the stakeholder group's felt
need to agitate. In the sense that this dilemma necessarily incorporated
communication between the organization and a stakeholder group,
communication that the CSD attempted to manage by creating a task
force, then, yes, it was a public relations dilemma.

Regardless of the initial motive for its formation, the task force
members formalized their group with bylaws approved by the CSD and
began to seriously gather and analyze data about highly capable
education, as well as the numerous other programs championed and
implemented by the school district. During this time period, numerous
CSD administrators spoke with the task force, ostensibly to provide
data or insight into the educational strategies and tactics of the school

district. By and large, these administrators adopted a competitive—some task force members would claim adversarial—approach. Several administrators were obviously upset by the creation of the task force as well as its charge to examine the delivery of education to a select group of students. This adversarial advocacy view led to a feeling among task force members that their eventual proposal would be severely challenged by certain administrators. This was most definitely stakeholder management through the implementation of competitive strategies as described by Savage et al. (1991).

One instance fairly well-along in the process is illustrative of the grounding of the school district's use of competitive strategies in Boulding's (1989) system of threat. One of the initial drafts of the Spectrum model eventually implemented was tentatively accepted by both the task force and the administrators charged with deciding the issue. This acceptance came only after several intense negotiating sessions between the parties. After reaching a collaborative agreement about the scope of the program, the deputy superintendent of schools released a report that significantly altered the location of the schools designated to be Spectrum schools. Indeed, her report eliminated one of the most heavily attended schools in the north end and moved the location to a central school, one that previously had only a token gifted program. This was viewed as a blatant threat, an attempt to "get even" with the majority of the parents on the task force whose children attended the school slated for elimination from the program. The intent of the change was met with skepticism and the threat that the entire process would disintegrate. Eventually, the matter was resolved, but only in the most tense of political negotiations.

Over time, as the task force rumbled and grumbled its way toward an educationally and politically acceptable proposal, a somewhat more collaborative frame was established. This came about primarily because the task force, seeking to gain support for highly capable education in a relatively hostile environment, expanded the scope of its original charge. The task force adopted a larger arena, one that allowed for the incorporation of numerous other programs, thereby alleviating fears of administrators and teachers. At best, it was a begrudging collaboration, a collaboration tinged with suspicion and continually in need of reassurance and renewal.

ANALYSIS

In analyzing this case, I use the concepts and ideas from chapter 10 as a starting point for examining several propositions about stakeholder communication choices. To that end I address briefly the

complexity of the issue.
insider/outsider frames of reference.
interdependence between organization and stakeholder.
symbolic communication behavior and creation.
instrumental and symbolic decision making.
stakeholder management strategies.

Each of these concepts helps better inform us about communication choices organizations should make regarding the richness of information and media necessary for interacting with particular stakeholder groups.

Complexity of the Issue

The issue of gifted or highly capable education is extremely complex. This conceptual complexity stems from vast differences on how to best define giftedness and how best to educate those children so designated. The issue is also organizationally complex for the City School District in that there were many voices with many perceptions, preconceived ideas, and emotional responses surrounding the issue. In this sense, the complexity of the issue demands rich information (Daft & Lengel, 1984). Highly complex phenomena can only be successfully managed with media that allow for high degrees of information richness.

Insider/Outsider Frames of Reference

Frames of reference about the issue of gifted education differed between the City School District insiders and the task force outsiders. Insider perceptions, especially those of key decision makers in the central administration, were bounded by the culture of the organization, which was described by many as being highly politicized, given to fiefdom-building by top administrators, often mistrustful of both staff as well as outsiders, and lacking in strong direction from the very top. The insiders' focus of interest was on organizational practices related to the maintenance of the presumed expertise of the administrative hierarchy.

Insider perspectives were also colored by a need to be perceived as demonstrating consistent CSD practice and ideals, primarily mainstreaming and moving away from separate classrooms for the gifted. An additional insider focus, an overriding concern with disproportionality in standardized achievement test scores between the ethnic groups in the school district, infused much of the district's decision making (and, as perceived by some task force members, led to far greater expenditure at the lower achieving levels of the district than the highly capable).

The most fundamental difference between the insider and outsider perspective was the personal (and subsequently highly emotional) view taken by the task force members, especially the parents of highly capable children. There were very few meetings over the course of 2 years in which a personal story was not shared with the group, a story that usually cast the school district in a negative light vis-à-vis the education of a particular child. The task force focus of interest was on organizational outputs (e.g., the child's education) rather than on current practices. The task force members were concerned with assessing the school district's ability to deliver an adequate educational program to the highly capable population.

The insider/outsider perspectives accentuated differences in frames of reference about what it meant to be highly capable as well as the use of limited resources available to the district. "Rich information is needed when information is processed to overcome different frames of reference" (Daft & Lengel, 1984, p. 215) between organization and stakeholder.

Organization–Stakeholder Interdependence

The district and the stakeholder groups were interdependent in that most of the members of the stakeholder group were parents extraordinarily interested in the outcomes of the district's decision-making process regarding highly capable education. Prior to the formal formation of the task force, the concerned parents were only loosely coupled with the district and with each other; the interactions between the two groups were sporadic, relatively negligible, and indirect. After the formalization of the task force, the interdependence between the stakeholder group and the organization was vastly increased, primarily because the group was accorded at least a symbolic semblance of legitimacy. The members of the task force were dependent on the school district for information resources, monetary resources, personnel, access to administrators, access to principals and teachers, and, ultimately, for approval or acceptance of the proposal. Interdependence, the "relationship between interdepartmental [stakeholder and organization] characteristics and coordination devices" (Daft & Lengel, 1984, p. 216) was high.

Using the framework proposed by Daft and Lengel (1984) shown in Fig. 11.3, the situation described in this case falls in Cell 2, high difference and high interdependence. This cell most particularly calls for the use of communication media that help create and sustain rich information to reduce the equivocality existing between insider and outsider frames of reference.

Symbolic Communication Versus Symbolic Creation Behaviors

The district, given its relatively parochial, insider view of the issue as well as its historically closed process of decision making, attempted to use symbolic communication behavior when communicating with the task force members. The insider, expert view, one grounded in the belief crudely summarized as "we're the experts, we know what's best," resulted in a great amount of symbolic communication behavior. In this sense, the district administrators attempted to define the issue using their terms and perceptions, communicating with symbols the meanings of which they ascribed (e.g., the formula by which a student was deemed eligible for the Horizon program). The very use of current educational jargon (e.g., heterogeneous grouping, outcome-based education, whole language, integrated curriculum, affective education) added to the symbolic communication behavior of the majority of the City School District administrators.

The task force members, on the other hand, although often given to their own insider view (the insider view of those on the outside), relatively early in the process adopted a symbolic creation behavior approach. The members of the task force, again particularly those on the executive committee, searched for symbolic meanings that expanded the range or definition of highly capable. In the process of this symbolic creation negotiation, new meanings were created and incorporated into the decision-making process. Interestingly enough, this caused severe strains in the task force membership, in that the internal negotiation led to a more inclusive definition of giftedness, one not solely based on cognitive ability. Given the distinctions made by Stryker and Statham (1985), the district administrators attempted to use a less information-rich style by using symbols about whose definition they agreed and sought to impose on the task force discussions. In response to the district's lack of responsiveness or willingness to recreate meanings, the members of the task force were forced to seek out rich information in their attempt to create new meanings.

Loosely Coupled Meanings

I characterize the situation described in the case study as being both tightly and loosely coupled. In that parents perceived the actions of the school district to be directly related to their child's education, the structure was perceived as being tightly coupled. At the same time, however, there was only the loosest of coupling between the symbolic and instrumental decision-making frames, especially as perceived by the task force members (Pfeffer, 1981a). The superintendent created the task force and charged it with its advisory mission. The superintendent was viewed, fairly or not, as being unfriendly toward highly capable education in general and the Horizon program in particular. Indeed, task force members reported that he was responsible for dismantling a similar program for gifted education in the school district he had previous led.

There was great uneasiness between the instrumental and symbolic coupling. This led to increased lack of trust in the administration on the part of numerous task force members. The motives of administrators, except the two directly attached to the task force who were perceived as good guys, were continually questioned. Comments such as "there is nothing to be trusted about the school district" and "we need to see this in writing" (referring to a school district proposal) are indicative of much of the tone of the task force participants, even those most committed to a collaborative model. Part of this dilemma in coupling is attributable to the school district's use of symbolic communication behavior rather than symbolic creation behavior.

Stakeholder Management Strategies

Using the Savage et al. (1991) schema of threat and opportunity, the highly capable task force began as the mixed blessing. The task force group, although having little power other than that ceded to it by the school district as an advisory board, did have the power to threaten the school district. Indeed, more than once, members of the task force (by and large highly educated and motivated) talked of actions more radical than simply creating an advisory plan of action (e.g., threatening legal action against the school district). At the same time, although many of the members of the task force were skeptical of the true meaning behind the district's creation of the task force, most were willing to at least give the district a chance to meet the needs of the highly capable students. There was an opportunity for collaboration, an opportunity that was greatly enhanced with the appointment of the second director of highly capable programs. Savage et al. (1991) suggested a management strategy geared toward collaboration with the mixed blessing stakeholder.

In summary, the situation presented by the City School District case study is one that demanded the use of communication media high in richness to allow for the collaborative advocacy interaction between stakeholder and organization. The process was painful, emotionally charged, extremely time-consuming, highly political, fraught with misunderstandings, physically demanding, and instrumentally symbolic. The 2 years of stakeholder–organization interaction resulted in a program that is successfully implemented. I was at a small party not long ago and overheard one man tell another how happy he and his wife were with the Spectrum program in which their son was enrolled at his neighborhood school. Perhaps a small token of success but an indicator nonetheless.

SUMMARY

The case study analysis leads me to propose several questions useful for public relations practitioners to pose as they enter into interactions with stakeholder groups. Certainly, the questions Savage et al. (1991) proposed are useful in determining a general sense of the stakeholder's position vis-a-vis the organization. Others of importance include:

1. How complex is the issue? Do those inside the organization define it differently than those outside the organization? How are the differences articulated? The more complex and the greater the difference, the more need there is for rich media.
2. To what degree are the stakeholder and organization interdependent? Is the stakeholder group located in the organization's institutional environment or technical environment? The greater the degree of interdependence (often found with institutional stakeholders), the more need there is for media high in richness.
3. Do all groups involved understand the symbols used during interactions? Are meanings relatively shared? The more the stakeholder and organization share meanings for symbols the more appropriate is a less rich form of communication (e.g., written brochure).
4. What characteristics of the insider frame preclude consideration of a collaborative advocacy approach to solving the dilemma?
5. Can the emotional stakes inherent in the issue be accurately assessed? The more emotional the issue to the stakeholders involved, the more necessity there is for a communication medium that allows for enhanced richness.

The responses to these questions or considerations will guide the organizational public relations manager in his or her selection of the appropriately rich communication medium. The questions also direct the practitioner to a much more strategic frame of reference for analyzing any stakeholder interaction.

Lauzen and Dozier (1992) suggested that the more complex an issue facing the organization becomes, the greater the necessity for the public relations practitioner to enact the manager role. The concepts presented in this chapter and in chapter 10 are ones with which public relations managers must be familiar if they are to succeed in helping their organization implement successful communication strategies. They are also crucial for understanding many of the ethical consider-ations that surround organizational–stakeholder interactions. It is to a consideration of ethics that I turn in chapter 12.

Practitioner Response to Chapter 11: Don't Hesitate, Collaborate!

Susan Macek
Director of Communications
Children's Hospital and Medical Center
Seattle, Washington

The collaborative advocacy framework for public relations practitioners promoted in chapter 11 can hardly evoke disagreement. Whether an
issue involves internal or external stakeholders, the ability to create
and maintain trust and to foster a sense of community among those
stakeholders directly correlates to an organization's sustainable success in achieving its goals. Savage's "Typology of Organizational
Stakeholders" grid outlining a stakeholder's potential threat to an
organization as opposed to a stakeholder's potential for cooperation
with an organization, coupled with Spicer's summary questions at the
end of chapter 11 lead me to share a timely example in an era of market
and business-driven initiatives to improve responsiveness to customer
needs while streamlining costs.

Such initiatives, although important to the substainability and
survival of many companies all across the country, are sure to elicit fear
and loathing among the very stakeholders who are key to the organization's successful adaptation to change employees. Concerns about
potential job loss could override their ability and incentive to actively
participate in the process of evaluating their work and even more
threatening questioning its value to the customer and recommending
ways to deliver the service differently. A strategy to consider as part of
an overall goal to help ensure the success of a dramatic change
initiative involves the creation of an employee feedback and communication group. Such a group is established as part of a well-defined
organizational structure for the change process that will be carried out
across the entire landscape of an organization. The role of this
staff-driven committee would be to provide feedback on communica-

tion issues related to the changes needing to occur, to recommend communication tactics that from the committee's perspective would be viewed as informative and useful by their peers, and ultimately to seek information about the changes occurring so as to serve as true advocates for change. The potential for such a group, as representatives of their constituents throughout the organization, to simultaneouly be ranked as "high" on Savage's scale of potential to threaten *and* to cooperate leads to their classification as a mixed blessing.

Change that calls for radical redesign of work processes requires repeated communication with staff through a variety of mechanisms to ensure an understanding of "why" behind the need to change (to be more responsive to customer needs and to be more cost competitive in the marketplace), "how" the changes will come about (through the involvement and ideas of staff at all levels of the organization), "when" all of this will take place (over a 2-year period, with a commitment to *continuously* seek ways to improve the operations thereafter), "where" the changes will occur (at all levels and in all areas of the organization), and perhaps most importantly from an employee's perspective, "who" will be involved and impacted (virtually all staff will be affected). No one denies that change is inevitable, but the way that change is initiated and communicated, particularly among employees, who will be expected to implement the changes, calls for information media or tools that are rich in honesty, accuracy, and timeliness. Forums, newsletters, hotlines, meetings, and regularly updated voice-mail and e-mail messages are examples of media that can effectively minimize rumors and anxiety and maximize opportunities for employees to embrace cultural and organizational changes. The level of support and commitment for senior management for such a committee of stakeholders is critical to the success of the dramatic changes required. For example, a meeting environment with staff and senior management that is viewed as safe, where risks are taken to ask questions for which sometimes there are no easy or known answers, takes time to cultivate and sustain, but on an ongoing basis, the open and honest dialogue in this setting can be replicated in other media, signaling the potential for collaborative advocacy to occur throughout all areas of an organization.

CHAPTER 12

Ethical Appraisals of Insiders and Outsiders

Well, that should be a short chapter.

A variety of colleagues on hearing this
last chapter was about public relations ethics

*CEOs need you [public relations practitioner] to tell them
what they need to hear. Is this right? is a question that
ought to be asked throughout any important decision
process.*

Dale A. Johnson, (1995),
Former CEO for a Fortune 500 company

The opening comments just presented represent the continuum of
perceptions about organizational public relations ethics. On one end of
the continuum is the perception that there is almost nothing ethical
about public relations, that the very combination of the words "ethical" and "public relations" represents a bizarre oxymoron much like
Bullwinkle's "military intelligence" or George Carlin's "jumbo
shrimp." The perceptions represented at this end were evident in our
discussions of the consequences of organizational arrogance presented
in chapter 2.

The second comment by a former CEO of a Fortune 500 company
represents a more enlightened perception about the role of organizational public relations practitioners. Johnson (1995) urged professional
communicators to help their CEO understand the complexity of organizational issues in relation to the consequences of organizational

decisions on stakeholders. He continues with an example from the Union Carbide disaster in Bhopal:

> Three years prior to the accident, one of Union Carbide's own internal safety records warned that the potential for serious safety problems existed. What might have been prevented had someone just asked, "Is this the right thing to do?" (Johnson, 1995, p. 4)

Johnson's question about the rightness of a decision speaks to the need to consider the other in much the same sense that communication theorists such as Habermas (1984) or Deetz (1992) advocated the consideration of the other. Johnson (1995) suggested that consideration of the organization's stakeholders must be accompished with an assessment about the rightness of any decision. Johnson (1995) proposed that organizational public relations practitioners practice from Boulding's (1989) integrative system. As evident in Exhibit 12.1, a number of Johnson's suggestions speak to Boulding's integrative frame.

The answers to the question, "Is it right?," fall squarely into the realm of organizational morality and the ethical dimensions of decision making.

I am not concerned with prescribing a set of ethical standards or guidelines for public relations practitioners. Practitioners have the Public Relations Society Code of Standards to guide decision making. Increasing professionalism in the public relations discipline has itself fostered a number of venues for the discussion of public relations and communication ethics (Barney & Black, 1994; Bivins, 1989). A recent issue of *Public Relations Review* was devoted to a discussion of ethical considerations inherent in the public relations profession (Heibert, 1993). Educators responsible for teaching public relations in colleges and universities are increasingly aware of the need to incorporate considerations of ethics in their case studies and textbooks (Pratt, 1991). The Public Relations Society of America (PRSA) Code of Ethics, professional concern, and the incorporation of ethical concerns in public relations education indicate an increasing and welcome awareness of the dimensions of ethical issues surrounding public relations dilemmas.

My purpose in this chapter is to sketch a framework to help organizational ombudspeople analyze ethical dilemmas from both an organizational and a stakeholder perspective. By so doing, I suggest that ombudspeople will be better equipped to identify areas of agreement and disagreement along the moral spectrum. In order to do so, I frame the question of organizational public relations ethics in a larger

EXHIBIT 12.1
Ten Ways Communicators Can Help the CEO Shine

There are "Ten Commandments" in communications—commandments that will help public relations professionals in their interactions with CEOs.

I. CEOs need you to understand their business. This means recognizing everything from the financial fundamentals and the product lines to the tone, style and collective attitudes of the organization. With this insight you can more accurately predict the potential impact on stakeholders. Moreover, you can design strategic communications programs to advance the organization's business goals—and that's the clearest way you can demonstrate to your CEO that you understand his or her business.

II. CEOs need you to create the foundation for effective communication. It's as basic as this: People can't communicate unless and until they share certain understandings. We need you to act as a catalyst for this process.

III. CEOs need you to put the communications message into terms the media, the public and stakeholders understand. Bring the group of business people together and they chatter about "dotted-line responsibilities," "reengineering," "matrix organization," "bottom-line" this and "top-of-the-line" that.

Oh, occasionally we sound lyrical—we talk about "white knights," "golden parachutes," "queen bees," and "baby bells." But it still doesn't mean anyone outside the corporate world knows what we're talking about.

We need your help to see the error of our ways. Helping executives understand how their messages fall on the others' ears is a real service to both CEOs and mankind.

IV. CEOs need you to use your understanding of business, communication skills, and audience-focused language to help them achieve corporate goals.

V. CEOs need you to objectively interpret how messages are received—both through your expertise in researching public attitudes and through being "plugged into the right grapevines."

VI. CEOs need you to tell them what they need to hear. "Is this right?" is a question that ought to be asked throughout any important decision process. Consider, for example, the disaster in Bhopal, India, where hundreds of people were killed or injured by a Union Carbide poisonous gas leak.

Three years prior to the accident, one of Union Carbide's own internal safety records warned that the potential for serious safety problems existed.

What might have been prevented had someone just asked, "Is this the right thing to do?"

VII. CEOs need you to serve as effective intermediaries with the media. You are in the best position to help executives understand the media's perspective while recognizing its dynamics.

VIII. CEOs need you to help anticipate and prepare for potential crises. No one can rehearse or plan for a crisis. This is all very unsettling to management. Management is all about predicting, preparing for, and controlling events.

IX. CEOs need you to advocate the appropriate degree of openness when a crisis situation arises. The company culture, the product line, the customer mix and the specific circumstances of the crisis dictate the degree of openness appropriate for each case.

X. CEOs need your help to manage in an era of radical and sometimes frightening change. More than ever, interdependence is a necessary condition of business.

As professional communicators, you hold the privilege and the responsibility of helping to explain what unites and connects us. The recognition of our interdependence may well become a survival issue as we speed our way through the 1990s.

From D. Johnson (1995). Ten ways communicators can help the CEO shine. *Public Relations Tactics, 2*(8), p. 4. Reprinted with permission of Dale A. Johnson, SPX Corporation.

context of organizational or business ethics. Business ethics has become a hot topic in recent years (Gioia, 1992; Hosmer, 1991; Kahn, 1990). Part of this concern emanates from the feeling by many in business and the public that the moral standards of those working in organizations have slipped in recent years. In an article, "The Challenge of Ethical Behavior in Organizations," Sims (1992) wrote:

> Many executives, administrators, and social scientists see unethical behavior as a cancer working on the fabric of society in too many of today's organizations and beyond. Many are concerned that we face a crisis of ethics in the West that is undermining our competitive strength. (p. 506)

In an earlier *Harvard Business Review* article titled, "Why 'Good' Managers Make Bad Ethical Choices," Gellerman (1986) estimated that almost two thirds of the Fortune 500 companies (the 500 largest) engaged in some form of illegal behavior.

Organizational concern stemming from illegal behaviors was evident in a content analysis of ethical policy statements regarding marketing activities in Fortune 500 firms by Hite, Bellizi, and Fraser (1988). The most frequently mentioned topics included the misuse of funds and improper accounting (66% of policy statements examined), conflicts of interest (64%), and dealing with public officials (61%). After discussing those topics most often addressed, the authors of the study comment that

> it is interesting to note the topics which were not covered by a large percentage of the firms. Only 18% of the firms provided specific guidance with regard to advertising/promotion/PR. Those that did cover the topic often stated that advertising should present the qualities and advantages of a product truthfully and with good taste. (Hite et al., 1988, p. 774)

Perhaps the creators of organizational ethics policies feel that those in their organization who create advertising, promote products, and engage in public relations are inherently ethical in their dealings with the larger public and, thus, need no specific mention in a company's statement of ethics.

An alternative view, however, is found in the ways in which top management seeks to constrain external communication (Sweep, Cameron, & Lariscy, 1994). Their results indicate that top management all too often thinks of

> communication as one-way, manipulating a range of publics that include adversarial news media. This view precludes consensus-building with publics, trust-building with the media and continues to define public relations as a tool for fixing perceptions, rather than building dialogue with publics. (Sweep et al., 1994, p. 327)

Sweep et al. (1994) found that management often attempts to limit the amount and type of information disclosed by the organization. They found, for example, that one of the statements with which public relations practitioners were most likely to agree was: "The administration insists that efforts be made to ignore or to conceal from various publics negative news about the institution" (Sweep et al., 1994, p. 323). This hardly represents an enlightened view of public relations. It also raises serious questions concerning organizational ethics in relation to communication with external stakeholders.

Given recent research on organizational or business ethics, I want to examine ethics from the perspective of organizational and external stakeholder interactions. The argument I elaborate on is grounded in my belief that organizations, as systems of management, use ethical reference points in decision making that are different from those used by stakeholders affected by the resulting decision. It is these differences in ethical frames that account for much of the ambiguity, both real and perceived, about organizational public relations ethics. In order to accomplish this simultaneous unpacking and elaboration of organizational–stakeholder public relations ethics, this chapter: (a) defines moral issues; (b) examines the linkages between espoused, enacted, and observed organizational values; (c) discusses the crucial differences between moral responsibilities applied by actors and observers (or insiders and outsiders); (d) discusses the foundations of moral theories based on utilitarianism, justice, and rights; and (e) distinguishes ways in which organizational and stakeholder conflicts are morally perceived by the different parties.

I begin with a couple of simple definitions to guide my thoughts on organizational public relations ethics.

MORAL ISSUES

It is instructive to remember that stakeholders coalesce around issues, around decision points that are often viewed differently by those inside the organization and those outside the organization. The art consultant who recommended selling the Henry Moore statue in the case presented in chapter 1 approached the decision of selling from an insider perspective. In his opinion, it was a good time to sell the Vertebrae statue and optimize profit that could be used to build the bank's art collection in another area. To art lovers outside the bank, the decision became an issue about the responsibility the bank owed the community regarding public art, in this case a statue that had become a downtown fixture.

Issues have a moral component when an organization's "actions, when freely performed, may harm or benefit others" (Jones, 1991, p. 367). Jones (1991) continued his definition of moral issue by suggesting that "the action or decision must have *consequences* for others and must involve choice, or *volition* on the part of the actor or decision maker" (p. 367). The notion of volition is important in that it implies a range of potential or possible responses to an issue. The nature of volition or discretion is at the core of most writings about moral obligation. Discretionary behavior indicates a higher level of responsibility than merely responding to legal mandates (Gatewood & Carroll, 1991). Equally important is the use of the word *harm*. We often phrase moral or ethical decisions in the negative, as in, do no harm to others or not to benefit one group at the expense of another group.

Jones (1991) defined a moral agent as "a person who makes a moral decision, *even though he or she may not recognize that moral issues are at stake"* (p. 367, italics added). An ethical decision, then, is one that is "both legal and morally acceptable to the larger community" (Jones, 1991, p. 367). In his issue-contingent model of ethical decision making, Jones (1991) argued that the values of the individual, the particular cultural characteristics of the organization, and characteristics of the "moral issue itself, collectively called *moral intensity*, are important determinants of ethical decision making and behavior" (p. 371). His focus on the moral attributes of the issue are important for expanding our thinking about public relations ethics and the communication of organizational decisions. To do so, I need to introduce the distinctions social psychologists make between the attributions of actors and observers.

ACTORS AND OBSERVERS

Moral judgments begin with the values of the individuals making moral decisions (Fritzsche, 1991; Liedtka, 1989; Zahra, 1989). At the same time, those individuals are situated in organizational contexts that also incorporate organizational value structures into the decision-making process (Beyer & Lutze, 1993; Conrad, 1994). Any moral decision is the result of the confluence of individual and organizational values.

Figure 12.1 shows a model of this confluence proposed by Beyer and Lutze (1993). Individuals (X_1, X_2) bring individual values (V_{11}, V_{12}) into the organization. Through organizational socialization processes, these values are moderated and transformed into shared internalized organizational values. At the same time, information from the environment (Y_1, Y_2) must be interpreted and assigned meaning through the organization's decision-making structure. The shared internalized values influence how the information bits from the environment are noticed and interpreted. According to Beyer and Lutze (1993), "this interpretation process, in turn, produces espoused values (what spokespersons for the organization say, perhaps to justify the decision) and enacted values (what people in the organization actually do)" (p. 43).

Beyer and Lutze (1993) proposed no relationship between espoused and enacted values, a situation similar to the loose coupling between instrumental and symbolic decision making proposed by Pfeffer (1981a). They "suggest that these two sets of values may operate relatively independently" (p. 43). They also propose that this independent relationship exists because both sets of values are "powerfully constrained by environmental and contextual factors" (p. 45), or in

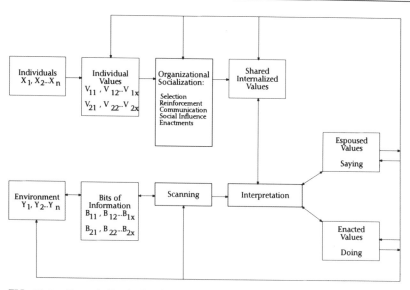

FIG. 12.1.   From individual values and environments to espoused and enacted values. From Beyer, J., & Lutze, S. (1993). The ethical nexus: Organization, values, and decision making. In C. Conrad (Ed.), *The ethical nexus* (pp. 23–45). Reprinted with permission of Ablex.

Jones' (1991) terms, the moral intensity of the issue. Finally, and most importantly for my purposes, Beyer and Lutze (1993) proposed that "enacted values will affect environments by sending signals to actors in the environment about what the organization stands for and whether that meets their demands and expectations" (p. 45). The demands and expectations of environmental actors—stakeholders—brings us to the cognitive psychology distinction between actor and observer.

The actor–observer differences observed in social psychology, particularly in attribution theories (Jones & Nisbett, 1971), are very similar to the distinctions already discussed about insider–outsider frames or schematas. The crucial link related to ethics is that actor–outsider differences influence the moral evaluation of organizational acts, as well as those of individuals. Drawing on earlier work by Ross and DiTecco (1975), Payne and Giacalone (1990) noted that the "moral evaluation of a person's conduct is based on a perception of that individuals responsibility for the conduct" (p. 653). Responsibility is attributed, at least in part, based on the perceived volition or discretion available to the actor making the decision.

Payne and Giacalone (1990) continued by noting that

the extent to which a person is viewed as responsible for a behavior is inversely related to the degree to which external factors are perceived to be determinants of the action. . . . An action may be perceived as more or less moral depending on whether it is the decision maker or actor making the judgment or another person who has observed the decision or action . . . Thus, if the individual decision maker sees his or her behavior as externally caused, the individual may well conclude that he or she is not responsible. (pp. 653–654)

The perception of responsibility is key to understanding ethical issues surrounding organization and stakeholder interactions, especially those resulting in conflict of interests.

In a study of the communication interaction between 21 sets of boycotting stakeholders and target organizations, Meyers and Garrett (1993) concluded that boycotters (outsiders–observers) and target organizations (insiders–actors) held differing perceptions of one another's communications. Given that responsibility is often inversely related to the constraints related to external factors the perceptions of the target organization managers interviewed is interesting. Meyers and Garrett (1993) reported that the respondents in the target organizations "believed that their role in the interaction process was to educate the protesters about business procedures and constraints that *limit their ability to act on the protesters' demands*" (p. 162, italics added). Here, then, we have an assessment of responsibility, one that is bounded by the external agents of "business procedures and constraints." If responsibility is parceled out or constrained by external factors, then the issue is not likely to be perceived as a moral one.

It is quite apparent that in many cases (e.g., Exxon Valdez, Kid's Place Hospital), affected stakeholders assign responsibility for the act to the organization. An analysis of the Exxon Corporation's response to the Valdez oil spill by Williams and Treadaway (1992) is instructive in showing the linkage between responsibility and perceptions of moral decision making. Williams and Treadaway (1992) noted that Exxon initially understated the severity of the accident by claiming that there would be little or no environmental damage resulting from the spill. Four days after the initial announcement, Exxon officials had to change their assessment.

Although officials of the Exxon Corporation admitted to environmental damage, they never accepted responsibility. A full-page advertisement placed in many magazines and newspapers throughout the nation briefly mentioned the environment. The Exxon advertisement's only statement about the environment was that the company has moved swiftly and competently to limit the effect the spill would have on the surrounding area, fish, and other wildlife.

Indeed, not only did Exxon deny responsibility, the corporation tried to shift the burden of responsibility by suggesting that others were also responsible for the crisis (Williams and Treadaway, 1992). Exxon tried, in turn, to blame the Pipeline Service Company, the Coast Guard, and Alaska state officials for their slow response to the cleanup efforts. Finally, Exxon attempted to place responsibility for the grounding on the captain and his third mate. Williams and Treadaway (1992) conclude their analysis with the assessment that Exxon did not understand its obligation to admit responsibility:

> By not accepting full responsibility, Exxon angered part of the general public and further distance itself from those already upset with the company. This response was the opposite of what was needed to restore stability with the public. (p. 63)

Assessments of responsibility for decisions taken by organization actors that will affect stakeholder observers is a crucial determinant of any resulting judgment concerning the morality of the decision. These differences in perceptions of responsibility lead to differences in the interpretation and use of ethical theories to guide and interpret organizational decision making.

THREE APPROACHES TO ETHICS

In their examination of the ethics of organizational politics, Cavanagh, Moberg, and Velasquez (1981), proposed three categories of normative ethics, as well as three kinds of moral theories:

> utilitarian theories (which evaluate behavior in terms of its social consequences), theories of rights (which emphasizes the entitlements of individuals), and theories of justice (which focus on the distributional effects of actions or policies). (p. 245)

I briefly describe each theoretical perspective before applying the Cavanagh et al., framework to our previous discussion of actor–observer distinctions in the assessment of responsibility.

Utilitarianism

This approach, grounded in 18th-century thinkers such as Bentham and Mill, emphasizes the adage that moral decisions produce the greatest good for the greatest number (Kidder, 1995). In many ways, the pluralistic approach to organizations discussed in chapter 5, emphasizes an utilitarian approach. One underlying assumption of pluralism is that decisions eventually negotiated by the various parties will be ones that serve the greatest good. The first article of the PRSA Code of Professional Standards, "A member shall conduct his or her professional life in accord with the public interest," emanates from a utilitarian philosophy (see Exhibit 12.2).

Classical utilitarian approaches are based on an evaluation of the act or decision. Moral evaluations of the greatest good are determined by assessing the consequences of the action taken. This focus on consequences is called *act utilitarianism*, in that each decision or action is separately evaluated as to its moral claim of providing the greatest public good. A second form of utilitarianism based on rules, has recently been proposed. The decision maker following a *rule utilitarian* philosophy would evaluate the decision based on an assessment of the validity of the rule under which the action falls (Fritzsche & Becker, 1984, p. 167) rather than the consequences of the act itself. Fritzsche and Becker (1984) suggested that "although following a chosen rule may not lead to the greatest benefit in every situation, over the long run the rule will result in decisions that lead to the greatest societal benefit when compared to all alternative rules" (p. 167).

Cavanagh et al. (1981) suggested that attempting to weigh and balance the interests of all parties potentially affected by any one decision in our increasingly complex society "can amount to a calculative nightmare" (p. 245). They accordingly suggest a number of shortcuts decision makers can use to reduce the complexity of the calculations. One of these involves adopting "a simplified frame of reference in evaluating the interests of affected parties" (p. 246), such as adopting an economic frame that only addresses decisions in terms of cost/benefit analysis.

Another shortcut allows the decision maker to place boundaries on his or her utilitarian calculations.

> For example, a decision maker can consider only the interests of those directly affected by a decision and thus exclude from analysis all indirect or secondary effects. Similarly, a decision maker can assume that by giving allegiance to a particular organizational coalition or set of goals (e.g., "official goals"), everyone's utilities will be optimized. (Cavanagh et al., 1981, p. 246)

Managers might, for example, consider only shareholders when making decisions about the necessity to downsize their organization, ignoring other stakeholders such as employees, community, or unions. Or, managers might make decisions based solely on perceptions of

EXHIBIT 12.2
Public Relations Code of Professional Standards

Declaration of Principles

Members of the Public Relations Society of America base their professional opinions on the fundamental values and dignity of the individual, holding that the free exercise of human rights, especially freedom of speech, freedom of assembly, and freedom of press, is essential to the practice of public relations.

In serving the interests of the clients and employers, we dedicate ourselves to the goals of better communication, understanding, and cooperation among the diverse individuals, groups, and institutions of society, and of equal opportunity of employment in the public relations profession.

We Pledge:

To conduct ourselves professionally, with truth, accuracy, fairness, and responsibility to the public;

To improve our individual competence and advance the knowledge and proficiency of the profession through the continuing research and education; and adhere to the articles of the Code of Professional Standards for the Practice of Public Relations as adopted by the governing Assembly of the Society.

Code of Professional Standards for the Practice of Public Relations

These articles have been adopted by the Public Relations Society of America to promote and maintain high standards of public service and ethical conduct among its members.

1. A member shall conduct his or her professional life in accord with the public interest.

2. A member shall exemplify high standards of honesty and integrity while carrying out dual obligations to a client or employer and to the democratic process.

3. A member shall deal fairly with the public, with past or present clients or employers, and with fellow practitioners, giving due respect to the ideal of free inquiry and to the opinions of others.

4. A member shall adhere to the highest standards of accuracy and truth; avoiding extravagant claims or unfair comparisons and giving credit for ideas and words borrowed from others.

5. A member shall not knowingly disseminate false or misleading information and shall act promptly to correct erroneous communications for which she or he is responsible.

(Continued)

6. A member shall not engage in any practice which has the purpose of corrupting the integrity of channels of communications or the processes of government.

7. A member shall be prepared to identify publicly the name of the client or employer on whose behalf any public communication is made.

8. A member shall not use any individual or organization professing to serve or represent an announced cause, or professing to be independent or unbiased, but actually serving another or undisclosed interest.

9. A member shall not guarantee the achievement of specified results beyond the member's direct control.

10. A member shall not represent conflicting or competing interests without the express consent of those concerned, given after a full disclosure of the facts.

11. A member shall not place himself or herself in a position where the member's personal interest is or may be in conflict with an obligation to an employer or client or others, without the full disclosure of such interest to all involved.

12. A member shall not accept fees, commissions, gifts in any other consideration from anyone except clients or employers for whom services are performed without their express consents, given after full disclosure of the facts.

13. A member shall scrupulously safeguard the confidences and privacy rights of present, former, and prospective clients or employers.

14. A member shall not intentionally damage the professional reputation or practice of another practitioner.

15. If a member had evidence that another member has been guilty of unethical, illegal, or unfair practices, including those in violation of this Code, the member is obligated to present the information promptly to the proper authorities of the Society for action in accordance with the procedure set forth in XII of the Bylaws.

16. A member called as a witness in a proceeding for enforcement of this Code is obligated to appear, unless excused for sufficient reason by the judicial panel.

17. A member shall, as soon as possible, sever relations with any organization or individual if such relationship requires conduct contrary to the articles of this Code.

what top management would want done (i.e., particular organizational coalition). Although these shortcuts help eliminate cumbersome calculations, they also present opportunities for misuse on the part of organizational decision makers. Important stakeholders might easily be excluded, or allegiance to one coalition might easily exclude the wishes and needs of another coalition.

Theory of Rights

The best example of a theory of rights is the American Bill of Rights, a document that guarantees certain inalienable rights thought to be held by all people. Ethical theories grounded in a rights perspective "can be summarized as providing a guide for the decision maker to insure respect for the rights of individuals" (Fritzsche & Becker, 1984, p. 167) or stakeholders. These rights include the right of free consent, right to privacy, right to freedom of conscience, right of free speech, and the right to due process (Cavanagh et al., 1981; Fritzsche & Becker, 1984; Kidder, 1995). The PRSA Declaration of Principles, states that members "base their professional principles of the fundamental value and dignity of the individual, holding that the free exercise of human rights, especially freedom of speech, freedom of assembly, and freedom of the press, is essential to the practice of public relations" (p. 1).

In an ethical system based on rights, decisions are judged ethical if they do not infringe on another's rights. The stakeholders in the Kid's Place Hospital case described in chapter 1, felt that their collective rights had been violated by the hospital's decision to build a helipad for emergency helicopter landings. Their right to consent in a decision that might possibly affect their lives (e.g., noise, potential crashes) was abridged. Indeed, if we count the noise argument we might conclude that their right to privacy (e.g., being able to anticipate quiet in the neighborhood during the night) was violated by the decision.

The importance of the rights philosophy to organizational interactions with external stakeholders is determining who has the right to be included in the decision process. As we saw in earlier chapters, many argue that the process of organizational decision making needs to be more inclusive of external stakeholders (Deetz, 1992, Mansbridge, 1980). The neighbors of Kid's Place Hospital certainly thought they had the "right" to be involved in the decision to build the helipad. Likewise, the parents in the City School District case examined in chapter 11 thought they had the "right" to be involved in decisions that would eventually affect their children's education. Determining who has the right to be included in the decision-making process is a continual dilemma for public relations practitioners.

Theories of Justice

"A theory of justice requires decision makers to be guided by equity, fairness, and impartiality" (Cavanagh et al., 1981, p. 247). Modern management practices, especially those related to employees, have elaborated a detailed set of working principles of justice governing rules and compensations (Scott, 1988). The first principle, distributive justice, states that similar individuals should be treated similarly. Second, rules should be clearly stated, understood by all, and administered fairly thereby avoiding expressions of partiality. Third, a theory of justice proclaims that "individuals should not be held responsible for matters over which they have no control . . . individuals should be compensated for the cost of their injuries by the party responsible for those injuries" (Cavanagh et al., 1981, p. 247).

A number of the articles of the PRSA code are concerned with issues of justice. "A member shall exemplify high standards of honesty and integrity while carrying out dual obligations to a client or employer and to the democratic process," (p. 1) speaks to the issue of equity. "A member shall deal fairly with the public, with past or present clients or employers and with fellow practitioners" (p. 1) speaks to the issue of fairness called forth by a theory of justice.

Based on an understanding of dialogue and grounded in philosophers such as Habermas, Pearson (1989b) outlined a prescription for ethical communication that unfolds from a theory of justice perspective. The core of his argument is that "ethical public relations practice is more fundamentally a question of implementing and maintaining interorganizational communication systems that question, discuss, and validate" (p. 82) the moral issues or actions that arise between organizations and their stakeholders. Pearson (1989b) proposed that central to this process is the implementation of an external communication system that is grounded in agreement about "communication rules that apply equally to the organization and to its publics" (p. 82). His emphasis on rules and the participants' (organization and stakeholder) understanding of and satisfaction with, clearly speaks to a system elaborated from a theory of justice that emphasizes equity and fairness.

From this framework, Pearson (1989b) proposed five dimensions regarding the perceived equity and fairness of communicative rules:

1. Degree of communicator understanding of and satisfaction with rules governing the opportunity for beginning and ending communicative interaction.

2. Degree of communicator understanding of and satisfaction with the rules governing the length of time separating messages, or a question from its answer.

3. Degree of communicator understanding of and satisfaction with rules governing opportunity for suggesting topics and initiating topic changes.

4. Degree of communicator satisfaction that a partner in communication has provided a response that counts as a response.
5. Degree of communicator understanding of and satisfaction with rules for channel selection (pp. 82–83).

The last dimension concerning rules for channel selection are particularly important, especially in light of the criteria Daft and Lengel (1984) suggested for using rich media as discussed in chapters 10 and 11.

Scott (1988) proposed that "justice in the form of due process is an instrumental means that must be managed to achieve organizational ends" (p. 281). Although writing primarily about justice in relation to the organization's employees, his ideas are equally pertinent to organizational–stakeholder interactions. Organizational due process includes procedural and substantive aspects that are called on to maintain the stability of relationships with external stakeholders. The two types differ in their purpose and in their implementation.

Procedural due process is based on rules designed to settle disputes over rights, in our case the rights of organizations and stakeholders. These disputes are managed by appealing to an external authority, such as a court of law or by appealing to some internal organizational mechanism established expressly for that purpose such as an ombudsperson function. Substantive due process has to do with the allocation of resources between the organization and stakeholder. These allocations are either made on the perceived fairness and benevolence of an internal organizational decision-making mechanism or, as in the City School District case study, participative decision making that includes the affected stakeholders. In that substantive due process involves the "allocation of resources according to interests," (p. 282) it falls squarely into the political metaphor of organization discussed in chapters 5 and 6. In this context, the political metaphor is most appropriate in our understanding of coalition building leading toward collaborative advocacy.

All three theories have strengths and weaknesses as shown in Table 12.1. Most interesting, in my view, is a weakness associated with utilitarianism. Cavanagh et al., (1981) proposed that utilitarianism "can result in an unjust allocation of resources, particularly when some individuals or groups lack representation or 'voice' " (p. 367, italics added). This matter of stakeholder voice is crucial in assessing organizational–stakeholder interactions and one that is returned to at the end of this chapter.

Figure 12.2 shows a decision tree adapted from Cavanagh et al. (1981). Their flow chart incorporates all three theories in a "yes" or

TABLE 12.1
Ethical Theories: Strengths and Weaknesses

Theory	Strengths as an Ethical Guide	Weaknesses as an Ethical Guide
Utilitarianism (Bentham, Ricardo, Smith)	1. Facilitates calculative short-cuts (e.g., owing loyalty to an individual, coalition, or organization).	1. Virtually impossible to assess the effects of a PBA on the satisfaction of all affected parties.
	2. Promotes the view that the interests accounted for should not be solely particularistic except under unusual circumstances (e.g., perfect competition).	2. Can result in an unjust allocation of resources, particularly when some individuals or groups lack representation or "voice."
	3. Can encourage entrepreneurship, innovation, and productivity.	3. Can result in abriding some persons' rights to accommodate utilitarian outcomes.
Theory of Rights (Kant, Locke)	1. Specifies minimial levels of satisfaction for all individuals.	1. Can encourage individualistic, selfish behavior—which, taken to an extreme, may result in anarchy.
	2. Establishes standards of social behavior that are independent of outcomes.	2. Reduces political prerogatives that may be necessry to bring about just or utilitarian outcomes.
Theory of Justice (Aristotle, Rawls)	1. Ensures that allocations of resources are determined fairly.	1. Can encourage a sense of entitlement that reduces entrepreneurship, innovation, and productivity.
	2. Protects the interests of those who may be underrepresented in organizations beyond according them minimal rights.	2. Can result in abriding some persons' rights to accommodate the canons of justice.

Note. From Cavanagh, G., et al. (1981). Ethical theories relevant to judging political behavior decisions. *Academy of Management Review, 6,* 248–249. Reprinted with permission.

''no'' question format. The flow of questions that should be asked of any decision that might affect external stakeholders is similar to the questions proposed by Laczniak and Murphy (1991) for fostering ethical marketing decisions as shown in Exhibit 12.3. The very asking of questions such as those proposed by Cavanagh et al. (1981) and Laczniak and Murphy (1991) go a long way in helping answer the question posed at the very beginning of this chapter, ''Is it right?''

Prevalence of Utilitarian Approach

Although all three theories—utilitarian, rights, and justice—are available for managers, including organizational public relations practition-

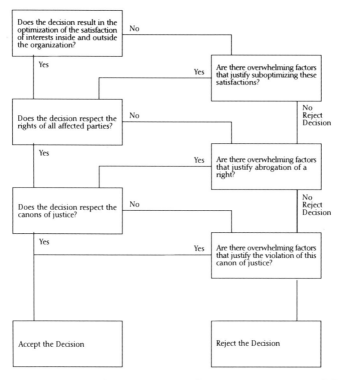

FIG. 12.2. Decision tree for incorporating ethics into organization–stakeholder interactions. From Cavanagh, G.,et al. (1981). Ethical theories relevant to judging political behavior decisions. *Academy of Management Review*, 6, 248–249. Reprinted with permission.

ers, to use, research indicates a particular fondness for utilitarian approaches. Some of the most intriguing research from a general business ethics point of view as well as the implications for public relations was conducted by Fritzsche and Becker (1984). Fritzsche and Becker (1984) created five vignettes that addressed five types of moral problems organizational members might face: (a) coercion and control, (b) conflict of interest, (c) environmental contamination, (d) autonomy versus consumer welfare, and (e) personal integrity. Respondents were asked to indicate the likelihood that they would engage in the behavior dictated by the vignette ("definitely would not" to "definitely would"). Respondents were then asked to provide a reason why the particular decision was made (Fritzsche and Becker, 1984, pp. 168–169).

The authors concluded that "the rationale provided by the respondents for their vignette decisions was predominantly of a utilitarian nature . . . such an orientation could be explained by the strong role

---

EXHIBIT 12.3
Questions to Improve Ethical Reasoning

Question 1: Does the contemplated action violate law?

Question 2: Is the contemplated action contrary to widely accepted moral obligations? (Such oral obligation might include *duties of fidelity* such as the responsibility to remain faithful to contracts, to keep promises, and to tell the truth; *duties of gratitude* which basically means that special obligations exist between relatives, friends, partners, cohorts, and employees; *duties of justice* which basically have to do with obligations to distribute rewards based upon merit; *duties of nonmaleficence* which consists of duties not to harm others; *duties of beneficence* which rest upon the notion that actions should be taken which improve the situation of others—if this can be readily accomplished.)

Question 3: Does the proposed action violate any other special obligations which stem from the type of marketing organization at focus? (For example, the special duty of pharmaceutical firms to provide safe products, the special obligation of toy manufacturers to care for the safety of children, the inherent duty of alcohol manufacturers to promote responsible drinking.)

Question 4: Is the *intent* of the contemplated action harmful?

Question 5: Are there any major damages to people or organizations that are likely to result from the contemplated action?

Question 6: Is there a satisfactory alternative action which produces equal or greater benefits to the parties affected than the proposed action?

Question 7: Does the contemplated action infringe upon the inalienable rights of the consumer (such as the right to information, the right to be heard, the right to choice, and the right to redress)?

Question 8: Does the proposed action leave another person or group less well off? Is this person or group already a member of a relatively underprivileged class?

From Laczniak, G., & Murphy, P. (1991). Fostering ethical marketing decisions. *Journal of Business Ethics, 10,* 267. Reprinted with kind permission from Kluwer Academic Publishers.

---

economics plays in managerial decision making" (Fritzsche & Becker, 1984, p. 174). Indeed, the respondents often invoked the economic shortcut described by Cavanagh et al. (1981). Respondents who invoked a rule utilitarian philosophy were somewhat more ethical in their responses. They were reluctant, for example, to provide information that would constitute a conflict of interest between their former and new employer. Those following an act utilitarian philosophy, on the other hand, were almost always more likely to succumb to the questionable ethical demands of the vignette. They were more likely to take action that would pollute the environment when a competitive advantage could be gained and more likely to suggest that those who wanted sensitive information they would like to publish could get that information from other sources anyway.

Fritzsche and Becker (1994) concluded that "individuals following a rule or a rights philosophy tend to place greater weight on ethical values relative to economic values, and individuals adhering to an act philosophy take the reverse position" (p. 174). Hosmer (1991) also suggested that in most organizational decision making, economic efficiency and competitive effectiveness are the criteria by which most consequences are judged. The focus on the act itself and its eventual consequences on affected stakeholders inherently results in two less than desirable traits of utilitarian decision making. First, focusing on the ends diminishes the process by which decisions are forged, especially in relation to the inclusion of external stakeholders. Second, a focus on the consequences of an organization's act promotes the need to contextualize the action in terms that are favorable to the organization. This is particularly true if harm to some stakeholder group results from the action.

ORGANIZATION–STAKEHOLDER DIFFERENCES IN MORAL ASSESSMENTS

To this point, I have defined organizational moral decisions as those for which there are consequences for a least one or more of the organization's stakeholders. Although consequences can certainly be beneficial, they are most often examined in light of the degree of potential harm resulting from the decision or act. We proceeded to the central notion that actors and observers—organizations and stakeholders—situate responsibility for actions differently. This difference, I suspect, leads to the use of different moral theories or philosophies to gauge the morality of the organizational decision. The three branches of normative ethics— utilitarianism, rights, and justice—were described in relation to the PRSA Code of Ethics as well as to other explorations of particular aspects of organizational and public relations ethics. I now turn to the ways in which stakeholders and organizations differentially apply and interpret the morality of organizational actions.

In his issue-contingent model of ethical decision making, Jones (1991) postulated that moral intensity can be characterized by six components: magnitude of consequences, social consensus, probability of effect, temporal immediacy, proximity, and concentration of effect (p. 374). Each of these components combines differently for different issues and comprises the construct Jones' labels moral intensity. In order to examine how organizations and stakeholders apply different ethical frameworks, we need to define each of Jones' (1991) components.

Magnitude of consequences is "the sum of the harms (or benefits) done to victims (or beneficiaries) of the moral act in question" (p. 374). An act that causes thousands of people to die, such as the actions that led to the Union Carbide accident in Bhopal, is of a greater magnitude than an action that causes that many people to experience only ill effects that eventually pass.

Social consensus is defined as "the degree of social agreement that a proposed act is evil (or good)" (p. 375). Jones suggests that "a high degree of social consensus reduces the likelihood that ambiguity [about the morality of the act] will exist" (p. 375). This component speaks to the appropriateness of the behavior or action in question. For example, it is fairly well-established as social consensus that public officials in the United States should not seek or accept bribes.

Probability of effect "is a joint function of the probability that the act in question will actually take place and the act in question will actually cause the harm (benefit) predicted" (p. 375). The probability of effect speaks to the utilitarian's need to weigh potential consequences in the calculative nightmare described by Cavanagh et al. (1981). A recent court decision in Washington State that overturned a law that allows for the indefinite incarceration of proven sexual predators is a case in point. Supporters of the law argue that the probabilities are high that a sexual predator will commit another crime after his or her release and that harm will come to the victim.

Temporal immediacy speaks to the length of time between the time the decision is made and the beginning of either intended or unintended consequences. Those who begin smoking cigarettes at a young age do not particularly think in terms of their future, when smoking might contribute to any number of illnesses. There is simply not much temporal immediacy in the decision to start smoking.

Proximity "is the feeling of nearness (social, cultural, psychological, or physical) that the moral agent has for victims (beneficiaries)" (p. 376) of the act. A long history on the effects of proximity leads to the conclusion that all things being equal, the closer we are to someone the more likely we are to feel compassion for that person. The financial crisis suffered by ABC University described in chapter 4 was physically, socially, and psychologically close and therefore more compelling than similar crises at other universities.

Concentration of effect "is an inverse function of the number of people affected by an act *of given magnitude*" (p. 377). Stealing from an individual, for example, has a greater concentration of effect than stealing from a large institution. The supporters of a small sales tax increase to support the construction of a new baseball stadium in Seattle used the concentration of effect component in their messages to the voting public by claiming that it would only cost the average taxpayer $7.50 a year because it was spread out among hundreds of thousands of taxpaying individuals.

Jones (1991) elaborated in interesting detail how the characteristics of moral intensity influence the remaining components of his model (recognize more issue, make moral judgment, establish moral intent, engage in moral behavior). The establishment of moral intent is similar to the organization's espoused values and engaging in moral behavior is similar to the organization's enacted values (Beyer & Lutze, 1993). Equally important is my contention that organizations and stakeholders will often assign different values to the six characteristics, thereby arriving at a very different assessment of the moral intensity of an issue.

The City School District case study provides an illustrative example of how stakeholders and organizations can (and often do) approach moral issues differently. In general, the parents of gifted children in the existing the Horizon program

1. thought that the magnitude of consequences was large (the elimination of the program would affect all of their children),
2. were in agreement (social consensus) that there needed to be some program for the gifted (although differences arose as to the type of program),
3. projected a high probability of effect that the school district would eliminate or seriously curtail gifted programs and that their children would definitely suffer from that action,
4. recognized that any action on the part of the school district would have immediate effects and was therefore viewed as having high temporal immediacy (typical concerns expressed by parents involved the immediacy of the next school year),
5. perceived that the eventual decision was very proximate physically and psychologically (physically in that parents wanted gifted programs relatively close to their neighborhoods and psychologically in that most parents agreed that highly capable children needed differential curricula), and
6. felt that there was a high concentration of effect in that more than 200 parents had originally come together rather than

facing school administrators one at a time (the parents felt singled out by the district).

The administrators of the school district, on the other hand, did not feel that the magnitude of consequences was that great in that they were only considering 2,200–2,300 students of the more than 45,000 in the district. They felt the probability of a negative effect accruing from eliminating or drastically changing the program was minimal in that they argued their other programs (e.g., early childhood model, individualized instruction) would take up any slack. The concentration of effect was perceived to be relatively small in that only a relative few were really affected. Although the issue was certainly close to the district, it was not as singularly focused on by administrators as it was for the parents. School district personnel did not feel that there would be any immediate adverse consequences inherent in dropping the gifted program so that temporal immediacy was not an issue. Finally, for the most part, the school district administrators were in consensus about their desire to incorporate gifted education into other programs.

The parents and school district administrators assessed the moral intensity of the situation differently. In that they assigned different values to the various components of the moral intensity construct, we might well imagine that they would bring different moral theories to judge the moral rightness of the process and the eventual decisions. And, indeed, such was the case. The task force members most often couched their appraisals of ethical issues in theories of rights (the right for their child to have the education he or she deserved or their right as parents to have a voice in decisions affecting their children) or theories of justice (fairness). Those administrators hostile to or nonsupportive of separate programs for the gifted most often framed their concerns in an act utilitarian philosophy (providing the best education for all students given limited resources).

Although all three theoretical perspectives are valid and appropriate, the use of different theories to support countering arguments led to constraints on meaning. Research on the moral climates of organizations indicates that subgroups in organizations (e.g., departments) may very well operate from differing ethical perspectives, "that various climate types can and do exist" (Victor, Cullen, & Boynton, 1993, p. 203). They note that, "the types of ethical climates in an organization or group [such as a stakeholder] influence the process by which conflicts are resolved" (p. 203). These authors imply that because each ethical perspective emphasizes different criteria for judging the ethical nature of a decision or action, the criteria themselves are often incompatible and lead to an additional source of disagreement.

The school district's use of the utilitarian act theory was viewed by parents as a ploy to get around providing for the needs of their highly capable children. Similarly, the use of rights and justice theories by the parents was seen as elitist by a number of the school district administrators. These differences led to an inability to collaboratively assess many of the arguments for and against the various plans and programs discussed and debated throughout the life of the task force.

SUMMARY

In summary, organizations and stakeholders will invoke different moral theories in their attempts to analyze and resolve issues. These differences emanate from differences in assessments of responsibility. As noted earlier in this chapter, responsibility for the moral consequences of an action are linked to an assessment of the degree of discretion or volition available to the decision maker. In those instances in which the decision maker is accorded little or no discretion, he or she is generally not held to be responsible (within limits, of course). In those instances in which the decision maker is accorded discretion, then he or she is held to higher standards of responsibility or accountability.

Organizational members—insiders–actors—are more likely to focus pragmatically on an issue and to attempt a resolution from previously established ways of doing. This position is notable in the interview data Meyers and Garrett (1993) gathered from the targets of boycotting stakeholders. The insider respondents often evoked arguments that extolled the virtues of their internal policies, thereby defending "their current value structure" (p. 159). Keough and Lake (1993) noted that the value of management rights (i.e., an insider perspective) "functions normatively to legitimize certain management tactics and prerogatives, it also functions as a domination structure, solidifying managerial control" (p. 175).

Insider–actors perceive themselves to have limited discretionary power or control because of their allegiance to the system in which they work—its culture, its rules, its historical approaches, its policy, and so on. In essence, the insider perspective binds the organizational manager, thereby limiting his or her discretion in decision making and action. This insider–actor perspective forces limits on the acceptance of responsibility, especially when moral issues are approached from the perspective of act utilitarianism. Those issues for which the insiders accept responsibility are those that can be controlled by management.

In this view, organizations are not responsible for those issues that fall outside the realm of managerial practice, pragmatics, and policy.

Outsider–observers (stakeholders) are far more likely to make assessments of organizational actions based on their perception of organizational sensitivity and responsiveness to their needs. Given the broader viewpoint of the outsiders, they are more likely to impute responsibility to the organizational actor than are the organizational actors themselves. In this manner, then, stakeholders are more likely to perceive that the organization has more discretion or volition than the organization either has, claims, or acknowledges.

Meyers and Garrett (1993) found that by going public with their arguments that a particular organization should be held accountable for certain decisions, boycotters ran the risk of forcing the organization to respond defensively. They note that "when pressures for accountability are intense, responses are typically used to legitimate and rationalize current and future courses of action" (p. 164). Ironically, the very pressure of the boycotters as observers gives "rise to communication that reproduces current organizational practices . . . the boycott agents create a rhetorical situation in which the organization feels compelled to argue for the credibility of its allegedly offensive policies and practices" (Meyers & Garrett, 1993, pp. 164–165). Situations of this type would be characterized as falling in Savage et al.'s (1991) nonsupportive category of stakeholders. It is for these very stakeholders that Savage et al. (1991) suggested a strategy of defensive communication, communication that is adversarial in its advocacy. The exchange of reproductive communication (Meyers & Garrett, 1993) leads to an ever-spiraling demand for assertion and counterassertion, for an adversarial exchange run amok with little hope for either understanding or satisfaction with the communication rules as suggested by Pearson (1989b).

It is this situation, finally, that conflict, as discussed throughout this book, is in most need of the public relations/communication ombudsperson. Granting that not all organizational-stakeholder interactions reach the intensity that results in a boycott of the organization. The themes uncovered by Meyers and Garrett (1993), however, have been evident in many of the case studies and examples presented throughout this discussion. There is undeniably a tendency of organizations to act like insiders, especially in the face of external demands for accountability. When faced with parents questioning their responsibility, many of the City School District administrators responded in ways similar to the target organization representatives interviewed by Meyers and Garrett (1993).

Ultimately, the inability or unwillingness to accept responsibility for decisions and actions leads to an organizational response set that fosters perceptions of arrogance evident in the examples in chapter 2. The moral assessment of the decision issue is narrowed, most often to an assessment based on act utilitarianism that incorporates an internal shortcut like those described by Cavanagh et al. (1981). It is in the assessment of the moral issue, the acceptance of reasonable responsibility, and the ability to incorporate an observer's stance that distinguishes the public relations manager as communication ombudsperson in getting to the heart of the question, ''What's the right thing to do?''

Practitioner Response to Chapter 12: It's Only Right to Remember Grandma

Katie Rossbach, President
Cascade Communication Associates
Seattle, Washington

Much of the public relations function involves serving as a mediator/ translator between internal and external audiences and concerns. In fact, PRSA describes the function as one that "brings private and public policies into harmony." The successful public relations manager must be able to understand both the internal and the external perspectives and to help each understand the other. The challenge faced by many in the profession is, "How can I earn a seat at the policy table, effectively offer the outside perspective, and not be asked to leave?"

Although advertising also reaches out to the external audience and must effectively cope with external sensibilities, it generally has the luxury of lengthy planning and access to research. A message's impact on its intended audience is well analyzed before it is ever publicly uttered. Situations addressed by the public relations staff tend to unfold spontaneously and decisions must often be justified to senior management based on instinct, not research.

As a result, PR people—perhaps more than any other in the organization—find themselves on the sharp edge of "team player versus outsider." Without empirical research to support a position, we resort to various renditions of playing the devil's advocate. It's a relatively safe way of saying, "I'm certainly an insider, but let's consider the perspective of *that* group."

When I served as spokesperson for a bank on the verge of insolvency, the "devil" was often my grandmother—a genuine bank customer and proud survivor of the Great Depression. It was rewarding to hear a senior vice president—with no specific PR background—parrot my standard line in a policy-setting meeting by reminding the decision makers to consider how "Katie's Grandma in Aberdeen" would react. Grandma had never actually talked about the bank's situation, but she had become an effective metaphor for an important group of outsiders the bank needed to consider!

The value of research should not be underestimated, although the most valuable is often more qualitative than quantitative. Situations often arise where the vast majority of a given population wholeheartedly agrees with the organization's goals and tactics. But a handful of resolute people can topple the entire program.

The research that is most valuable to public relations is not the study that gives demographics, but the hands-on, in-the-field, who's-who knowledge of constituencies. It comes from taking the time to set up personal relationships and building channels to carry information (both ways!) between the organization and its audiences.

An approach that is often underutilized is a methodical program of involving employees in the community, coupled with insuring that employees understand the organization's positions. The associations and friendships that employees have with people in their communities can be the most effective channels of communication for a company facing difficult issues. Knowing which senior managers are represented on which boards, actively identifying and recruiting for others, and supporting employee's volunteer activities is more that just something "nice to do" or "because we're a good citizen." With a little effort, it can be a way to gather information about concerns and passions of people outside the company. When listening to the external audience becomes the responsibility of everyone at the decision-making table, the public relations manager no longer stands alone. Of course, this tactic needs to be coupled with a solid employee communications program that entrusts employees with information by covering issues thoroughly.

Accurately understanding the perspective of outside groups is the art of public relations and the mark of a truly talented practitioner. It can also be thankless. Success often means that a potential problem never materializes, and what credit can there be in that?

References

Acharya, L. (1981, August). *Effects of perceived environmental uncertainty on public relations roles.* Paper presented at the meeting of the Public Relations Division, Association for Education in Journalism, East Lansing, MI.

Acharya, L. (1985) Public relations environments. *Journalism Quarterly, 62,* 577–584.

Aldrich, H. E. (1979). *Organizations and environments.* Englewood Cliffs, NJ: Prentice-Hall.

Aldrich, H. E. (1992). Incommensurable paradigms? Vital signs from three perspectives. In M. Reed & M. Hughes (Eds.), *New directions in organizational theory and analysis* (pp. 17–45). London: Sage.

Aldrich, H., & Mindlin, S. (1978). Uncertainty and dependence: Two perspectives on environment. In L. Karpik (Ed.), *Organization and environment: Theory, issues and reality* (pp. 149–170). Beverly Hills, CA: Sage.

Allen, R. W., Madison, D. L., Porter, L. W., Renwick, P. A., & Mayes, B. T. (1979). Organizational politics: Tactics and characteristics of its actors. *California Management Review, 22*(1), 77–82.

Applegate, J. L., & Woods, E. (1991). Construct system development and attention to face wants in persuasive situations. *Southern Communication Journal, 56,* 194–204.

Aronoff, C. (1975). Credibility of public relations for journalists. *Public Relations Review, 1,* 45–56.

Art-sale blunder hurts bank image. (1986, September). *Seattle Times,* p. A4.

At-Twaijri, M. I. A., & Montanari, J. R. (1987). The impact of context and choice on the boundary-spanning process: An empirical extension. *Human Relations, 40,* 783–798.

Awad, J. (1985). *The power of public relations.* New York: Prager.

Axley, S. R. (1984). Managerial and organizational communication in terms of the conduit metaphor. *Academy of Management Review, 9,* 428–437.

Bacharach, S. B., & Lawler, E. J. (1980). *Power and politics in organizations.* San Francisco: Jossey-Bass.

Baddeley, S., & James, K. (1986). Political management: Developing the management portfolio. *Journal of Management Development, 9*(13), 42–59.

Bahls, J. E. (1992). What credentials do you seek when you hire? *Public Relations Journal, 48*(9), 22.

298

Bailey, F. G. (1983). *The tactical uses of passion: An essay on power, reason and reality.* Ithaca, NY: Cornell University Press.

Banks, S. P. (1991, August). *Telling true stories in public relations: An application of the narrative paradigm.* Paper presented at the meeting of the Association for Education in Journalism and Mass Communication, Boston.

Barney, R. D., & Black, J. (1994). Ethics and professional persuasive communications. *Public Relations Review, 20,* 233–248.

Bartunek, J. M., & Moch, M. K. (1987). First-order, second- order, and third-order change and organization developments interventions: A cognitive approach. *The Journal of Applied and Behavioral Science, 23,* 483–500.

Baskin, O., & Aronoff, C. (1992). *Public relations: The profession and the practice* (3rd. ed.). Dubuque, IA: Wm. C. Brown.

Bates, S. (1995). *Realigning journalism with democracy: The Hutchins Commission, its times and ours.* Washington, DC: The Annenberg Washington Program.

Baum, B. (1994, April 24). Former foes team up to save salmon. *The Seattle Times,* B2.

Baum, H. S. (1989). Organizational politics against organizational culture: A psychoanalytic perspective. *Human Resource Management, 28,* 191–206.

Baxter, L. (1993). Two codes of communication in an academic institution. *Journal of Applied Communication Research 21,* 313–326.

Belz, A., Talbott, A., & Starck, K. (1989). Using role theory to evaluate specialized magazines and commication channels. In J. E. Grunig & L. A. Grunig (Eds.), *Public relations research annual* (Vol. 1, pp. 114–125). Hillsdale, NJ: Lawrence Erlbaum Associates.

Bennis, W. (1989). *Why leaders can't lead.* San Francisco: Jossey-Bass.

Berns, D. (1992, May 4). Ethical society honors head of women's clinic. *St. Louis Post-Dispatch,* 3A.

Bettman, J., & Weitz, B. (1983). Attributions in the boardroom: Causal reasoning in corporate annual reports. *Administrative Science Quarterly, 28,* 165–183.

Beyer, J., & Lutze, S. (1993). The ethical nexus: Organization, values, and decision making. In C. Conrad (Ed.), *The ethical nexus* (pp. 23–45). Norwood, NJ: Ablex.

Bishop, R. L. (1988). What newspapers say about public relations. *Public Relations Review, 14,* 50–52.

Bivins, T. (1987). Applying ethical theory to public relations. *Journal of Business Ethics, 6,* 195–200.

Bivins, T. (1989). Ethical implications of the relationship of purpose to role and function in public relations. *Journal of Business Ethics, 8,* 65–73.

Bluedorn, A. C. (1993). Pilgrim's progress: Trends and convergence in research on organizational size environments. *Journal of Management, 19,* 163–191.

Bluedorn, A. C., Johnson, R., Cartwright, D., & Barringer, B. (1994). The interface and convergence of the strategic management and organizational environment domains. *Journal of Management, 20*(2), 201–262.

Boeker, W., & Goodstein, J. (1991). Organizational performance and adaptation: Effects of environment and performance on changes in board composition. *Academy of Management Journal, 34*(4), 805–826.

Bolman, L. G., & Deal, T. E. (1991). *Reframing organizations: Artistry, choice, and leadership.* San Francisco: Jossey-Bass.

Botan, C. H. (1993). Introduction to the paradigm struggle in public relations. *Public Relations Review, 19,* 107–110.

Boulding, K. E. (1989). Social indicators of one-way transfers in organizations. In J. A. Anderson (Ed.), *Communication yearbook 12* (pp. 670–674). Newbury Park, CA: Sage.

Bourgeois, L. J., III. (1980). Strategy and environment: A conceptual integration. *Academy of Management Review, 5*(1), 25–39.

Bourgeois, L. J., III, & Singh, J. U. (1983). Organizational slack and political behavior among top management teams. In K. H. Chung (Ed.), *Academy of Management Proceedings* (pp. 43–47). Wichita, KS: Wichita State University.

Brody, E. W. (1985). Changing roles and requirements of public relations. *Public Relations Review, 11*(4), 22–28.

Broom, G. M. (1986, May). *Public relations roles and systems theory: Functional and historicist causal models.* Paper presented at the meeting of the International Communication Association, Chicago.

Broom, G. M., & Dozier, D. M. (1986). Advancement for public relations role models. *Public Relations Review, 12*(1), 37–56.

Broom, G. M., & Smith, G. D. (1979). Testing the practitioner's impact on clients. *Public Relations Review, 5*(3), 47–59.

Brousell, D. R. (1993). IBM's job 1: Customer confidence. *Datamation, 39*(10), 124.

Browning, L. D., & Henderson, S. C. (1989). One-way communication in loosely coupled systems. In J. A. Anderson (Ed.), *Communication yearbook 12* (pp. 638–669). Newbury Park, CA: Sage.

Bullis, C. (1993). Organizational socialization research: Enabling, constraining, and shifting perspectives. *Communications Monographs, 60*, 10–17.

Burrell, G., & Morgan, G. (1979). *Social paradigms and organizational analysis.* London, England: Heinemann.

Cage, M. (1992). Humanizing the debate: The dialogue experience in Wisconsin. *Conscience*, 10–11.

Carnevale, P. J., & Pruitt, D. G. (1992). Negotiation and mediation. *Annual Review of Psychology, 43*, 531–582.

Castrogiovanni, G. J. (1991). Environmental munificence: A theoretical assesment. *Academy of Management Review, 16*, 542–565.

Cavanagh, G. F., Moberg, D. J., & Velasquez, M. (1991). The ethics of organizational politics. *Academy of Management Review, 6*, 363–374.

Cheney, G. (1991). *Rhetoric in organizational society: Managing multiple identities.* Columbia, SC: University of South Carolina Press.

Cheney, G., & Dionisopoulos, G. N. (1989). Public relations? No, relations with publics: A rhetorical-organizational approach to contemporary corporate communications. In C. H. Botan & V. Hazleton, Jr. (Eds.), *Public relations theory* (pp. 135–158). Hillsdale, NJ: Lawrence Erlbaum Associates.

Cheney, G., & Vibbert, S. L. (1987). Corporate discourse: Public relations and issue management. In F. M. Jablin, L. L. Putnam, K. H. Roberts, & L. W. Porter (Eds.), *Handbook of organizational communication: An interdisciplinary perspective* (pp. 165–194). Newbury Park, CA: Sage.

Child, J. (1972). Organizational structures, environment and performance: The role of strategic choice. *Sociology, 6*, 1–22.

Clegg, S. (1983). Organizational democracy, power and participation. In C. Crouch & F. Heller (Eds.), *Organizational democracy & political processes* (pp. 3–31). New York: Wiley.

Cline, C. (1982). The image of public relations in mass communication texts. *Public Relations Review, 8*(4), 63–72.

Cobb, A. T. (1986). Political diagnosis: Applications in organization development. *Academy of Management Review, 11*(3), 482–496.

Conlon, E. J., & Stone, T. H. (1992). Absence schema and managerial judgment. *Journal of Management, 18*, 435–454.

Conrad, C. (1992). Book review. *Quarterly Journal of Speech, 78*, 508–509.

Conrad, C. (1994). *Strategic organizational communication: Toward the twenty-first century.* (3rd ed.). New York: Harcourt Brace.

Cook, B. M. (1991). Quality: The pioneers survey the landscape. *Industry Week, 240*(20), 68–73.

Coombs, W. (1993). Philisophical underpinnings: Ramifications of a pluralist paradigm. *Public Relations Review, 19,* 111–119.

Cooper, M. (1989). *Analyzing public discourse.* Prospect Heights, IL: Waveland Press.

Covey, R. (1989). *The seven habits of highly effective people: Restoring the character ethic.* New York: Simon & Schuster.

Cox, W. R. (1984). Government relations. In B. Cantor & C. Burger (Eds.), *Experts in action: Inside public relations (pp. 7–30).* New York: Longman.

Creedon, P. (1993). Acknowledging the infrasystem: A critical feminist analysis of systems theory. *Public Relations Review, 19,* 157–166.

Crosby, P. B. (1992). Managerial arrogance. *Across the Board, 29*(10), 32–35.

Culbertson, H. (1985). Practitioner roles: Their meaning for educators. *Public Relations Review, 11,* 5–21.

Cyert, R. M., & March, J. G. (1963). *A behavioral theory of the firm.* Englewood Cliffs, NJ: Prentice-Hall.

Daft, R., & Weick, K. (1984). Toward a model of organizations as interpretation systems. *Academy of Management Review, 9,* 284–295.

Daft, R. L., & Lengel, R. H. (1984). Information richness: A new approach to managerial behavior and organization design. In B. M. Staw & L. L. Cummings (Eds.), *Research in organizational behavior* (pp. 191–233). Greenwich, CT: JAI Press.

Daft, R. L., Wiginton, J. C. (1979). Language and organization. *Academy of Management Review, 4,* 179–191.

Deal, T., & Kennedy, A. (1982). *Corporate cultures.* Reading, MA: Addison-Wesley.

Deetz, S. A. (1992). *Democracy in an age of corporate colonization: Developments in communication and the politics of everyday life.* Albany: State University of New York Press.

DeFleur, M. L., & Ball-Rokeach, S. (1989). *Theories of mass communication.* New York: Longman.

DeLamarter, R. (1986). *Big blue.* New York: Dodd, Mead & Company.

Dess, G., & Origer, N. (1987), Environment, structure, and consensus in strategy formulation: A conceptual integration. *Academy of Management Review, 12,* 313–330.

DiMaggio, P. (1988). Interest and agency in institutional theory. In L. G. Zucker (Ed.), *Institutional patterns and organizations* (pp. 3–21). Cambridge, MA: Ballinger.

Dobos, J., Bahniuk, M., & Hill, S. (1987). Power-gaining communication strategies and career success. *The Southern Communication Journal, 52,* 35–48.

Dodge, K. A. (1993). Social-cognitive mechanisms in the development of conduct disorder and depression. *Annual Review Psychology, 44,* 559–584.

Dozier, D. M. (1990). The innovation of research in public relations practice. In L. A. Grunig & J. E. Grunig (Eds.), *Public relations research annual* (Vol. 2, pp. 9–28). Hillsdale, NJ: Lawrence Erlbaum Associates.

Dozier, D. M., & Broom, G. M. (1995). Evolution of the manager role in public relations practice. *Journal of Public Relations Research, 7*(1), 3–26.

Driskill, L., & Goldstein, J. (1986). Uncertainty: Theory and practice in organizational communication. *Journal of Business Communication, 23*(3), 41–56.

Drory, A., & Beaty, D. (1991). Gender differences in the perception of organizational influence tactics. *Journal of Applied and Behavioral Science, 12,* 249–258.

Drory, A., & Romm, T. (1988). Politics and organization and its perception within the organization. *Organizational Studies, 9,* 165–179.

Drory, A., & Romm, T. (1990). The definition of organizational politics: A review.

Human Relations, 43, 1133–1154.

Dunbar, R. L. M., & Ahlstrom, D. (1995). Seeking the institutional balance of power: Avoiding the power of a balanced view. *Academy of Management Review, 20,* 171–192.

Dutton, J. E., Fahey, L., & Narayanan, V. K. (1983). Toward understanding strategic issue diagnosis. *Strategic Management Journal, 4,* 307–323.

Dutton, J. E., & Ottensmeyer, E. (1987). Strategic issue management systems: Forms, functions, and contexts. *Academy of Management Review, 12,* 355–365.

Edelman, M. (1985). *The symbolic uses of politics.* Chicago: Illinois University Press.

Ehling, W. P. (1989, January, 24). *Public relations management and marketing management: Different paradigms and different missions.* Speech presented at A Challenge to the Calling: Public Relations Colloqium, San Diego, CA.

Eisenberg, E. M. (1984). Ambiguity as strategy in organizational communication. *Communication Monographs, 51,* 227–242.

Engstrom, J. (1992, July 16). Bad press better than no press to Burke. *Seattle Post-Intelligencer,* C1.

Entman, R. M. (1993). Framing: Toward clarification of a fractured paradigm. *Journal of Communication, 43*(4), 51–58.

Erera, I. P. (1992). Social support under conditions of organizational ambiguity. *Human Relations, 45,* 247–264.

Euske, N. A., & Roberts, K. H. (1987). Evolving perspectives in organization theory: Communication implications. In R. M. Jablin, L. L. Putnam, K. H. Roberts, & L. W. Porter (Eds.), *Handbook of organizational communication* (pp. 41–69). Newbury Park, CA: Sage.

Feldman, S. (1990). Stories as cultural creativity: On the relation between symbolism and politics in organizational change. *Human Relations, 43,* 809–828.

Ferguson, K. (1984). *The feminist case against bureaucracy.* Philadelphia: Temple University Press.

Ferris, G. R., Fedor, D. B., Chachere, J. G., & Pondy, L. R. (1989). Myths and politics in organizational contexts. *Group and Organizational Studies, 14*(1), 83–103.

Ferris, G. R., & Kaemar, K. M. (1992). Perceptions of organizational politics. *Journal of Management, 18,* 93–116.

Ferris, G. R., & King, T. R. (1991). Politics in human resource decisions: A walk on the dark side. *Organizational Dynamics, 20*(2), 59–73.

Fiedler, F. E., & Garcia, J. E. (1987). *New approaches to effective leadership.* New York: Wiley.

Finkelstein, S. (1992). Power in top management teams: Dimensions, measurement, and validation. *Academy of Management Review, 35,* 505–538.

Fiol, C. M. (1995). Corporate communications: Comparing executives' private and public statements. *Academy of Management Journal, 38,* 522–536.

Fiske, S. T., & Taylor, S. E. (1984). *Social cognition.* Reading, MA: Addison Wesley.

Fitzgerald, M., & Hildebrand, C. (1992). Name alone won't win PC sales or restore customer confidence. *Computerworld, 26*(13), 1.

Freeman, S. A., Littlejohn, S. W., & Pearce, W. B. (1992). Communication and moral conflict. *Western Journal of Communication, 56,* 311–329.

French, J., & Raven, B. (1959). The bases of social power. In D. Cartwright (Ed.), *Studies in structural power* (pp. 150–167). Ann Arbor: Institute for Social Research, University of Michigan.

Fritzsche, D. (1991). A model of decision-making incorporating ethical values. *Journal of Business Ethics, 10,* 841–852.

Fritzsche, D., & Becker, H. (1984). Linking management behavior to ethical philosophy—an empirical investigation. *Academy of Management Journal, 27*(1), 166–175.

Frolik, J. (1993, January 17). Demons fade in abortion debate. *Cleveland Plain Dealer*, pp. 1-C, 4-C.

Frost, P., & Egri, C. (1991). The political process of innovation. *Research in Organizational Behavior, 13*, 229-295.

Frost, P. J., Mitchell, V., & Nord, W. R. (1992). *Organizational reality: Reports from the firing line* (4th ed.). New York: HarperCollins.

Furst, A. (1991). *Dark star.* New York: St. Martin's Press.

Galbraith, J. (1977). *Strategies of organization design.* Reading, MA: Addison-Wesley.

Gandz, J., & Murray, V. V. (1980). The experience of workplace politics. *Academy of Management Journal, 23*, 237-251.

Gatewood, R., & Carroll, A. (1991). Assessment of ethical performance of organization members: A conceptual framework. *Academy of Management Review, 4*, 667-690.

Gellerman, S. W. (1986). Why "good" managers make bad ethical choices. *Harvard Business Review, 64*(4), 85-90.

Gerloff, E., Muir, N., & Bodensteiner, W. (1991). Three components of perceived environmental uncertainty: An exploratory analysis of the effects of aggregation. *Journal of Management, 17*, 749-768.

Gibson, D. (1991). The communication continuum: A theory of public relations. *Public Relations Review, 17*, 175-183.

Gilligan, C. (1982). *In a different voice.* Cambridge, MA: Harvard University Press.

Ginsberg, A. (1990). Connecting diversification to performance: A sociocognitive approach. *Academy of Magagement Review, 15*, 514-535.

Gioia, D. A. (1992). Pinto fires and personal ethics: A script analysis of missed opportunities. *Journal of Business Ethics, 11*, 379-389.

Gioia, D., & Pitre, E. (1990). Multiparadigm perspectives on theory building. *Academy of Management Review, 15*, 584-602.

Glassman, R. B. (1973). Persistence and loose coupling in living systems. *Behavioral Sciences, 18*, 83-98.

Goffman, E. (1974). *Frame analysis: An essay on the organization of experience.* Cambridge, MA: Harvard University Press.

Gordon, G. G. (1991). Industry determinants of organizational culture. *Academy of Management Review, 16*, 396-415.

Greening, D., & Gray, B. (1994). Testing a model of organizational response to social and political issues. *Academy of Management Journal, 37*, 467-498.

Greenwald, J. (1992). Are America's corporate giants a dying breed? (How managerial arrogance has weakened mega-corporations). *Time, 140*(26), 28.

Grunig, J. E. (1989). Symmetrical presuppositions as a framework for public relations theory. In C. H. Botan & V. Hazelton, Jr. (Eds.), *Public relations theory* (pp. 17-44). Hillsdale, NJ: Lawrence Erlbaum Associates.

Grunig, J. E. (1992). *Excellence in public relations and communication management: Contributions to effective organizations.* Hillsdale, NJ: Lawrence Erlbaum Associates.

Grunig, J. E. (1993). Images and substance: From symbolic to behavioral relationships. *Public Relations Review, 19*, 121-139.

Grunig, J. E., & Grunig, L. A. (1989). Toward a theory of the public relations behavior of organizations: Review of a program of research. In J. E. Grunig & L. A. Grunig (Eds.), *Public relations research annual* (Vol. 1, pp. 27-63). Hillsdale, NJ: Lawrence Erlbaum Associates.

Grunig, J. E., & Grunig, L. A. (1990). Models of public relations and communication. In J. E. Grunig & L. A. Grunig (Eds.), *Public relations research annual* (Vol. 2, pp. 115-155). Hillsdale, NJ: Lawrence Erlbaum Associates.

Grunig, J. E., & Grunig, L. A. (1992). Models of public relations and communication. In J. E. Grunig (Ed.), *Excellence in public relations and communication management* (pp. 285–325). Hillsdale, NJ: Lawrence Erlbaum Associates.

Grunig, J. E., & Hunt, T. (1984). *Managing public relations.* New York: Holt, Rinehart and Winston.

Grunig, J. E., & White, J. (1992). The effect of world views on public relations theory and practice. In J. E. Grunig (Ed.), *Excellence in public relations and communication management: Contributors to effective organizations* (pp. 31–64). Hillsdale, NJ: Lawrence Erlbaum Associates.

Grunig, L. A. (1990a). An exploration of the causes of job satisfaction in public relations. *Management Communication Review, 3,* 355–375.

Grunig, L. A. (1990b). Power in the public relations department. In L. A. Grunig & J. E. Grunig (Eds.), *Public relations research annual* (Vol. 1, pp. 27–63). Hillsdale, NJ: Lawrence Erlbaum Associates.

Habermas, J. (1970). On systematically distorted communication. *Inquiry, 13,* 205–218.

Habermas, J. (1973). *Theory and practice.* (T. McCarthy, Trans.). Boston: Beacon Press.

Habermas, J. (1979). *Communication and the evolution of society.* (T. McCarthy, Trans.). Boston: Beacon Press.

Habermas, J. (1984). *The theory of communicative action, volume 1: Reason and the rationalization of society.* (T. McCarthy, Trans.). Boston: Beacon Press.

Habermas, J. (1991). *Moral consciousness and communicative action.* Cambridge, MA: MIT Press.

Hackett, R. (1986a, August 28). City losing a landmark sculpture. *Seattle Post-Intelligencer,* p. A1, A28.

Hackett, R. (1986b, October 9). It's a deal! "Vertebrae" is staying. *Seattle Post-Intelligencer,* p. A1, A15.

Hage, J. (1972). *Techniques and problems of theory construction in sociology.* New York: Wiley.

Hage, J. (1980). *Theories of organizations: Form, process and transformation.* New York: Wiley.

Hallahan, K. (1993). The paradigm struggle and public relations practice. *Public Relations Review, 19,* 197–205.

Hample, D., & Dallinger, J. M. (1987). Individual differences in cognitive editing standards. *Human Communication Research, 14,* 123–144.

Hansen, E. (1991). *Motoring with Mohammed: Journeys to Yemen and the Red Sea.* New York: Vintage.

Harari, O. (1993a). The danger of success. *Management Review, 82(7),* 29–32.

Haynes, W. L. (1988). Of that which we cannot write: Some notes on the phenomenology of media. *Quarterly Journal of Speech, 74,* 71–101.

Hazelton, V., Jr. & Cutbirth, C. (1992). Public relations in Europe: An alternative educational paradigm. *Public Relations Review, 19,* 187–196.

Heath, R., & Nelson, R. (1986). *Issues management: Corporation, public policy making in an information society.* Newbury Park, CA: Sage.

Heath, R. L. (1991). Public relations research and education: Agendas for the 1990s. *Public Relations Review, 17,* 185–194.

Heath, R. L. (1993). A rhetorical approach to zones of meaning and organizational perspectives. *Public Relations Review, 19,* 141–155.

Heibert, R. E. (Ed.). (1993). Special issue: Public relations ethics. *Public Relations Review, 19(1).*

Hellweg, S. A. (1989, May). *The application of Grunig's symmetry-asymmetry public relations models to internal communication systems.* Paper presented at the meeting of the International Communication Association, San Francisco.

Hennestad, B. W. (1990). The symbolic impact of double bind leadership: Double bind and the dynamics of organizational culture. *Journal of Management Studies, 27,*

265–280.

Herbiniak, L. G., & Joyce, W. F. (1985). Organizational adaptation: Strategic choice and environmental determinism. *Administrative Science Quarterly, 30,* 336–349.

Hickson, D. J., Astley, W. G., Butler, J. R., & Wilson, D. C. (1981). *Organization as power.* Greenwich, CT: JAI Press.

Hite, R., Bellizi, J., & Fraser, C. (1988). A content analysis of ethical policy statements regarding marketing activities. *Journal of Business Ethics, 7,* 771–776.

Hosmer, L. T. (1991). Managerial responsibilities on the micro level. *Business Horizons,* July-August, 49–55.

Huber, G. P., & Daft, R. L. (1987). The information environment of organizations. In F. M. Jablin, L. L. Putnam, K. H. Roberts, & L. W. Porter (Eds.), *Handbook of organizational communication* (pp. 130–164). Newbury Park, CA: Sage.

Huff, A. S. (1988). Politics and argument as a means of coping with ambiguity and change. In L. R. Pondy, R. J. Boland, Jr., & H. Thomas (Eds.), *Managing ambiguity and change* (pp. 79–90). New York: Wiley.

Ice, R. (1991). Corporate publics and rhetorical strategies: The case of Union Carbide's Bhopal crisis. *Management Communication Quarterly, 4,* 341–362.

Infante, D. A., Rancer, A. S., & Womack, D. F. (1993). *Building communication theory* (2nd ed.). Prospect Heights, IL: Waveland Press.

Isaacson-Jones, B. J. (1992, Autumn). Adversaries, not enemies: Prochoice and prolife activists find common ground in St. Louis. *Conscience,* 11–12.

Isaacson-Jones, B. J., Puzder, A. F., Wagner, L., & Cavender, J. (1991, June 9). Common ground: Common sense requires recognition of common humanity. *St. Louis Post-Dispatch,* 3B.

Jackall, R. (1988). *Moral mazes: The world of corporate managers.* Oxford, NY: Oxford University Press.

Jackson, N., & Pippa, C. (1992). Postmodern management: Past-perfect or future-imperfect? *International Studies of Management & Organization, 22*(3), 11–26.

Jacobellis v. State of Ohio, 378 U.S. (1964).

Jacobson, D. Y., & Tortorello, N. J. (1992). Seventh annual salary survey. *Public Relations Journal, 48,* 9–21.

Jauch, L., & Kraft, K. (1986). Strategic management of uncertainty. *Academy of Management Review, 11,* 777–790.

Johnson, D. A. (August, 1995). Ten ways communicators can help the CEO shine. *Public Relations Tactics, 2*(8), p. 4.

Johnson, D. J., & Acharya, L. (1982, July). *Organizational decision making and public relations roles.* Paper presented at the meeting of the Association for Education in Journalism, Athens, OH.

Johnson, K. L. (1989). Desperation and successful men. *Broker World, 9*(11), 114–120, 144.

Jones, D. C. (1992). Insurance industry deserves bad image. *National Underwriter, 96*(26), 9–10.

Jones, E., & Nisbett, R. E. (1971). *The actor and observer: Divergent perceptions of the causes of behavior.* Morristown, NJ: General Learning Press.

Jones, T. M. (1991). Ethical decision making by individuals in organizations: an issue-contingent model. *Academy of Management Review, 16,* 366–395.

Jongbloed, L., & Frost, P. J. (1985). Pfeffer's model of management: An expansion and modification. *Journal of Management, 11*(3), 97–110.

Jordan, G. (1990). The pluralism of pluralism: an anti-theory? *Political Studies, 38,* 286–301.

Kahn, W. A. (1990). Toward an agenda for business ethics research. *Academy of Management Review, 15,* 311–328.

Kalupa, F. B., & Allen, T. H. (1982). Future directions in public relations education. *Public Relations Review, 8,* 31–45.

Kanter, D., & Mirvis, P. (1991). Cynicism: The new American malaise. *Business and Social Review, 77,* 57–61.

Kanter, R. M. (1977). *Men and women of the corporation.* New York: Basic Books.

Kanter, R. M. (1979). Power failure in management circuits. *Havard Business Review, 57* (July/August), 65.

Kast, F., & Rosenzweig, J. (1972). The modern view: A systems approach. In J. Beishon & G. Peters (Eds.), *Systems behaviour* (pp. 14–28). England: The Open University Press.

Katriel, T., & Philipsen, G. (1981). What we need is communication: Communication as a cultural category in some American speech. *Communications Monographs, 48,* 301–317.

Katz, D., & Kahn, R. (1966). *The social psychology of organizations.* New York: John Wiley & Sons, Inc.

Katzman, J. B. (1993). What's the role of public relations? *Public Relations Journal, 48*(4), 11–15.

Keough, C., & Lake, R. A. (1993). Values as structuring properties for contract negotiations. In C. Conrad (Ed.), *The ethical nexus* (pp. 171–189). Norwood, NJ: Ablex.

Kidder, R. M. (1995). *How good people make tough choices.* New York: William Morrow.

Kolb, D. M., & Putnam, L. L. (1992). Introduction: The dialectics of disputing. In D. M. Kolb & J. M. Bartunek (Eds.), *Hidden conflict in organizations: Uncovering behind-the-scenes disputes* (pp. 1–31). Newbury Park, CA: Sage.

Kopenhaver, L. L. (1985). Aligning values of practitioners and journalists. *Public Relations Review, 11,* 34–42.

Kotter, J. P. (1978). *Organizationanl dynamics: Diagnosis and intervention.* Reading, MA: Addison-Wesley.

Kramer, M. (1994). The next big election. *Time Magazine, 144*(22), 31.

Krefting, L., & Frost, P. (1985). Untangling webs, surfing waves, and wildcatting. In P. Frost, L. Moore, M. Louis, C. Lundberg, & J. Martin (Eds.), *Organizational culture* (pp. 155–168). Beverly Hills, CA: Sage.

Kreiner, P., & Bhambri, A. (1991). Influence and information in organization-stakeholder relationships. *Management Corporate Social Performance and Policy, 12,* 3–36.

Krippendorf, K., & Eleey, M. F. (1986). Monitoring a group's symbolic environment. *Public Relations Review, 12*(1), 13–36.

Krone, K. J., Jablin, F. M., & Putnam, L. L. (1987). Communication theory and organizational communication: Multiple perspectives. In F. M. Jablin, L. L. Putnam, K. H. Roberts, & L. W. Porter (Eds.), *Handbook of organizational communication: An interdisciplinary approach* (pp. 18–40). Newbury Park, CA: Sage.

Kruckeberg, D., & Starck, K. (1988). *Public relations and community: A reconstructed theory.* New York: Prager Publishing.

Kuhn, T. S. (1970). *The structure of scientific revolutions.* Chicago: Illinois University Press.

Laczniak, G. R., & Murphy, P. E. (1991). Fostering ethical marketing decisions. *Journal of Business Ethics, 10,* 259–271.

Lakoff, G., & Johnson, M. (1980). *Metaphors we live by.* Chicago: Univeristy of Chicago Press.

Lange, J. (1993). The logic of competing information campaigns: Conflict over old growth and the spotted owl. *Communication Monographs, 60,* 239–257.

Lapierre, R. (1990a). How to get maximum benefit from public relations by positioning it properly in the organization. *PR Reporter: Tips and Tactics, 28*(10), 1–2.

Lapierre, R. (1990b). Positioning public relations, part II: "I try to be optimistic, but . . ." An interview with retiring maverick educator Bill Ehling. *PR Reporter: Tips and Tactics, 28*(11), 1–2.

Lauzen, M. (1992). Public relations roles, intraorganizational power, and encroachment. *Journal of Public Relations Research, 4*, 61–80.

Lauzen, M., & Dozier, D. (1992). The missing link: The public relations manager role as mediator of organizational environments and power consequences for the function. *Journal of Public Relations Research, 4*, 205–220.

Lawrence, P., & Lorsch, J. (1967). *Organization and environment.* Boston: Harvard University Press.

Leichty, G., & Springston, J. (1993). Reconsidering public relations models. *Public Relations Review, 19*, 327–339.

Leifer, R., & Delbecq, A. (1978). Organizational/environmental interchange: A model of boundary spanning activity. *Academy of Management Review, 3*, 40–50.

Lengel, R. H. (1983). *Managerial information processing and communication-media source selection behavior.* Unpublished doctoral dissertation, Texas A&M University.

Liedtka, J. (1989). Value congruence: The interplay of individual and organizational value systems. *Journal of Business Ethics, 8*, 805–815.

Liedtka, J. (1991). Organizational value contention and managerial mindsets. *Journal of Business Ethics, 10*, 543–557.

Long, L. W., & Hazleton, V., Jr. (1987). Public relations: A theoretical and practical response. *Public Relations Review, 13*, 3–13.

Louis, M. R. (1980). Surprise and sense-making in organizations. *Administrative Science Quarterly, 25*, 226–251.

Lucas, R. (1987). Political-cultural analysis of organizations. *Academy of Management Review, 12*, 144–156.

Lysonski, S. (1985). A boundary theory investigation of the product manager's role. *Journal of Marketing, 49*, 26–40.

Madison, D. L., Allen, R. W., Porter, L. W., Renwick, P. A., & Mayes, B. T. (1980). Organizational politics: An exploration of managers' perceptions. *Human Relations, 33*(2), 79–100.

Mansbridge, J. (1980). *Beyond adversary democracy.* New York: Basic Books.

Maranville, S. J. (1989). You can't make steel without having some smoke: A case study in stakeholder analysis. *Journal of Business Ethics, 8*, 57–63.

March, J., & Olsen, J. (1979). *Ambiguity and choice in organizations.* Oslo, Norway: Universitetsforlaget.

Marshall, J. (1989). Re-visioning career concepts: A feminist invitation. In M. B. Arthur, D. T. Hall, & B. S. Lawrence (Eds.), *Handbook of career theory* (pp. 275–291). Cambridge, UK: Cambridge University Press.

Marshall, J. (1993). Viewing organizational communication from a feminist perspective: A critique and some offerings. In S. A. Deetz (Ed.), *Communication yearbook 16* (pp. 122–143). Newbury Park, CA: Sage.

Martin, P. (1989). The moral politics of organizations: Reflections of an unlikely feminist. *Journal of Applied Behavioral Science, 25*, 451–470.

Mason, R. O., & Mitroff, I. I. (1981).*Challenging strategic planning assumptions.* New York: Wiley.

Mayes, B., & Allen, R. (1977). Toward a definition of organizational politics: Conceptual notes. *Academy Management Review, 2*, 672–679.

McCabe, D. L. (1990). The assessment of percieved environmental uncertainty and economic performance. *Human Relations, 43*, 1203–1218.

McCaskey, M. B. (1988). The challenge of managing ambiguity and change. In L. R.

Pondy, R. J. Boland, & H. Thomas (Eds.), *Managing ambiguity and change* (pp. 1–15). New York: Wiley.

McFarland, D. E. (1986). *The managerial imperative: The age of macromanagement.* Cambridge, MA: Ballinger.

Meindl, J. R., (1985). Spinning on symbolism: The liberating potential of symbolism. *Journal of Management, 11*(2), 99–100.

Meisenhelder, T. (1989). Habermas and feminism: The future of critical theory. In R. A. Wallace (Ed.), *Feminism and sociological theory* (pp. 199–132). Newbury Park, CA: Sage.

Meyer, A. D. (1982). Adapting to environmental jolts. *Administrative Science Quarterly, 27,* 515–537.

Meyer, J. W., & Rowan, B. (1977). Institutionalized organizations: Formal structure as myth and ceremony. *American Journal of Sociology, 83,* 440–463.

Meyer, J. W., & Rowan, B. (1992). The structure of educational organizations. In J. W. Meyer & W. R. Scott (Eds.), *Organizational environments* (pp. 71–98). Newbury Park, CA: Sage.

Meyer, J. W., & Scott, W. R. (1992). *Organizational environments: Ritual and rationality.* Newbury Park, CA: Sage.

Meyers, R. A., & Garrett, D. E. (1993). Contradictions, values, and organizational argument. In C. Conrad (Ed.), *The ethical nexus* (pp. 149–170). Norwood, NJ: Ablex.

Meyerson, D., & Martin, J. (1987). Cultural change: An integration of three different views. *Journal of Management Studies, 24*(6), 623–643.

Miles, R. E., & Snow, C. C. (1984). Fit, failure and the hall of fame. *California Management Review, 26*(3), 10–28.

Miles, R. H. (1980). *Macro organizational behavior.* Santa Monica, CA: Goodyear Publishing Company.

Miller, G. R. (1989). Persuasion and public relations: Two "Ps" in a pod. In C. H. Botan & V. Hazleton, Jr. (Eds.), *Public relations theory* (pp. 45–66). Hillsdale, NJ: Lawrence Erlbaum Associates.

Miller, G. R., & Burgoon, M. (1978). Persuasion research: Review and commentary. In B. D. Ruben (Ed.), *Communication yearbook 2* (pp. 29–47). New Brunswick, NJ: Transaction Books.

Milliken, F. J. (1987). Three types of percieved uncertainty about the environment: State, effect, and response uncertainty. *Academy of Management Review, 12*(1), 133–143.

Mintzberg, H. (1983). *Power in and around organizations.* Englewood Cliffs, NJ: Prentice-Hall.

Mintzberg, H. (1985). The organization as political arena. *Journal of Management Studies, 22*(2), 133–154.

Mintzberg, H., Raisinghani, D., & Theoret, A. (1976). The structure of "unstructured" decision processes. *Administrative Science Quarterly, 21,* 246–275.

Mitroff, I., & Linstone, H. (1993). *The unbounded mind: Breaking the chains of traditional business thinking.* New York: Oxford University Press.

Mitroff, I. I. (1983). *Stakeholders of the organizational mind.* San Fransisco, CA: Jossey-Bass.

Mitroff, I. I., & Emshoff, J. R. (1979). On strategic assumption making: A dialectical approach to policy and planning. *Academy of Management Review, 4,* 1–12.

Moch, M. K. (1990). Creating alternative realities at work. *Journal of Applied and Behavioral Sciences, 23*(4), 1–13.

Moch, M. K., & Bartunek, J. M. (1990). *Creating alternative realities at work: The quality of work life experiment at Foodcom.* New York: Harper & Row.

Morgan, G. (1986). *Images of organization.* Newbury Park, CA: Sage.

Morgan, G. (1989). *Creative organization theory: A resource book.* Newbury Park, CA:

Sage.

Morris, W. (Ed.). (1973). *The American heritage dictionary of the English language.* Boston: American Heritage Publishing.

Moussavi, F., & Evans, D. (1993). Emergence of organizational attributions: The role of a shared cognitive schema. *Journal of Management, 19*(1) 79–95.

Mumby, D. K. (1987). The political function of narrative in organizations. *Communication Monographs, 54,* 113–126.

Mumby, D. K. (1988). *Communication and power in organizations: Discourse, ideology, and domination.* Norwood, NJ: Ablex.

Mumby, D. K. (1993). Feminism and the critique of organizational communication studies. In S. A. Deetz (Ed.), *Communication yearbook 16* (pp. 155–166). Newbury Park, CA: Sage.

Mumby, D. K., & Putnam, L. (1992). The politics of emotion: A feminist reading of bounded rationality. *Academy of Management Review, 17,* 465–486.

Murphy, P. (1991). How "bad" PR decisions get made: A roster of faulty judgment heuristics. *Public Relations Review, 17*(2), 117–129.

Nadler, D. A., & Tushman, M. L. (1980). A congruence model for diagnosing organizational behavior. In R. H. Miles (Ed.), *Resource book in macro-organizational behavior* (pp. 30–49) Santa Monica, CA: Goodyear Publishing.

Nie, N. H., Hull, C. H., Jenkins, J. G., Steinbrenner, K., & Bent, D. H. (1975). *SPSS: Statistical package for the social sciences.* New York: McGraw-Hill.

Noble, A. (1986a, August 29). Realty firm defends sale of sculpture. *Seattle Post-Intelligencer,* C1, C2.

Noble, A. (1986b, September 3). Who sold the Moore sculpture? *Seattle Post-Intelligencer,* A1, A5.

Noble, A., & Sevem, R. (1986, September 4). "Vertebrae" promised to 2 potential buyers at once, sources say. *Seattle Post-Intelligencer,* A3.

Nooteboom, B. (1989). Paradox, identity and change in management. *Human Systems Management, 8,* 291–300.

Nutt, P. C. (1984). Types of organizational decision process. *Administrative Science Quarterly, 29,* 414–450.

Olasky, M. N. (1987). *Corporate public relations: A new historical perspective.* Hillsdale, NJ: Lawrence Erlbaum Associates.

Olasky, M. N. (1989). The aborted debate within public relations: An approach through Kuhn's paradigm. In J. E. Grunig & L. A. Grunig (Eds.), *Public relations research annual* (Vol. 1, pp. 87–95). Hillsdale, NJ: Lawrence Erlbaum Associates.

Oliver, C. (1991). Strategic responses to institutional processes. *Academy of Management Review, 16*(1), 145–179.

Ondaatje, M. (1992). *The English patient.* New York: Alfred A. Knopf.

Orton, J. D., & Weick, K. E. (1990). Loosely coupled systems: A reconceptualization. *Academy of Management Review, 15,* 203–223.

Pauchant, T. C., & Mitroff, I. I. (1992). *Transforming the crisis-prone organization: Preventing individual, organizational, and environmental tragedies.* San Francisco: Jossey-Bass.

Pavlik, J. (1987). *Public relations: What research tells us.* Beverly Hills. CA: Sage.

Payne, S., & Giacalone, R. (1990). Social psychological approaches to the perception of ethical dilemas. *Human Relations, 43,* 649–665.

Pearson, R. (1989a). Albert J. Sullivan's theory of public relations ethics. *Public Relations Review, 15*(2), 52–62.

Pearson, R. (1989b). Beyond ethical relativism in public relations: Coorientation, rules, and the idea of communication symmetry. In J. E. Grunig & L. A. Grunig (Eds.), *Public relations research annual* (Vol. 1, pp. 67–86). Hillsdale, NJ: Lawrence Erlbaum

Associates.

Pearson, R. (1990a). Ethical values or strategic values: The two faces of systems theory in public relations. In L. A. Grunig & J. E. Grunig (Eds.), *Public relations research annual* (Vol. 2, pp. 219–234). Hillsdale, NJ: Lawrence Erlbaum Associates.

Pearson, R. (1990b). Perspectives on public relations history. *Public Relations Review, 16*(3), 27–88.

Perrow, C. (1984). *Normal accidents: Living with high-risk technologies.* New York: Basic Books.

Perry, J. L., & Angle, H. L. (1979). The politics of organizational boundary roles in collective bargaining. *Academy of Management Review, 4,* 487–496.

Peters, T. (1989, September 19). Fifteen observations to consider on the issue of ethics. *Seattle Post-Intelligencer,* B5.

Peters, T., & Waterman, R. (1982). *In search of excellence.* New York: Warner Communications.

Pfeffer, J. (1981a). Management as symbolic action. *Research in Organizational Behavior, 3,* 1–52.

Pfeffer, J. (1981b). *Power in organizations.* Marshfield, MA: Pitman Publishing.

Pfeffer, J. (1982). *Organizations and organizational theory.* Marshfield, MA: Pitman Publishing.

Pfeffer, J. (1992). Understanding power in organizations. *California Management Review, 34*(2), 29–50.

Pfeffer, J., & Salancik, G. R. (1978). *The external control of organizations: A resource dependence perspective.* New York: Harper and Row.

Pincus, J. D., Rimer, T., Rayfield, R. E., & Cropp, F. (1991, August). *Newspaper editors' perceptions of public relations: How business, news and sports editors differ.* Paper presented at the annual meeting of the Association for Education in Journalism and Mass Communication, Boston.

Pitta, J. (1991). The arrogance was unnecessary. *Forbes, 48*(5), 138.

Pondy, L., Frost, P., Morgan, G., & Dandridge, T.(Eds.) (1983). *Organizational symbolism.* London, England: JAI Press.

Pondy, L. R., Boland, R. J., Jr., & Thomas, H. (1988). *Managing ambiguity and change.* New York: Wiley.

Porter, L. W., Allen, R. W., & Angle, H. L. (1981). The politics of upward influence in organizations. *Organizational Behavior, 3,* 109–149.

Posner, B., & Schmidt, W. (1984). Values and the American manager: An update. *California Management Review, 26,* 202–216.

Powell, T. C. (1992). Organizational alignment as competitive advantage. *Strategic Management Journal, 13,* 119–134.

Powell, W. W. (1988). Institutional effects on organizational structure and performance. In L. G. Zucker (Ed.), *Institutional patterns and organizations* (pp. 115–136). Cambridge, MA: Ballinger.

Powell, W. W. , & DiMaggio, P. J. (1991). *The new institutionalism in organizational analysis.* Chicago: University of Chicago Press.

Prasad, P. (1993). Symbolic processes in the implementation of technological change: A symbolic interactionist study of work computerization. *Academy of Management Journal, 36,* 1400–1429.

Pratt, C. (1991). Public relations: The empirical research on practitioner ethics. *Journal of Business Ethics, 10,* 229–236.

Pringle, R. (1988). *Secretaries talk.* London: Verso Publishing.

Public Relations Journal (September 1992), 48.

Public Relations Journal (June/July 1994), 50.

Putnam, L., & Pacanowsky, M. E. (Eds.). (1983). *Communication and organizations: An interpretive approach.* Newbury Park, CA: Sage.

Puzder, A. (1989, December 26). Common ground on abortion. *St. Louis Post-Dispatch,* 3B.

Ramsay, K., & Parker, M. (1992). Gender, bureaucracy and organizational culture. In A. Witz & S. M. Savage (Eds.), *Gender and bureaucracy* (pp. 253–278). England: Blackwell.

Rasberry, W. (1992, August). Only the brave can find common ground. *St. Louis Post-Dispatch,* 3C.

Reddy, M. (1979). The conduit metaphor—a case frame conflict in our language about language. In A. Ortony (Ed.), *Metaphor and thought* (pp. 284–324). Cambridge, England: Cambridge University Press.

Refashioning IBM: Don't just stand there, listen to something (1990, November 17). *The Economist, 317,* 21–24.

Rice, R. E. (1992). Task analyzability, use of new media, and effectiveness: A multi-site exploration of media richness. *Organization Science, 3,* 475–500.

Riley, P. (1983). A structurist account of political culture. *Administrative Science Quarterly, 28,* 414–437.

Robbins, S. P. (1987). *Organization theory: Structure, design, and application* (2nd ed.). Englewood Cliffs, NJ: Prentice-Hall.

Ross, M., & DiTecco, D. (1975). An attributional analysis of moral judgments. *Journal of Social Issues, 31,* 91–109.

Ross, L., & Stillinger, C. (1991). Barriers to conflict resolution. *Negotiation Journal, 7,* 389–404.

Ruben, B. D. (1972). General system theory: An approach to human communication. In R. W. Budd & B. D. Ruben (Eds.), *Approaches to human communication* (pp. 120–144). Rochelle Park, NJ: Hayden Book Company.

Russell, A. (1993). How firms can attract, retain . . . or lose clients. *Public Relations Journal, 49*(6), 33–36.

Ryan, M. (1987a). Organizational constraints on corporate public relations practitioners. *Journalism Quarterly, 64,* 473–482.

Ryan, M. (1987b). Participative versus authoritative public relations environments. *Journalism Quarterly, 64,* 853–857.

Ryan, M., & Martinson, D. L. (1988). Journalists and public relations practitioners: Why the antagonism? *Journalism Quarterly, 62,* 131–140.

Sale threatens "public treasure." (1986, August 29). *Seattle Post-Intelligencer,* p. A10.

Savage, G., Nix, T., Whitehead, C., & Blair, J. (1991). Strategies for assessing and managing organizational stakeholders. *Academy of Management Executive, 5,* 61–75.

Savage, M., & Witz, A. (1992). *Gender and bureaucracy.* Oxford, UK: Blackwell Publishers.

Schiappa, E. (1989). Spheres of argument as topoi for the critical study of power/knowledge. In B. E. Gronbeck (Ed.), *Spheres of argument: Proceedings of the sixth SCA/AFA conference on argumentation* (pp. 47–56). Annandale, VA: Speech Communication Association.

Schmitz, J., & Fulk, J. (1991). Organizational colleagues, media richness, and electronic mail. *Communication Research, 18,* 487–523.

Schneider, L. (1985). The role of public relations in four organizational types. *Journalism Quarterly, 62,* 567–594.

Schwartz, D. G., Yarbrough, J. P., & Shakra, M. T. (1992). Does public relations education make the grade? *Public Relations Journal, 48*(9), 18–21, 24–25.

Scott, W. R. (1981). *Organizations.* Englewood Cliffs, NJ: Prentice-Hall.

Scott, W. R. (1987). The adolescence of institutional theory. *Administrative Science Quarterly, 32,* 493–511.

Scott, W. R. (1988). The management governance theories of justice and liberty. *Journal of Management, 14*, 277–298.

Scott, W. R. (1992). The organization of environments: Network, cultural, and historical elements. In J. Meyer & W. Scott (Eds.), *Organizational environments* (pp. 155–175). Newbury Park, CA: Sage.

Scott, W. R., & Hart, D. (1989). *Organizational values in America.* New Brunswick, NJ: Transaction Publications.

Seitel, F. P. (1987). *The practice of public relations* (3rd ed.). Englewood Cliffs, NJ: Prentice-Hall.

Seitel, F. P. (1995). No-tell Intel learns silence isn't golden. *Public Relations Tactics, 2*(1), p. 1.

Serini, S. A. (1993). Influences on the power of public relations professionals in organizations: A case study. *Journal of Public Relations Research, 5*(1), 1–25.

Shapley, T. (1993, June 3). Concerned teachers flunk controversy. *Seattle Post-Intelligencer*, A11.

Shepherd, G. J. (1992). Communication as influence: Definitional exclusion. *Communication Studies, 43*, 203–219.

Sims, R. (1992). The challenge of ethical behavior in organizations. *Journal of Business Ethics, 11*, 505–513.

Slater, M. D., Chipman, H., Auld, G., Keefe, T., & Kendall, P. (1992). Information processing and situational theory: A cognitve response analysis. *Journal of Public Relations Research, 4*, 189–203.

Smiley, T. (1992). Helping subordinates grow: Managers as "schemata modifiers." *Journal of Managerial Psychology, 7*, 25–30.

Smircich, L. (1983). Concepts of culture and organizational analysis. *Administrative Science Quarterly, 28*, 339–358.

Smith, M. J. (1990). Pluarlism, reformed pluralism and neopluralism: The role of pressure groups in policy-making. *Political Studies, 38*, 302–322.

Spicer, C. H. (1988, November). *Hospitals in competition: A root metaphor analysis.* Paper presented at the meeting of the Speech Communication Association, New Orleans.

Spicer, C. H. (1991). Communication functions performed by public relations and marketing practitioners. *Public Relations Review, 17*, 293–305.

Spicer, C. H. (1993). Images of public relations in the print media. *Journal of Public Relations Research, 5*, 47–61.

Spicer, C. H. (1994, November). *Public relations and organizational politics: Influencing effectiveness.* Presented at Speech Communication Association annual meeting, New Orleans.

Springston, J., Keyton, J., Leichty, G. B., & Metzger, J. (1992). Field dynamics and public relations theory: Toward the management of multiple publics. *Journal of Public Relations Research, 4*, 81–100.

Sproule, J. M. (1988). The new managerial rhetoric and the old criticism. *Quarterly Journal of Speech, 74*, 468–486.

Sproule, J. M. (1989). Organizational rhetoric and the public sphere. *Communication Studies, 40*, 258–265.

Stevenson, W. B., Pearce, J. L., & Porter, L. W. (1985). The concept of "coalition" in organization theory and research. *Academy of Management Review, 10*, 256–268.

Stewart, J. R. (1990). *Bridges, not walls* (5th ed.). New York: McGraw-Hill.

Stork, D., & Sapienza, A. (1992). Task and human message over the project life cycle. *Project Management Journal, 22*, 44–49.

Stryker, S., & Statham, A. (1985). Symbolic interaction and role theory. In G. Lindsay & E. Aronson (Eds.), *Handbook of social psychology* (3rd ed., Vol 1, pp. 311–378). New

York: Random House.

Sullivan, A. J. (1965). Values in public relations. In O. Lerbinger & A. Sullivan (Eds.), *Information, influence and communication: A reader in public relations* (pp. 412–439). New York: Basic Books.

Sweep, D., Cameron, G., & Lariscy, R. (1994). Rethinking constraints on public relations practice. *Public Relations Review, 20,* 319–331.

Terkel, S. (1972). *Working.* New York: Avon.

Thomas, J. B., Clark, S. M., & Gioia, D. A. (1993). Strategic sensemaking and organizational performance: Linkages among scanning, interpretation, action, and outcomes. *Academy of Management Journal, 33,* 286–306.

Thomas, K. W. (1976). Conflict and conflict management. In M. Dunnette (Ed.), *Handbook of industrial and organizational psychology* (pp. 889–935). Chicago: Rand McNally.

Thomas, K. W. (1977). Toward multi-dimensional values in teaching: The example of conflict behaviors. *Academy of Management Review, 2,* 484–490.

Thomas, K. W., & Kilmann, R. H. (1975). *The Thomas-Killman conflict mode survey.* Tuxedo, NY: Xicom.

Tompkins, P., & Cheney, G. (1985). Communication and unobtrusive control in contemporary organizations. In R. McPhee & P. Tompkins (Eds.), *Organizational communication* (pp. 179–210). Beverly Hills, CA: Sage.

Toth, E. L. (1992). The case for pluralistic studies of public relations: Rhetorical, critical, and systems perspectives. In E. L. Toth & R. L. Heath (Eds.), *Rhetorical and critical approaches to public relations* (pp. 3–16). Hillsdale, NJ: Lawrence Erlbaum Associates.

Toth, E. L., & Heath, R. (Eds.). (1992). *Rhetorical and critical approaches to public relations.* Hillsdale, NJ: Lawrenece Erlbaum Associates.

Trevino, L. K., Lengel, R. H., & Daft, R. L. (1987). Media symbolism, media richness, and media choice in organizations. *Communication Research, 14,* 553–574.

Trujillo, N., & Toth, E. (1987). Organizational perspectives for public relations research and practice. *Management Communications Quarterly, 1,* 199–231.

Tuchman, G. (1978). *Making news: A study in the construction of reality.* New York: Free Press.

Turk, J. V. (1989). Management skills need to be taught in public relations. *Public Relations Review, 15*(1), 38–52.

Tushman, M. L. (1977). A political approach to organizations: A review and rationale. *Academy of Management Review, 2,* 206–216.

Valacich, J., Paranka, D., George, J., & Nunamaker, J. (1993). Communication concurrency and the new media. *Communication Research, 20,* 249–276.

Vanderford, M. (1989). Villification and social movements: A case study of pro-life and pro-choice rhetoric. *Quarterly Journal of Speech, 75,* 166–182.

Victor, B., Cullen, J., & Boynton, A. (1993). Toward a general framework of organizational meaning systems. In C. Conrad (Ed.), *The ethical nexus* (pp. 193–215). Norwood, NJ: Ablex.

Virgin, B. (1995, March). Esterline stock up 73 percent in a year. *Seattle Post-Intelligencer,* p. B1, B6.

Vredenburgh, D. J., & Maurer, J. G. (1984). A process framework of organizational politics. *Human Relations, 37*(1), 47–66.

Wakefield, G., & Cottone, L. P. (1987). Knowledge and skills required by public relations employers. *Public Relations Review, 13*(3), 24–32.

Weick, K. E. (1976). Educational organizations as loosely coupled systems. *Administrative Science Quarterly, 21,* 1–19.

Weick, K. E. (1979). *The social psychology of organizing* (2nd ed.). Reading, MA:

Addison-Wesley.

Weick, K. E. (1982). Management of organizational change among loosely coupled elements. In P. S. Goodman (Ed.), *Change in organizations: New perspectives on theory, research, and practice* (pp. 375–408). San Francisco: Jossey-Bass.

Weick, K. E. (1985). Sources of order in underorganized systems: Themes in recent organizational theory. In Y. S. Lincoln (Ed.), *Organizational theory and inquiry: The paradigm revolution* (pp. 106–136). Beverly Hills, CA: Sage.

Weiser, D. (1988). Two concepts of communication as criteria for collective responsibility. *Journal of Business Ethics, 7,* 735–744.

Werhane, P. H. (1991). Engineers and management: The challenge of the Challenger accident. *Journal of Business Ethics, 10,* 605–616.

Williams, D. E., & Olaniran, B. A. (1994). Exxon's decision-making flaws: The hypervigilant response to the Valdez grounding. *Public Relations Review, 20*(1), 5–18.

Williams, D., & Treadaway, G. (1992). Exxon and the Valdez accident: A failure in crisis communication. *Communication Studies, 43,* 56–64.

Wilstein, S. (1994, March). Inner torment of Eric Snow. *Seattle Post-Intelligencer,* D2.

Witz, A., & Savage, M. (1992). Theoretical introduction. In A. Witz & M. Savage (Eds.), *Gender and bureaucracy* (pp. 3–64). England: Blackwell.

Wright, D. K. (1983). Implications of the IPRA "Gold Paper." *Public Relations Review, 9*(2), 3–6.

Yagoda, B. (1990). Cleaning up a dirty image. *Business Month, 135*(4), 48–51.

Zahra, S. (1989). Executive values and the ethics of company politics: Some preliminary findings. *Journal of Business Ethics, 8,* 15–29.

Zaleznik, A. (1970). Power and politics in organizational life. *Harvard Business Review, 81*(3), 47–60.

Zauderer, D. G. (1992). Integrity: An essential executive quality. *Business Forum, 17*(4), 12–16.

Author Index

Gray, B., 60, 87, 158, 168, 169, 171, 224, 253
Greening, D., 60, 87, 158, 168, 169, 171, 224, 253
Greenwald, J., 29
Grunig, J. E., 17, 22, 23, 34, 53, 56, 58, 59, 60, 61, 65, 66, 67, 68, 70, 97, 98, 100, 155, 156, 178, 182, 191, 202, 209, 224
Grunig, L. A., 61, 65, 67, 84, 136, 141

H

Habermas, J., 92, 207, 209, 210, 211, 213, 218, 271
Hackett, R., 2, 3, 4
Hage, J., 57, 71
Hallahan, K., 69
Hample, D., 213
Hansen, E., 24
Harari, O., 29
Hart, D., 84, 216
Haynes, W. L., 192
Hazleton, Jr., V., 19, 20, 54, 55, 56, 59, 69, 86, 97, 124, 140, 153, 154, 155, 173, 189, 191, 192, 194, 234, 260
Heath, R., 58, 60, 68, 177, 180, 208
Heibert, R. E., 271
Hellweg, S. A., 65
Henderson, S. C., 248
Hennestad, B. W., 227
Herbiniak, L. G., 158, 169, 172
Hickson, D. J., 133
Hildebrand, C., 29
Hill, S., 129
Hite, R., 273, 274
Hosmer, L. T., 273, 289
Huber, G. P., 158, 159, 160
Huff, A. S., 249
Hull, C. H., 147
Hunt, T., 22, 53, 56, 61, 68, 70, 98, 178, 191, 224

I

Ice, R., 61
Infante, D. A., 57, 58
Isaacson-Jones, B. J., 204, 205

J

Jablin, F. M., 94
Jackall, R., 21, 31, 32, 33, 36, 48, 97
Jackson, N., 227
Jacobson, D. Y., 13, 40, 41
James, K., 129
Jauch, L., 157, 158, 161, 167, 173

Jenkins, J. G., 147
Johnson, D. A., 270, 271, 273
Johnson, D. J., 37
Johnson, K. L., 78
Johnson, M., 107, 108
Johnson, R., 60, 87, 91, 169
Jones, D. C., 29
Jones, E., 277
Jones, T. M., 275, 276, 277, 289, 290, 291
Jongbloed, L., 238
Jordan, G., 68
Joyce, W. F., 158, 169, 172

K

Kaemar, K. M., 110, 130, 137, 146, 147
Kahn, R., 57
Kahn, W. A., 273
Kalupa, F. B., 38
Kanter, D., 78, 132
Kanter, R. M., 110, 130, 133
Kast, F., 57
Katriel, T., 178, 179, 180
Katz, D., 57
Katzman, J. B., 180, 181
Keefe, T., 190
Kendall, P., 190
Kennedy, A., 17, 94, 96
Keough, C., 293
Keyton, J., 61
Kidder, R. M., 279, 283
Kilmann, R. H., 250, 251
King, T. R., 103, 138
Kolb, D. M., 249
Kopenhaver, L. L., 40, 41
Kotter, J. P., 87, 88, 91, 154
Kraft, K., 157, 158, 161, 167, 173
Kramer, M., 235
Krefting, L., 107
Kreiner, P., 15, 153, 158, 169, 170, 171, 173, 224, 253, 255
Krippendorf, K., 234
Krone, K. J., 94
Kruckeberg, D., 23, 34, 53, 54
Kuhn, T. S., 58

L

Laczniak, G. R., 286, 288
Lake, R. A., 293
Lakoff, G., 107, 108
Lange, J., 193, 194, 195, 196, 197, 203
Lapierre, R., 34, 39, 135
Lariscy, R., 274
Lauzen, M., 58, 97, 135, 141, 155, 158, 172, 173, 253, 267
Lawler, E. J., 117, 120

Pitta, J., 29
Pondy, L. R., 107, 138, 226, 227
Porter, L. W., 121, 122, 130, 136, 137, 138, 139
Posner, B., 30
Powell, T. C., 90
Powell, W. W., 168, 169
Prasad, P., 96, 97
Pratt, C., 271
Pringle, R., 214
Pruitt, D. G., 249
Putnam, L. L., 94, 107, 133, 216, 217, 249
Puzder, A. F., 204, 205

R

Raisinghani, D., 107
Ramsay, K., 212, 213
Rancor, A. S., 57, 58
Raspberry, W., 205
Raven, B., 133, 134, 149
Rayfield, R. E., 40, 41, 47
Reddy, M., 189, 190, 192, 196
Renwick, P. A., 130, 136, 137, 138, 139
Rice, R. E., 90, 239
Riley, P., 96, 117
Rimer, T., 40, 41, 47
Robbins, S. P., 97
Roberts, K. H., 57, 58
Romm, T., 137, 139
Rosenzweig, J., 57
Ross, L., 251
Ross, M., 277
Rowan, B., 85, 167, 236
Ruben, B. D., 57, 58
Russell, A., 18, 19
Ryan, M., 40, 41, 42, 47, 84, 132, 136

S

Salancik, G. R., 59, 158
Sapienza, A., 239
Savage, G., 15, 16, 254, 255, 256, 261, 265, 266, 294
Savage, M., 212, 214
Schiappa, E., 217
Schmidt, W., 30
Schmitz, J., 239
Schneider, L., 140
Schwartz, D. G., 38
Scott, W. R., 57, 60, 84, 87, 158, 168, 169, 216, 235, 284, 285
Seitel, F. P., 37, 64
Serini, S. A., 136, 141
Sevem, R., 3
Shakra, M. T., 38
Shapley, T., 80

Shepherd, G. J., 213
Sims, R., 29, 273
Singh, J. U., 139
Slater, M. D., 190
Smiley, T., 92
Smircich, L., 94, 96, 107
Smith, G. D., 37
Smith, M. J., 68
Snow, C. C., 90
Spicer, C. H., 38, 43, 46, 48, 112, 130, 131, 132, 141, 144
Springston, J., 61, 65, 67, 190
Sproule, J. M., 56, 192, 193, 196, 247
Starck, K., 23, 34, 41, 53, 54
Statham, A., 240, 241, 264
Steinbrenner, K., 147
Stevenson, W. B., 121, 122
Stewart, J. R., 22
Stillinger, C., 251
Stone, T. H., 92
Stork, D., 239
Stryker, S., 240, 241, 264
Sullivan, A. J., 35, 36, 197, 202
Sweep, D., 274

T

Talbott, A., 41
Taylor, S. E., 94
Terkel, S., 77, 78, 84
Theoret, A., 107
Thomas, H., 226, 227
Thomas, J. B., 232
Thomas, K. W., 249, 250, 251, 252
Tompkins, P., 79
Tortorello, N. J., 13, 40, 41
Toth, E. L., 11, 58, 70
Treadaway, G., 278, 279
Trevino, L. K., 239
Trujillo, N., 11, 70
Tuchman, G., 42
Turk, J. V., 38
Tushman, M. L., 60, 110, 137

V

Valacich, J., 239
Vanderford, M., 203
Velasquez, M., 14, 279, 280, 283, 284, 285, 286, 287, 288, 295
Vibbert, S. L., 70, 191, 224, 231
Victor, B., 292
Virgin, B., 156
Vredenburgh, D. J., 137

W

Wagner, L., 205
Wakefield, G., 38

Subject Index

321

32442513